Fodor's

# OAHU

# Welcome to Oahu

The island known as "The Gathering Place" has many charms, from Honolulu's bright city lights and Waikiki Beach buzz to the North Shore's big-wave meccas. Learn to surf or paddle an outrigger canoe, sample shave ice, and feast at a luau—all in one day. Slow down with a thought-provoking visit to Pearl Harbor or a leisurely drive along the coast and into the countryside. Take in Oahu's stunning beaches and bays as well as the island's beautiful valleys and mountains. This truly is an island that has it all. As you plan your upcoming travels, please confirm that places are still open and let us know when we need to make updates by writing to us at editors@fodors.com.

## TOP REASONS TO GO

★ **Pearl Harbor:** This historic memorial in Honolulu is a sobering, don't-miss sight.

★ **Waikiki:** Busy but beautiful, with a perfect beach for first-time surfers.

★ **Great food:** Simple plate lunches, fresh sushi, creative Hawaii regional cuisine.

★ **History:** Around Oahu, sights such as Iolani Palace illuminate Hawaii's past.

★ **Nightlife:** From upscale jazz bars to local hangouts, Honolulu comes alive after dark.

★ **North Shore:** Shave ice, big waves, pro surfers, and a slower pace add appeal here.

# Contents

Fodor's Features

## MAPS

Chapter 1



# EXPERIENCE OAHU

# 25 ULTIMATE EXPERIENCES

Oahu offers terrific experiences that should be on every traveler's list. Here are Fodor's top picks for a memorable trip.

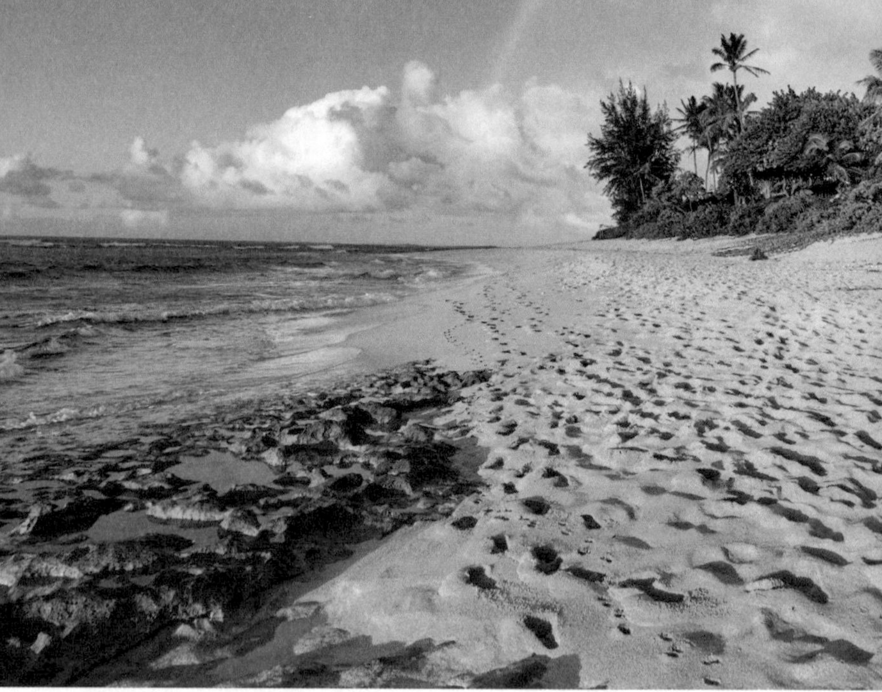

## 1 Explore the North Shore

Spend a day on the North Shore. Start off in Kaneohe on the windward side and drive up Kamehameha Highway to Haleiwa, stopping at fruit stands, shrimp trucks, beaches, world-famous surfing spots (don't miss Waimea Bay), and scenic overlooks. *(Ch. 5)*

## 2 Watch a Hula Show

For a more traditional, less touristy introduction to hula and Hawaiian music, go to the free hula show that's held several nights a week at Kuhio Beach Park. *(Ch. 3)*

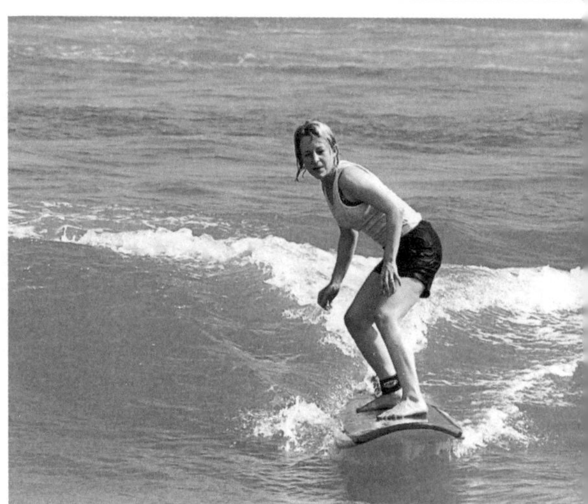

## 3 Learn to Surf

Waikiki's surf schools are popular with beginners. Less-crowded White Plains Beach Park in Kapolei has better novice conditions plus surf amenities. *(Ch. 3, 4)*

## 4 Have a Plate Lunch

Everyone should try this bargain-priced Hawaii lunch tradition: an entrée with white rice and a scoop of macaroni salad. It's an island favorite. *(Ch. 3, 4, 5, 6)*

## 5 Relax at Kailua Beach

Looking for that idyllic, unpopulated stretch of white sandy beach and turquoise-blue water? Visit Kailua Beach for easy swimming waves and maximum sand. *(Ch. 6)*

## 6 Paradise Cove Luau

Paradise Cove is where locals like to take visitors for traditional Hawaiian foods (give *poi* a chance) and a genuinely fun experience. *(Ch. 4)*

## 7 Munch on Malasadas

A must-eat, these deep-fried, sugar-coated doughnuts without holes (first brought to the islands by Portuguese immigrants) are an island fixture. *(Ch. 3, 4, 5, 6)*

## 8 Byodo-In Temple

Part of the Valley of the Temples cemetery complex, Byodo-In is a smaller version of the 11th-century original in Uji, Japan, but it's every bit as beautiful and peaceful. *(Ch. 6)*

## 9 Makapuu Lighthouse Trail

Less crowded than Diamond Head, Makapuu—popular with families because of its paved trail—offers an equally beautiful coastal panorama. *(Ch. 6, 7)*

## 10 Seek a Waterfall on the Manoa Falls Trail

Manoa Falls is an easy (though occasionally muddy), 1½-mile rain-forest hike in Manoa Valley with the reward of a 150-foot waterfall at its end. *(Ch. 3, 7)*

## 11 Explore Chinatown

Honolulu's Chinatown is a jumble of the historic and hip, with a revitalized dining scene, plus a mix of galleries, shops, and cultural sites. *(Ch. 3)*

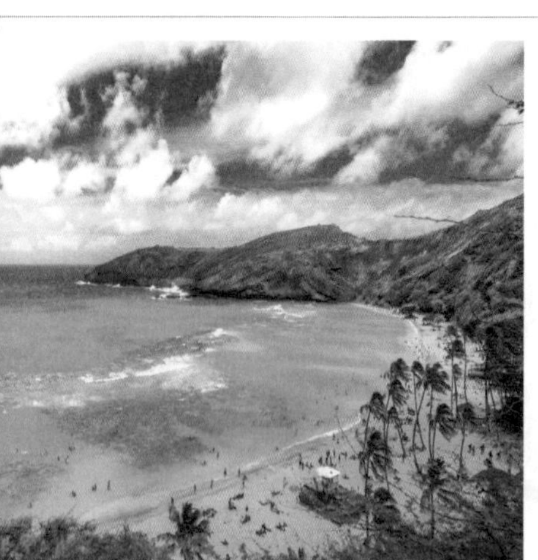

## 12 Snorkel at Hanauma Bay

This nature preserve nestled in a volcanic crater with a vibrant reef is a phenomenal, family-friendly place to see colorful fish and other sea life. Advance reservations are required. *(Ch. 6, 7)*

## 13 Explore the Kakaako Neighborhood

Filled with shops, restaurants, bars, and intriguing wall murals, this Honolulu district is vibrant, fun, and very cool. *(Ch. 3)*

## 14 Walk through Waikiki

The best way to enjoy Waikiki's famed tourist strip is by foot: skip the traffic, burn off some mai tai calories, and catch the sights you might otherwise miss. *(Ch. 3)*

## 15 Take a Cruise or Kayak Trip

You've got to get out on the water, whether it's on a sunset catamaran cruise, a whale-watching trip, or a kayak excursion in the Mokulua Islands. *(Ch. 6, 7)*

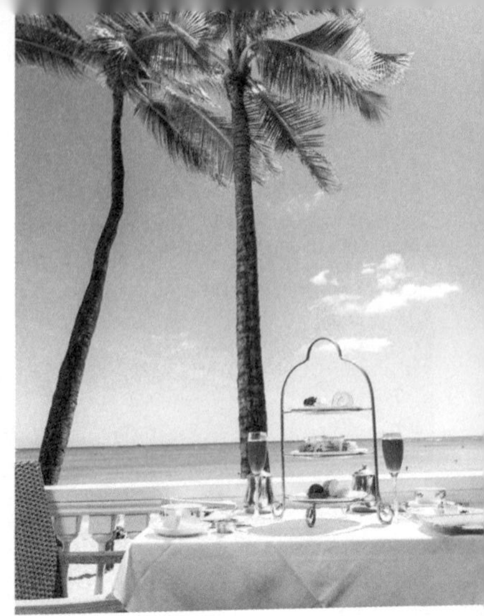

## 16 Take Tea at the Moana

Relaxed and refined at the same time, the Moana Surfrider offers high tea on its oceanfront Veranda, complete with dainty sandwiches, desserts, and a dose of glamour. *(Ch. 3)*

## 17 Visit Iolani Palace

The only royal residence in the United States gives you an introduction to the era of Hawaii's monarchy, which ended with the overthrow of Queen Liliuokalani in 1893. *(Ch. 3)*

## 18 Eat Out in Kaimuki

This unassuming neighborhood east of Waikiki and north of Diamond Head offers a diverse array of restaurants (both upscale and more affordable) in a part of town with a distinct local vibe. *(Ch. 3)*

## 19 Explore the Nature Preserve at Kaena Point

Striking, stark, solitary: Kaena Point requires an easy (though not shaded) hike out to the island's westernmost point, which is considered a sacred spot. *(Ch. 5, 7)*

## 20 Relive History at Pearl Harbor

You can't go to Oahu and skip a visit to Pearl Harbor National Memorial, which preserves the USS *Arizona* and other World War II sites. *(Ch. 3)*

## 21 Treat Yourself to Shave Ice at Island Snow

Matsumoto's on the North Shore may offer the most well-known shave ice, but we (and former president Barack Obama) prefer Island Snow in Kailua. *(Ch. 6)*

## 22 Try a Spam Musubi

If you want to eat like a local, you've got to try what is basically Spam sushi—sticky rice with seasoned, fried Spam wrapped up in seaweed. It's surprisingly tasty. *(Ch. 3, 4, 5, 6)*

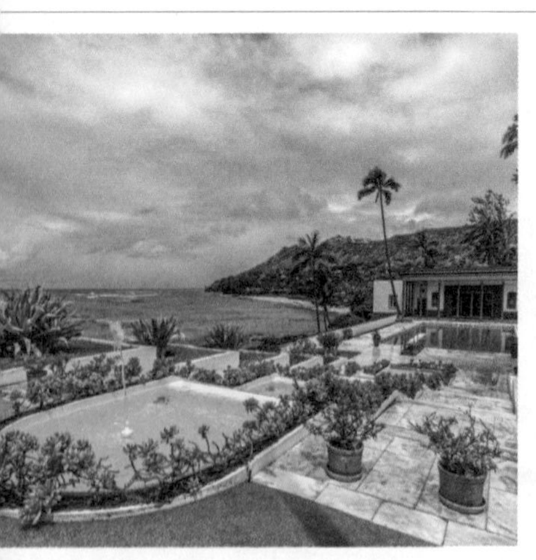

## 23 Visit Doris Duke's Shangri La

Tobacco heiress Doris Duke's incredible waterfront mansion, now a museum, was inspired by the Middle East, South Asia, and North Africa. Don't miss it. *(Ch. 3, 6)*

## 24 Feel the Wind at Nuuanu Pali Lookout

On especially windy days, you can actually lean up against the wind, and on most days, you get spectacular views. *(Ch. 6)*

# 25 Watch the Pros Surf at Waimea Bay

During winter, when waves can crest past 20 feet, Waimea Bay is one of the best places in the world to watch the pros catch the big ones. *(Ch. 5, 7)*

# WHAT'S WHERE

**1 Honolulu and Pearl Harbor.** The vibrant state capital, Honolulu is home to the nation's only royal palace and has free concerts under the tamarind trees in the financial district and art galleries, breweries, fun bars, and outdoor markets in Chinatown, Kakaako, and other neighborhoods. It also encompasses Waikiki—dressed in lights at the base of Diamond Head, famous for its world-class resorts, shopping, restaurants, and surf—and Pearl Harbor, Hawaii's largest natural harbor and the resting place of the USS *Arizona*, sunk on December 7, 1941.

**2 West (Leeward) and Central Oahu.** The island's rugged western side has become a suburban destination with golf courses and resorts surrounding lagoons in Ko Olina. It's also home to the new Wai Kai entertainment complex (opened in 2023), featuring a massive wave pool. Although the interstate cuts through the region, fertile Central Oahu is an integral part of Hawaii's rich cultural history. This valley, between the Waianae and Koolau

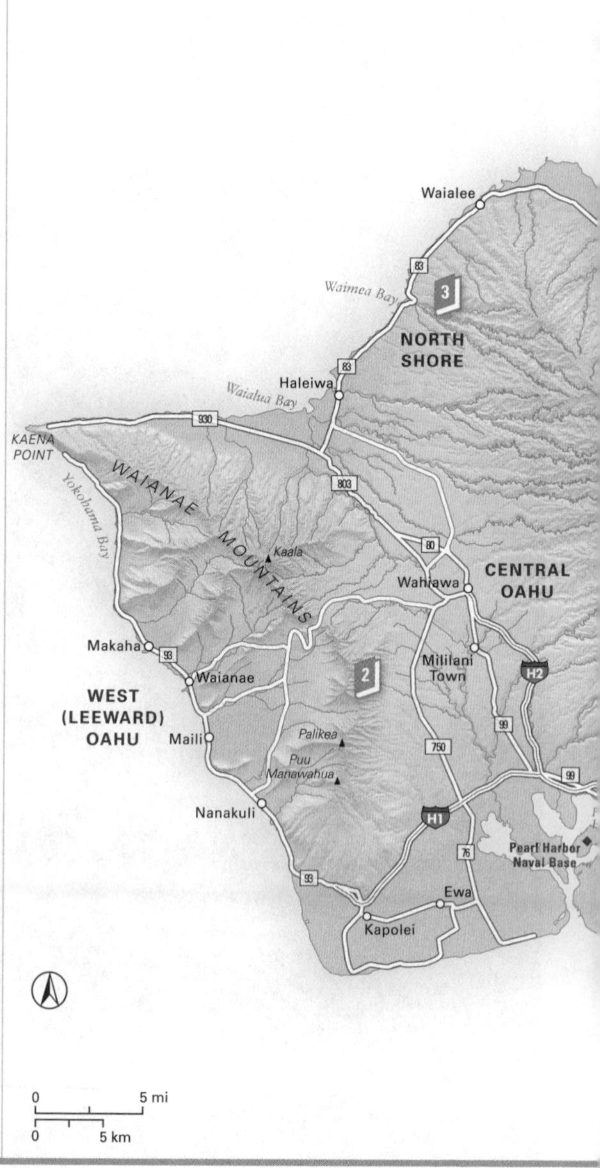

mountain ranges, is a mix of farms, planned communities, and strip malls.

**3 North Shore.** Best known for its miles of first-rate surf breaks and green sea turtle sightings, the world-famous North Shore is home to the legendary laid-back surf town of Haleiwa. This plantation area also has farms, restaurants, and scenic hiking trails.

**4 East (Windward) Oahu.** The sleepy neighborhoods at the base of the majestic Koolau Mountains offer a respite from bustling Honolulu, with charming eateries, long stretches of sandy beaches, ancient Hawaiian fishponds, and offshore islands to explore. In the southeastern corner of Oahu, Honolulu's main bedroom communities crawl up the steep valleys that flow into Maunalua Bay. Also here are snorkelers' favorite Hanauma Bay and a string of wild and often hidden beaches.

# Oahu Today

The island of Oahu, often referred to as "The Gathering Place," is usually the first Hawaiian destination that travelers visit. It's the third largest of the Hawaiian islands and also the most populated, with about 75% of the state's 1.4 million residents.

## OVERTOURISM AND THE COST OF LIVING

Oahu truly features the best of both worlds, with a big-city vibe alongside tropical sandy beaches and turquoise ocean waves. The half-million visitors arriving each month find not only a world-famous surf destination but also one rich in natural beauty and Hawaiian heritage. Although tourism fuels Hawaii's heartbeat, the COVID-19 pandemic prompted a shift toward creating a more environmentally friendly and culturally meaningful experience for visitors. To address overtourism and protect some strained natural resources, a statewide plan introduced new fees and reservation requirements limiting the number of visitors at certain popular destinations, such as Diamond Head. Visitors should check reservation policies before visiting sites such as Hanauma Bay Nature Preserve.

Despite Oahu's beauty, beneath the surface lie ongoing challenges for locals. Reliance on tourism strains the island's resources, creating daily traffic jams and soaring housing prices. Today most residents' salaries do not nearly match Hawaii's high cost of living. It's not unusual for locals to hold multiple jobs, share homes with extended family, and endure long commutes to Honolulu.

Locals are also dealing with the consequences of Bill 89 (City Ordinance 19-18). Introduced in 2019, it limits short-term residential/apartment rentals. Some residents relied on rentals for added income, while others remain firmly against rentals. At this writing, short-term rentals are only allowed in Waikiki, Ko Olina, and Turtle Bay. Despite these hurdles, Oahu's allure persists.

## SUSTAINABILITY

Embracing a forward-thinking ethos regarding climate change and sustainability, Oahu is promoting environmental practices spearheaded by a 2021 mandate by the city of Honolulu to create a carbon-neutral economy focusing on renewable energy and sustainable infrastructure. In recent years, too, Hawaii has launched an educational initiative to identify the best ways to preserve the land, beaches, and marine life. Oahu's commitment includes tangible measures, such as banning plastic straws and single-use bags. Today, all sunblock sold in Hawaii is reef-safe. The state is also considering a "climate fee" for tourists that would support Hawaii's unique natural resources.

Overall, the island is moving toward a more eco-friendly mindset. Hawaii Tourism's Malama Hawaii program (🌐 *www.gohawaii.com/malama*) echoes this earth-friendly approach, offering travelers opportunities to engage with natural sites and culture responsibly. Encouraging "malama" (which means "to care for"), the initiative promotes voluntourism and supporting local businesses. Many hotels across Hawaii offer special Malama packages so guests can participate in eco-friendly experiences.

## HONORING HAWAIIAN CULTURE

In the late 1700s, the arrival of Western Europeans launched a chain of events that negatively impacted Hawaiian culture, nearly leading to its eradication. The situation worsened after Hawaii became a U.S. state in 1959, with Americanization efforts including banning the Hawaiian language in schools and prohibiting celebrations.

Since the 1970s, a cultural renaissance has unfolded as Hawaiians reclaim their heritage through hula, lei making, music, and traditional practices like pounding poi and learning the nutritional properties of native plants. Waikiki, the island's main tourist destination, offers some immersive experiences to visitors. Landmark hotels like the Royal Hawaiian and Moana Surfrider provide free, captivating historical tours, and other resorts offer lei-making sessions, sunrise ceremonies, and more.

Additionally, a turnaround is seen in Oahu's Native Hawaiian population, which is increasing for the first time since the 18th century. Considered the first of its kind, Puuhonua o Waimanalo is a unique settlement developed in 1994 in partnership with the state. It houses over 200 mostly Indigenous residents on nearly 50 acres of land. This community is actively dedicated to preserving and promoting Hawaii's culture and traditions.

## IMPACT OF NEIGHBORHOOD DEVELOPMENT

Several Oahu neighborhoods are experiencing increased development. In Honolulu, the Kakaako neighborhood has been transformed from its industrial roots into a trendy hub with bars, restaurants, and street art. However, despite its allure, most of the luxury high-rises are owned by nonresidents.

Located about 40 minutes west of Waikiki, popular Ko Olina is home to opulent resorts and man-made lagoons. Nearby, in Ewa Beach, the new Wai Kai entertainment complex, with its massive wave pool and several restaurants, is ushering in development to this residential community. On the windward side, the beach town of Kailua has become a sought-after destination, requiring parking restrictions and crowd management. As these areas grow, maintaining the unique character of each locale is becoming essential to locals.

## TRANSPORTATION

For public transportation within Waikiki and around Oahu, there's TheBus, the Waikiki Trolley, and taxi or ride-share options. In 2023, the first segment of the Honolulu Rail Transit system, called Skyline, opened, running from East Kapolei to Aloha Stadium. This multiyear elevated train project is expected to cost over $10 billion dollars when it fully opens in 2031, extending to Honolulu's Ala Moana Center. Currently, the Skyline is not near Honolulu or Waikiki, so it is of limited use to most visitors.

## AGRICULTURE AND OAHU'S CULINARY SCENE

Hawaii's agricultural landscape used to center on sugarcane and pineapple, but sugarcane is now gone, and pineapples are grown only on a small scale. Despite the state's reliance on imports (about 80%), a statewide push for a sustainable food supply has rejuvenated local agriculture.

Today restaurants on Oahu take pride in serving farm-to-table cuisine, aligning with the movement to prioritize fresh, locally sourced produce. Popular farmers' markets display a spectrum of delights, from papayas to artisanal honey. Oahu's culinary scene, particularly in Waikiki and Kakaako, is bustling, with a surge of independent eateries across the island. Diners can savor diverse cuisines, spanning casual beach bites to elaborate and expensive tasting menus, that feature a fusion of global flavors. Traditional Hawaiian favorites like plate lunches endure, though, and other menus reflect a modern Hawaiian flair.

# Oahu's Best Beaches

**SUNSET (PAUMALU) BEACH PARK, NORTH SHORE**
As its name implies, this beautiful beach, just down the road from the world-famous Banzai Pipeline, is a favorite place to catch the sun's last brilliant rays before it dips below the horizon. It also offers calm waters and fun snorkeling in summer and big waves in winter.

**ALA MOANA REGIONAL PARK, HONOLULU**
Just a few steps away from the Ala Moana Center's shops and restaurants, this beach offers extraordinarily fine sand and smaller crowds than Waikiki, which is about 20 minutes away. With lifeguards, amenities (though little shade), and a protective reef, this is a family-friendly spot with plenty of activity in and out of the water, including stand-up paddleboarding and snorkeling, as well as bicycling and picnicking. It's also a favorite local surfing spot, with several popular breaks just offshore.

**WAIMANALO BAY BEACH PARK, EAST (WINDWARD) OAHU**
Picturesque and family-friendly, Waimanalo Bay Beach Park is an eastward-facing stretch of white sand and turquoise water that's famous for spectacular sunrises, shady ironwood trees, and strong afternoon breezes. In addition to the stunning views, there are good amenities: lifeguards, showers, picnic tables, restrooms, and ample parking.

**HALEIWA ALII BEACH PARK, NORTH SHORE**
This legendary surfing spot attracts professional surfers all winter long. Its beach park is popular (and often busy), with shade, picnic tables, showers, and other amenities. In summer, the beach becomes one of the North Shore's few that are considered safe for swimmers. It's also great for snorkelers and novice surfers. Soak in some authentic island vibes by checking out the town of Haleiwa's shops and surf culture.

**KO OLINA BEACH, WEST (LEEWARD) OAHU**
Four picture-perfect, totally protected, man-made lagoons in front of three major resorts—including Disney's incredible Aulani—offer soft sand and calm, turquoise water. The Ko Olina area was truly made for family-friendly fun, with kayaks, SUPs (stand-up paddleboards), and snorkel gear readily available for rent and plenty of room for everyone, with grassy areas for relaxing and enjoying a pleasant beach day.

**KUALOA REGIONAL PARK, EAST (WINDWARD) OAHU**
With lots of shade and green space, this expansive park makes it possible for campers and other beachgoers to spread out. The sand itself isn't very wide, but the waves are gentle, and it's a great spot for swimming, kayaking, and paddleboarding. If the wind is kicking up, you might see locals flying large, two-handed kites. The scenery here is lovely, too, with the Koolau Mountains forming a distant backdrop and Mokolii Island visible offshore.

Ko Olina, Leeward (West) Oahu

**LANIKAI BEACH, EAST (WINDWARD) OAHU**

Tucked away in a quiet residential neighborhood, this beach offers powdery white sand and crystal clear water but very limited shade. It's worth getting here before dawn, as it's a gorgeous place to catch the sunrise. Unlike at nearby Kailua Beach Park, no food, water, or facilities are available here, so bring whatever you think you will need to enjoy the tranquil setting. Access to this beach is through several narrow pedestrian walkways that you can see from the street, but parking is very limited.

**SANDY BEACH PARK, EAST (WINDWARD) OAHU**

This south shore, Hawaii Kai–area beach features plenty of room to spread out atop the fine golden sand and enjoy the scenery, including, if the tides are right, a glimpse of the nearby Halona Blowhole. Popular with locals and known for its crashing shorebreak, this beach has lifeguards and facilities. If the waves are rough, though, it's best to retire to the shoreline and watch the activity—which might include kites performing acrobatics in the gusts—from your lounge chair.

**WHITE PLAINS BEACH, WEST (LEEWARD) OAHU**

A go-to beach for surfing, stand-up paddleboarding, and bodyboarding, White Plains is a favorite among locals (and, often, seals). Not only is it known to be less crowded than Waikiki, but it also has beautiful azure water and a smooth, sandy bottom. The currents and wind can be strong and unpredictable, but there are lifeguards watching over the swimmers. You'll also find abundant parking, as well as many other amenities.

**WAIMEA BAY BEACH PARK, NORTH SHORE**

During the summer, the snorkeling is simply magical at this popular, jaw-droppingly beautiful beach. But in winter, surf's up, so be careful if you don't know what you're doing. Major contests are held here, as waves frequently reach 20 feet. "The Eddie" surf competition honors big-wave surfer Eddie Aikau, attracting fans from across the Islands, so arrive early in the morning to claim your seat on the dunes.

# Oahu's Most Incredible Natural Wonders

**WAIMEA BAY AND VALLEY, NORTH SHORE**
The scenic and legendary Waimea Bay is famous for powerful, big waves in winter and calm water in summer. Nearby is the lush and expansive Waimea Valley, with exquisite scenery, including waterfalls (there's an admission charge to enter this preserve).

**HALONA BLOWHOLE, EAST (WINDWARD) OAHU**
North of the picturesque Hanauma Bay, the Halona Blowhole can be viewed easily from a lookout just off the Kalanianaole Highway. Formed by ancient lava tubes, this blowhole blasts a forceful spray about 30 feet in the air when the tide is right.

**MANOA FALLS, HONOLULU**
In the lush Manoa Valley, a trail leads to this beautiful and ancient waterfall, which drops 150 feet into a pool. Surrounding it is a tropical rain forest with soaring bamboo, trees, and flowers. It will come as no surprise that the cascade is a popular filming location.

**DIAMOND HEAD, HONOLULU**
Legendary and majestic, Oahu's breathtaking Diamond Head crater is an iconic symbol of the island. Looming large above Waikiki's coastline, the former military outpost is now a popular place to hike. Panoramic views from the top are truly splendid, but it's a steep climb and always best to go in the early morning to see the sunrise. Advance reservations are required for the hike.

**KAENA POINT, WEST (LEEWARD) OAHU AND NORTH SHORE**
Wild and remote, Kaena Point is the westernmost point on Oahu. Featuring picturesque coves and sweeping ocean views, this spot can only be reached by hiking a rocky (and often muddy) trail along the rough coastline that offers extraordinary vistas. It's home to a bird sanctuary and nature reserve. The point has two entrances (Kaena Point State Park and Mokuleia), from West Oahu and the North Shore, so you can trek for about 5 miles round-trip.

**HANAUMA BAY, EAST (WINDWARD) OAHU**
On the island's southeast coast, Hanauma Bay is one of Oahu's most popular snorkeling spots. With white sand and shallow, calm water, this nature preserve is teeming with tropical fish and marine life. Over the years, it's become increasingly crowded, so visitors are now capped at 1,400 per day. The entrance fee is $25, and tickets must be booked and

Diamond Head

paid for in advance on the website (🌐 *hanaumabay-statepark.com*).

**NUUANU PALI LOOKOUT, EAST (WINDWARD) OAHU**

As part of the Koolau mountain range, the renowned Nuuanu Pali Lookout is situated along the road in Nuuanu Pali State Park and offers a panoramic view of Oahu. At nearly 1,000 feet high, this notoriously windy spot offers views far across the island's windward coast and the ocean beyond. It also played a major role in King Kamehameha I's epic victory over the troops of Oahu. This viewpoint can get very busy.

**KOOLAU MOUNTAINS, EAST (WINDWARD) OAHU**

Stretching nearly 40 miles, this majestic volcanic mountain formation features an abundance of steep trails that lead to gorgeous waterfalls and streams. The most recognizable section of this mountain range is the cliff that rises to about 2,000 feet on the eastern side.

**MAKAPUU POINT, EAST (WINDWARD) OAHU**

On the island's southeastern tip, the Makapuu Point lookout is located off the side of the Kalanianaole Highway. A paved walkway leads to an overlook with a breathtaking panoramic view of Windward Oahu's dramatic sea cliffs and lovely Makapuu Beach Park (or you can take a short hike to the lighthouse nearby). It's also known as a great spot for whale-watching.

**HOOMALUHIA BOTANICAL GARDEN, EAST (WINDWARD) OAHU**

This beautiful garden destination, created by the U.S. Army Corps of Engineers, is free to enjoy and is home to tropical trees, plants, and flowers from across the world, all grouped by region.

# Flora and Fauna in Hawaii

**PLUMERIA**
Also known as frangipani, this fragrant flower is named after Charles Plumier, the noted French botanist who discovered it in Central America in the late 1600s. Plumeria come in shades of white, yellow, pink, red, and orange. The hearty, plentiful blossoms are frequently used in lei.

**GARDENIA**
The gardenia is a favorite for lei makers because of its sweet smell. The plant is native to tropical regions throughout China and Africa, but there are also endemic gardenias in Hawaii. The nanu gardenia is found only in the Islands and has petite white blossoms.

**HONU**
The *honu*, or Hawaiian green sea turtle, is a magical sight. The graceful reptile is an endangered and protected species in Hawaii. It's easier to encounter *honu* during a snorkeling or scuba-diving excursion, but they occasionally can be spotted basking on beaches.

**KUKUI**
The kukui, or candlenut, is Hawaii's state tree, and Hawaiians have had many uses for it. Oil was extracted from its nuts and burned as a light source and also rubbed on fishing nets to preserve them. The juice from the husk's fruit was used as a dye. The small kukui blossoms and nuts also have medicinal purposes.

**HUMPBACK WHALES**
Each year, North Pacific humpback whales make the long journey to Hawaii from Alaska. With its warm, protected waters, Hawaii provides the ideal place for the marine mammals to mate and to birth and to nurse their young. They arrive between November and May, and their presence is an anticipated event. You can see them up close during whale-watching boat tours.

**MONK SEAL**
Known as the *ilio holo i ka uaua*, meaning "dog that runs in rough water," monk seals are endemic to Hawaii and critically endangered. The majority of these mammals, which can grow to more than 7 feet long, live in the remote, uninhabited Northwestern Hawaiian Islands.

**TROPICAL FISH**
Approximately 25% of the fish species in the Islands are endemic. Snorkeling in Hawaii is a unique, fun opportunity to see colorful fish found nowhere else on Earth. Interestingly, Hawaii's state fish, the *humuhumunukunukuapuaa*, or reef trigger, is not endemic to the state.

**NENE GOOSE**
Pronounced *nay-nay*, the endemic nene goose (Hawaii's state bird) is one of the world's rarest. A descendant of the Canada goose, it has been bred back from the edge of extinction and reintroduced into the wild. Use caution driving in national and state parks, which they frequent.

**HIBISCUS**
In 1923, the Territory of Hawaii passed a law designating hibiscus as Hawaii's official flower. While there are more than 30 introduced species of the large, colorful flowers throughout the Islands, there are five endemic types. The endemic hibiscus has yellow blossoms and is known in Hawaiian as *mao hau hele*, which means the "traveling green tree."

**PIKAKE**
These small, delicate blossoms are known for their hypnotic, sweet scent. The jasmine flower was introduced from India and was a favorite of Princess Kaiulani. *Pikake*, which is the Hawaiian word for the blossom as well as for a peacock—another favorite of the princess—is the subject of many *mele*, or Hawaiian songs.

# What to Eat and Drink in Hawaii

**SHAVE ICE**

Shave ice is simple in its composition—fluffy ice drizzled in Technicolor syrups. Shave ice traces its roots to Hawaii's plantation past. Japanese laborers would use the machetes from their field work to finely shave ice from large frozen blocks and then pour fruit juice over it.

**MUSUBI**

*Musubi* are Hawaii's answer to the perfect snack. Portable, handheld, and salty, *musubi* are a great go-to any time of day. The local comfort food is a slice of fried Spam encased in packed white rice and snugly wrapped with nori, or dried seaweed. Available everywhere, *musubi* are usually just a few dollars.

**MAI TAI**

When people think of a Hawaiian cocktail, the colorful mai tai often comes to mind. It's the unofficial drink to imbibe at a luau and refreshingly tropical. This potent concoction has a rum base and is traditionally made with orange curaçao, orgeat, fresh-squeezed lime juice, and simple syrup.

**HAWAIIAN PLATE LUNCH**

The Hawaiian plate lunch comprises the delicious, traditional foods of Hawaii, all on one heaping plate. You can find these combo meals anywhere, from roadside lunch wagons to five-star restaurants. Get yours with the melt-in-your-mouth shredded kalua pig, pork, or chicken *laulau* (cooked in ti leaves) with *lomi lomi* salmon (diced salmon with tomatoes and onions) on the side and the coconut-milk *haupia* for dessert. Most Hawaiian plates come with the requisite two scoops of white rice. Don't forget to try *poi*, or pounded and cooked taro.

**POKE**

In Hawaiian, *poke* is a verb that means to slice and cut into pieces. It perfectly describes the technique Hawaiians have used for centuries to prepare poke the dish. The cubed raw fish, most commonly *ahi* (yellowfin tuna), is traditionally tossed with Hawaiian sea salt, *limu kohu* (red seaweed), or *inamona* (crushed kukui nuts). Today, countless varieties of this must-try dish are served in all kinds of restaurants across the Islands. Poke shacks offer no-frills, made-to-order poke.

**SAIMIN**

This only-in-Hawaii noodle dish is the culinary innovation of Hawaii plantation workers in the late 1800s who created a new comfort food with ingredients and traditions from their home countries.

Poke

**MANAPUA**

When *kamaaina*, or Hawaii residents, are invited to a potluck, business meeting, or even an impromptu party, inevitably there will be a box filled with *manapua*. Inside these airy white buns are pockets of sweet *char siu* pork. Head to cities and towns around the Islands, and you'll find restaurants with manapua on their menus, as well as manapua takeout places serving a variety of fillings. There's sweet potato, curry chicken, *lap cheong* (or Chinese sausage)—and even sweet flavors, such as custard and *ube*, a purple yam popular in Filipino desserts.

**MALASADA**

*Malasadas* are a beloved treat in Hawaii. The Portuguese pastries are about the size of a baseball and are airy, deep-fried, and dusted with sugar. They are best enjoyed hot and filled with custard; fillings are a Hawaiian variation on the original.

**LOCO MOCO**

The traditional version of one of Hawaii's classic comfort-food dishes consists of white rice topped with a hamburger patty and fried eggs and generously blanketed in rich, brown gravy. Cafe 100 in Hilo on the Big Island is renowned as the home of the *loco moco*, but you'll find this popular staple everywhere. It can be eaten any time of day.

**KONA COFFEE**

In Kona, on the Big Island, coffee reigns supreme. There are roughly 600 coffee farms dotting the west side of the island, each producing flavorful (and quite expensive) coffee grown in the rich, volcanic soil. Kona coffee is typically hand-harvested from August through December.

# What to Buy in Hawaii

**LEI**

As a visitor to Hawaii, you may well receive a lei, either a shell, kukui nut, or fragrant flower variety, as a welcome to the Islands. *Kamaaina* (Hawaii residents) mark special occasions by gifting lei.

**LAUHALA**

The hala tree is most known for its long, thin leaves and the masterful crafts that are created from them. Lauhala weavers make baskets, hats, mats, jewelry, and more, using intricate traditional patterns and techniques.

**JEWELRY**

Island-inspired jewelry comes in many styles. Tahitian pearl pendants and earrings are a local favorite, as are delicate, inexpensive shell pieces. The most coveted are Hawaiian heirloom bracelets in gold or silver with one's name enameled in Old English script.

**MACADAMIA NUT CANDY**

Macadamia nuts are native to Australia, but the gumball-sized nut remains an important crop in Hawaii. It was first introduced in the late 1880s as a windbreak for sugarcane crops. Today, mac nuts are a popular local snack and are especially good baked in cookies or other desserts.

**ALOHA WEAR**

Aloha wear in Hawaii has come a long way from the polyester fabrics with too-bright, kitschy patterns (although those still exist). Local designers have been creating dressy, modern aloha attire with softer prints that evoke Island botanicals, heritage, and traditional patterns. Hawaii residents don aloha wear for everything from work to weddings.

**HAWAIIAN COFFEE**

Reminisce about your Hawaii getaway each time you brew a cup of aromatic, full-bodied coffee, whether it's from Kona or Kauai. All the main islands grow distinctive coffee. Stores and cafés sell bags of varying sizes, and in some places you can buy directly from a farmer.

**HAWAIIAN HONEY**

With its temperate climate and bountiful foliage, Hawaii is ideal for honeybees. Its unique ecosystem yields honeys with robust flavors and textures, including elixirs extracted from the blossoms of the macadamia nut tree, the lehua flower, and the invasive Christmas berry shrub.

**KOA WOOD**

If you're looking for an heirloom keepsake from the Islands, consider a koa wood product. Grown only in Hawaii, the valuable koa is some of the world's rarest and hardest wood. Hawaiians traditionally made surfboards and canoes from these trees, which today grow only in upland forests.

**HAWAIIAN SEA SALT**

A long tradition of harvesting salt beds by hand continues today on all the Islands. The salt comes in various colors, including inky black and brick red—the result of the salt reacting and mixing with activated charcoal and *alaea* (volcanic clay). It is renowned by chefs around the state.

**UKULELE**

In Hawaiian, *ukulele* means "the jumping flea." The small instrument made its way to the Islands in the 1880s via Portuguese immigrants who brought with them the four-string, guitarlike *machete de braga*. It is famous as a solo instrument today, with virtuoso artists like Jake Shimabukuro and Taimane Gardner popularizing the ukulele's versatile sound.

# What to Read and Watch

### *HAWAIIAN MYTHOLOGY* BY MARTHA BECKWITH

This exhaustive work of ethnology and folklore was researched and collected by Martha Beckwith over decades and published when she was 69. *Hawaiian Mythology* is a comprehensive look at the Hawaiian ancestral deities and their importance throughout history.

### *HAWAII'S STORY BY HAWAII'S QUEEN* BY LILIUOKALANI

This poignant book by Queen Liliuokalani chronicles the 1893 overthrow of the Hawaiian monarchy and her plea for her people. It's an essential read to understand the political undercurrent and the push for sovereignty that exists in the Islands more than 125 years later.

### *LETTERS FROM HAWAII* BY MARK TWAIN

In 1866, when Samuel Clemens was 31, he sailed from California and spent four months in Hawaii. He eventually mailed 25 letters to the *Sacramento Union* newspaper about his experiences. Along the way, Twain sheds some cultural biases as he visits Kilauea Volcano, meets with Hawaii's newly formed legislators, and examines the sugar trade.

### *SHOAL OF TIME: A HISTORY OF THE HAWAIIAN ISLANDS* BY GAVAN DAWS

Perhaps the most popular book by this best-selling Honolulu author is *Shoal of Time*. Published in 1974, the account of modern Hawaiian history details the colonization of Hawaii and everything that was lost in the process.

### *MOLOKAI* BY ALAN BRENNERT

The writer's debut novel, set in the 1890s, follows a Hawaiian woman who contracts leprosy as a child and is sent to the remote, quarantined community of Kalaupapa on the island of Molokai, where she then lives. The Southern California–based author was inspired to write the book during his visits to Hawaii.

### *HAWAII SAYS "ALOHA"* BY DON BLANDING

First published in 1928, this volume of enchanting, rhyming verse about Hawaii evokes the rich details about the Islands that mesmerized the author in the 1920s and for the rest of his life. Blanding also illustrated this and many other books and was later named Hawaii's poet laureate.

### *THE DESCENDANTS*

Based on the book by local author Kaui Hart Hemmings, the film adaptation starring George Clooney and directed by Alexander Payne was filmed on Oahu and Kauai. It spotlights a contemporary, upper-class family in Hawaii as they deal with family grief and landholdings in flux.

### *BLUE HAWAII*

The 1961 musical features the hip-shaking songs and moves of Elvis Presley, who plays tour guide Chadwick Gates. Elvis famously sings "Ke Kali Nei Au," or "The Hawaiian Wedding Song," at the iconic and now-shuttered Coco Palms Resort on Kauai. (The resort has remained closed since 1992 following Hurricane Iniki.)

### *MOANA*

The release of *Moana* in 2016 was celebrated by many in Hawaii and the Pacific for showcasing Polynesian culture. The now-beloved animated movie, which tells the story of the demigod Maui, features the voice talents of Auli'i Cravalho and Dwayne Johnson. In 2018, *Moana* was rerecorded and distributed in Olelo Hawaii, or the Hawaiian language, with Cravalho reprising her role. It marked the first time a Disney movie was available in Hawaiian.

# Kids and Families

## CHOOSING A PLACE TO STAY

**Resorts:** All the big resorts make programs for kids a priority. When booking your room, ask about *keiki* (children's) menus at restaurants, free on-property activities, and pools and water parks designed specifically for the younger set. In Waikiki, your best bet for kids is the Hilton Hawaiian Village, where there's a large beach, lagoon, and loads of kids' programs. Also good choices: the Alohilani Resort, which has a roster of family-friendly cultural activities, and the beachfront Sheraton Waikiki, where the Helumoa Playground features two pools and a water slide.

**Condos:** You can cook your own food and get twice the space of a hotel room for much less. Ask about the size of the complex's pool and barbecue availability. For the ultimate family condo experience on Oahu, Marriott's Ko Olina Beach Club is ideal thanks to its sheltered beaches, four pools, barbecues, children's play areas, large kitchens, and an on-site grocery store. In Waikiki, try the Waikiki Shore and Luana Waikiki. ■ **TIP→ Some hotels and resorts offer free beach towels, chairs, and other amenities. Be sure to check on such things in advance.**

## OCEAN ACTIVITIES

**On the beach:** In Waikiki, your best beach bets for young children are Kuhio Beach Park and Fort DeRussy Beach Park, both protected from a strong shore break and with a wide stretch of sand, with lifeguards on duty. On the windward side, try Kailua Beach Park, with its shady trees and good bathroom/shower facilities. North Shore beaches are recommended for children only in the summer months, and of these, Waimea Bay, with its wide stretch of sand and good facilities, is best for kids. On the leeward side, Ko Olina's protected coves with calm waters are great for families with small children.

**On the waves:** Waikiki is *the* place for everyone to learn to surf, including kids. Some hotels, including the Royal Hawaiian, the Halekulani, and the Outrigger Waikiki Beach Resort, offer in-house surf schools steps from these mellow waves. For a less crowded surfing experience, try White Plains beach.

**The underwater world:** Hawaii is a great place to introduce your kids to snorkeling. Even without the mask and snorkel, they'll be able to see colorful fish darting around coral reefs, and they may also spot endangered Hawaiian green sea turtles and dolphins. On Oahu, the quintessential snorkeling experience is at Hanauma Bay, where kids can see hundreds of species of fish in protected waters and enjoy a wide stretch of beach. In summer months only, Shark's Cove on the North Shore is an interesting experience for older kids who already have snorkeling basics.

## LAND ACTIVITIES

Oahu has the greatest variety of land-based experiences in the Islands. Kids can visit the Honolulu Zoo for twilight tours, explore the undersea world at the Waikiki Aquarium, or husk a coconut at the Polynesian Cultural Center. Hoomaluhia Botanical Garden offers wide-open spaces and a duck pond, while Kualoa Ranch is the place for horseback riding.

## AFTER DARK

At night, children get a kick out of a luau. Older kids are likely to enjoy the handful of more modern luau, incorporating acrobatics, lively music, and fire dancers. Check on the status of Hilton Hawaiian Village's free Friday night fireworks shows, which are especially fun to watch from the beach in Waikiki.

# The History of Hawaii

## THE POLYNESIANS

Years before the eras of the Vikings and Christopher Columbus, Polynesian seafarers embarked on journeys across the boundless ocean in wooden, double-hulled canoes. These were no chance voyages—these adventurers possessed an intricate understanding of celestial navigation and sailing. Originating from western Polynesia, they navigated between Samoa, Fiji, Tahiti, the Marquesas, and the Society Isles. By AD 300, they had established settlements in far-flung places like Hawaii and Easter Island.

Around AD 1200, the pinnacle of Polynesian voyaging was reached. Following this, the distant Hawaiian Islands evolved independently, fostering distinct cultural practices and ways of life. The community on these islands beautifully blended religion, mythology, science, and artistry. Each settlement, overseen by an *alii*, a chief, existed within an *ahupuaa*, a pie-shaped division of land that extended from the mountains, through the valleys to the shores. Everyone played a crucial role such as crafting canoes, fishing, or farming.

## THE HAWAIIAN KINGDOM

In 1778, when Captain James Cook arrived in Kealakekua Bay on the Big Island, the Hawaiians welcomed him warmly with a sense of great importance. The trade that followed, including the acquisition of guns from foreign ships, provided Kamehameha the Great, the chief of the Big Island, with a strategic advantage over other chiefs. This led to the unification of Hawaii into a single kingdom in 1810, putting an end to the frequent interisland battles that had long defined Hawaiian life.

However, the new kingdom faced many challenges. Native religion was abandoned, and traditions, including *kapu* (laws and regulations) were eventually discarded. In addition, the European explorers brought devastating diseases that decimated the Native Hawaiian population within a few decades.

The fabric of pre-contact Hawaii began to unravel with new laws affecting land ownership and religious practices. As Western influences permeated Hawaiian culture, social unrest took root, marking a major shift in the island's way of life, including the loss of the Hawaiian language.

## MODERN HAWAII

In 1893, Queen Liliuokalani, the last Hawaiian monarch, was overthrown by American and European leaders, backed by an armed militia. This upheaval created the Republic of Hawaii, paving the way for 60 years as a U.S. territory. The scars of lost sovereignty and the terms of annexation have lingered, haunting the Hawaiian people since the monarchy's abrupt end.

In 1941, the attack on Oahu's Pearl Harbor thrust the U.S. into World War II. This surprise bombing destroyed or damaged many military ships and airplanes, and killed over 2,000 people. Visitors are encouraged to visit the memorial, which includes the battleships USS *Arizona* and USS *Missouri,* to pay tribute to the fallen.

Hawaii's complex history continued to evolve and in 1959, Hawaii officially became the 50th U.S. state. Despite ongoing challenges, a cultural revival known as the Hawaiian Renaissance began in the 1960s among the Native Hawaiian community, including resurrecting the hula, reviving voyaging canoes, and reinvigorating Hawaiian art, music, and language. Today, tourists can learn about the culture and even volunteer through the *Malama Aina* project, (meaning "to care for the land").

# HAWAIIAN CULTURAL TRADITIONS HULA, LEI, AND LUAU

# HULA: MORE THAN A FOLK DANCE

Hula has been called "the heartbeat of the Hawaiian people" and also "the world's best-known, most misunderstood dance." Both are true. Hula isn't just dance. It is storytelling.

Chanter Edith McKinzie calls it "an extension of a piece of poetry." In its adornments, implements, and customs, hula integrates every important Hawaiian cultural practice: poetry, history, genealogy, craft, plant cultivation, martial arts, religion and protocol. So when 19th-century Christian missionaries sought to eradicate a practice they considered depraved, they threatened more than just a folk dance.

With public performance outlawed and private hula practice discouraged, hula went underground for a generation. The fragile verbal link by which culture was transmitted from teacher to student hung by a thread. Even increasing literacy did not help because hula's practitioners were a secretive and protected circle.

As if that weren't bad enough, vaudeville, Broadway, and Hollywood got hold of the hula, giving it the glitz treatment in an unbroken line from "Oh, How She Could WickyWackyWoo" to "Rock-A-Hula Baby." Hula became shorthand for paradise: fragrant flowers, lazy hours. Ironically, this development assured that hundreds of Hawaiians could make a living performing and teaching hula. Many danced *'auana* (modern form) in performance; but taught *kahiko* (traditional) quietly, at home or in hula schools.

Today, decades after the cultural revival known as the Hawaiian Renaissance, language immersion programs have assured a new generation of proficient chanters, songwriters, and translators. Visitors can see more—and more authentic—traditional hula now than at any other time in the last 200 years.

Like the culture of which it is the beating heart, hula has survived.

Lei poo. Head lei. In *kahiko,* greenery only. In auana, flowers.
Face emotes appropriate expression. Dancer should not be a smiling automaton.
Shoulders remain relaxed and still, never hunched, even with arms raised. No bouncing.
Eyes always follow leading hand.
Lei. Hula is rarely performed without a shoulder lei.
Arms and hands remain loose, relaxed, below shoulder level—except as required by interpretive movements.
Traditional hula skirt is loose fabric, smocked and gathered at the waist.
Hip is canted over weight-bearing foot.
Knees are always slightly bent, accentuating hip sway.
*Kupee.* Ankle bracelet of flowers, shells, or foliage.
In *kahiko*, feet are flat. In *'auana*, they may be more arched, but not tiptoes or bouncing.

At backyard parties, hula is performed in bare feet and street clothes, but in performance, adornments play a key role, as do rhythm-keeping implements such as the *pahu* drum and the *ipu* (gourd).

In hula *kahiko* (traditional style), the usual dress is multiple layers of stiff fabric (often with a pellom lining, which most closely resembles *kapa*, the paperlike bark cloth of the Hawaiians). These wrap tightly around the bosom but flare below the waist to form a skirt. In pre-contact times, dancers wore only kapa skirts. Men traditionally wear loincloths.

Monarchy-period hula is performed in voluminous muumuu or high-necked muslin blouses and gathered skirts. Men wear white or gingham shirts and black pants.

In hula *'auana* (modern), dress for women can range from grass skirts and strapless tops to contemporary tea-length dresses. Men generally wear aloha shirts, but sometimes grass skirts over pants or even everyday gear.

### BASIC MOTIONS

Speak or sing

Moon or sun

Grass shack or house

Mountains or heights

Love or caress

### SURPRISING HULA FACTS

- Grass skirts are not traditional; workers from Kiribati (the Gilbert Islands) brought this custom to Hawaii.
- In olden-day Hawaii, *mele* (songs) for hula were composed for every occasion—name songs for babies, dirges for funerals, welcome songs for visitors, celebrations of favorite pursuits.
- Hula *mai* is a traditional hula form in praise of a noble's genitals; the power of the *alii* (royalty) to procreate gave *mana* (spiritual power) to the entire culture.
- Hula students in old Hawaii adhered to high standards: scrupulous cleanliness, no sex, daily cleansing rituals, certain food prohibitions, and no contact with the dead. They were fined if they broke the rules.

### WHERE TO WATCH

If you're interested in "the real thing," there are annual hula festivals on each island. Check the individual island visitors' bureaus websites at *www.gohawaii.com.*

If you can't make it to a festival, there are plenty of other hula shows—at most resorts, many lounges, and even at certain shopping centers. Ask your hotel concierge for performance information.

# ALL ABOUT LEI

Lei brighten every occasion in Hawaii, from birthdays to bar mitzvahs to baptisms. Creative artisans weave nature's bounty—flowers, ferns, vines, and seeds—into gorgeous creations that convey an array of heartfelt messages: "Welcome," "Congratulations," "Good luck," "Farewell," "Thank you," "I love you." When it's difficult to find the right words, a lei expresses exactly the right sentiment.

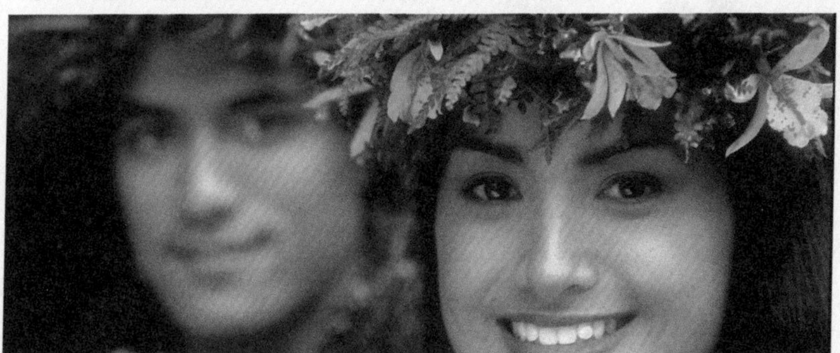

## WHERE TO BUY THE BEST LEI

Most airports in Hawaii have lei stands where you can buy a fragrant garland upon arrival. Every florist shop in the Islands sells lei; you can also treat yourself to a lei while shopping for provisions at any supermarket or box store. And you'll always find lei sellers at crafts fairs and outdoor festivals.

## LEI ETIQUETTE

- To wear a closed lei, drape it over your shoulders, half in front and half in back. Open lei are worn around the neck, with the ends draped over the front in equal lengths.
- Pikake, ginger, and other sweet, delicate blossoms are "feminine" lei. Men opt for cigar, crown flower, and ti leaf lei, which are sturdier and don't emit as much fragrance.
- Lei are always presented with a kiss, a custom that supposedly dates back to World War II when a hula dancer fancied an officer at a U.S.O. show. Taking a dare from members of her troupe, she took off her lei, placed it around his neck, and kissed him on the cheek.
- You shouldn't wear a lei before you give it to someone else. Hawaiians believe the lei absorbs your mana (spirit); if you give your lei away, you'll be giving away part of your essence.

| | |
|---|---|
|  | **ORCHID**<br>Growing wild on every continent except Antarctica, orchids—which range in color from yellow to green to purple—comprise the largest family of plants in the world. There are more than 20,000 species of orchids, but only three are native to Hawaii—and they are very rare. The pretty lavender vanda you see hanging by the dozens at local lei stands has probably been imported from Thailand. |
|  | **MAILE**<br>Maile, an endemic twining vine with a heady aroma, is sacred to Laka, goddess of the hula. In ancient times, dancers wore maile and decorated hula altars with it to honor Laka. Today, "open" maile lei usually are given to men. Instead of ribbon, interwoven lengths of maile are used at dedications of new businesses. The maile is untied, never snipped, for doing so would symbolically "cut" the company's success. |
|  | **ILIMA**<br>Designated by Hawaii's Territorial Legislature in 1923 as the official flower of the island of Oahu, the golden ilima is so delicate it lasts for just a day. Five to seven hundred blossoms are needed to make one garland. Queen Emma, wife of King Kamehameha IV, preferred ilima over all other lei, which may have led to the incorrect belief that they were reserved only for royalty. |
|  | **PLUMERIA**<br>This ubiquitous flower is named after Charles Plumier, the noted French botanist who discovered it in Central America in the late 1600s. Plumeria ranks among the most popular lei in Hawaii because it's fragrant, hardy, plentiful, inexpensive, and requires very little care. Although yellow is the most common color, you'll also find plumeria lei in shades of pink, red, orange, and "rainbow" blends. |
| 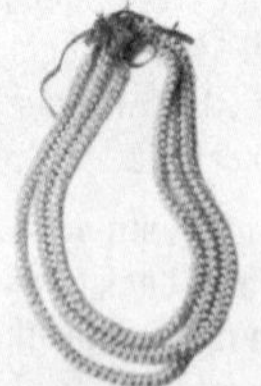 | **PIKAKE**<br>Favored for its fragile beauty and sweet scent, pikake was introduced from India. In lieu of pearls, many brides in Hawaii adorn themselves with long, multiple strands of white pikake. Princess Kaiulani enjoyed showing guests her beloved pikake and peacocks at Ainahau, her Waikiki home. Interestingly, pikake is the Hawaiian word for both the bird and the blossom. |
|  | **KUKUI**<br>The kukui (candlenut) is Hawaii's state tree. Early Hawaiians strung kukui nuts (which are quite oily) together and burned them for light; mixed burned nuts with oil to make an indelible dye; and mashed roasted nuts to consume as a laxative. Kukui nut lei may not have been made until after Western contact, when the Hawaiians saw black beads from Europe and wanted to imitate them. |

# LUAU: A TASTE OF HAWAII

The best place to sample Hawaiian food is at a backyard luau. Aunts and uncles are cooking, the pig is from a cousin's farm, and the fish is from a brother's boat.

But even locals have to angle for invitations to those rare occasions. So your choice is most likely between a commercial luau and a Hawaiian restaurant.

Some commercial luau are less authentic; they offer little of the traditional diet and are more about umbrella drinks, spectacle, and fun.

For greater culinary authenticity, folksy experiences, and rock-bottom prices, visit a Hawaiian restaurant (most are in anonymous storefronts in residential neighborhoods). Expect rough edges and some effort negotiating the menu.

In either case, much of what is known today as Hawaiian food would be as foreign to a 16th-century Hawaiian as risotto or chow mien. The pre-contact diet was simple and healthy—mainly raw and steamed seafood and vegetables. Early Hawaiians used earth ovens and heated stones to cook seafood, taro, sweet potatoes, and breadfruit and seasoned their food with sea salt and ground kukui nuts. Seaweed, fern shoots, sweet potato vines, coconut, banana, sugarcane, and select greens and roots rounded out the diet.

Successive waves of immigrants added their favorites to the ti leaf–lined table. So it is that foods as disparate as salt salmon and chicken long rice are now Hawaiian—even though there is no salmon in Hawaiian waters and long rice (cellophane noodles) is Chinese.

## AT THE LUAU: KALUA PORK

The heart of any luau is the *imu*, the earth oven in which a whole pig is roasted. The preparation of an imu is an arduous affair for most families, who tackle it only once a year or so, for a baby's first birthday or at Thanksgiving, when many Islanders prefer to imu their turkeys. Commercial luau operations have it down to a science, however.

### THE ART OF THE STONE

The key to a proper imu is the *pohaku*, the stones. Imu cook by means of long, slow, moist heat released by special stones that can withstand a hot fire without exploding. Many Hawaiian families treasure their imu stones, keeping them in a pile in the backyard and passing them on through generations.

### PIT COOKING

The imu makers first dig a pit about the size of a refrigerator, then lay down *kiawe* (mesquite) wood and stones, and build a white-hot fire that is allowed to burn itself out. The ashes are raked away, and the hot stones covered with banana and ti leaves. Well-wrapped in ti or banana leaves and a net of chicken wire, the pig is lowered onto the leaf-covered stones. *Laulau* (leaf-wrapped bundles of meats, fish, and taro leaves) may also be placed inside. Leaves—ti, banana, even ginger—cover the pig followed by wet burlap sacks (to create steam). The whole is topped with a canvas tarp and left to steam for the better part of a day.

### OPENING THE IMU

This is the moment everyone waits for: The imu is unwrapped like a giant present and the imu keepers gingerly wrestle out the steaming pig. When it's unwrapped, the meat falls moist and smoky-flavored from the bone, looking just like Southern-style pulled pork, but without the barbecue sauce.

### WHICH LUAU?

Most resort hotels have luau on their grounds that include hula, music, and, of course, lots of food and drink. Each island also has at least one "authentic" luau. For lists of the best luau on each island, visit the Hawaii Visitors and Convention Bureau website at 🌐 *www.gohawaii.com.*

## MEA AI ONO: GOOD THINGS TO EAT.

### LAULAU

Steamed meats, fish, and taro leaf in ti-leaf bundles: fork-tender, a medley of flavors; the taro resembles spinach.

### LOMI LOMI SALMON

Salt salmon in a piquant salad or relish with onions and tomatoes.

### POI

*Poi*, a paste made of pounded taro root, may be an acquired taste, but it's a must-try during your visit.

Consider: The Hawaiian Adam is descended from *kalo* (taro). Young taro plants are called "keiki" (children). Poi is the first food after mother's milk for many Islanders. *Ai*, the word for food, is synonymous with poi in many contexts.

Not only that, locals love it. "There is no meat that doesn't taste good with poi," the old Hawaiians said.

But you have to know how to eat it: with something rich or powerfully flavored. "It is salt that makes the poi go in," is another adage. When you're served poi, try it with a mouthful of smoky kalua pork or salty *lomi lomi* salmon. Its slightly sour blandness cleanses the palate. And if you don't like it, smile and say something polite. (And slide that bowl over to a local.)

Laulau

Lomi lomi salmon

Poi

## E HELE MAI AI! COME AND EAT!

Local-style Hawaiian restaurants tend to be inconveniently located in well-worn storefronts with little or no parking, outfitted with battered tables and clattering Melmac dishes, but they personify aloha, invariably run by local families who welcome tourists who take the trouble to find them.

Many are cash-only operations and combination plates, known as "plate lunches," are a standard feature: one or two entrées, two scoops of steamed rice, one scoop of macaroni salad, and—if the place is really old-style—a tiny portion of coarse Hawaiian salt and some raw onions for relish.

Most serve some foods that aren't, strictly speaking, Hawaiian, but are beloved of *kamaaina* (locals), such as salt meat with watercress (preserved meat in a tasty broth), or *akubone* (skipjack tuna fried in a tangy vinegar sauce).

# Weddings and Honeymoons

There's no question that Hawaii is one of the country's top honeymoon destinations, but it's also popular for destination weddings.

## THE BIG DAY

**Choosing the perfect place:** You really have two choices to make: the ceremony location and where to have the reception. For the former, Oahu offers beaches, sea-hugging bluffs, gardens, private residences, resort lawns, and, of course, places of worship. As for the reception, there are these same choices, as well as restaurants and even a luau. If you decide to go with the outdoors, have a backup plan for inclement weather.

**Finding a wedding planner:** If you intend to invite more than an officiant and your betrothed, seriously consider hiring a wedding planner who can help select a location, design the floral scheme, and recommend a florist and photographer. They can also plan the menu and choose a restaurant, caterer, or resort, and suggest Hawaiian traditions to incorporate into your ceremony.

If it's a resort wedding, most properties have on-site wedding coordinators who can provide guidance and one-stop shopping. Resorts also have indoor-outdoor space for ceremonies, private dining areas for any size reception, and stunning on-site photography spots. However, many independent wedding planners around Oahu specialize in certain types of ceremonies. Share your budget, and get a detailed written proposal before you proceed.

**Getting your license:** There's no waiting period in Hawaii, no residency or citizenship requirements, and no required blood test or shots. You can apply and pay the fee online; however, both the bride and groom must appear together in person before a marriage-license agent to receive the marriage license at the State Department of Health in Honolulu. You'll need proof of age—the legal age to marry is 18. Upon approval, a marriage license is immediately issued and costs $65. After the ceremony, your officiant—who must be licensed by the Hawaii Department of Health—will mail the marriage certificate to the state, and you'll get your copy about four months later. There's an informative instructional video on the state's official website (🌐 *emrs.ehawaii.gov/emrs/public/home.html*).

**Wedding attire:** In Hawaii, basically anything goes, from long, formal dresses with trains to casual attire—even bathing suits! For men, a pair of solid-color trousers with a nice aloha shirt is appropriate. If you're planning a wedding on the beach, barefoot is the way to go.

**Local customs:** The most obvious traditional Hawaiian wedding custom is the lei exchange in which the bride and groom take turns placing a lei around the neck of the other—with a kiss. Bridal lei are usually floral, whereas the groom's is typically made of *maile,* for a green leafy garland that drapes the neck. Brides often also wear a *lei poo*—a circular floral headpiece. Other Hawaiian customs include the blowing of the conch shell, hula, chanting, and Hawaiian music.

## THE HONEYMOON

Do you dream of champagne and strawberries delivered to your room each morning? A breathtaking swimming pool in which to float? A five-star restaurant in which to dine? Then a resort is ideal. A small inn or condominium is also good if you're on a tight budget or don't plan to spend much time in your room. The good news is that Waikiki's accommodations are almost as plentiful as the beaches, and there are many options to ensure your honeymoon is extra-special.

Chapter 2

# TRAVEL SMART



Updated by
Marla Cimini

**★ CAPITAL:**
Honolulu

**POPULATION:**
1,000,890

**LANGUAGE:**
English, Hawaiian

**$ CURRENCY:**
U.S. dollar

**AREA CODE:**
808

**EMERGENCIES:**
911

**DRIVING:**
On the right

**ELECTRICITY:**
120–220 V/60Hz; plugs have two or three rectangular prongs

**TIME:**
Hawaii-Aleutian Standard time, five (or six) hours behind New York

**WEB RESOURCES:**
www.gohawaii.com
www.hawaii.com
www.hawaii-guide.com

**AIRPORT:**
HNL

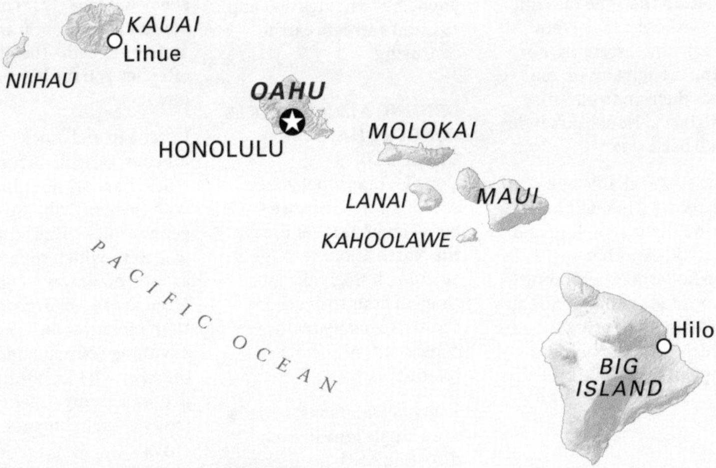

# Know Before You Go

Planning a trip to Oahu? It's better to be prepared. Here are some important pieces of information you should know while making your plans.

### THERE ARE SEVERAL AIRPORT TRANSFER OPTIONS

The Daniel K. Inouye International Airport in Honolulu is 20 minutes (60 minutes during rush hour) from Waikiki. Car-rental companies have booths at baggage claim. Shuttle buses then take you to the car-pickup areas.

Sometimes taxis are waiting in a line. If not, the airport taxi system requires you to line up for a dispatcher who radios for cars (about $45–$55 to Waikiki). A rideshare via Uber or Lyft is an alternative, but you meet the drivers in a different location than the taxi line. Regardless, ask drivers to take Interstate H1, not Nimitz Highway, or your introduction to paradise will be via Honolulu's industrial back side.

The city's reliable bus system ($3) makes stops throughout Honolulu and Waikiki. Another option is the Roberts Hawaii shuttle (from $25 or $180, available as a shared or private ride), which transports you to any hotel in Waikiki.

### IT'S BEST TO BOOK RENTAL CARS IN ADVANCE

You can get away with not renting a car if you're staying in Waikiki. For exploring the rest of the island, though, there's no substitute for having your own wheels. To ensure you get a rental car (and the best rates), reserve in advance, especially around holidays and summer breaks.

Avoid renting candy-color convertibles or other flashy cars, and never leave anything valuable inside a vehicle, even if you lock it. Get a portable GPS navigator or make sure your phone has a navigation app, as Oahu's streets can be confusing.

### DRIVING ALWAYS TAKES LONGER THAN EXPECTED

Don't let maps fool you. Although the distance between Waikiki and, say, the North Shore is roughly 40 miles, it may take more than an hour to get there, thanks to heavy traffic, construction, and other factors.

Many of Oahu's main roads are a single lane in each direction, with no alternate routes. So if you're stuck behind a slow-moving vehicle, you may have no other choice than to hope it turns soon. Heavy traffic moving toward downtown can begin as early as 6 am, with after-work traffic starting at 3 pm.

### OAHU IS EXPENSIVE, BUT THERE ARE WAYS TO SAVE

A vacation to Hawaii doesn't have to break the bank. Online sources, like Groupon or Yelp, offer discounted rates for everything from dinner cruises to massages. Buy your souvenirs at Longs or ABC Stores rather than at shops catering to tourists, and you'll likely get the same type of goods for less money.

You don't need to stay at a pricier waterfront hotel when, in Waikiki, almost all hotels are a short walk to the shore. Access to beaches and most hiking trails on the island is free to the public. For inexpensive fresh fruit and produce, check out weekly farmers' markets and farm stands along the road—they'll often let you try before you buy.

For cheap and quick lunches, consider a food truck. Part of the culinary landscape of Oahu for generations, these lunch wagons—which rove around downtown and other areas—charge less than restaurants. Take advantage of *pau hana* time (happy hour) for cheaper drinks and appetizers at many establishments.

**SEEING PEARL HARBOR REQUIRES PLANNING**
Consider whether you want to see only the USS *Arizona* Memorial or the USS *Bowfin* and USS *Missouri* as well. You can also visit the nearby Pearl Harbor Aviation Museum on Ford Island. Note, however, that tickets to the USS *Arizona* Memorial are free but must be reserved online in advance for a $1 processing fee. Same-day tickets are not available.

Allow approximately 1 hour and 15 minutes for the USS *Arizona* tour, which includes a 23-minute documentary of the Pearl Harbor attack and a short ferry ride to the memorial itself. Also allow time for the visitor center, which has two state-of-the-art exhibits that tell the story of the attack on December 7, 1941.

Strict security measures prohibit any sort of bag (purses, backpacks, diaper bags, camera cases—even small ones), although cameras are allowed. Strollers are allowed in the visitor center but not in the theaters or on the shuttle boats. Baggage storage is available for a $5 fee. Also, check ahead on any remaining COVID-19 requirements, and don't forget to bring your ID.

Children under four years of age are not allowed on the USS *Bowfin* for safety reasons, and they may not enjoy the crowds or waiting in line at other sights. Older kids are likely to find the more experiential, hands-on history of the USS *Bowfin* and USS *Missouri* memorable. The Pearl Harbor Aviation Museum's vintage planes are bonus attractions, if you have the time.

**THERE'S MORE TO SEE THAN JUST WAIKIKI**
Although Waikiki is a great place to stay, especially for first-time visitors, be sure to leave the hustle and bustle of Oahu's most popular neighborhood and explore the island's other notable areas. Consider, for example, a day trip to the North Shore, home to 10- to 20-foot monster swells in the winter.

Another must-visit neighborhood is Kailua, on Oahu's windward side. Since 2000, it has become a buzzing beach town (and beaches have picnic tables, showers, and rest rooms). The area also features hip boutiques as well as restaurants featuring dishes made with locally sourced ingredients.

**SAFETY IS A FACTOR WHEN EXPLORING OAHU'S OUTDOORS**
Hawaii's natural wonders, while beautiful, can also be perilous if you're not careful. While at the beach, don't turn your back to the ocean; waves can be unpredictable. It's best to go with a buddy if you're planning to swim, snorkel, or surf. Check ahead on hazardous conditions, such as shorebreaks and rip currents. Remember the adage: when in doubt, don't go out.

Since Hawaii is close to the equator, the sun's rays are strong in the Islands, so you should use sunscreen with an SPF of at least 50. Save room in your luggage and protect the environment by buying sunscreen after you arrive. Today, any sunblock purchased in Hawaii is officially reef safe. Locally bought products can no longer contain oxybenzone and octinoxate, two chemicals proven to cause coral bleaching.

**MOSQUITOES CAN REALLY BUG YOU**
To protect against mosquitoes, which are most abundant during the summer months, apply repellent containing DEET, and wear a long-sleeve shirt and pants during outdoor activities such as hiking.

**RESPECT LOCAL CULTURE**
Hawaii is a unique place with a vibrant, rich culture. Your visit to the Islands will be much more rewarding if you learn about the history and traditions of Hawaii and its peoples. Places such as Bishop Museum and Iolani Palace offer interesting, educational glimpses into Hawaii's storied past. The Royal Hawaiian Hotel and some other resorts offer exceptional historical tours as well. When you're exploring the outdoors, be mindful of cultural sites, such as the rock wall remains of a temple or Hawaiian petroglyphs. Treat such areas with respect.

**BRING YOUR OWN SHOPPING BAGS**
Hawaii has banned single-use plastic bags. When you go shopping, carry your own bags or be prepared to purchase one at the register.

# Getting Here and Around

A few major landmarks can help you navigate Oahu. The island is made up of three extinct shield volcanoes, which form two mountain ranges: Waianae and Koolau. The Waianae range curves from Kaena State Park, on the island's westernmost point, past Makaha, Waianae, and Nanakuli to Ko Olina on the sunny leeward shore. The extinct craters of Diamond Head and Koko Head are usually visible from anywhere along the island's leeward coast. The jagged Koolau range runs from the island's eastern tip along the windward coast to the famous surfing center on the North Shore.

## Air

Flying time to Oahu is about 10 hours from New York, 8 hours from Chicago, and 5 hours from Los Angeles. From the U.S. mainland, Alaska, American, Delta, Hawaiian, Southwest, and United are the primary U.S. carriers to serve Honolulu.

All the major airline carriers serving Hawaii fly direct to Honolulu; some also offer nonstops to Maui, Kauai, and the Big Island, though most flights to the latter two come from the West Coast only. Daniel K. Inouye International Airport in Honolulu, although open-air and seemingly more casual than most major airports, can be very busy. Allow extra travel time during rush-hour mornings and afternoons.

Plants and plant products are subject to regulation by the Department of Agriculture, both on entering and leaving Hawaii. Upon leaving, you must have your bags x-rayed and tagged at the airport's agricultural inspection station before proceeding to check-in. Pineapples and coconuts with the packer's agricultural inspection stamp pass freely; papayas and certain other fruits must be treated, inspected, and stamped. But most other fruits are banned for export to the U.S. mainland. Flowers pass except for citrus-related flowers, fruits, or parts; jade vine; and mauna loa. Also banned are insects, snails, soil, cotton, cacti, sugarcane, and all berry plants.

Bringing your dog or cat with you is a tricky process and not something to be undertaken lightly. Hawaii is a rabies-free state and requires animals to pass strict quarantine rules, which you can find online (🌐 *hdoa.hawaii.gov/ai*). Most airlines do not allow pets to travel in the cabin on flights to Hawaii (though Alaska Airlines and Hawaiian Airlines are notable exceptions). If specific pre- and post-arrival requirements are met, most animals qualify for a five-day-or-less quarantine. You can also check whether masks and proof of vaccination or a negative COVID test are required to visit the animal quarantine facilities.

### AIRPORT

The Daniel K. Inouye International Airport (HNL) is roughly 20 minutes (9 miles) west of Waikiki (60 minutes during rush hour) and is served by most of the major domestic and international carriers. To travel to other islands from Honolulu, you can depart from either the interisland terminal or the commuter terminal, located in two separate structures adjacent to the main overseas terminal building. A free Wiki-Wiki shuttle bus operates between terminals.

## Bicycle

Biki Bikeshare Hawaii (🌐 *gobiki.org*) has 1,300 aqua, cruiser-style bicycles at 130 solar-powered stations in the Waikiki and Honolulu corridor. You can unlock a bike from a station using your credit card, without having to sign up for the member pass. A one-way fare costs $4.50 for 30 minutes. There's also a multistop pass for $30, which gets you 300 minutes of riding time. ■ **TIP→ A $50 security hold is placed on your card when you check out a bike.**

##  Bus

Getting around by bus is convenient and affordable on Oahu, particularly in the most heavily touristed areas of Waikiki. Options include Honolulu's municipal transit system, affectionately known as TheBus; the Waikiki Trolleys, brass-trimmed, open-air, hop-on-hop-off vehicles that look like trolleys or large double-decker buses; and brightly painted private buses, some of them free, that shuttle you to such commercial attractions as dinner cruises, shopping centers, and the like.

TheBus is one of the best bargains on Oahu. You can use it to travel around the island or just down Kalakaua Avenue for $3. Buses stop in Waikiki every 10–15 minutes to take passengers to nearby shopping areas. Although free transfers have been discontinued, you can purchase a one-day pass for $7.50. Just ask the driver when boarding. Exact change is required, and dollar bills are accepted. Monthly passes cost $80.

The company's website has timetables, route maps, and real-time bus tracking, or you can download the free DaBus2 app for your smartphone. You can call to speak with a representative for route advice, or you can find privately published booklets at most drugstores and other convenience outlets.

The Waikiki Trolley has three lines—each beginning and ending in Waikiki—and dozens of stops that allow you to plan your own itinerary. A one-day single line pass starts at $18 (but just $5 for the Pink Line) and $55 for all lines. Four-day ($65) and seven-day ($75) all-line passes are also available.

The Ocean/Diamond Head Tour (Blue Line) stops at the Duke Kahanamoku statue; along Diamond Head and Kahala; the Halona Blow Hole; Sea Life Park; and Koko Marina. As its name suggests, the Ala Moana Shopping Tour (Pink Line) goes to the Ala Moana Center, a sprawling outdoor mall. The City Arts District Tour (Red Line) travels between Waikiki, Chinatown, and Kakaako and includes stops at the Honolulu Museum of Art, the capitol, Iolani Palace, Punchbowl Crater, and Ala Moana.

##  Car

Thanks to public transit, you don't need a car in Waikiki. Elsewhere on the island, though, a car can be invaluable. Avoid the obvious tourist cars—candy-color convertibles, for example—and never leave anything valuable inside, even if you've locked the vehicle. A GPS (either on your smartphone or a separate device) will help guide you through Oahu's sometimes-confusing streets.

Reserve in advance to ensure availability (rentals can book up, especially during holidays and summer breaks) and to get the best rates. Also, be prepared to pay for parking; most hotels in Honolulu (and many outside of Honolulu) charge for parking.

Except for one area around Kaena Point, major highways follow Oahu's shoreline and traverse the island at two points. Rush-hour traffic (6:30–9:30 am and 3 or 3:30–6 pm) can be frustrating around Honolulu and the outlying areas. Winter swells also bring heavy traffic to the North Shore, as people hoping to catch

# Getting Here and Around

the surfing action clog the two-lane Kamehameha Highway. Parking along many streets is curtailed during these times, and tow-away zones are strictly enforced. Read curbside signs before leaving your vehicle, even at a meter.

Asking for directions will almost always produce a helpful explanation from the locals, but you should be prepared for a Hawaiian term or two. Instead of using compass directions, remember that Hawaii residents refer to places as being either *mauka* (toward the mountains) or *makai* (toward the ocean).

Other directions depend on your location. In Honolulu, for example, people say to "go Diamond Head," which means toward that famous landmark, or to "go *ewa*," meaning in the opposite direction. A shop on the *mauka*–Diamond Head corner of a street is on the mountain side of the street on the corner closest to Diamond Head. It all makes perfect sense once you get the lay of the land.

### CAR RENTALS

Hotel parking garages charge upward of $40 per day, so if you're staying in Waikiki, where you can easily walk or take public transit to many area attractions, consider renting a car only for sightseeing elsewhere on the island. Even though the city bus is a wonderfully affordable way to explore much of Oahu, having your own car gives you flexibility, especially if you're planning lots of stops.

You can rent anything from an econobox and motorcycle to a Ferrari while on Oahu. Rates in Honolulu begin at about $35 a day for an economy car with air-conditioning, automatic transmission, and unlimited mileage. This does not include the airport concession fee, general excise tax, rental-vehicle surcharge, or vehicle-license fee. Note that rates are sometimes better if you reserve through a rental agency's website. Some rental companies even offer coupons for discounts at various attractions.

It's wise to make reservations far in advance, especially if visiting during peak seasons. When you book, ask about cancellation penalties and drop-off charges, should you plan to pick up the car in one location and return it to another, and request extras, such as GPS and car seats. ■ **TIP→ Be sure that a confirmed reservation guarantees you a car. Agencies sometimes overbook, particularly for busy weekends and holiday periods.**

In Hawaii you must be 21 years of age to rent a car, and you must have a valid driver's license (which you can use to drive a rental for up to 90 days) and a major credit card. Those under 25 will pay a daily surcharge of around $25. Hawaii's Child Passenger Restraint Law requires that all children under four be in an approved child safety seat in the back seat of a vehicle. Children ages four to seven must be seated in a rear booster seat or child safety seat with a restraint such as a lap and shoulder belt. Car seats and boosters run from $6 to $14 per day.

Allow plenty of time to return your vehicle before your flight home. Traffic in Honolulu is terrible during morning and afternoon rush hours. Give yourself 3½–4 hours prior to departure during these peak times; otherwise, plan on 2½–3 hours.

### DRIVING

Driving on Oahu involves traversing a mix of one-way country roads and congested city streets. As in most major cities, traffic in and around Honolulu is bad, especially during rush hour. The H1 highway travels from Kapolei on the west side to Kahala in East Oahu. Weekday rush-hour traffic on the H1 tends to run from 6 to 9 am and again from 3 to 7 pm. During

## Car Rental Resources

| | | |
|---|---|---|
| **Automobile Associations** | | |
| AAA | 800/222–4357 for roadside assistance | www.aaa.com |
| National Automobile Club | 883/622–7377 | www.nacroadservice.com (CA residents only) |
| **Major Agencies** | | |
| Alamo | 888/233–8749 | www.alamo.com |
| Avis | 800/633–3469 | www.avis.com |
| Budget | 800/218–7992 | www.budget.com |
| Hertz | 800/704–4473 | www.hertz.com |
| National Car Rental | 884/382–6875 | www.nationalcar.com |
| Thrifty Car Rental | 800/847–4389 | www.thrifty.com |

these times, it may take 45 minutes to travel only 10 miles, so plan ahead.

### GASOLINE

Gasoline is noticeably more expensive on Oahu than on most of the U.S. mainland. At the time of this writing, the average price of a gallon of gas was $4.68.

### PARKING

In Honolulu's densest neighborhoods (Chinatown, Kakaako, Ala Moana, Kaimuki, and downtown), parking is often limited and expensive. While there are a variety of parking lots, parking structures, and street parking, you will always have to pay. The same goes for nearly everywhere in Waikiki. Some businesses validate for parking, so it's always good to ask in advance. As you head out west to Kapolei or Haleiwa or northeast to Kailua, parking is easier to come by and often free.

### ROAD CONDITIONS

Oahu is relatively easy to navigate. Roads, although their names are often a challenge for a visitor's tongue, are usually well marked. Free publications containing helpful maps are found at most hotels throughout Waikiki.

Be mindful of the many one-way streets in Waikiki and the Honolulu neighborhoods of Chinatown, Kakaako, and Kaimuki. Also, watch for the Hawaii Visitors and Convention Bureau's red-caped King Kamehameha signs, which mark major attractions and scenic spots.

### ROADSIDE EMERGENCIES

If you have a cell phone, call the roadside assistance number on your car-rental contract or AAA Help. If your car has been broken into or stolen, report it immediately to your rental-car company. If it's an emergency and someone is hurt, call *911*.

### RULES OF THE ROAD

Hawaii has a strictly enforced mandatory seat-belt law for front- and back-seat passengers. Children under four must be in a car seat (available from car-rental agencies), and children ages four to seven must be seated in a booster seat or child safety seat with a restraint such as a lap and shoulder belt.

# Getting Here and Around

Hawaii prohibits texting or talking on the phone (unless you are over 18 and using a hands-free device) while driving. The highway speed limit is usually 55 mph. In-town traffic travels 25–40 mph. Jaywalking is not uncommon, so watch for pedestrians. Unauthorized use of a parking space reserved for persons with disabilities can net you a $250–$500 fine.

Oahu's drivers are generally courteous, and you rarely hear a horn. People will slow down and let you into traffic with a wave of the hand. A friendly wave back is customary. If a driver sticks a hand out the window in a fist with the thumb and pinkie sticking straight out, this is a good thing: it's the *shaka,* the gesture for "hang loose" that's often used to say "thanks."

## Cruise Ship

Several major lines offer seasonal cruises to and from the Hawaiian Islands (typically from Los Angeles, San Francisco, or San Diego) with interisland cruise components. But you can also hop aboard a strictly interisland cruise with Norwegian Cruise Line's ship *Pride of America* or UnCruise Adventures' smaller yacht.

## Ride-Sharing

Both Uber and Lyft operate on Oahu, including in designated locations at the airport. Although you may still want to rent a car while you're on island—especially if you're staying in or visiting the North Shore or towns on the east side of Oahu—ride-shares are good for quick trips and evenings out when you want to avoid parking or you want to imbibe.

## Scooter

Mopeds and scooters (both standard and electric versions) are a common form of transportation in the Islands, both for locals and visitors. They're easier and sometimes cheaper than renting a car, costing around $40 a day or less for multiday rentals. Some companies even rent to people as young as 18. But these freedoms come with a few caveats. Mopeds and scooters aren't allowed on any highways, and renting a scooter requires a valid motorcycle license.

## Taxi

Taxis cost $4.30 at the drop of the flag, and each additional 1/8 mile is $0.56. Taxi and limousine companies can provide a car and driver for half- or full-day island tours, and a number of companies also offer personal guides. Remember, however, the rates are steep for these services, running $100 to $200 or more per day.

## Train

The first phase of the Skyline rail project, a 10-mile section between Halawa/Aloha Stadium near Pearl Harbor and East Kapolei, opened in 2023. Three stations have park-and-ride lots. This section is mostly for residents, though it may be useful for visitors to some West Oahu attractions. The next phase, opening in 2025, will include a stop at the airport; by 2031, the line will extend to Kakaako in Honolulu. The fare is $3, the same as TheBus; riders need to have a HOLO card, available at stations and various stores. For more information, visit the Hawaii Transportation website (*honolulu.gov/transportation*).

# Essentials



##  Dining

Oahu has undergone a renaissance at both ends of the dining spectrum. Consider budgeting for a meal in at least one pricey restaurant, where chefs such as Roy Yamaguchi, Lee Ann Wong, Vikram Garg—or others you've seen on the Food Network and Travel Channel—put a sophisticated spin on local foods and flavors. Dishes that take cues from Japan, China, Korea, the Philippines, the United States, and Europe are often filtered through an island sensibility. Take advantage of the location and order the superb local fish—mahimahi, *opakaka* (Hawaiian pink snapper), ono, and opah.

Spend the rest of your food dollars where budget-conscious locals do: in plate-lunch places and small eateries serving global fare, at lunch wagons, or at window-in-the-wall delis. Snack on a *musubi* (a handheld rice ball wrapped with seaweed and topped with Spam), slurp shave ice with red-bean paste, or order Filipino pork adobo with rice and macaroni salad.

In Waikiki, you can find everything from upscale dining rooms with a view to nondescript Japanese noodle shops. By going just a few miles in any direction, you can save money and eat like a local. On Kaimuki's Waialae Avenue, for example, a foodie favorite, you'll find restaurants with diverse cusines from elevated Hawaiian food to barbecue—all in three blocks and 10 minutes from Waikiki.

Chinatown, 15 minutes in the other direction and easily reached by the Waikiki Trolley, is another dining (and shopping) treasure, not only for Chinese but also for Vietnamese, Filipino, Burmese, and Mexican food. There's even a chic little tea shop. Kakaako, the vibrant, urban area between Waikiki and Chinatown, also offers a mix of local eateries, upscale restaurants, and international takeout.

Although restaurants are fewer outside Honolulu and Waikiki, they tend to be filled with locals and are cheaper and more casual. Thanks to popular beaches such as Kailua and Lanikai, Windward Oahu's dining scene features everything from plate lunches to creative regional offerings. Kapolei in Leeward Oahu, once dominated by Mainland chains and fast-food joints, is now another area with a variety of quality eateries.

### DISCOUNTS AND DEALS

If you eat early or late, you may be able to take advantage of prix fixe deals not offered at peak hours. Many upscale restaurants offer great lunch deals with special menus at cut-rate prices designed to give customers a true taste of the place.

### MEALS AND MEALTIMES

People dine early here—the most sought-after dinner reservations are between 6 and 8, while many restaurants offer happy hour food specials daily. A few places that may serve dinner later are sushi bars, Japanese taverns, a few 24-hour diners, and popular new restaurants. Many island eateries offer takeout and delivery options.

### PARKING

In Waikiki, downtown Honolulu, or Chinatown, walk, take a cab, or call Lyft or Uber when you are going out for dinner; it can be cheaper and easier than dealing with parking or high valet rates. Elsewhere on Oahu, free or reasonably priced parking is available.

### PAYING

Most restaurants take credit cards, but some smaller places do not. It's worth asking. Servers expect a 20% tip at restaurants; some add an automatic gratuity for groups of six or more.

# Essentials

### PRICES

⇨ *Restaurant prices are the average cost of a main course at dinner or, if dinner is not served, at lunch. Prices do not include taxes.*

| What It Costs in U.S. Dollars | | | |
|---|---|---|---|
| $ | $$ | $$$ | $$$$ |
| **RESTAURANTS** | | | |
| Under $20 | $20–$30 | $31–$40 | Over $40 |

### RESERVATIONS AND DRESS

At Honolulu's top upscale restaurants, book your table from home weeks in advance. For other places, you can usually reserve when you get into town.

Most top restaurants abide by the dressy casual (i.e., "aloha wear") standard, where dark jeans are acceptable. A select few of Honolulu's nicest spots ask men to wear a jacket.

### SMOKING

Smoking is prohibited in enclosed areas open to the public, including restaurants, bars, and clubs.

## Health and Safety

Hawaii is known not only as the Aloha State, but also as the Health State. The life expectancy here is 81 years, the longest in the nation. Balmy weather makes it easy to remain active year-round, and the low-stress attitude seems to contribute to the general well-being. When visiting the Islands, however, there are a few health issues to keep in mind.

### COVID-19

Although COVID-19 brought travel to a virtual standstill in 2020 and 2021, vaccinations have made travel possible and safe again. The state of Hawaii and the island of Oahu dropped negative-test requirements in early 2022. Check online (🌐 *hawaiicovid19.com*) for the latest information.

In case travel is curtailed abruptly again, consider buying trip insurance. Just be sure to read the fine print: not all travel-insurance policies cover pandemic-related cancellations.

### MOSQUITO-BORNE ILLNESSES

The Islands have their share of insects. Most are harmless but annoying—like cockroaches—but dengue fever, a mosquito-borne disease, has been reported on Oahu. For hiking and other outdoor activities, wear long-sleeve shirts and pants, and use mosquito repellent containing DEET. In remote areas, it's a good idea to carry a first aid kit, too.

In damp places, you may encounter the dreaded local centipedes, which are brown and blue and measure up to eight inches long. Their painful sting is similar to those of bees and wasps. When camping, shake out your sleeping bag and check your shoes, as the centipedes like cozy places.

### SAFETY PRECAUTIONS

Although Oahu is generally a safe tourist destination, there is crime here, so it's wise to follow the same common-sense safety precautions you would in your own hometown. Rental cars are magnets for break-ins, so don't leave any valuables in the car, not even in a locked trunk. Avoid poorly lighted areas, beach parks, and isolated areas after dark as a precaution. **■ TIP→ Distribute your cash, credit cards, IDs, and other valuables between a deep front pocket, an inside jacket or vest pocket, and a hidden money pouch. Don't reach for the money pouch once you're in public.**

## Lodging

If you like the action and choices of big cities, consider Waikiki, a 24-hour playground with everything from surf to karaoke bars. For an escape from urban life, look to the island's leeward or windward sides or to the North Shore, where the surf culture creates a laid-back atmosphere.

Most of Oahu's major hotels and resorts are in busy Waikiki, where you don't need a car to reach key sights and amenities. Public transportation can get you around town as well as around the island. You'll find places to stay along the entire stretches of both Kalakaua and Kuhio Avenues, with smaller and quieter hotels and condos at the eastern end of Waikiki and more business-centric accommodations on the western edge, near the Hawaii Convention Center, Ala Moana Center, and downtown.

Leeward Oahu, in the Ko Olina resort area, is about 20 minutes from Honolulu International Airport (40 minutes from Waikiki) and has great golf courses and quiet beaches that make for a relaxing getaway. Note, though, that you'll need a car to explore, and all the resorts in this area charge hefty parking fees.

Other low-key options are on Windward Oahu or the North Shore, home to Turtle Bay, one of the island's premier resorts. Both areas have quaint eateries and coffee shops, local boutiques, and some of the island's best beaches.

### CONDOS AND VACATION RENTALS

Vacation rentals give you the convenience of staying at a home away from home and getting to know Oahu the way the locals do. You can often save money as well, since you have a kitchen, can cook your meals, and don't pay for hotel parking. Prices, amenities, and locations of vacation homes vary considerably, meaning you should be able to find the perfect getaway.

Properties managed by individual owners can be found in online vacation-rental directories, as well as on the Oahu Visitors Bureau website (🌐 *www.gohawaii.com/islands/oahu*). Don't be surprised to see the same homes advertised on different sites and with different names. Compare companies, as some offer online specials and free nights when booking, and make sure that there will be an on-island point of contact in case any issues arise during your stay.

Also ask about the home's licensing as a vacation rental, since not all properties advertised carry the necessary license. Technically, rentals of less than 30 days are illegal on Oahu unless the property has a license for short-term vacation rentals or is a hotel with apartment units. The state does take a stand from time to time to enforce vacation rental laws, and you'll have more protection and assurance that you aren't on your own if something goes wrong.

### FACILITIES

Assume that all hotel rooms have private baths, phones, and TVs, unless otherwise indicated, but many rentals do not have air-conditioning, especially outside of the Waikiki high-rises. Breakfast is noted when it is included in the rate. Most hotels have pools, but many home rentals do not.

### PARKING

Most resorts on Oahu charge for parking, even those not in Ko Olina and Waikiki (where virtually all hotels charge for parking), so be sure to ask before you rent a car. Sometimes parking is included in the hotel's resort fee, but often it is not.

# Essentials

## Where to Stay on Oahu

| NEIGHBORHOOD | LOCAL VIBE | PROS | CONS |
|---|---|---|---|
| Honolulu | Lodging options are limited in downtown Honolulu, but if you want an urban feel, look no farther. | Access to a wide selection of art galleries, boutiques, and restaurants, as well as Chinatown. | No beaches within walking distance. If you're looking to get away from it all, this is not the place. |
| Waikiki | Lodgings abound in Waikiki, from youth hostels to five-star accommodations. The area is always abuzz with activity, and anything you desire on vacation is within walking distance. | You can surf in front of the hotels, wander miles of beach, and explore restaurants and bars. | This is tourist central. Prices are high, and you are not going to get the true Hawaii experience. |
| East (Windward) Oahu | More in tune with the local experience, this is where you'll find many privately listed (e.g., on Airbnb or Vrbo) places and enjoy the lush side of Oahu. | From beautiful vistas to green jungles, this side really captures the tropical paradise most people envision when dreaming of a Hawaii vacation. | The lushness comes at a price—it rains a lot on this side. Also, luxury is not the specialty here; if you want pampering, stay elsewhere. |
| The North Shore | This is true country living, with one luxurious resort exception. The area bustles in the winter (when the surf is up) and is slower-paced in the summer. | Amazing surf and long stretches of sand truly epitomize the beach culture in Hawaii. Historic Haleiwa has enough stores to keep shopaholics busy. | There is no middle ground for accommodations; you're either in backpacker cabanas or $300-a-night suites. There is also zero nightlife, and traffic can be heavy during winter months. |
| West (Leeward) Oahu | This is the resort side of the rock; there isn't much outside these resorts but plenty on the grounds to keep you occupied for a week. | Ko Olina's lagoons offer the most kid-friendly swimming on the island, and the golf courses are magnificent. Rainy days are rare out here. | You are isolated from the rest of Oahu, with fewer shopping options or jungle hikes. |

### PRICES

Before you book a room, try calling hotels directly. Sometimes on-property reservationists can get you the best deals, and they usually have the most accurate information about rooms, availability, and hotel amenities. Remember that many reservations centers are not on Oahu.

⇨ *Hotel prices are for two people in a standard double room in high season, excluding taxes. Condo price categories reflect studio and one-bedroom rates.*

| What It Costs in U.S. Dollars | | | |
|---|---|---|---|
| $ | $$ | $$$ | $$$$ |
| **HOTELS** | | | |
| Under $200 | $200–$280 | $281–$380 | Over $380 |

### RESERVATIONS

Always make a reservation. Hotels often fill up, and rooms can be particularly hard to come by at the beginning of festival season in late March or early April as well as in May, when students at the many local colleges graduate.

## Nightlife

Oahu is the best of all the Islands for nightlife. The island's few clubs are in Waikiki, but bars are just about everywhere. On weeknights, it's likely that you'll find the working crowd, still in their business-casual attire, downing chilled beers even before the sun goes down. Though you might call it happy hour, the locals call it *pau hana,* which translates to "done with work." Those who don't have to wake up early in the morning should change into a fresh outfit and start the evening closer to 10 pm.

On the weekends, it's typical to have dinner at a restaurant before hitting the bars at around 9:30. Some barhoppers start as early as 7, but even they usually don't patronize more than two establishments a night because getting from one Oahu nightspot to the next often requires transportation. Happily, cab services and rideshares (Uber and Lyft) are plentiful.

The drinking age is 21 on Oahu and throughout Hawaii. Many bars will admit younger people but will not serve them alcohol. By law, all establishments that serve alcoholic beverages must close by 2 am. The only exceptions are a handful in Waikiki with a cabaret license, which allows them to stay open until 4 am.

**■ TIP→ Some places have a cover charge of $5–$10, but with many establishments, arriving early means you don't have to pay.**

## Packing

Outside of a few upscale restaurants that might require a jacket for dinner and golf courses that have collared-shirt or other dress codes, Oahu is casual. Sandals, bathing suits, and comfortable, informal clothing are the norm. The aloha shirt is accepted dress for business and most social occasions. There's no need to overpack, as shorts are acceptable daytime attire, along with a T-shirt or polo shirt. Plenty of stores around Waikiki sell just about everything, so you can easily buy bathing suits, hats, cover-ups, sundresses and shoes. It's a good idea to purchase sunblock in Hawaii, as all brands sold here are reef safe and environmentally friendly.

In summer, synthetic slacks and shirts, although easy to care for, can be uncomfortably warm. If you're visiting in winter or are planning to visit a high-altitude area, bring a sweater or light- to medium-weight jacket. A hoodie is ideal and makes a great impromptu pillow. Note that there's no need to buy expensive sandals before you travel—here, you can get flip-flops (locals call them slippers) and off-brand sandals for a reasonable price.

## Passports and Visas

United States citizens do not need a passport to visit Hawaii. But all visitors to the United States require a passport that is valid for six months beyond your expected period of stay.

Except for citizens of Canada and Bermuda, most visitors to the United States must have a visa. If you are from one of the 41 designated members of the Visa Waiver Program, then you only require an ESTA (Electronic System for Travel Authorization) as long as you are staying for 90 days or less.

Note, though, that nationals of Visa-Waiver nations who have traveled to Iran, Iraq, Libya, North Korea, Somalia, Sudan, Syria, or Yemen no longer qualify for ESTA. Also, if you have been denied a visa to visit the United States, your application for the ESTA program most likely will be denied.

## Performing Arts

Oahu has a thriving arts and culture scene, especially in the summer. Check local newspapers (or their websites), such as the *Honolulu Star-Advertiser* or *MidWeek*, for the latest events, or *Honolulu* magazine (🌐 *www.honolulumagazine.com*). Websites like 🌐 *gohawaii.com* and 🌐 *livemusichawaii.com* also have listings; the latter is the website of a music company but has a useful performance calendar.

## Shopping

Savvy shoppers hunt for luxury goods at high-end malls *and* scout tiny boutiques and galleries for items created by local artists and artisans. Honolulu's Chinatown and Kakaako neighborhoods, Kailua on the windward side, and Haleiwa on the North Shore often have the most original merchandise. ABC Stores are everywhere in Waikiki and sell just about everything you need, including food, clothing, beach gear, and sunblock. Some small stores carry island-made clothes and gifts reflecting the heritage of the makers—a reminder that, on this island halfway between Asia and the United States, shopping is a multicultural experience.

## Taxes

A 17.962% combined tax will be added to your hotel bill. This includes the State General Excise tax at 4.712%, Hawaii Transient Accommodations tax at 10.25%, and Oahu Transient Accommodations tax at 3%. In addition, almost every hotel has a "resort fee" or "amenity fee" (plus tax per night).

For car rentals, a $6-per-day road tax is also assessed on each rental vehicle, plus a daily rental-facility surcharge and some other charges; it adds up, so do ask about fees. Although Hawaii doesn't have a statewide sales tax, 4.7% will be tacked onto goods and services you purchase on Oahu.

## Tipping

People who work in the service industry rely on tips, so gratuities are not only common, but expected.

| Tipping Guide for Oahu | |
|---|---|
| Bartender | $1–$5 per round of drinks, depending on the number and cost of the drinks |
| Bellhop | $1–$5 per bag, depending on the level of the hotel |
| Hotel concierge | $5 or more, depending on the service |
| Hotel doorstaff | $1–$5 for help with bags or hailing a cab |
| Hotel maid | $2–$5 each time your room is cleaned |
| Hotel room service waiter | $1–$2 per delivery, even if a service charge has been added |
| Restroom attendants | $1 per vist |
| Skycap at airport | $1–$3 per bag checked |
| Spa personnel | 15%–20% of the cost of your service |
| Taxi driver | 15%–20% of the fare |
| Tour guide | 15%–20% of the cost of the tour, per person |
| Valet parking attendant | $2–$5 each time your car is brought to you |
| Server | 20%; nothing additional if a service charge is added to the bill |

## Visitor Information

Before you go to Hawaii, contact the Oahu Visitors Bureau (OVB) for a free vacation planner and map. The OVB website (*gohawaii.com/islands/oahu*) has online listings for accommodations, activities, attractions, dining venues, services, transportation, travel professionals, and wedding information. The website also has a calendar of events.

## When to Go

**Low season:** The fall (September through mid-December) is a slower time for tourism in Oahu. During this period, you can find better rates on just about everything. That beach you want to lounge on will be less crowded, too.

**Shoulder season:** Mid-April through June is an in-between time. Because of Hawaii's warm weather, though, this season still attracts plenty of visitors.

**High season:** The busiest time is generally from mid-December to March or mid-April, when Hawaii weather is good and temperatures are moderate. The height of summer (July and August) is also considered high season. Make all reservations well in advance, and don't expect to find deals on accommodations.

### WEATHER

In Hawaii, the thermometer generally hovers between the mid-70s and the mid-80s (degrees Fahrenheit). There are essentially just two seasons: summer and winter. Winters, from November through April, are rainier and a bit cooler than the summer months, May through October. But even if it's raining in one part of Oahu, chances are it's dry and sunny on the other coast. Oahu's leeward (western) coast is warmer and more arid than its windward (eastern) side, which is usually cooler and wetter.

# Hawaiian Vocabulary

Although an understanding of Hawaiian is by no means required on a trip to the Aloha State, a *malihini,* or newcomer, will find plenty of opportunities to pick up a few of the local words and phrases. Traditional names and expressions are widely used in the Islands. You're likely to read or hear at least a few words each day of your stay.

Simplifying the learning process is the fact that the Hawaiian language contains only seven consonants—*H, K, L, M, N, P, W,* and the silent *'okina,* or glottal stop, written '—plus one or more of the five vowels. All syllables, and therefore all words, end in a vowel. Each vowel; with the exception of a few diphthongized double vowels, such as *au* (pronounced "ow") or *ai* (pronounced "eye"), is pronounced separately. Thus *'Iolani* is four syllables (ee-oh-la-nee), not three (yo-la-nee). Although some Hawaiian words have only vowels, most also contain some consonants, but consonants are never doubled.

Pronunciation is simple. Pronounce *A* "ah" as in *father*; *E* "ay" as in *weigh*; *I* "ee" as in *marine*; *O* "oh" as in *no*; *U* "oo" as in *true*.

Consonants mirror their English equivalents, with the exception of *W.* When the letter begins any syllable other than the first one in a word, it is usually pronounced as a *V.* *'Awa,* the Polynesian drink, is pronounced "ava," *'ewa* is pronounced "eva."

Almost all long Hawaiian words are combinations of shorter words; they are not difficult to pronounce if you segment them. *Kalaniana'ole,* the highway running east from Honolulu, is easily understood as *Kalani ana 'ole.* Apply the standard pronunciation rules—the stress falls on the next-to-last syllable of most two- or three-syllable Hawaiian words—and Kalaniana'ole Highway is as easy to say as Main Street.

Now about that fish. Try *humu-humu nuku-nuku āpu a'a.*

The other unusual element in Hawaiian language is the *kahakō,* or macron, written as a short line (¯) placed over a vowel. Like the accent (´) in Spanish, the kahakō puts emphasis on a syllable that would normally not be stressed. The most familiar example is probably *Waikīkī.* With no macrons, the stress would fall on the middle syllable; with only one macron, on the last syllable, the stress would fall on the first and last syllables. Some words become plural with the addition of a macron, often on a syllable that would have been stressed anyway. No Hawaiian word becomes plural with the addition of an *S,* since that letter does not exist in the language.

*Note that Hawaiian diacritical marks are not printed in this guide.*

### PIDGIN

You may hear Pidgin English, the unofficial language of Hawaii. It is a Creole language, with its own grammar, evolved from the mixture of English, Hawaiian, Japanese, Portuguese, and other languages spoken in 19th-century Hawaii, and it is heard everywhere.

## GLOSSARY

What follows is a glossary of some of the most commonly used Hawaiian words. Hawaiian residents appreciate visitors who at least try to pick up the local language.

**'a'ā:** rough, crumbling lava, contrasting with *pāhoehoe,* which is smooth.

**'ae:** yes.

**aikane:** friend.

**āina:** land.

**akamai:** smart, clever, possessing savoir faire.

**akua:** god.

**ala:** a road, path, or trail.

**ali'i:** a Hawaiian chief, a member of the chiefly class.

**aloha:** love, affection, kindness; also a salutation meaning both greetings and farewell.

**'ānuenue:** rainbow.

**'a'ole:** no.

**'apōpō:** tomorrow.

**'auwai:** a ditch.

**auwē:** alas, woe is me!

**'ehu:** a red-haired Hawaiian.

**'ewa:** in the direction of 'Ewa plantation, west of Honolulu.

**hala:** the pandanus tree, whose leaves (*lau hala*) are used to make baskets and plaited mats.

**hālau:** school.

**hale:** a house.

**hale pule:** church, house of worship.

**hana:** to work.

**haole:** foreigner. Since the first foreigners were Caucasian, *haole* now means a Caucasian person.

**hapa:** a part, sometimes a half; often used as a short form of *hapa haole,* to mean a person who is part-Caucasian.

**hau'oli:** to rejoice. *Hau'oli Makahiki Hou* means Happy New Year. *Hau'oli lā hānau* means Happy Birthday.

**heiau:** an outdoor stone platform; an ancient Hawaiian place of worship.

**he mea iki** or **he mea 'ole:** you're welcome.

**holo:** to run.

**holoholo:** to go for a walk, ride, or sail.

**holokū:** a long Hawaiian dress, somewhat fitted, with a yoke and a train. It was worn at court, and at least one local translates the word as "expensive muumuu."

**holomū:** a post–World War II cross between a *holokū* and a mu'umu'u, less fitted than the former but less voluminous than the latter, and having no train.

**honi:** to kiss; a kiss. A phrase that some tourists may find useful, quoted from a popular hula, is *Honi Ka'ua Wikiwiki:* Kiss me quick!

**honu:** turtle.

**ho'omalimali:** flattery, a deceptive "line," bunk, baloney, hooey.

**huhū:** angry.

**hui:** a group, club, or assembly. A church may refer to its congregation as a *hui* and a social club may be called a *hui.*

**hukilau:** a seine; a communal fishing party in which everyone helps to drive the fish into a huge net, pull it in, and divide the catch.

# Hawaiian Vocabulary

**hula:** the dance of Hawaii.

**iki:** little.

**ipo:** sweetheart. Commonly seen as "ku'uipo," or "my sweetheart."

**ka:** the. This is the definite article for most singular words; for plural nouns, the definite article is usually *nā.* Since there is no *S* in Hawaiian, the article may be your only clue that a noun is plural.

**kahuna:** a priest, doctor, or other trained person of old Hawaii, endowed with special professional skills that often included prophecy or other supernatural powers.

**kai:** the sea, saltwater.

**kalo:** the taro plant from whose root *poi* (paste) is made.

**kamā'aina:** literally, a child of the soil; it refers to people who were born in the Islands or have lived there for a long time.

**kanaka:** originally a man or humanity, it is now used to denote a male Hawaiian or part-Hawaiian, but is occasionally taken as a slur when used by non-Hawaiians. *Kanaka maoli* is used by some Native Hawaiian rights activists to embrace part-Hawaiians as well.

**kāne:** a man, a husband. If you see this word (or *kane*) on a door, it's the men's room.

**kapa:** also called by its Tahitian name, *tapa,* a cloth made of beaten bark and usually dyed and stamped with a repeat design.

**kapakahi:** crooked, cockeyed, uneven. You've got your hat on *kapakahi.*

**kapu:** keep out, prohibited. This is the Hawaiian version of the more widely known Tongan word *tabu* (taboo).

**kēia lā:** today.

**keiki:** a child; *keikikāne* is a boy, *keikiwahine* a girl.

**kōkua:** to help, assist. Often seen in signs like "Please *kōkua* and throw away your trash."

**kona:** the leeward side of the Islands, the direction (south) from which the *kona* wind and *kona* rain come.

**kula:** upland.

**kuleana:** a homestead or small plot of ground on which a family has been installed for some generations without necessarily owning it. By extension, *kuleana* is used to denote any area or department in which one has a special interest or prerogative. You'll hear it used this way: "If you want to hire a surfboard, see Moki; that's his *kuleana.*"

**kupuna:** grandparent; elder.

**lā:** sun.

**lamalama:** to fish with a torch.

**lānai:** a porch, a balcony, an outdoor living room.

**lani:** heaven, the sky.

**lauhala:** the leaf of the *hala,* or pandanus tree, widely used in handicrafts.

**lei:** a garland of flowers.

**lōlō:** feeble-minded, crazy.

**luna:** a plantation overseer or foreman.

**mahalo:** thank you.

**mahina:** moon.

**makai:** toward the ocean.

**mālama:** to take care of, preserve, protect

**malihini:** a newcomer to the Islands.

**mana:** the spiritual power that the Hawaiians believe inhabits all things and creatures.

**manō:** shark.

**manuahi:** free, gratis.

**mauka:** toward the mountains.

**mauna:** mountain.

**mele:** a Hawaiian song or chant, often of epic proportions.

**Mele Kalikimaka:** Merry Christmas (a transliteration from the English phrase).

**Menehune:** a Hawaiian pixie. The Menehune were a legendary race of little people who accomplished prodigious work, such as building fishponds and temples in the course of a single night.

**moana:** the ocean.

**mu'umu'u:** the voluminous dress in which the missionaries enveloped Hawaiian women. Culturally sensitive locals have embraced the Hawaiian spelling but often shorten the spoken word to "mu'u." Most English dictionaries include the spelling "muumuu."

**nani:** beautiful.

**nui:** big.

**'ohana:** family.

**'ono:** delicious.

**pāhoehoe:** smooth, unbroken, satiny lava.

**palapala:** document, printed matter.

**pali:** a cliff, precipice.

**pānini:** prickly pear cactus.

**paniolo:** a Hawaiian cowboy, a rough transliteration of *español,* the language of the Islands' earliest cowboys.

**pau:** finished, done.

**pilikia:** trouble. The Hawaiian word is much more widely used here than its English equivalent.

**pū:** large conch shell used to trumpet the start of luau and other special events.

**puka:** a hole.

**pule:** prayer, blessing. Often performed before a meal or event.

**pupule:** crazy, like the celebrated Princess Pupule. This word has replaced its English equivalent in local usage.

**pu'u:** volcanic cinder cone.

**tūtū:** grandmother

**waha:** mouth.

**wahine:** a female, a woman, a wife, and a sign on the ladies' room door; the plural form is *wāhine.*

**wai:** freshwater, as opposed to saltwater, which is *kai.*

**wailele:** waterfall.

**wikiwiki:** to hurry, hurry up (since this is a reduplication of *wiki,* quick, neither *W* is pronounced as a *V*).

# Great Itineraries

## Highlights of Oahu

From *mauka* (mountains) to *makai* (sea), Oahu is probably the Hawaiian island most likely to please all types of travelers—whether you're an outdoorsy type, a beach bum, a foodie, or a family—and a week should give you enough time to see the highlights. You can either use the bus or take taxis or rideshares while you're in Honolulu, but rent a car to get out on the island and get a true feel for all things Oahu.

### DAY 1: WAIKIKI

Due to the time difference between Hawaii and the rest of the United States, you'll probably be jet-lagged. Grab coffee and head for a beach: Waikiki, Sans Souci, or Fort DeRussy. You'll see locals on their morning jogs at Kapiolani Park and catching waves at their favorite shore break.

When you're ready to explore the city, hit Kalakaua Avenue on foot, the best way to shop and sightsee. Got kiddos in tow? Try the Waikiki Aquarium or the Honolulu Zoo. Get some refreshments with tea at the Moana Surfrider, the oldest hotel in Waikiki, or mai tais and *pupu* (hors d'oeuvres) at Duke's Waikiki (a better deal at lunch). In the afternoon, take a surf lesson in the beginner-friendly waves of Waikiki. Finish your day with a seaside dinner.

### DAY 2: PEARL HARBOR

Give yourself a whole day for Pearl Harbor. Note that only the USS *Arizona* and the visitor center, which are operated by the National Park Service, are free; the other sights are operated by private entities and charge admission. Also, you must reserve tickets for the USS *Arizona* Memorial online in advance (for a small fee).

After your ferry ride out to the memorial, you can also explore the USS *Bowfin* submarine or take a shuttle to Ford Island and visit the restored USS *Missouri* battleship (the "Mighty Mo") and the Pearl Harbor Aviation Museum. Return to Waikiki for some late-afternoon beach time and a good dinner.

### DAY 3: DOWNTOWN HONOLULU AND CHINATOWN

Take a bus or taxi to downtown Honolulu for a guided tour of the royal residence, Iolani Palace, where you'll get an excellent overview of Hawaii's monarchical era, from the early 1800s through its overthrow in 1893. For more historical highlights, walk between Honolulu Hale (Hawaiian for "house"), Kawaiahao Church, the Hawaiian Mission Houses Historic Site and Archives, the Hawaii State Capitol, Washington Place, and the King Kamehameha I statue in the courtyard of Aliiolani Hale (now home of Hawaii Supreme Court). Several companies offer guided walks of the area.

Continue walking the ½ mile through Honolulu's business district into Chinatown for lunch at one of its eclectic eateries. Browse the shops, art galleries, and cultural sites, like Maunakea Marketplace, Chinatown Cultural Plaza, the Izumo Taishakyo Mission, and Kuan Yin Temple.

### DAY 4: DIAMOND HEAD AND KAIMUKI

Today you will go the opposite direction from downtown. Tours of Shangri La, the opulent former waterfront home of heiress Doris Duke, with its museum of Islamic art and architecture, book up well in advance. It's well worth the effort to make an online reservation for a small surcharge. (Note: Shuttles to the Kahala home-turned-museum start and end at the Honolulu Museum of Art, located on the other side of Waikiki).

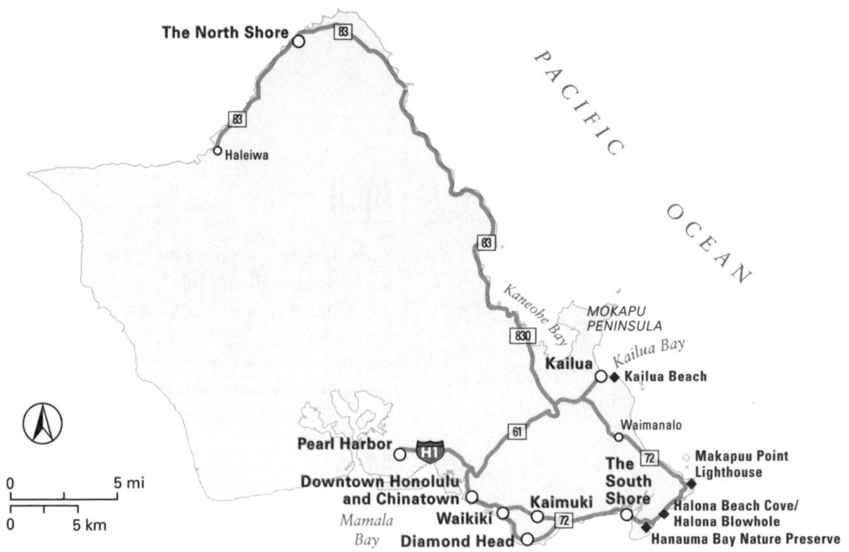


Another option is to hike Diamond Head State Monument (early morning is recommended to avoid the midday sun). Reservations must be made in advance to enter the area for the park's steep 1½-hour, 1½-mile (round-trip) trail up and down this dormant volcano. Keep in mind there is little shade, and bring water.

For either option, enjoy afternoon beach time and finish the day with dinner in the foodie neighborhood of Kaimuki.

### DAY 5: KAILUA AND THE SOUTH SHORE

Head to Windward Oahu for a stop in Kailua, a swim at its quintessential beach, and lunch at Kalapawai Cafe & Deli. Next, drive along the southeastern shore via Waimanalo, and choose your afternoon adventure: 1) do the easy, stroller-friendly hike at Makapuu Point Lighthouse, with great whale-watching views in winter and spring; 2) snorkel at the pristine Hanauma Bay Nature Preserve, where you'll have more space to swim with the fish after the morning-to-midday rush. Reservations must be made ahead; entrance fee is $25; or 3) stop at the Halona Blowhole lookout and the *From Here to Eternity* Halona Beach Cove nearby.

## Tips

- If this is your first visit, stay in Waikiki, which has most of the island's hotels.
- You don't need a car in Honolulu, but you'll need one to explore farther afield.
- Don't forget your hat, sunscreen, and good walking shoes.
- Be sure to reserve your free USS *Arizona* Memorial tickets online in advance ($1 charge). Also reserve ahead to hike Diamond Head.

### DAY 6: THE NORTH SHORE

The stunning beaches here are home to some of the world's most famous surf breaks. Each winter, surfers converge to catch barreling waves of 15 feet or higher. The cute town of Haleiwa is filled with surf shops, boutiques, and restaurants. Grab lunch from Haleiwa Joe's Seafood Grill or Uncle Bo's Haleiwa. Enjoying a frozen treat at Matsumoto Shave Ice is a sweet way to end the day.

# On the Calendar

Local events are a fun way to experience Oahu's diverse culture, and with festivals, parades, concerts, tournaments, surfing events, and more happening every month across the island, you're sure to find something to please everyone. It's still a good idea to check the format of a festival or event (in-person, virtual, or hybrid) that you're interested in.

## January

**Sony Open in Hawaii.** The Sony Open in Hawaii is held at the Waialae Country Club in east Honolulu in early to mid-January. Part of the PGA tour, the tournament attracts many of the top players in professional golf. It's also one of the largest charity sports events in the Islands. ☎ *808/523–7888* 🌐 *www.sonyopeninhawaii.com.*

## March

**Honolulu Festival.** Every year this event attracts participants and spectators from the Pacific Rim and beyond. The three-day celebration presents a variety of Asian, Pacific, and Hawaiian cultures in exhibits and events, including a craft market with artisans from across the world and a parade on Kalakaua Avenue in the center of Waikiki. 🌐 *honolulufestival.com.*

**King's Runner 10K.** The annual race may not be as well recognized as December's Honolulu Marathon, but it's now the largest 10K in Hawaii. Thousands of runners (walkers and strollers are welcome, too) race through a 6.2-mile course that begins in Honolulu, near the Neal S. Blaisdell Center, weaves through Kakaako, and parallels the beautiful beaches of Ala Moana. 🌐 *thehapalua.com/our-events/kings-runner-10k.*

## April

**Spam Jam.** Hawaii loves its Spam, which is spotlighted during this late-April food event. It's a Waikiki block party with live entertainment, Spam merchandise, and food booths offering unique snacks, desserts, and more made with the canned meat. 🌐 *spamjamhawaii.com.*

## May

**Lei Day.** Hawaii's version of May Day is a treasured celebration. Festivities take place every May 1 at Kapiolani Park near Waikiki and include lei-making demonstrations and contests, hula, crafts, food, and live music.

## June

**King Kamehameha I Day.** The celebration honoring the monarch who united the Hawaiian Kingdom takes place every June 11 with parades and other events throughout the Islands. On Oahu, the parade is held in Waikiki and features floats and traditional *pau* (skirt) riders—namely, women on horseback draped in lei and wearing ornate, colorful skirts.

## July

**Hawaii Ukulele Festival.** At this annual event, performers *kani ka pila,* or make music, with Hawaii's favorite instrument, the ukulele. The festival is a reimagined version of a longtime event and also includes a craft village and a food court. 🌐 *www.hawaiiukulelefestival.com.*

## August

**Duke's Oceanfest.** This weeklong, mid-month festival celebrates waterman Duke Kahanamoku, an Olympian and ambassador of Aloha who loved to swim, surf, and paddle. Surfing and stand-up paddleboarding competitions, outrigger races, and more are held along Waikiki Beach. Some events have been virtual and may still be, so check the website before heading out. 🌐 *dukesoceanfest.com.*

## September

**The Aloha Festivals.** This quintessential late-September event celebrates the storied, vibrant culture of the Islands. Festivities traditionally include a block party, parade, music, and hula. Some events offered in-person and virtual options, so check ahead to see the format. 🌐 *www.alohafestivals.com.*

## October

**Honolulu Pride.** One highlight of Oahu's Pride Month is the Honolulu Pride parade, a day-long, Waikiki event complete with Technicolor floats, live music, and food. 🌐 *hawaiilgbtlegacyfoundation.com.*

## November

**Hawaii Food & Wine Festival.** Held over several days at upscale locations across the Islands, this event features notable chefs from Hawaii, the Mainland, and abroad, as well as mixologists and wine producers. You'll eat some of the best foods the Islands have to offer. 🌐 *hawaiifoodandwinefestival.com.*

## December

**Honolulu City Lights.** Celebrate the holidays, Oahu style, throughout December. Honolulu Hale, where the city government is located, is transformed with twinkling lights. Other highlights include dozens of uniquely decorated Christmas trees, Shaka Santa, and Tutu Mele. 🌐 *www.honolulucitylights.org.*

# Contacts

## Air

**AIRPORT Daniel K. Inouye International Airport.** *(HNL).* *300 Rodgers Blvd., Airport Area* *808/836–6411* *airports.hawaii.gov/hnl.*

**GROUND TRANSPORTATION Roberts Hawaii.** *Honolulu* *808/539–9400* *www.robertshawaii.com/airport-shuttle.*

**LOCAL AIRLINES Mokulele Airlines.** *866/260–7070* *www.mokuleleairlines.com.*

**MAJOR AIRLINES Alaska Airlines.** *800/252–7522* *www.alaskaair.com.* **American Airlines.** *800/433–7300* *www.aa.com.* **Delta Airlines.** *800/221–1212 for U.S. reservations, 800/241–4141 for international reservations* *www.delta.com.* **Hawaiian Airlines.** *800/367–5320* *www.hawaiianairlines.com.* **Southwest.** *800/435–9792* *www.southwest.com.* **United Airlines.** *800/864–8331 for U.S. reservations* *www.united.com.*

## Bus

**CONTACTS TheBus.** *Honolulu* *808/848–5555* *www.thebus.org.* **Waikiki Trolley.** *Waikiki Shopping Plaza, 2250 Kalakaua Ave., Honolulu* *808/591–2561, 808/465–5543 Waikiki kiosk* *waikikitrolley.com.*

## Cruise

**CONTACTS Norwegian Cruise Line.** *866/234–7350* *www.ncl.com.* **UnCruise Adventures.** *888/862–8881* *www.uncruise.com.*

## Taxi

**CONTACTS TheCAB.** *808/422–2222* *www.thecabhawaii.com.* **Carey Honolulu.** *888/405–1792* *www.careyhonolulu.com.* **Charley's Taxi.** *808/233–3333* *www.charleystaxi.com.* **Elite Limousine Service.** *808/735–2431* *www.elitelimohawaii.com.*

## Vacation Rentals

**CONTACTS Hawaiian Villa Rentals.** *808/247–7521* *www.hawaiianvillarentals.com.* **Private Homes Hawaii.** *808/896– 9580* *www.privatehomeshawaii.com.*

## Visitor Information

**CONTACTS Hawaii Tourism Authority.** *800/464–2924 for brochures* *www.gohawaii.com.* **Oahu Visitors Bureau.** *800/464–2924* *www.gohawaii.com/islands/oahu.*

## Websites

**CONTACTS Hawaii Beach Safety.** *hawaiibeachsafety.com.* **Hawaii Department of Land and Natural Resources.** *dlnr.hawaii.gov.* **State of Hawaii Portal.** *portal.ehawaii.gov.*

Chapter 3

# HONOLULU AND PEARL HARBOR



Updated by
Anna Weaver

Sights
★★★★★

Restaurants
★★★★★

Hotels
★★★★★

Shopping
★★★★★

Nightlife
★★★★★

# WELCOME TO HONOLULU AND PEARL HARBOR

## TOP REASONS TO GO

★ **Variety:** The city has something for everyone: beaches, shopping, restaurants, sightseeing, nightlife, and hiking.

★ **History:** Honolulu, like the rest of the island, is saturated in Hawaiian history, from ancient times to the modern day. Pearl Harbor is Oahu's most visited attraction.

★ **Excellent food:** The capital is a melting pot of food and drink and a hub for Hawaii's farm-to-table dining scene.

★ **Great hotels:** An excellent selection of urban resorts, many on or near the beach, makes it easy to find accommodations that suit different budgets.

★ **The great outdoors:** Beaches offer every oceanside activity imaginable, from lounging and swimming to surfing and snorkeling. Diamond Head is a memorable hike.

**1 Waikiki and Diamond Head.** Most of Oahu's hotels are in Waikiki, as are shops, restaurants, and that famous beach. Beautiful Diamond Head, a great hiking spot but also a good destination for food, is just to the east.

**2 Pearl Harbor.** History is preserved and presented at multiple memorials and museums at this still-active naval base.

**3 Salt Lake.** There's no lake in this neighborhood; a serene park is the main draw.

**4 Mapunapuna.** What is mostly a warehouse and office area also has some hidden-gem restaurants and shops.

**5 Iwilei.** Stop in Iwilei for a number of good restaurants alongside the working harbor and farther inland.

**6 Downtown.** The business district is bustling during weekdays but dead in the evening. The historic district is easily walkable.

**7 Chinatown.** Chock-full of history and culture, Chinatown also has some of Honolulu's trendiest bars, restaurants, and boutiques alongside long-time local shops, markets, and restaurants.

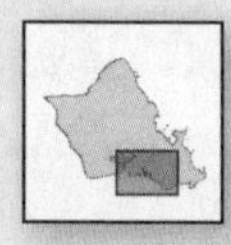

**8 Kakaako.** Completely transformed since the early 2010s, Kakaako is now a great place to shop, eat, and absorb street art.

**9 Ala Moana.** Come here for the shopping and food at the state's largest mall and enjoy the beachfront park.

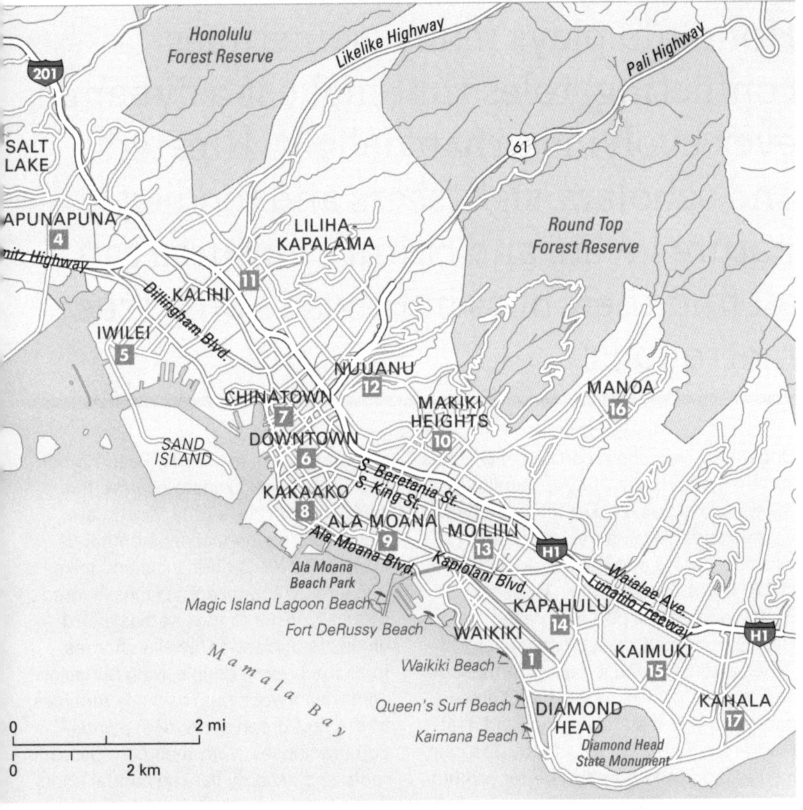


**10 Makiki Heights.** Head up Tantalus for stunning views from *mauka* to *makai* (mountain to ocean).

**11 Kalihi-Liliha-Kapalama.** Fabulous food spots popular with locals are the hallmarks of this working-class district.

**12 Nuuanu.** This largely residential valley with several interesting sights is intersected by the Pali Highway.

**13 Moiliili.** The excellent and varied restaurants here fall largely along King Street in this neighborhood overlapping with the McCully area.

**14 Kapahulu.** From Waikiki, head north along Kapahulu Avenue for low-key shops and restaurants.

**15 Kaimuki.** Since the 2010s, Kaimuki has emerged as a paradise for foodies.

**16 Manoa.** Home of the largest branch of the University of Hawaii, Manoa is also known for its historic homes.

**17 Kahala.** This upscale residential area has a beachfront hotel to match and a good-size mall.

As the seat of government, a center of commerce and shipping, and an entertainment and recreation mecca, Honolulu plays many (sometimes conflicting) roles that make it a dynamic, ever-evolving urban delight. Hipsters and scholars, sightseers and foodies, nature lovers and culture vultures can all find their bliss in Hawaii's only true metropolis.

---

Once there was the broad bay of Mamala and the narrow inlet of Kou, fronting a dusty plain occupied by a few thatched houses and the great Pakaka *heiau* (shrine). Nosing into the narrow passage in 1794, British sea captain William Brown named the port Fair Haven. Later, Hawaiians would call it Honolulu, or "sheltered bay," and it gained further importance in 1804, when King Kamehameha I built a stately compound near the harbor here after reluctantly abandoning his Big Island home to better protect Hawaiian interests.

As shipping traffic increased, the settlement grew into a Western-style town of streets and buildings, tightly clustered around the single freshwater source, Nuuanu Stream. Not until piped water became available in the early 1900s did Honolulu spread across the greening plain, becoming both a city and a county. Today, the entire island is, in a sense, Honolulu, which has no official boundaries, extending across flatlands, from Pearl Harbor to Waikiki, and high into the hills.

The main areas of Waikiki, Pearl Harbor, downtown, and Chinatown have the lion's share of the sights, but greater Honolulu's residential neighborhoods also have a lot to offer, including folksy restaurants and takeout places favored by locals. Visits to these areas afford glimpses of classic Hawaiian homes, from the breezy, double-wing bungalows, with their swooping, Thai-style rooflines, to the tiny, green-and-white, plantation-era houses, with their corrugated tin roofs and window-flanked central doors and porches.

Also common are "Grandma-style" gardens and *ohana* houses, with smaller backyard homes or apartments allowing extended families to live together. In these districts, carports rarely shelter cars but instead serve as rec rooms. Beneath the roof, parties are held and neighbors sit to "talk story," and atop it, gallon jars of pickled lemons ferment in the sun.

# Planning

## Getting Here and Around

### AIR

Honolulu's Daniel K. Inouye International Airport (HNL) is Hawaii's busiest, with the most nonstop flights from the mainland United States as well as the majority of the state's international flights.

Some hotels have their own pickup and drop-off service, though they may charge a fee. Taxi service is available on the center median just outside baggage-claim areas. Look for the yellow-shirted taxi dispatchers, who willl radio for a taxi. The fare to Waikiki is about $45, plus 60¢ per bag and tip. An oversize baggage fee may apply. Uber and Lyft also serve the airport.

Another option is to take a private shuttle like Roberts Hawaii. The company will greet you at the arrival gate, escort you to baggage claim, and take you to your hotel. Call ahead for the service, which costs $26 per person one-way to Waikiki.

TheBus, the municipal bus, will take you into Waikiki for only $3, but all bags must fit on your lap or under your legs.

**CONTACTS Roberts Hawaii.** ☎ *808/539–9400* 🌐 *robertshawaii.com.*

### BUS

Buses are convenient and affordable, particularly in the most heavily touristed areas of Waikiki. Options include Honolulu's municipal transit system, affectionately known as TheBus, which also travels to and from the airport; the Waikiki Trolleys, brass-trimmed, open-air vehicles that look like trolleys or large double-decker buses; and brightly painted private buses, some of them free, that shuttle you to such commercial attractions as dinner cruises, shopping centers, and the like.

TheBus is one of Oahu's best bargains. You can use it to travel around the island or just down Kalakaua Avenue for $3, with buses regularly stopping in Waikiki to take passengers to nearby shopping areas. Exact change (dollar bills are accepted) and the system's HOLO cards are accepted. Indeed, you can ride all day for $7.50 using a HOLO card; monthly passes cost $80. Look into downloading the free DaBus2 or HEA app for your smartphone.

The hop-on-hop-off Waikiki Trolley has four lines—each beginning and ending in Waikiki—and dozens of stops that allow you to plan your own itinerary. A one-day pass costs $30 ($18 for the Green Line, $5 for the Pink Line) for a single line and $55 for all lines. Four-day ($65) and seven-day ($75) all-line passes are also available.

The Coastline & Local Grindz Tour (Blue Line) includes stops at the Duke Kahanamoku statue, along Diamond Head and Kahala, at the Halona Blowhole, Sea Life Park, and Koko Marina, plus stops at local eateries. As its name suggests, the Ala Moana Shopping Tour (Pink Line) goes to the Ala Moana Center, a sprawling outdoor mall. The Heroes and Legends Tour (Red Line) travels between Waikiki, Chinatown, and Kakaako and includes stops at the Honolulu Museum of Art, the capitol, Iolani Palace, Punchbowl Crater, Chinatown, and Ala Moana. The Diamond Head Shuttle (Green Line) takes you from Waikiki to Diamond Head with a Saturday morning option to stop at the popular KCC Farmers' Market.

**CONTACTS TheBus.** ✉ *Honolulu* ☎ *808/848–5555* 🌐 *thebus.org.* **Waikiki Trolley.** ✉ *Honolulu* ☎ *808/591–2561* 🌐 *waikikitrolley.com.*

### CAR

If you plan on spending most of your time in Hawaii in Honolulu, it doesn't pay to rent a car for your entire trip, especially if you are staying in Waikiki. Hotels typically charge (a lot) for parking, gas is expensive, and traffic can be heavy, especially during rush hour.

But having a car will make exploring the rest of Oahu easier, so consider renting only for a couple of days. Just be sure to reserve your vehicle as far ahead as possible. Note, too, that the post-pandemic rental-car shortage saw business boom for car-sharing companies like Turo (🌐 *turo.com*), which help you rent cars from private owners as an alternative to traditional car-rental agencies.

For those with a Costco card, the least expensive gas on the island is at the three Costco stations. The one in Honolulu is on Alakawa Street, between Dillingham Boulevard and Nimitz Highway; the one in Waipio is at 94-1231 Ka Uka Boulevard; and the one in Kapolei is at 4589 Kapolei Parkway.

### TAXI

In Honolulu, taxis cost $4.30 at the drop of the flag, and each additional 1/8 mile is $0.56. Taxi and limousine companies can provide a car and driver for half-day or daylong island tours. Several companies also offer personal guides, though rates for such services can be steep, running a few hundred dollars or more per day. Uber and Lyft also serve Oahu, including for airport pickups.

## Hotels

Most hotels in Honolulu are in Waikiki, with a few downtown and in the Ala Moana area between downtown and Waikiki. Elsewhere on Oahu, accommodations range from quiet bed-and-breakfasts and cottages to less expensive hotels that are a great value. There are also a few luxury resorts, where you'll truly feel like you're getting away from it all.

⇨ *Hotel prices are the lowest cost of a standard double room in high season. Hotel reviews have been shortened. For full information, visit Fodors.com.*

**What It Costs in U.S. Dollars**

| $ | $$ | $$$ | $$$$ |
|---|---|---|---|
| **HOTELS** | | | |
| under $200 | $200–$280 | $281–$380 | over $380 |

## Nightlife

Gone are the days when there was nothing to do in Honolulu at night. In fact, many people who arrive on Oahu expecting little more than white-sand beaches are surprised by a nighttime scene so vibrant that it can be hard to pick which DJ to see at which club or which art show opening to attend. After a day on the beach, though, lingering beneath the swaying palms to watch the sun set over Waikiki, you might want to head back to your hotel and dress up: more and more Honolulu clubs are enforcing a dress code. It's also a good idea to check with a bar or club to see if they require reservations.

## Performing Arts

If all-night dancing isn't for you, Oahu also has a thriving arts and culture scene, with community-theater productions, outdoor concerts, film festivals, and chamber-music performances, most of it centered in Honolulu. Major Broadway shows, dance companies, musicians, and comedians come through, too. Check local newspapers (and their accompanying websites)—the *Honolulu Star-Advertiser* or *MidWeek*—and *HONOLULU Magazine* for the latest events.

# Restaurants

There's no lack of choices when it comes to dining in Honolulu, where you'll find everything from the haute cuisine of heavy-hitting top-notch chefs to a wide variety of Asian specialties to reliable and inexpensive American favorites.

⇨ *Restaurant prices are the average cost of a main course at dinner or, if dinner is not served, at lunch. Restaurant reviews have been shortened. For full information, visit Fodors.com.*

**What It Costs in U.S. Dollars**

| | $ | $$ | $$$ | $$$$ |
|---|---|---|---|---|
| **RESTAURANTS** | under $20 | $20–$30 | $31–$40 | over $40 |

# Shopping

There are two distinct types of shopping experiences: vast malls with the customary department stores or tiny boutiques with specialty items. That said, three Honolulu malls provide a combination of the standard stores and interesting shops showcasing original paintings and woodwork from local artists and craftspeople.

Although it's easy enough to find designer merchandise and other items you can get back home, with a little effort, you can also find unusual Asian imports. Be sure to scout the malls for the slightly hidden shops, where a sale bin might contain the perfect, and truly unique, souvenir or gift.

In Waikiki, stores open at around 9 or 10 am, and many don't close until 10 or even 11 pm.

# Tours

Guided tours are convenient; you don't have to worry about finding a parking spot or getting admission tickets. Most of the tour guides have taken special classes in Hawaiian history and lore, and many are certified by the state of Hawaii. On the other hand, you won't have the freedom to proceed at your own pace, nor will you have the ability to take a detour trip if something else catches your attention.

## BUS AND VAN TOURS

**Oahu Nature Tours**

**BUS TOURS** | The company's full-day, all-inclusive Ultimate Circle Island Tour has pickups from central locations in Waikiki and includes lunch at a North Shore shrimp truck and a walk to the Waimea Valley waterfalls. Among other highlights are the Halona Blowhole, Pali Lookout, Byodo-in Temple, Sunset Beach, and Dole Plantation. ✉ *Honolulu* ☎ *808/924–2473* 🌐 *www.oahunaturetours.com* 🎟 *$149.*

**Polynesian Adventure**

**BUS TOURS** | This company leads tours of Pearl Harbor and other Oahu sights and also offers a circle-island tour. ☎ *877/930–1740* 🌐 *polyad.com* 🎟 *From $62.*

## THEME TOURS

**Discover Hawaii Tours**

**SPECIAL-INTEREST TOURS** | In addition to circle-island and other Oahu-based itineraries on motor coaches and minicoaches, this company can also get you from Waikiki to the lava flows of the Big Island or to Maui's Hana Highway and back in one day. ☎ *808/824–3995* 🌐 *discoverhawaiitours.com* 🎟 *From $89.*

**E Noa Tours**

**SPECIAL-INTEREST TOURS** | This outfitter's certified tour guides conduct circle-island and Pearl Harbor tours, with pickups from Ko Olina and Waikiki. E Noa also owns Waikiki Trolley. ☎ *808/591–2561* 🌐 *enoa.com* 🎟 *From $61.*

# Waikiki and Diamond Head

Waikiki, approximately 3 miles east of downtown Honolulu, is Oahu's primary resort area. A mix of historic and modern hotels and condos front the sunny 2-mile stretch of beach, and many have clear views of Diamond Head. The area is home to much of the island's dining, nightlife, and shopping—from posh boutiques to hole-in-the-wall eateries to craft booths at Duke's Marketplace.

Waikiki was once a favorite retreat for Hawaiian royalty. In 1901, the Moana Hotel debuted, introducing Waikiki as an international travel destination. The region's fame continued to grow when Duke Kahanamoku, known as the "Father of Modern Surfing," helped popularize the sport by offering surf lessons to visitors at Waikiki. You can see Duke immortalized in a bronze statue, with a surfboard, on Kuhio Beach in the heart of it all.

Today there is a decidedly "urban resort" vibe here. Streets are clean, gardens are manicured, and the sand feels softer than at beaches farther down the coast. At first glance, there isn't much of a local culture—it's mainly tourist crowds—but if you explore the neighborhood, you can still find the relaxed surf-y vibe and friendly aloha spirit that have drawn people here for more than a century.

Diamond Head Crater is perhaps Hawaii's most recognizable natural landmark. The crater got its name from sailors who thought they had found precious gems on its slopes; these later proved to be calcite crystals, a much more common mineral. Hawaiians saw a resemblance between the sharp angle of the crater's seaward slope and the oddly shaped head of the ahi fish and so called it Leahi, though later they Hawaiianized the English name to Kaimana Hila. It is commemorated in a widely known hula—*A ike i ka nani o Kaimana Hila, Kaimana Hila, kau mai i luna* ("We saw the beauty of Diamond Head, Diamond Head set high above"). Today Diamond Head State Monument is so popular that visitors must reserve and pay ahead to make the steep climb.

Sprawling Kapiolani Park lies in the shadow of Diamond Head, which is just beyond the easternmost limits of Waikiki. King David Kalakaua established the park in 1877, naming it after his queen and dedicating it "to the use and enjoyment of the people." In this 500-acre expanse, you can go for a stroll, play all sorts of field sports, enjoy a picnic, see wild animals and tropical fish at the Honolulu Zoo and the Waikiki Aquarium, and hear live music at the Waikiki Shell or the Kapiolani Park Bandstand.

### GETTING HERE AND AROUND

Bounded by the Ala Wai Canal on the north and west, the beach on the south, and the Honolulu Zoo to the east, Waikiki is compact and easy to walk around. TheBus runs multiple routes here from the airport and downtown Honolulu. By car, finding Waikiki from H1 can be tricky; look for the Punahou exit for the west end of Waikiki and the King Street exit for the eastern end.

## Sights

**★ Diamond Head State Monument**

**STATE/PROVINCIAL PARK | FAMILY** | Panoramas from this 760-foot extinct volcanic peak, which was once used as a military fortification, extend from Waikiki and Honolulu in one direction and out to Koko Head in the other, with surfers and windsurfers scattered like confetti on the cresting waves below. The 360-degree perspective is a great orientation for first-time visitors. On a clear day, look east past Koko Head to glimpse the outlines of the islands of Maui and Molokai.

**Despite the steep climb, Diamond Head, an extinct volcanic crater on the eastern edge of Waikiki, is one of Honolulu's most popular hiking destinations.**

Reservations to enter this popular park are required in advance for those who are not Hawaii residents, and an entrance and parking fee must be paid via credit card. You can reserve up to 30 days in advance; the last reservation is 4 pm. From Waikiki, take Kalakaua Avenue east, turn left at Monsarrat Avenue, head a mile up the hill, and look for a sign on the right. Drive through the tunnel to the inside of the crater. The ¾-mile trail to the top begins at the parking lot, and the hike up to the crater is steep, with numerous stairs to climb. So if you aren't in the habit of getting occasional exercise, this might not be for you. At the top, you have a somewhat awkward scramble through a dark tunnel and bunker out into the open air, but the view is worth it.

As you walk, note the color of the vegetation: if the mountain is brown, Honolulu has been without significant rain for a while, but if the trees and undergrowth glow green, you'll know it's the wet season (winter) without looking at a calendar. Winter is when rare Hawaiian marsh plants revive on the floor of the crater. Wear closed-toe shoes or sneakers, a hat, and take bottled water with you to stay hydrated under the tropical sun. There are no water stations (or any shade) along the hike. Keep an eye on your watch if you're here at day's end: the gates close promptly at 6 pm. ■ **TIP→ To beat the heat and the crowds, rise early and make the hike before 8 am.** ✉ *Diamond Head Rd., at 18th Ave., Waikiki* ☎ *808/587–0300* 🌐 *dlnr.hawaii.gov/dsp/parks/oahu* 🎫 *$5 per person (for nonresidents of Hawaii), $10 parking per non-commercial vehicle.*

### Honolulu Zoo

**ZOO** | **FAMILY** | The world definitely has bigger and newer zoos, but this 42-acre facility features well-paved, walkable trails amid a lush garden with tropical flowers. To get a glimpse of the endangered nene, the Hawaii state bird, check out the zoo's Kipuka Nene Sanctuary. Other highlights include a Japanese Giant

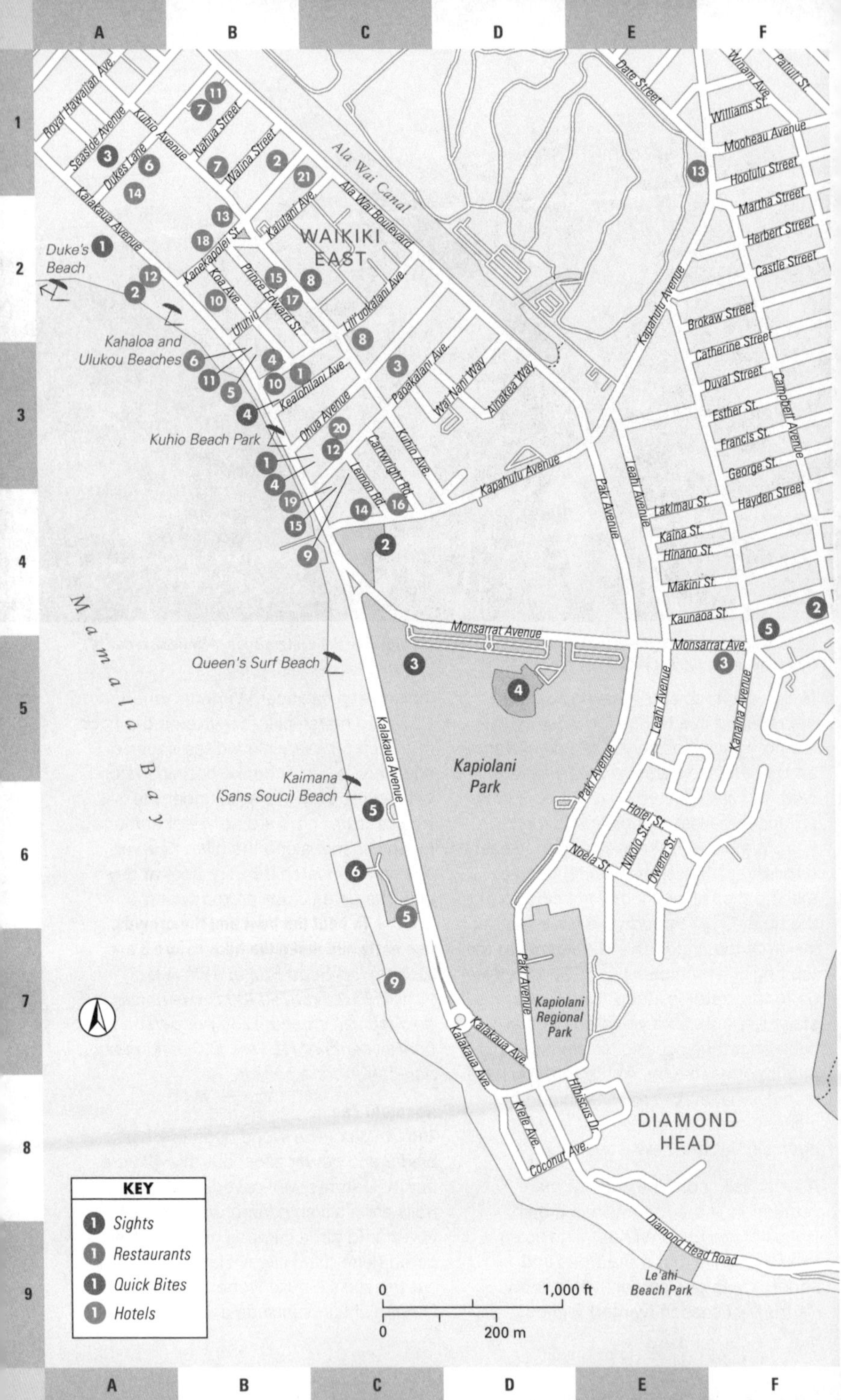

WAIKIKI EAST
Ala Wai Canal
Ala Wai Boulevard
Royal Hawaiian Ave.
Seaside Avenue
Kuhio Avenue
Nahua Street
Walina Street
Dukes Lane
Kalakaua Avenue
Duke's Beach
Kanekapolei St.
Kaiulani Ave.
Koa Ave.
Prince Edward St.
Uluniu
Lili'uokalani Ave.
Kahaloa and Ulukou Beaches
Kealohilani Ave.
Ohua Avenue
Kuhio Beach Park
Paoakalani Ave.
Wai Nani Way
Ainakea Way
Cartwright Rd.
Kuhio Ave.
Lemon Rd.
Kapahulu Avenue
Date Street
Winam Ave.
Paliuli St.
Williams St.
Mooheau Avenue
Hoolulu Street
Martha Street
Herbert Street
Castle Street
Brokaw Street
Catherine Street
Duval Street
Esther St.
Francis St.
George St.
Hayden Street
Campbell Avenue
Lakimau St.
Kaina St.
Hinano St.
Makini St.
Kaunaoa St.
Monsarrat Ave.
Leahi Avenue
Paki Avenue
Monsarrat Avenue
Mamala Bay
Queen's Surf Beach
Kaimana (Sans Souci) Beach
Kapiolani Park
Kanaina Avenue
Hotei St.
Nikolo St.
Owena St.
Noela St.
Kapiolani Regional Park
Kalakaua Ave.
Kiele Ave.
Hibiscus Dr.
Coconut Ave.
DIAMOND HEAD
Diamond Head Road
Le'ahi Beach Park
KEY
Sights
Restaurants
Quick Bites
Hotels
0
1,000 ft
0
200 m
A B C D E F
1 2 3 4 5 6 7 8 9

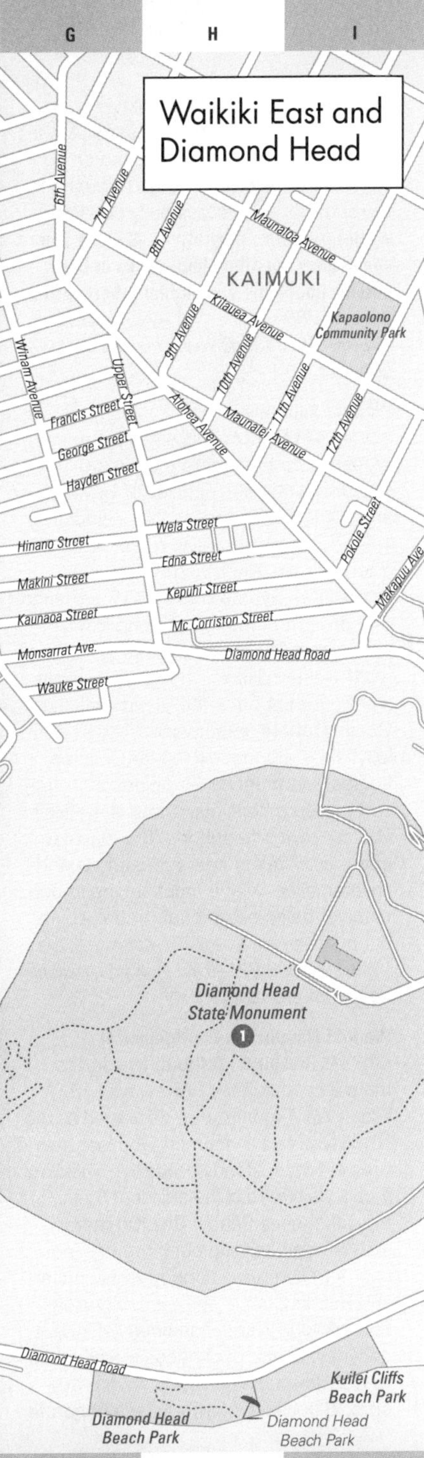


## Sights

1 Diamond Head State Monument........ **H7**
2 Honolulu Zoo............. **C4**
3 Kapiolani Park Bandstand............... **C5**
4 Tom Moffatt Waikiki Shell............ **D5**
5 Waikiki Aquarium........ **C6**
6 Waikiki Natatorium War Memorial........... **C6**

## Restaurants

1 Arancino di Mare........ **C3**
2 Beachhouse at the Moana.............. **A2**
3 Bogart's Café............ **F5**
4 d.k Steakhouse.......... **C3**
5 Hau Tree................. **C6**
6 Herringbone Waikiki.................. **A1**
7 Heyday................... **B1**
8 Hy's Steak House........ **C2**
9 Michel's at the Colony Surf............... **C7**
10 Morimoto Asia Waikiki.................. **B3**
11 Mugen.................. **B3**
12 Queensbreak............ **C3**
13 Side Street Inn Kapahulu................ **E1**
14 Teddy's Bigger Burgers.......... **C4**
15 Tiki's Grill and Bar........ **C4**

## Quick Bites

1 Banán.................... **A2**
2 Diamond Head Market & Grill.................... **F4**
3 Holey Grail Donuts...... **A1**
4 Kai Coffee Hawaii...... **B3**
5 South Shore Grill......... **F4**

## Hotels

1 Alohilani Resort Waikiki Beach........... **B3**
2 Aqua Aloha Surf Waikiki.............. **B1**
3 Aston at the Waikiki Banyan.......... **C3**
4 Aston Waikiki Beach Tower............ **B3**
5 Aston Waikiki Circle Hotel.............. **B3**
6 Espacio – The Jewel of Waikiki........ **B3**
7 Hilton Garden Inn Waikiki Beach........... **B1**
8 Hilton Waikiki Beach.... **C2**
9 Hotel Renew.............. **C3**
10 Hyatt Regency Waikiki Beach Resort & Spa.... **B2**
11 Ilima Hotel............... **B1**
12 Moana Surfrider, A Westin Resort & Spa, Waikiki Beach........... **A2**
13 Ohana Waikiki East by Outrigger............. **B2**
14 Outrigger Waikiki Beachcomber Hotel...................... **A1**
15 Pacific Monarch........ **B2**
16 Queen Kapiolani Hotel....................... **C4**
17 Royal Grove Waikiki.... **B2**
18 Sheraton Princess Kaiulani....... **B2**
19 Twin Fin Hotel........... **C4**
20 Waikiki Beach Marriott Resort & Spa... **C3**
21 Wayfinder Waikiki....... **C1**

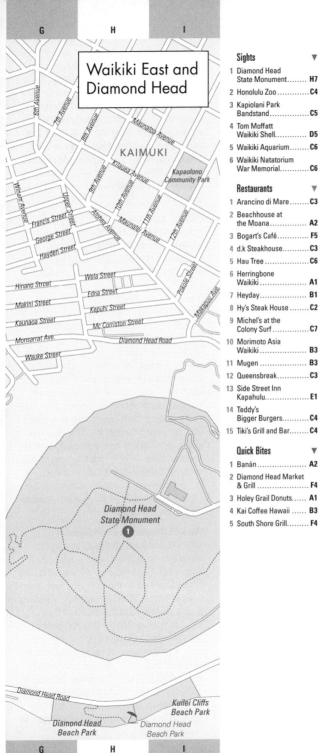

Salamander habitat and an ectotherm complex, which houses a Burmese python, elongated tortoises, and a giant African snail. Though many animals prefer to remain invisible—particularly the big cats—the monkeys and elephants appear to enjoy being seen and are a hoot to watch. It's best to get to the zoo when it opens because the animals are livelier in the cool of the morning. Children adore the petting zoo, where they can make friends with a llama or stand in the middle of a koi pond.

There's an exceptionally good gift shop. On weekends, the Art on the Zoo Fence, on Monsarrat Avenue on the Diamond Head side outside the zoo, has affordable artwork by local contemporary artists. Metered parking is available along the *makai* (ocean) side of the park and in the lot next to the zoo. Parking is free at the lot across the street (at the Waikiki Shell), but it can fill up early. TheBus makes stops here along the way to and from Ala Moana Center and Sea Life Park (Routes 8 and 22). ✉ *151 Kapahulu Ave., Waikiki* ☎ *808/971–7171* 🌐 *www.honoluluzoo.org* 🎫 *$21.*

**Kapiolani Park Bandstand**

**PERFORMANCE VENUE** | **FAMILY** | The Victorian-style bandstand, built in the late 1890s, is Kapiolani Park's stage for community entertainment and concerts. Founded by King Kamehameha III in 1836, the Royal Hawaiian Band is the nation's only city-sponsored band and performs free concerts at the bandstand as well as at Iolani Palace and the center stage at Ala Moana Center. Visit the band's website for concert dates (🌐 *www.rhb-music.com*), and check event-listing websites and the *Honolulu Star-Advertiser*—Oahu's local newspaper—for information on other coming bandstand attractions. ✉ *2805 Monsarrat Ave., Waikiki* ☎ *808/922–5331.*

**Tom Moffatt Waikiki Shell**

**PERFORMANCE VENUE** | Grab one of the 6,000 "grass seats" (that is, spots on the lawn, though there are actual seats as well) for music under the stars. An eclectic array of musical acts put on concerts at this landmark venue throughout the summer and occasionally during the winter, weather permitting. **■ TIP→ This venue does not allow backpacks or large purses. Check the website for other restrictions.** ✉ *2805 Monsarrat Ave., Waikiki* ☎ *808/768–5400* 🌐 *www.blaisdellcenter.com.*

**Waikiki Aquarium**

**AQUARIUM** | **FAMILY** | This small yet fun attraction harbors more than 3,500 organisms and 500 species of Hawaiian and South Pacific marine life, including an endangered Hawaiian monk seal and a zebra shark. The Living Reef exhibit showcases diverse corals and fascinating reef environments found along Hawaii's shorelines. Check out exhibits on the Northwestern Hawaiian Islands (explaining the formation of the island chain) and Ocean Drifters (about various types of jellyfish). A 60-foot exhibit houses sea horses, sea dragons, and pipefish. A free, self-guided mobile audio tour is available via your own smartphone. The aquarium offers activities of interest to adults and children alike, with a focus on the importance of being eco-friendly and keeping our oceans clean. ✉ *2777 Kalakaua Ave., Waikiki* ☎ *808/923–9741* 🌐 *www.waikiki-aquarium.org* 🎫 *$12.*

**Waikiki Natatorium War Memorial**

**NOTABLE BUILDING** | Although closed to the public, this Beaux Arts–style, 1927 World War I monument, dedicated to the 101 Hawaiian servicemen who lost their lives in battle, stands proudly in Waikiki and is visible from the adjacent Sans Souci/Kaimana Beach. The 100-meter saltwater swimming pool, the training spot for Olympians Johnny Weissmuller and Buster Crabbe and the U.S. Army during World War II, has been closed for decades, as the pool needs repair. Plans to tear down the natatorium were put on hold because of efforts by a nonprofit

## Beach Safety on Oahu

Hawaii's beautiful, world-renowned beaches can be dangerous at times, primarily due to large waves and strong currents. Be mindful of wave hazards, which the state rates using three signs: a yellow square (caution), a red stop sign (high hazard), and a black diamond (extreme hazard). Signs are updated three times daily or as conditions change.

Visiting beaches with lifeguards is strongly recommended, and you should swim only when there's a normal caution rating. Never swim alone or dive into unknown water or shallow breaking waves. When close to the shoreline, don't turn your back to the ocean as sudden waves can wash you out to sea. If you're caught in a rip current, instead of fighting the pull, tread water and wave your arms in the air to signal for help.

Even in calm conditions, you need to be mindful of other water dangers, including razor-sharp coral, jellyfish, eels, and sharks. Jellyfish, including the tiny, blue Portuguese man-of-war, cause the most injuries. They're found on the island year-round, and signs are posted along beaches when they're present. The Waikiki Aquarium also has a box jellyfish advisory calendar (🌐 *www.waikikiaquarium.org/interact/box-jellyfish-calendar*). If you're stung, pick off the tentacles with tweezers, rinse the affected area with vinegar, and apply heat.

Shark attacks in Hawaii are rare. Of the 40 species found here, tiger sharks are considered the most dangerous because of their size and feeding behavior. They're easily recognized by their blunt snouts and vertical bars on their sides. Here are a few tips to reduce your shark-attack risk:

- Swim, surf, or dive with others at beaches patrolled by lifeguards.
- Avoid swimming at dawn or dusk or at night, when some shark species move inshore to feed.
- Don't enter the water if you have open wounds or are bleeding.
- Avoid murky waters; harbor entrances; and areas near stream mouths, channels, or steep drop-offs.
- Don't wear high-contrast swimwear or shiny jewelry.
- Don't swim near dolphins, which are often prey for large sharks.
- If you spot a shark, leave the water quickly and calmly; never provoke or harass a shark.

The Hawaii Beach Safety website (🌐 *hawaiibeachsafety.com*) provides statewide beach-hazard maps, as well as weather and surf advisories; 🌐 *hioceansafety.com* has good information for beachgoers.

group that continues fighting to save it. With massive environmental and funding issues, though, the proposed refurbishment remains in flux. ✉ *2777 Kalakaua Ave., Waikiki* 🌐 *natatorium.org.*

## Beaches

Waikiki Beach is a bustling, 2-mile stretch of sand that runs from Hilton Hawaiian Village on one end to Kapiolani Park and Diamond Head on the other. You can easily walk along the shoreline (and some paved pathways such as the Beach Walk) fronting some hotels for the entire distance. The beach itself was widened in 2021, when the area underwent a major sand-replenishment project that added about 20,000 cubic yards to the shoreline.

Although it's one contiguous strand, Waikiki Beach is as varied as the people who inhabit the Islands. Whether you want to kick back and watch the action from the shade or enjoy the ocean, you can find everything available here for a lively day on the world's most famous beach.

If you're staying outside the area and driving here, it's easiest to park at either end of the beach and walk in. The city has started upgrading parking meters to include the Park Smarter mobile app, which takes electronic payments. If you can find a spot, metered parking is affordable ($1.50 per hour) and available to the west, at Ala Wai Harbor, and to the east, at Kapiolani Park and the Honolulu Zoo. Resorts also have parking, but the hourly rates are high.

**Diamond Head Beach Park**

**BEACH** | You have to do a little hiking to reach this beautiful, remote spot at the base of Diamond Head Crater. Although the beach is just a small, narrow strip of sand with lots of coral in the water, the views from the point are breathtaking, and it's fun to watch the windsurfers skimming along. From the parking area, look for an opening in the wall where an unpaved trail leads down to the beach. Even for the unadventurous, a stop at the lookout point is well worth the time. **Amenities:** parking (no fee); showers. **Best for:** solitude; sunset; surfing; windsurfing. ✉ *At base of Diamond Head, 3500 Diamond Head Rd., Diamond Head ⊕ Park at crest of Diamond Head Rd. and walk down.*

**Duke's Beach**

**BEACH | FAMILY** | Named for Duke Kahanamoku, Hawaii's famous Olympic swimming champion and waterman, this hard-packed beach fronting the Hilton Hawaiian Village Waikiki Beach Resort is great for families. It's the only stretch of Waikiki with shade trees on the sand, and its waters are very calm thanks to a rock wall that creates a semiprotected cove. The ocean clarity here is not as good as elsewhere, but this is a small price to pay for peace of mind about youngsters. **Amenities:** food and drink; parking (fee); showers; toilets. **Best for:** sunset; swimming; walking. ✉ *2005 Kalia Rd., Waikiki.*

**★ Fort DeRussy Beach Park**

**BEACH | FAMILY** | A wide, soft, ultra-white shore with gently lapping waves makes this fine beach a family favorite for running-jumping-frolicking fun. Other bonuses include the shaded, grassy grilling area, pickleball courts, and many aquatic rental options. The beach fronts the Hale Koa Hotel as well as Fort DeRussy. **Amenities:** food and drink; lifeguards; showers; toilets; water sports. **Best for:** swimming; walking. ✉ *2161 Kalia Rd., Waikiki.*

## Outrigger Canoes

If catching a wave on a 10-foot surfboard was a rush, wait until you catch one aboard a 30-foot outrigger canoe! You'll need to paddle a bit, but the captains and beach boys will guide you in and out of the breaks.

Look for the long, skinny boats in front of the Royal Hawaiian Resort, where the family-run, family-friendly **Waikiki Beach Services** (🌐 *www.waikikibeachservices.com*) is one option. A 30-minute experience costs about $35; booking in advance is suggested.

**Gray's Beach**

**BEACH** | In the 1920s, a little guesthouse called Gray's-by-the-Sea stood on what is now a very narrow strip of sand that's best for walking, admiring the ocean, and imagining a Waikiki of yesteryear. (Note that the tides often put sand space at a premium, so you have to use the elevated concrete walkway most of the time.) Catamaran charters launch from this beach throughout the day, sailing out for views of Diamond Head and Waikiki Beach. You can get a great view of Diamond Head here, and you can also sip a mai tai at House Without a Key, a legendary beach restaurant at the Halekulani hotel a few steps away. **Amenities:** food and drink; lifeguards; parking (fee); showers; toilets. **Best for:** walking. ✉ *2199 Kalia Rd., Waikiki.*

**Kahaloa and Ulukou Beaches**

**BEACH** | This busy beach has everything: famous for the Canoes surf break, it's the launching spot for most of the catamaran charters that sail out to Diamond Head several times a day, as well as the place for surfing lessons and outrigger canoe rentals. Chair and umbrella rentals are available, and great music and outdoor dancing beckon at the lively Duke's restaurant, where shirt and shoes not only aren't required, they're discouraged. The Royal Hawaiian Hotel and Moana Surfrider are here. **Amenities:** food and drink; lifeguards; parking (fee); showers; toilets; water sports. **Best for:** partiers; surfing. ✉ *2259 Kalakaua Ave., Waikiki.*

**Kaimana (Sans Souci) Beach**

**BEACH** | **FAMILY** | Across from the zoo, at the eastern end of Waikiki along what is known as the Gold Coast, this small rectangle of sand is a local-favorite sunning spot for beach lovers of all ages. Although it's usually quieter than the stretches of beach in the heart of town, it's also close to the conveniences of Waikiki. Children can splash safely in its shallow waters, which are protected (for now) by the walls of the historic natatorium, a long-closed, Olympic-size, saltwater swimming arena. Serious swimmers and triathletes also train in the channel beyond the reef here. The Kaimana Beach Hotel and popular Hau Tree lanai restaurant are next door. **Amenities:** lifeguards; parking (fee); showers; toilets. **Best for:** swimming; walking. ✉ *2776 Kalakaua Ave., Waikiki* ✣ *Across from Kapiolani Park, between New Otani Kaimana Beach Hotel and Waikiki Natatorium War Memorial.*

**Kuhio Beach Park**

**BEACH** | **FAMILY** | Featuring a bronze statue of Duke Kahanamoku, the father of modern-day surfing, this lively beach is bordered by a landscaped walkway with a few benches and some shade. It's great for strolls and people-watching any time of day. Check out the Kuhio Beach hula mound Tuesday, Thursday, and Saturday at 6:30 (at 6, November–January) for free hula and Hawaiian-music performances and a sunset torch-lighting ceremony. Surf lessons for beginners are available from the beach center every half hour. **Amenities:** food and drink; lifeguards; showers; toilets; water sports. **Best for:** surfing; walking. ✉ *2461 Kalakaua Ave., Waikiki* ✣ *Go past Moana Surfrider Hotel to Kapahulu Ave. pier.*

**Queen's Surf Beach**

**BEACH** | **FAMILY** | Once the site of Queen Liliuokalani's beach house, this strand near the Honolulu Zoo draws locals and tourists of all ages. Lovely banyan trees offer shade, the bronze *Surfer on a Wave* sculpture by artist Robert Pashby honors surfing, volleyball nets welcome pros and amateurs alike, and waters that are part of an aquatic reserve provide superb snorkeling opportunities. The beach is also near what is considered the area's premier bodyboarding spot: the break called The Wall. Be sure to walk out to the gazebo (where experienced boarders jump into the ocean) for stellar views of Waikiki and beyond. **Amenities:** lifeguards; showers; toilets. **Best for:** snorkeling;

swimming; walking. ✉ *2598 Kalakaua Ave., Waikiki* ✣ *Across from entrance to Honolulu Zoo.*

##  Restaurants

Waikiki has become a great destination for food lovers, with a new generation of innovative chefs and a renewed focus on using local ingredients, indigenous produce, and farm- and ocean-to-table cuisine. Although there are a number of familiar chain restaurants and traditional steak houses here, you can also find some solid choices for a variety of delectable meals at all price points—from upscale dining rooms with a view to budget-friendly poke bowls and Japanese noodle shops.

**Arancino di Mare**
**$$$ | ITALIAN** | Three locations in town offer fresh seafood, hand-trimmed beef, pastas cooked to order, handmade pizza and bread, homemade desserts, and meats and cheeses imported from Italy. Customer favorites include spaghetti *pescatore* (with shrimp, calamari, mussels, and clams) and a pizza topped with shrimp and Maui onions. **Known for:** fresh, authentic ingredients; local favorite; small and casual in Waikiki, elegant date-night setting in Kahala. $ *Average main: $33* ✉ *Waikiki Beach Marriott Resort, 2552 Kalakaua Ave., Waikiki* ☎ *808/931–6273* 🌐 *www.arancino.com* ⏲ *No lunch.*

**Azure Restaurant**
**$$$$ | MODERN HAWAIIAN** | This legendary indoor-outdoor restaurant has views of Diamond Head and an expansive terrace on the same level as the beach, so you'll feel the calm, island vibes as soon as you arrive. Azure offers a sophisticated atmosphere and features the chef's multicourse tasting menu, which spotlights local seafood, meat, and produce. **Known for:** world-class cuisine and excellent service; beautifully presented dishes; priceless views and pricey (prix fixe) menu. $ *Average main: $130* ✉ *Royal Hawaiian Resort, 2259 Kalakaua Ave., Waikiki* ☎ *808/931–7440* 🌐 *www.azurewaikiki.com* ⏲ *Closed Mon. and Tues. No lunch.*

**Bali Oceanfront**
**$$$$ | STEAK HOUSE** | Spacious and sprawling, this many-windowed, multilevel room at Hilton Hawaiian Village takes delightful advantage of its perch above the beach, facing Diamond Head. The wine list is exceptional, and the extensive contemporary menu features seafood, steaks, salads, and chops accented with East–West fusion flavors; desserts are impressive too. **Known for:** partnerships with local producers for farm-to-table offerings; attentive staff; reservations are essential. $ *Average main: $50* ✉ *Hilton Hawaiian Village, 2005 Kalia Rd., Waikiki* ☎ *808/941–2254* 🌐 *www.hiltonhawaiianvillage.com/bali* ⏲ *Closed Sun. and Mon. No lunch.*

**Beachhouse at the Moana**
**$$$$ | MODERN HAWAIIAN** | At this elegant, indoor-outdoor restaurant in Waikiki's oldest hotel, try for a table on the veranda, which overlooks the courtyard and a majestic banyan tree. Although the adjacent Veranda restaurant serves breakfast—and an exquisite afternoon tea Friday through Sunday—the Beachhouse is an especially delightful spot for a sunset dinner, featuring three- or four-course tasting menu options that use fresh, local ingredients. **Known for:** oceanfront dining; good cocktails and a long wine list; romantic setting. $ *Average main: $50* ✉ *Moana Surfrider Hotel, 2365 Kalakaua Ave., Waikiki* ☎ *808/921–4600* 🌐 *www.beachhousewaikiki.com* ⏲ *Closed Mon. and Tues.*

★ **Bogart's Café**
**$$ | AMERICAN** | Well established as a local favorite, this unassuming café is situated in a strip mall near Diamond Head and away from the bustle of Waikiki. It's a great spot to grab a quick, delicious breakfast or brunch, including best-sellers such as the *loco moco*, açai bowl, bagel sandwiches, French toast, omelets,

and other morning staples. **Known for:** a neighborhood staple and local favorite; Mama's fried rice; some outdoor seating. *Average main: $24 3045 Monsarrat Ave., Waikiki 808/739–0999 www.bogartscafe.com No dinner.*

**★ Chart House Waikiki**

$$$$ | **AMERICAN** | Enjoy sunset views over the yacht harbor, live music, and signature "Guy-Tai" cocktails at this Waikiki landmark opened in 1969 by surfing legend Joey Cabell. The extensive menu maintains the mid-century notion of fine dining, with oysters Rockefeller, shrimp cocktail, and steaks (including a bison tenderloin from Ted Turner's ranch) alongside poke, macadamia-nut-crusted mahimahi, and the fan-favorite "Joey's ahi mignon." Early birds can take advantage of the "surf break" menu, and there's a very popular weekend brunch (book in advance). **Known for:** sought-after tables on the lanai (book well in advance); old-time steak-house atmosphere with live music and strong cocktails; generations of regulars, and popular weekend brunch. *Average main: $52 1765 Ala Moana Blvd., Waikiki 808/941–6669 charthousewaikiki.com No lunch.*

**d.k Steakhouse**

$$$$ | **STEAK HOUSE** | D. K. Kodama serves steaks that are free from hormones, antibiotics, and steroids—and come straight from Oahu's first dry-aging room. Consider trying the 22-ounce *paniolo* (cowboy) rib eye—dry-aged 30 days on the bone and seasoned with a house-made rub—accompanied by a side of the popular and addictive potatoes au gratin, topped with Maui onions and Parmesan. **Known for:** local flavors, local ownership, and locally sourced produce and select meats; gluten-free and vegan options; sunset views from outdoor tables. *Average main: $55 Waikiki Beach Marriott Resort & Spa, 2552 Kalakaua Ave., Waikiki 808/931–6280 dkrestaurants.com/d-k-steak-house No lunch.*

**Doraku Sushi**

$$ | **JAPANESE** | From entrepreneur Kevin Aoki, son of Benihana founder Rocky Aoki, comes this low-lit, bells-and-whistles, sushi-roll chain (with two additional locations in Hawaii and another in Miami) featuring indoor-outdoor seating, as well as happy hours and a late-night bar scene that keeps the place packed. Newer dishes, such as the sake bomb or stuffed jalepeño rolls, are offered alongside favorites like the tuna *tataki* or the Emperor Roll, a seafood extravaganza of tuna, crab, shrimp, and scallop crusted in panko bread crumbs and flash-fried. **Known for:** a buzzing bar scene, with happy hour from 4 to 5 pm; tempura everything, including brownies; creative rolls. *Average main: $28 Royal Hawaiian Center, 2233 Kalakaua Ave., Waikiki 808/922–3323 www.dorakusushi.com.*

**Duke's Waikiki**

$$ | **AMERICAN** | **FAMILY** | Locals often bring Mainland visitors to this open-air restaurant, which has a lively bar and a beachfront setting facing Waikiki's famed Canoes surf break. Named for the father of modern surfing and filled with Duke Kahanamoku memorabilia, this casual spot offers lots of pupu (appetizers), a large salad bar, and crowd-pleasing entrées that include fish, prime rib, and *huli huli* (rotisserie). **Known for:** iconic local spot with great views and a perfect location; Duke's on Sunday is so renowned that musician Henry Kapono wrote a song about it; bar seating usually offers faster service. *Average main: $28 Outrigger Waikiki Beach Resort, 2335 Kalakaua Ave., Waikiki 808/922–2268 www.dukeswaikiki.com.*

**★ El Cielo**

$$$$ | **SPANISH** | In the heart of Waikiki, El Cielo was opened in 2023 by chef Masa "Arnaldo" Gushiken, who creates incredible Spanish tapas and other international specialties based on his global expertise in places such as Japan, Los

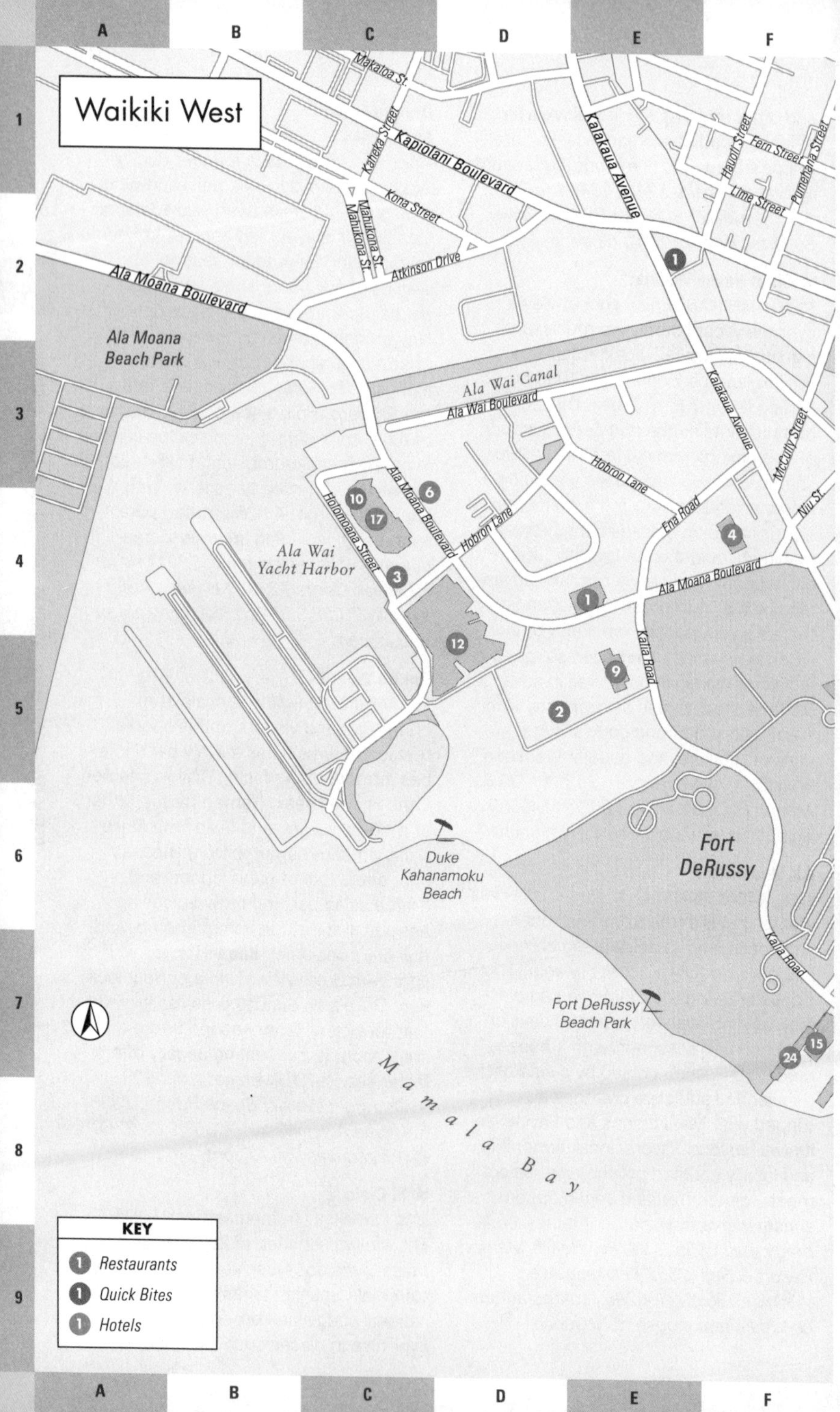
Waikiki West
A
B
C
D
E
F
1
2
3
4
5
6
7
8
9
Makaloa St.
Kaheka Street
Kapiolani Boulevard
Kalakaua Avenue
Hauoli Street
Fern Street
Pumehana Street
Lime Street
Kona Street
Mahukona St.
Atkinson Drive
Ala Moana Boulevard
Ala Moana Beach Park
Ala Wai Canal
Ala Wai Boulevard
Kalakaua Avenue
McCully Street
Hobron Lane
Ena Road
Niu St.
Holomoana Street
Hobron Lane
Ala Wai Yacht Harbor
Kalia Road
Fort DeRussy
Duke Kahanamoku Beach
Kalia Road
Fort DeRussy Beach Park
Mamala Bay
KEY
Restaurants
Quick Bites
Hotels

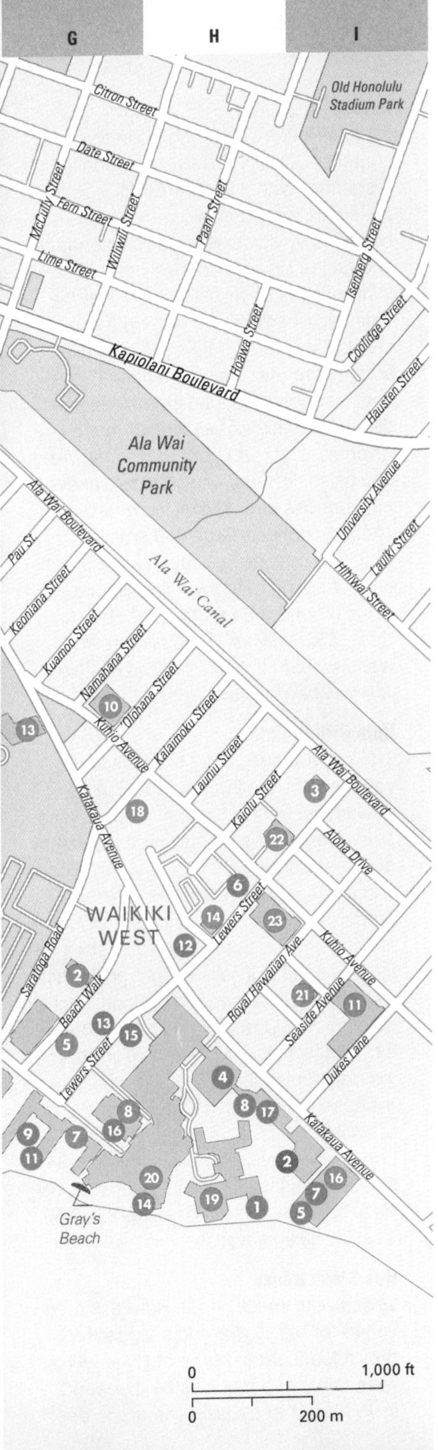


### Restaurants

1 Azure Restaurant....... H8
2 Bali Oceanfront......... D5
3 Chart House Waikiki..... C4
4 Doraku Sushi............ H7
5 Duke's Waikiki............ I8
6 El Cielo.................. H6
7 Hula Grill Waikiki.......... I8
8 Island Vintage Wine Bar................ H7
9 La Mer.................. G7
10 100 Sails Restaurant & Bar........ C4
11 Orchids.................. G8
12 The Pupu House........ H6
13 Roy's Waikiki............ G7
14 RumFire Waikiki......... G8
15 Taormina Sicilian Cuisine.......... G7
16 UMI by Vikram Garg.... G7
17 Wolfgang's Steakhouse by Wolfgang Zwiener...... H7

### Quick Bites

1 Honolulu Coffee Experience............... E2
2 Waikiki Food Hall....... H8

### Hotels

1 Aqua Palms Waikiki..... E4
2 The Breakers Hotel..... G6
3 Coconut Waikiki Hotel.............. I5
4 DoubleTree by Hilton Alana – Waikiki Beach............ F4
5 Embassy Suites by Hilton Waikiki Beach Walk.... G7
6 The Equus................ C3
7 Halekulani Hotel........ G7
8 Halepuna Waikiki by Halekulani............... G7
9 Hilton Hawaiian Village Waikiki Beach Resort... E5
10 Holiday Inn Express Waikiki, an IHG Hotel... G5
11 Hyatt Centric Waikiki Beach............. I7
12 Ilikai Hotel & Luxury Suites............ D5
13 Luana Waikiki Hotel & Suites.................. G5
14 Oasis Hotel Waikiki..... H6
15 Outrigger Reef Waikiki Beach Resort... F7
16 Outrigger Waikiki Beach Resort............. I8
17 Prince Waikiki............ C4
18 The Ritz-Carlton Residences, Waikiki Beach........... G5
19 The Royal Hawaiian, a Luxury Collection Resort, Waikiki.......... H8
20 Sheraton Waikiki Beach Resort........... H8
21 Shoreline Hotel Waikiki.............. I7
22 Surfjack Hotel & Swim Club............... H6
23 Waikiki Malia............ H6
24 Waikiki Shore............ F7

Angeles, and Spain. The interior's serene, minimalist design establishes a sophisticated but relaxed ambience in several dining rooms. **Known for:** authentic tapas by award-winning chef; creative paellas and main dishes; an away-from-the-beach gem serving a unique cuisine for Waikiki. *Average main: $44 346 Lewers St., Waikiki 808/772–4533 www.elcielo-hawaii.com No lunch.*

**Hau Tree**

$$ | **AMERICAN** | Countless anniversaries, birthdays, and other milestones have been celebrated under this lanai restaurant's spectacular *hau* tree, where it's said that even Robert Louis Stevenson found shade as he mused and wrote about Hawaii. Diners are captivated by beach views and spectacular sunsets, and fan-favorites dishes at this lovely, restaurant inside the Kaimana Beach Hotel include several versions of eggs Benedict in the morning and Kauai shrimp or grilled lamb chops later in the day. **Known for:** the romantic beach dining spot folks dream about (and reserve ahead); gorgeous views of moonlit water by night; an updated menu and attentive service. *Average main: $29 Kaimana Beach Hotel, 2863 Kalakaua Ave., Waikiki 808/921–7066 www.kaimana.com.*

**Herringbone Waikiki**

$$$ | **SEAFOOD** | Upstairs at International Marketplace and featuring a 2,000-square-foot lanai dining area, casual-chic Herringbone is a lively place for craft cocktails and dinner. Emphasizing locally sourced seafood, produce, and other ingredients, the menu includes many raw bar options, as well as lobster rolls, king salmon, whole fish, salads, and flatbreads. **Known for:** large outdoor dining space; beef and chicken options for those who don't love seafood; good weekend brunch. *Average main: $40 International Marketplace, 2330 Kalakaua Ave., Waikiki 808/797–2435 aokigroup.com/herringbonewaikiki No lunch weekdays.*

**Heyday**

$$$ | **AMERICAN** | Although it's in the center of Waikiki, this lively outdoor restaurant with a retro, tropical vibe feels a bit tucked away, with a bamboo-lined walkway leading to its entrance and tables set around the pool at the White Sands Hotel. Grab a drink at the whimsical bamboo bar, where a cool crowd sits and sips tiki-style cocktails, and peruse the "new continental" menu with a variety of pupu (appetizers) and decadent desserts, as well as such favorites as the B.O.L.T. (bacon, smoked ono salad, lettuce, and tomato) sandwich on a brioche bun. **Known for:** great food and armosphere; large and small plates, including options like vegan lumpia (a type of spring roll); swinging wooden seats around the bamboo bar. *Average main: $35 White Sands Hotel, 431 Nohonani St., Waikiki 808/475–6864 www.heydayhawaii.com.*

**Hula Grill Waikiki**

$$$$ | **HAWAIIAN** | **FAMILY** | The placid younger sibling of boisterous Duke's, downstairs, resembles an open-air, plantation-period summer home with kitschy decor, stone-flagged floors, warm wood, and floral prints. The food is carefully prepared and familiar—with the occasional intriguing Asian touch—and dishes include steaks, locally caught grilled fish, and a few island-inspired options, such as *loco moco* and tropical pancakes. **Known for:** spectacular beach views from the window tables (ask for one); reliable local dining experience with the right amount of Waikiki kitsch; nice bar scene for drinks and snacks. *Average main: $45 Outrigger Waikiki Beach Resort, 2335 Kalakaua Ave., Waikiki 808/923–4852 www.hulagrillwaikiki.com.*

**Hy's Steak House**

$$$$ | **STEAK HOUSE** | If the Rat Pack reconvened for big steaks and a bigger red, they'd feel right at home at Hy's, which hasn't changed much since it opened in 1976. The formula: prime-grade beef

cooked over an open kiawe-wood (mesquite) fire, "old-school" service, a clubby atmosphere, and a wine list recognized for excellence by *Wine Spectator*. In addition to the signature steaks, specialties include beef Wellington, miso-marinated sea bass, and ahi sashimi fresh from the auction. **Known for:** dark woods, club chairs, banquettes, and that fabulous 1970s feel; reservations are essential; desserts flambéed tableside. *Average main: $60 Waikiki Park Heights Hotel, 2440 Kuhio Ave., Waikiki 808/922–5555 hyswaikiki.com No lunch.*

### ★ Island Vintage Wine Bar

$$ | **WINE BAR** | Tucked away on the second floor of the Royal Hawaiian Center, this stylish, sleek, and cozy spot has a selection of more than 40 international wines by the glass—all served via a high-tech vending machine that uses prepaid cards. The food menu is limited, but a few favorites are braised beef sandwiches, poke bites with nori chips, and charcuterie plates. **Known for:** vending-machine wines by the glass is a bit gimmicky but fun; a subdued happy hour; nice cheese items from burrata to Brie. *Average main: $26 Royal Hawaiian Center, 2301 Kalakaua Ave., Bldg. C, Level 2, Waikiki 808/799–9463 www.islandvintagewinebar.com.*

### ★ La Mer

$$$$ | **FRENCH** | With spectacular Diamond Head views and an elegant, art deco–tinged interior, La Mer is an epic dining experience, where the second-floor restaurant's windows are open to the breezes and the sounds of the ocean and Halekulani Hotel's nightly hula show. Ideal for special occasions, the three-, four-, or seven-course French-influenced dinners might feature steamed Big Island *kampachi* (amberjack) tartare with fennel soup, Chilean sea bass with a vegetable "sphere," roasted duck breast with kumquat confit, or rib eye with vegetables. **Known for:** it doesn't get more romantic than this, and reservations are essential; impressive wine list and a sommelier to match; classy bar with cocktail and small-bite pairings. *Average main: $160 Halekulani Hotel, 2199 Kalia Rd., Waikiki 808/923–2311 www.halekulani.com/dining/la-mer Closed Sun. and Mon. No lunch Long-sleeved, collared (or aloha) shirts required for men.*

### Michel's at the Colony Surf

$$$$ | **FRENCH** | This romantic restaurant on Waikiki's tranquil Gold Coast features beachside sunset views and traditional French fare. It opened in 1962, and the surroundings reflect this, with lots of wood and stone, bow-tied servers preparing the restaurant's "famous" lobster bisque and steak tartare table-side, and a charm that's beloved by old-time locals but sometimes lost on younger diners. **Known for:** the sound of the surf and live music most nights; classic French cuisine with some local twists; reserve ahead for the pricey experience and retro vibe. *Average main: $75 Colony Surf, 2895 Kalakaua Ave., Waikiki 808/923–6552 www.michelshawaii.com No lunch.*

### Morimoto Asia Waikiki

$$$$ | **JAPANESE FUSION** | Iron Chef Masaharu Morimoto serves classics and new fusion favorites at his second-floor restaurant—a sleek modern, most neutral-hued space with a lanai (and water views), a gorgeous bar, and a dining room designed for entertaining clients or celebrating with friends. Enjoy some Morimoto specialties, including *ishiyaki buri bop* (yellowtail seared tableside with pickled daikon, royal fern, and egg yolk) or spicy black pepper steak, as well as dim sum, sushi, and creative specialty rolls. **Known for:** attentive service and great food; casual elegance in a lovely spot; Asian-fusion menu with enough classics to draw loyalists. *Average main: $41 Alohilani Resort, 2490 Kalakaua Ave., Waikiki 808/922–0022 morimotoasiawaikiki.com.*

**Mugen**

$$$$ | **ASIAN FUSION** | Food lovers in the know—including the Obamas, who have eaten here—recognize that this exclusive French-Japanese restaurant offers a truly memorable Waikiki dining experience in the luxurious Espacio hotel. The perfectly plated dishes on the multicourse tasting menu change seasonally, and guests here experience sublime service as well. **Known for:** superb cocktails and wine list; intimate space; reservations are required for dinner. *Average main: $195* *Espacio – The Jewel of Waikiki, 2452 Kalakaua Ave., Waikiki* *808/377–2247* *www.mugenwaikiki.com.*

**100 Sails Restaurant & Bar**

$$$$ | **ECLECTIC** | **FAMILY** | The spacious, airy 100 Sails continues the everything-you-can-imagine buffet tradition (with crab legs and prime rib, of course), along with plenty of à la carte small bites, an emphasis on locally sourced ingredients, and a commitment to knockout presentation. And then there are the views—night after night, the sunsets over the harbor deliver stunning shows of color. **Known for:** high-quality international buffet for every meal; views and sunsets to rival those anywhere else in Waikiki; good happy hour platter. *Average main: $60* *Hawaii Prince Hotel Waikiki, 100 Holomoana St., Waikiki* *808/944–4494* *www.100sails.com.*

**★ Orchids**

$$$$ | **SEAFOOD** | Perched along the seawall at historic Gray's Beach, in the luxe Halekulani resort, Orchids is a locus of power breakfasters, ladies who lunch, and those celebrating special occasions at Sunday brunch or dinner. The louvered walls are open to the breezes, sprays of orchids add color, the contemporary international dishes are perfectly prepared, and the wine list is intriguing. **Known for:** ocean sounds and views, plus stellar service and a varied menu; live music at sunset; reservations are essential. *Average main: $42* *Halekulani Hotel, 2199 Kalia Rd., Waikiki* *808/923–2311* *www.halekulani.com* *Collared shirts required for men.*

## Pupu

Entertaining Hawaii-style means having a lot of *pupu*—the local term for appetizers or hors d'oeuvres—which are often served during *pau hana*, the Islands-style happy hour when locals wind down from the workday and enjoy a couple of drinks. Popular pupu include sushi, tempura, teriyaki chicken or beef skewers, barbecued meat, and the favorite: *poke* (pronounced "po-keh"), or raw fish, seasoned with seaweed, shoyu, and other flavorings.

**The Pupu House**

$$$$ | **ECLECTIC** | **FAMILY** | With a fun, tiki-bar vibe and great food, this cheerful new (opened 2023) place is located in the center of Waikiki and just a short walk from the beach. Featuring a large menu with something for everyone, including an assortment of delectable pupu (appetizers) and main dishes, it's ideal for a casual, laid-back dinner. **Known for:** lively spot with an island vibe and late-night cocktails upstairs; locally owned family business; popular, so there's often a wait at prime time. *Average main: $42* *301 Lewers St., Waikiki* *www.thepupuhouse.com* *No lunch.*

**Queensbreak**

$$$ | **AMERICAN** | **FAMILY** | Across from popular Kuhio Beach, and three floors up from busy Waikiki on the pool deck at the Waikiki Beach Marriott Resort & Spa, this laid-back, multilevel, terrace restaurant is a great place to grab a casual bite (fish tacos, poke, Caesar salad, burgers) and a beer, a glass of wine, or a tropical cocktail. In addition to ocean views, you can enjoy happy hour specials and live music.

**Known for:** live music in the evening; familiar favorites on the menu; outdoor dining. *Average main: $40 Waikiki Beach Marriott Resort & Spa, 2552 Kalakaua Ave., Waikiki 808/922–6611 www.queensbreak.com.*

**Roy's Waikiki**

$$$$ | **MODERN HAWAIIAN** | **FAMILY** | Enjoy a taste of modern Hawaiian cuisine from the chef who started it all, Roy Yamaguchi. Situated in the center of Waikiki, the sprawling, stylish restaurant has been serving innovative pan-Asian dishes since 2007 and remains a fan favorite. **Known for:** signature spicy ahi hand rolls; nightly happy hour on the lanai; indoor and outdoor seating. *Average main: $42 226 Lewers St., Waikiki 808/923–7697 www.royyamaguchi.com No lunch.*

**RumFire Waikiki**

$$$ | **ASIAN FUSION** | If the perfect sunset happy hour means cocktails, bite-size shareable plates, tropical breezes, ocean sounds, and flaming oversize torches, then make it a point to dine at RumFire, situated beachfront in the Sheraton Waikiki. Enjoy such dishes as lemon-herb mahimahi, island fish tacos, and "local style" sesame-ahi poke; sip signature concoctions like the RumFire Mai Tai or the Fire Runner, made with spiced rum and tropical juices. **Known for:** beachside nightlife scene with great food and cocktails; fabulous location right on the beach; hip vibe that attracts young professionals. *Average main: $34 Sheraton Waikiki, 2255 Kalakaua Ave., Waikiki 808/922–4422 www.rumfirewaikiki.com.*

**Side Street Inn Kapahulu**

$$ | **ECLECTIC** | **FAMILY** | The original Hopaka Street pub is famous as the place where celebrity chefs gather after hours; this second Kapahulu Avenue location is also popular and closer to Waikiki. Local-style bar food—salty pan-fried pork chops with a plastic tub of ketchup, *lup cheong* fried rice, and passion fruit–glazed ribs—is served in huge, shareable portions. **Known for:** gets busy, so best to make a reservation; popular local spot with a crowd of regulars; sports-bar feel with lots of fried food. *Average main: $27 614 Kapahulu Ave., Waikiki 808/739–3939 www.sidestreetinn.com No lunch weekdays.*

**Taormina Sicilian Cuisine**

$$$ | **ITALIAN** | Honolulu has its share of Italian restaurants, and Taormina, taking its culinary cues from Sicily, is considered one of the best by foodies, locals, and visitors alike. In a sleek, elegant room (there is outdoor seating, but this is one place it's best to dine indoors), you can dine on well-executed classics, such as porcini risotto with sautéed foie gras and a breaded veal chop "*alla Taormina*" (the restaurant's take on veal Parmesan). **Known for:** reserve ahead for this intimate, quiet respite in bustling Waikiki; authentic Sicilian cuisine, including signature sea urchin with tagliatelle; extensive wine list. *Average main: $36 Waikiki Beach Walk, 227 Lewers St., Waikiki 808/926–5050 www.taorminarestaurant.com.*

**Teddy's Bigger Burgers**

$ | **BURGER** | **FAMILY** | Modeled after 1950s diners, this casual spot serves classic, tender, messy burgers—including the Hawaiian teriyaki burger with grilled pineapple and the Kailua with Swiss cheese, mushrooms, and grilled onions—along with turkey and veggie burgers, salads, and chicken breast and fish sandwiches. The fries are crispy, and the shakes rich and sweet. **Known for:** tangy Super Sauce; diner-style service, with food to go; local chain for dependable quick lunches across Oahu. *Average main: $16 Waikiki Grand Hotel, 134 Kapahulu Ave., Waikiki 808/926–3444 www.teddysbb.com.*

★ **Tiki's Grill and Bar**

$$$ | **MODERN HAWAIIAN** | Tiki's is the kind of fun place people come to Waikiki for: a retro–South Pacific spot with a back-of-the-bar faux volcano, open-air lounge with live local music, indoor-outdoor

Waikiki and Honolulu, looking toward Diamond Head

dining, and a fantastic view of the beach across the street. Chef Ronnie Nasuti turns out beautifully composed plates and puts fresh twists on the super-familiar—like spicy "volcano" chicken wings, watermelon and feta salad, or Thai-style shrimp puttanesca. **Known for:** surprisingly good food in a made-for-TV setting that attracts locals; Pacific Rim menu inspired by a noted Islands chef; can get pricey, but a fun experience worthy of a hana hou (encore). *Average main: $35 ✉ Twin Fin Hotel, 2570 Kalakaua Ave., Waikiki ☎ 808/923–8454 🌐 www.tikisgrill.com.*

### ★ UMI by Vikram Garg

**$$$$ | SEAFOOD** | Stylish, spacious, and accented with subtle modern art, this seafood-focused restaurant—*umi* means "sea"—by acclaimed chef Vikram Garg offers a feast for the senses in the stunning Halepuna Waikiki, the boutique sister property of the Halekulani Hotel. Garg works culinary magic in the kitchen with dinner specialties such as popcorn soup (with lotus leaves) and steamed branzino with takana rice (fried rice with pickled mustard greens), and food lovers can also discover unique breakfast choices such as the mai tai pancake and masala omelet. **Known for:** beautifully plated specialties served in a serene setting; boundary-stretching global menus; thoughtful drink options. *Average main: $45 ✉ Halepuna Waikiki by Halekulani, 2233 Helumoa Rd., Waikiki ☎ 808/744–4244 🌐 www.umibyvikramgarg.com ⏲ No dinner Mon. and Tues.*

### Wolfgang's Steakhouse by Wolfgang Zwiener

**$$$$ | STEAK HOUSE** | The Honolulu outpost of the New York–based original serves good steaks that have been dry-aged on-site, as well as classic shrimp cocktails, slabs of Canadian bacon, crab cakes, creamed spinach, broiled jumbo lobster, and the token grilled fish selection. If it sounds like Peter Luger's on the Pacific, then it won't come as a surprise to learn that owner Wolfgang Zwiener was once head waiter at that legendary Brooklyn steak house. **Known for:** classic steak-house vibe, food, and attentive

## Malasadas

*Malasadas* are a contribution of the Portuguese, who came to the Hawaiian Islands to work on the plantations. Roughly translated, the name means "half-cooked," as these deep-fried, heavily sugared treats are said to have been created as a way to use up scraps of rich, buttery egg dough. They are similar to fluffy doughnuts and are offered in many flavors; some are filled with fruit or cream.

You'll find malasadas at farmers' markets, fairs, and carnivals. A few Honolulu bakeries specialize in them, including **Leonard's Bakery** (✉ *933 Kapahulu Ave.*) and **Kamehameha Bakery** (✉ *1284 Kalani St., Unit D-106*). Some Honolulu restaurants serve upscale versions, stuffed with fruit puree. Regardless, eat them fresh and hot or not at all.



service; great location in the heart of Waikiki; surprisingly varied brunch menu (with a killer Bloody Mary). *Ⓢ Average main: $65* ✉ *Royal Hawaiian Center, 2201 Kalakaua Ave., Waikiki* ☎ *808/922–3600* 🌐 *wolfgangssteakhouse.jp/waikiki/en.*

## Coffee and Quick Bites

### ★ Banán

$ | **HAWAIIAN** | **FAMILY** | Follow a narrow beach pathway (between The Cheesecake Factory and Outrigger Waikiki Beach Resort) lined with surfboards to reach this takeout spot specializing in banán, a frozen, vegan-friendly dessert made with local bananas and containing no added sugar. Other snack options include smoothies, smoothie bowls, and *ulu* (breadfruit) waffles. **Known for:** plant-based frozen desserts; locally owned; refreshing snack on a hot day. *Ⓢ Average main: $10* ✉ *2301 Kalakaua Ave., Waikiki* ☎ *808/691–9303* 🌐 *banan.co.*

### Diamond Head Market & Grill

$ | **AMERICAN** | **FAMILY** | Just five minutes from Waikiki's hotels is chef Kelvin Ro's one-stop food shop—indispensable if you have accommodations with a kitchen or want a quick grab-and-go meal. Join surfers, beachgoers, and Diamond Head hikers at the takeout window to order gourmet sandwiches and plates, such as hand-shaped burgers, portobello mushroom sandwiches, Korean *kalbi* ribs, and grilled ahi with wasabi-ginger sauce, rice, and salad. Selections include sandwiches, bento boxes, and salads. **Known for:** excellent desserts and scones; picnic fare for the beach; well-priced grab-and-go dinners. *Ⓢ Average main: $15* ✉ *3158 Monsarrat Ave., Waikiki* ☎ *808/732–0077* 🌐 *www.diamondheadmarket.com.*

### Holey Grail Donuts

$ | **BAKERY** | **FAMILY** | Locals love the scrumptious taro-based confections and delightful coffee beverages created by this family-run outfit. Fried in coconut oil, the doughnuts are known for their light texture, splashy colors and designs, and sophisticated flavors, as well as fun names like Island Chocolate, Pineapple Express, Miso Honey, Kale'n It, and Prosperity (with kumquat and poppy seeds). **Known for:** taro-based doughnuts; locally sourced, fresh ingredients; weekly tasting boxes and seasonal special flavors. *Ⓢ Average main: $8* ✉ *325 Seaside Ave., Waikiki* ☎ *808/634–8838* 🌐 *www.holeygraildonuts.com.*

### Honolulu Coffee Experience

$ | **CAFÉ** | A massive, antique roaster is the centerpiece of this beautifully appointed, spacious, and airy coffeehouse, the largest and most unique branch of the Waikiki chain, situated near the convention center. There are plenty of options for tea drinkers, too, in addition to pastries, breakfast sandwiches, and açai bowls. **Known for:** high-quality coffee; variety of baked goods; lovely spot to relax. *$ Average main: $12 ✉ 1800 Kalakaua Ave., Waikiki ☎ 808/202–2562 🌐 www.honolulucoffee.com.*

**Kai Coffee Hawaii**

$ | **CAFÉ** | Serving up delicious coffee made with Hawaii-grown and -roasted beans, Kai Coffee Hawaii is an island favorite and has several locations. Featuring various coffee styles (including pour over and French press), this is a trusted spot for a fresh cup of gourmet brew or other beverages, such as hibiscus iced tea. **Known for:** açai bowls and crepes; variety of house-made snacks; welcoming vibe and friendly service. *$ Average main: $14 ✉ Alohilani Resort, 2490 Kalakaua Ave., Suite 131, Waikiki ☎ 808/926–1131 🌐 www.kaicoffeehawaii.com.*

**South Shore Grill**

$ | **AMERICAN** | Popular with locals, this casual counter-service spot is just minutes from Waikiki, on trendy Monsarrat Avenue near the base of Diamond Head. It has something for everyone: generous plate lunches (try the wahoo—a type of mackerel—coated with macadamia-nut pesto and served with a tangy slaw), fish tacos, burritos, burgers, ciabatta-roll sandwiches, and entrée salads. **Known for:** casual surfer vibe (no reservations); takeout for the beach; Peanut Butter Temptations for dessert. *$ Average main: $15 ✉ 3114 Monsarrat Ave., Diamond Head ☎ 808/734–0229 🌐 www.southshoregrill.com.*

**★ Waikiki Food Hall**

$ | **FOOD HALL** | **FAMILY** | At this bright, lively, upscale food court on the third floor of the Royal Hawaiian Center, you can feast on local and Japanese options ranging from massive, juicy burgers to spicy shrimp tacos to exquisite smoothies topped with colorful, edible designs—all emphasizing the use of fresh, local ingredients. Vendors here include Five Star Shrimp, Milk, JTRRD, Meatally Boys, POTAMA (Pork Tamago Onigiri), Honolulu Burger Co., Surfer's Cafe, and Tap Bar. **Known for:** modern and spacious, with ample seating; options you can mix and match; Hawaiian craft beer at Tap Bar. *$ Average main: $14 ✉ Royal Hawaiian Center, 2301 Kalakaua Ave., Bldg. C, 3rd fl., Waikiki ⊕ Above the Cheesecake Factory ☎ 808/922–2299 for Royal Hawaiian Center 🌐 www.waikikifoodhall.com.*

## Hotels

A stay in Waikiki puts you in the heart of the action, and though parking can be difficult and pricey, you really don't need a car as there's ready access to the beach, restaurants, activities, and affordable public transportation. To be slightly removed from the main scene, however, opt for accommodations on the *ewa* (western) end of Waikiki.

The hotel selection ranges from superluxe resorts to small, no-frills places where surfers and beachgoers hang out in the lobby. Room sizes, styles, and configurations can vary tremendously even in the same hotel, so ask questions to ensure that you get an ocean view, lanai, or have other requirements met. Also inquire about extras: for instance, some hotels—even if they aren't right on the sand—provide their guests with sunblock, towels, chairs, and other beach accessories.

**★ Alohilani Resort Waikiki Beach**

$$$ | **HOTEL** | **FAMILY** | The centerpiece of this modern, stylish high-rise, across the street from the beach in the middle of Waikiki, is the lobby's mesmerizing aquarium, filled with nearly 300,000 gallons of seawater and colorful marine life. **Pros:** new and modern, with several on-site restaurants; cutting-edge fitness facilities and spa; excellent guest lounge. **Cons:** resort fee is $50 per day; large hotel that can feel impersonal; you must

cross the street for the beach. $ *Rooms from: $339* ✉ *2490 Kalakaua Ave., Waikiki* ☎ *808/922–1233* 🌐 *www.alohilaniresort.com* 🛏 *839 rooms* 🍽 *No Meals.*

**Aqua Aloha Surf Waikiki**

$ | **HOTEL** | **FAMILY** | This affordable property two blocks from Waikiki Beach appeals to the young (and young at heart) with surfer-chic rooms and suites, a cool blue-and-green color scheme, and lounge chairs throughout. **Pros:** in-room refrigerators and microwaves; pool with sundeck and cabanas; on-site coin-operated laundry. **Cons:** hotel is dated overall; no daily housekeeping services; no view and 10-minute walk to beach. $ *Rooms from: $169* ✉ *444 Kanekapolei St., Waikiki* ☎ *866/970–4160, 808/954–7410* 🌐 *www.aquaaston.com/hotels/aqua-aloha-surf-waikiki* 🛏 *204 rooms* 🍽 *No Meals.*

**Aqua Palms Waikiki**

$ | **HOTEL** | **FAMILY** | The 12-story Aqua Palms was revitalized in 2020, giving many of its rooms and suites (some with kitchens) energy-efficient air-conditioning and new furnishings, carpeting, drapes, bedding, and lighting fixtures. **Pros:** recent refurbishments; short walk to park, beach, and convention center; free coffee and tea in the lobby. **Cons:** beach access is through the Hilton Hawaiian Village, across the street; resort fee is $30 per day; not all rooms have lanai. $ *Rooms from: $169* ✉ *1850 Ala Moana Blvd., Waikiki* ☎ *808/954–7424 reservations local number, 866/970–4165 reservations toll-free, 808/947–7256 direct to hotel's front desk* 🌐 *www.aquaaston.com/hotels/aqua-palms-waikiki* 🛏 *262 units* 🍽 *No Meals.*

**Aston at the Waikiki Banyan**

$$ | **RESORT** | **FAMILY** | Families and active travelers love the convenience and action of this high-rise hotel, often referred to as "the Banyan," just a block from Waikiki Beach, the aquarium, the zoo, and bustling Kalakaua Avenue. **Pros:** many suites have great views, and many have kitchens; massive recreation deck for the entire family; heated swimming pool. **Cons:** suites are individually owned, so conditions can vary greatly; resort fee is $25 per day; sharing hotel with residents. $ *Rooms from: $200* ✉ *201 Ohua Ave., Waikiki* ☎ *808/922–0555, 877/997–6667 toll-free for reservations* 🌐 *www.aquaaston.com/hotels/aston-at-the-waikiki-banyan* 🛏 *876 suites* 🍽 *No Meals.*

**Aston Waikiki Beach Tower**

$$$$ | **RESORT** | **FAMILY** | Here, in the center of Waikiki, you get the elegance of a luxury all-suites condominium combined with the intimacy and service of a boutique hotel. **Pros:** roomy suites with kitchens and quality amenities; great private lanai and views; a recreation deck with something for everyone. **Cons:** resort fee is $39 per day; you must cross a busy street to the beach; space, amenities, and location don't come cheap. $ *Rooms from: $699* ✉ *2470 Kalakaua Ave., Waikiki* ☎ *808/926-6400, 855/776–1766 toll-free* 🌐 *aquaaston.com/hotels/aston-waikiki-beach-tower* 🛏 *140 suites* 🍽 *No Meals.*

**Aston Waikiki Circle Hotel**

$$ | **HOTEL** | Built to resemble a Chinese lantern, this circular, 14-story hotel is a Waikiki landmark, with a charming interior design that brings the Pacific inside, beginning at check-in with breezes that flow through an open-air lobby. **Pros:** unbeatable location; lanai with a view in every room; on-site surfboard lockers and complimentary beach gear. **Cons:** small rooms, with showers only; busy location in Waikiki; resort fee is $25 per day. $ *Rooms from: $269* ✉ *2464 Kalakaua Ave., Waikiki* ☎ *808/923–1571, 877/997–6667 toll-free for reservations* 🌐 *aquaaston.com/hotels/aston-waikiki-circle-hotel* 🛏 *104 rooms* 🍽 *No Meals.*

**The Breakers Hotel**

$ | **HOTEL** | With a homey atmosphere and a vintage vibe, this small, low-rise complex—two blocks from the beach and close to the Waikiki Beach Walk entertainment, dining, and retail

## Hotel Cultural Programs

In 2022, the state launched its Malama Hawaii program (🌐 *gohawaii.com/malama*), which encourages visitors to learn about and care for the land and to seek authentic Island experiences. As part of this program, some hotels are offering special packages and voluntourism opportunities. Be sure to ask about them when booking.

Many of the larger hotels and resorts offer a variety of cultural activities for guests of all ages. In addition to lei-making and hula lessons, you can learn how to strum a ukulele, listen to Grammy Award–winning Hawaiian musicians, watch a revered master *kumu* (teacher) share the art of ancient hula and chant, chat with a marine biologist about Hawaii's endangered species, learn about the island's sustainability efforts, or get a lesson in the Hawaiian language or in the art of canoe making.

complex—transports its guests back to 1960s-era Hawaii. **Pros:** intimate atmosphere with fabulous poolside courtyard; great location; kitchenettes and lanai. **Cons:** a bit worn down and dated; parking is extremely limited (but free); showers only. *Rooms from: $199 250 Beach Walk, Waikiki 808/923–3181, 800/923–7174 toll-free www.breakers-hawaii.com 63 rooms No Meals.*

**Coconut Waikiki Hotel**
**$ | HOTEL | FAMILY** | Overlooking the Ala Wai Canal, this reasonably priced boutique hotel has a more residential feel than the typical resort, with a cobblestone driveway, a lobby with rattan furnishings, a small fitness center, and a tiny swimming pool tucked in a backyard. **Pros:** no resort fee if booked directly; good bet for larger groups; some rooms have two bathrooms. **Cons:** walking three blocks to and from the beach on a busy street can be tiresome; only valet parking available, and free continental breakfast is limited; area is residential and removed from the action, particularly at night. *Rooms from: $179 450 Lewers St., Waikiki 866/974–2626 toll-free, 808/923–8828 www.coconutwaikikihotel.com 81 rooms Free Breakfast.*

**DoubleTree by Hilton Alana – Waikiki Beach**
**$$ | HOTEL** | A convenient location—a 10-minute walk from the Hawaii Convention Center or the beach—a professional staff, pleasant public spaces, and a 24-hour business center and small gym draw a global clientele to this reliable chain hotel. **Pros:** walkable to the beach and Ala Moana mall; walk-in glass showers with oversize rain showerheads; heated outdoor pool and 24-hour fitness center. **Cons:** lanai have city views; little local flavor; resort fee is $30 per day. *Rooms from: $259 1956 Ala Moana Blvd., Waikiki 808/941–7275 www.hilton.com/en/hotels/hnlkadt-doubletree-alana-waikiki-beach 317 rooms No Meals.*

**Embassy Suites by Hilton Waikiki Beach Walk**
**$$$ | RESORT | FAMILY** | In a place where space is at a premium, this resort in the heart of the Waikiki Beach Walk dining and shopping area offers families and other groups spacious, one- and two-bedroom suites stylishly decorated in relaxing earth tones with splashes of color. **Pros:** no resort fee; spacious and modern rooms with kitchenettes; free hot breakfast and happy hour reception daily. **Cons:**

no direct beach access; lobby feels more like a business hotel; property can seem busy and noisy. *Rooms from: $329 ✉ 201 Beach Walk, Waikiki ☎ 800/362–2779 toll-free, 808/921–2345 direct to hotel ⊕ www.embassysuiteswaikiki.com ⇨ 369 suites 🍽 Free Breakfast.*

**The Equus**

$ | **HOTEL** | **FAMILY** | On the *ewa* (western) end of Waikiki, a block from both the Ala Moana Center and Ala Moana Beach Park, this modern, family-owned, boutique hotel has a Hawaiian country theme that pays tribute to Hawaii's polo-playing history. **Pros:** free beach towels, chairs, and umbrellas; attentive staff; nicely furnished rooms. **Cons:** busy, hectic area; must cross a major road to reach the beach; resort fee is $25 a day. *Rooms from: $169 ✉ 1696 Ala Moana Blvd., Waikiki ☎ 808/949–0061 ⊕ www.equushotel.com ⇨ 67 rooms 🍽 No Meals.*

**Espacio – The Jewel of Waikiki**

$$$$ | **HOTEL** | **FAMILY** | As its name suggests, this is one of the most luxurious hotel experiences in Hawaii, with nine designer suites, each occupying an entire floor and featuring smart-home technology, a large private lanai with a hot tub, two or three bedrooms, a gourmet kitchen, and spacious bathrooms with saunas. **Pros:** incredible ocean views; height of opulence and luxury; highest level of service. **Cons:** swimming pool is shared and on the small side; across the street from the beach; exceptionally expensive. *Rooms from: $3,000 ✉ 2452 Kalakaua Ave., Waikiki ☎ 855/945–4089 toll-free, 808/377–2246 direct to hotel ⊕ www.espaciowaikiki.com ⇨ 9 suites 🍽 Free Breakfast.*

**★ Halekulani Hotel**

$$$$ | **RESORT** | Its name translates to the "house befitting heaven," and this beachfront haven does, indeed, seem like a slice of heaven thanks to impeccable service and spacious guest rooms that are artfully appointed with marble and wood, neutral color schemes, modern furniture, updated technology, and bathrooms with oversize soaking tubs as well as showers. **Pros:** exquisite interior and exterior spaces; award-winning spa and wonderful bars and restaurants; no resort fee. **Cons:** might feel a bit formal for Waikiki; narrow beachfront with little room for sunbathing; lofty room rates. *Rooms from: $759 ✉ 2199 Kalia Rd., Waikiki ☎ 808/923–2311 direct to hotel, 800/367–2343 reservations toll-free ⊕ www.halekulani.com ⇨ 453 rooms 🍽 No Meals.*

**★ Halepuna Waikiki by Halekulani**

$$$ | **HOTEL** | The outstanding service and attention to detail at this high-rise boutique property are the same as what's offered at its elegant sister hotel, the Halekulani, but without the beachfront location and higher prices. **Pros:** fresh, modern, and well appointed; great access to Waikiki Beach and Beach Walk shopping and dining; no resort fee. **Cons:** no direct beach access; rooms can be small; swimming pool can get busy. *Rooms from: $376 ✉ 2233 Helumoa Rd., Waikiki ☎ 808/921–7272 direct to hotel, 800/422–0450 reservations toll-free ⊕ www.halepuna.com ⇨ 297 rooms 🍽 No Meals.*

**Hilton Garden Inn Waikiki Beach**

$$ | **HOTEL** | **FAMILY** | Most of the rooms at this expansive midrange chain hotel in the heart of Waikiki have a lanai with seating and feature a partial ocean or a Waikiki city view. **Pros:** near International Marketplace's shops and restaurants; rooftop pool; no resort fee. **Cons:** the large resort can feel impersonal; valet-only parking; two-block walk to the beach. *Rooms from: $229 ✉ 2330 Kuhio Ave., Waikiki ☎ 808/892–1820 ⊕ www.hilton.com/en/hotels/hnlkugi-hilton-garden-inn-waikiki-beach ⇨ 623 rooms 🍽 No Meals.*

**Hilton Hawaiian Village Waikiki Beach Resort**

$$$ | **RESORT** | **FAMILY** | Location, location, location: this five-tower mega-resort sprawls over 22 acres on Waikiki's widest

stretch of beach, with the greenery of neighboring Fort DeRussy creating a buffer zone between it and central Waikiki's high-rise lineup. **Pros:** activities and amenities keep you and the kids busy for weeks (including Friday night fireworks); stellar spa and fitness center; a large variety of room options. **Cons:** size of property can be overwhelming; resort fee is $50 per day; parking is expensive ($49 per day for self-parking). *Rooms from: $325 2005 Kalia Rd., Waikiki 808/949–4321, 800/774–1500 toll-free hilton.com/en/hotels/hnlhvhh-hilton-hawaiian-village-waikiki-beach-resort 4499 rooms No Meals.*

**Hilton Waikiki Beach**

$$ | **HOTEL** | On the Diamond Head end of Waikiki and two blocks from Kuhio Beach, this 37-story high-rise is great for travelers who want to be near the action but not right in it. **Pros:** central location; every room has a lanai; pleasant, comfortable public spaces. **Cons:** resort fee is $30 per day; $45 a day (valet only parking); older property that shows some wear. *Rooms from: $259 2500 Kuhio Ave., Waikiki 808/922–0811 direct to hotel, 888/370–0980 toll-free hilton.com/en/hotels/hnlwahf-hilton-waikiki-beach 609 rooms No Meals.*

**★ Holiday Inn Express Waikiki, an IHG Hotel**

$ | **HOTEL** | **FAMILY** | Thanks to wallet-friendly rates and unexpected perks, this 44-story chain hotel—with compact but stylish and smartly equipped and configured rooms—bustles, so its speedy elevators are often full. **Pros:** free breakfast has large selection; modern conveniences abound; select rooms have great views. **Cons:** resort fee is $25 per day; busy hotel and lobby can feel crowded; three-block walk to the beach. *Rooms from: $199 2058 Kuhio Ave., Waikiki 877/859–5095 toll-free for reservations, 808/947–2828 direct to hotel www.ihg.com 596 rooms Free Breakfast.*

**Hotel Renew**

$ | **HOTEL** | Just a block from Waikiki Beach, this unassuming but stylish boutique hotel focuses on wellness and renewal, making it a calm alternative to the big, bustling resorts that dominate the area. **Pros:** free beach supplies, including towels, chairs, umbrellas, and snorkel gear; personalized, upscale service; close to zoo, aquarium, and beach. **Cons:** no pool or on-site restaurant; daily amenity fee of $35; rooms are small. *Rooms from: $185 129 Paoakalani Ave., Waikiki 808/687–7700, 877/997–6667 toll-free www.hotelrenew.com 72 rooms No Meals.*

**Hyatt Centric Waikiki Beach**

$$ | **HOTEL** | Modern and stylish, with an urban beach vibe, the Hyatt Centric has a friendly staff, rooms in several sizes and configurations, and a sprawling, seventh-floor lobby with a breakfast café and lovely outdoor pool area. **Pros:** fresh, modern, and right in the middle of Waikiki; spacious rooms and bathrooms; lovely pool deck. **Cons:** resort fee is $33 per day; rooms don't have lanai; not on the beach. *Rooms from: $225 349 Seaside Ave., Waikiki 808/237–1234 www.hyatt.com 230 rooms No Meals.*

**Hyatt Regency Waikiki Beach Resort & Spa**

$$$ | **RESORT** | **FAMILY** | There's no other resort between the ocean and this high-rise hotel, which is across the street from Kuhio Beach and features a lively, atrium-style lobby with three levels of shopping (including a farmers' market on Tuesday and Thursday afternoons), a two-story waterfall, gardens, and free live evening entertainment. **Pros:** on-site spa and many shopping and dining options; spacious rooms with soaring windows and lanai; beach chairs and towels for guests. **Cons:** in a very busy and crowded part of Waikiki; small on-site pool; resort fee is $45 per day. *Rooms from: $325 2424 Kalakaua Ave., Waikiki 808/923–1234 direct to hotel, 800/633–7313 toll-free for reservations*

🌐 www.hyatt.com 🛏 1230 rooms 🍴 No Meals.

**Ilikai Hotel & Luxury Suites**

**$$$ | HOTEL | FAMILY** | At Waikiki's *ewa* (western) edge, overlooking Ala Wai Harbor and a five-minute walk from Ala Moana Beach Park, this high-rise resort is a Honolulu landmark—Jack Lord's character, Steve McGarrett, appears on a lanai here in the opening of the original *Hawaii Five-0* TV series. **Pros:** sunset views from most ewa-side rooms; removed from some of the bustle yet still close to everything; spacious rooms with kitchens. **Cons:** resort fee is $25 per day; five-minute walk to the beach; despite renovations, it still shows its age. *$ Rooms from: $325 ✉ 1777 Ala Moana Blvd., Waikiki ☎ 808/954–7417, 866/536–7973 toll-free 🌐 www.ilikaihotel.com 🛏 779 rooms 🍴 No Meals.*

**Ilima Hotel**

**$ | HOTEL | FAMILY** | Tucked away on a residential side street near Waikiki's Ala Wai Canal, this locally owned, 17-story, condo-style hotel is a throwback to old Waikiki, offering partially refreshed, large units that are ideal for families. **Pros:** free parking (first-come, first-served); spacious rooms with separate bedrooms and kitchens; friendly and helpful service. **Cons:** dated bathrooms (renovations planned for 2025); resort fee is $38 per day; no ocean views. *$ Rooms from: $175 ✉ 445 Nohonani St., Waikiki ☎ 808/923–1877, 800/801–9366 🌐 www.ilima.com 🛏 98 units 🍴 No Meals.*

**Luana Waikiki Hotel & Suites**

**$$ | HOTEL | FAMILY** | If you like Hawaiiana and appreciate a bit of kitsch in your decor, this welcoming hotel with both rooms and condo units is a great option. **Pros:** some rooms have kitchenettes or full kitchens; sundeck with pool and barbecue grills; on-site coin-operated laundry facilities. **Cons:** no direct beach access; resort fee is $25 per day; pool is small. *$ Rooms from: $235 ✉ 2045 Kalakaua Ave., Waikiki ☎ 808/955–6000 direct to hotel, 855/747–0755 toll-free 🌐 www.aquaaston.com/hotels/luana-waikiki-hotel-and-suites 🛏 225 units 🍴 No Meals.*

**★ Moana Surfrider, a Westin Resort & Spa, Waikiki Beach**

**$$$$ | RESORT** | Waikiki's oldest hotel (1901) is still a wedding and honeymoon favorite, with a sweeping main staircase and Victorian furnishings in its historic and expensive Moana Wing and more contemporary rooms in its 1950s-era Diamond Head Tower and refurbished Surfrider Tower, where oceanfront suites have two separate lanai—one for sunrise and another for sunset. **Pros:** elegant, historic property; lovely beach bar that often features live music; can't beat the location. **Cons:** you'll likely dodge bridal parties in the lobby; resort fee is $42 per day; expensive parking ($35 per day for self-parking across the street). *$ Rooms from: $499 ✉ 2365 Kalakaua Ave., Waikiki ☎ 808/922–3111, 866/716–8112 toll-free 🌐 marriott.com 🛏 791 rooms 🍴 No Meals.*

**Oasis Hotel Waikiki**

**$ | HOTEL | FAMILY** | An open-air lobby of Italian marble, a koi pond, hanging egg chairs, and a guava smoothie greet you on arrival at this hideaway a five-minute stroll from Kalakaua Avenue through one of the many public-access ways to the beach. **Pros:** all rooms have lanai; Japanese restaurant adjacent to lobby; on-site coin-operated laundry. **Cons:** rooms are slightly dated; trip to the beach can be a bit of a haul if you're carrying lounge chairs; valet parking only. *$ Rooms from: $169 ✉ 320 Lewers St., Waikiki ☎ 808/923–2300 🌐 oasishotelwaikiki.com 🛏 96 rooms 🍴 Free Breakfast.*

**Ohana Waikiki East by Outrigger**

**$$ | HOTEL | FAMILY** | If you want to be in central Waikiki and don't want to pay beachfront lodging prices, consider the Ohana Waikiki East, which is a mere two blocks from the beach and within walking distance of shopping, restaurants, and nightlife. **Pros:** reasonable rates close to the beach; some rooms have kitchenettes; spacious accommodations. **Cons:** very basic public spaces; an older property with signs of wear and tear; resort fee is $27 per day and parking fee is $35 per night. *Rooms from: $269* *150 Kaiulani Ave., Waikiki* *808/922–5353 direct to hotel, 866/956–4262 toll-free* *www.outrigger.com/hawaii/oahu/ohana-waikiki-east-by-outrigger* *441 rooms* *No Meals.*

**Outrigger Reef Waikiki Beach Resort**
**$$$ | HOTEL | FAMILY** | A prime location and aloha spirit keep guests returning to the Outrigger Reef, where rooms were renovated and the beach was widened in 2021, with 23 new rooms, a beachfront restaurant, and a luxury guest lounge added in 2022. **Pros:** on the beach; direct access to Waikiki Beach Walk; attentive staff. **Cons:** pool is not beachfront; views from nonoceanfront rooms are uninspiring; resort fee is $45 per day. *Rooms from: $325* *2169 Kalia Rd., Waikiki* *808/923–3111 direct to hotel, 866/956–4262 toll-free* *outrigger.com* *669 rooms* *No Meals.*

**Outrigger Waikiki Beach Resort**
**$$$$ | RESORT | FAMILY** | Outrigger's star property sits on one of the finest sections of Waikiki Beach, a location that, along with an array of cultural and dining options and great live-music and bar scenes, makes it a favorite. **Pros:** the best beach bar in Waikiki; on-site activities and amenities (including a spa) abound; excellent lounge that's worth splurging on an upgrade to access. **Cons:** a busy property (often used as a pedestrian throughway to the beach); resort fee is $45 per day; rooms are dated. *Rooms from: $450* *2335 Kalakaua Ave., Waikiki* *808/923–0711, 808/956–4262, 800/442–7304 toll-free* *outrigger.com* *525 rooms* *No Meals.*

**Outrigger Waikiki Beachcomber Hotel**
**$$ | HOTEL | FAMILY** | Almost directly across from the Royal Hawaiian Center and next to International Marketplace, the Beachcomber is a well-situated high-rise hotel for families as well as those looking for a boutique feel in the heart of the action. **Pros:** great beach views from some rooms; renovated and stylish; lovely pool area. **Cons:** very busy area in the thick of Waikiki action; not beachfront; resort fee is $35 per day. *Rooms from: $275* *2300 Kalakaua Ave., Waikiki* *808/922–4646, 877/418–0711* *outrigger.com* *496 rooms* *No Meals.*

## Looking for a Private Beach?

**Oahu's oldest hotels—the Royal Hawaiian and Moana Surfrider—are also the only hotels in Waikiki with property lines that extend into the sand. They have created private, roped-off beach areas with lounge chairs and umbrellas that can be accessed only by hotel guests for a fee. The areas are crowded and adjacent to the hotel properties at the top of the beach. They usually require reservations during the busy season, and guests often line up early in the morning to rent the chairs and umbrella sets.**

**Pacific Monarch**
**$$ | HOTEL | FAMILY** | One block from the western end of Waikiki Beach, this 34-story condominium resort offers sweeping views of Waikiki and the Pacific Ocean, especially from its rooftop deck, complete with a small pool, hot tub, and sauna. **Pros:** fantastic views from upper floors; hospitality lounge; all rooms have lanai. **Cons:** stairs to the pool deck are fairly steep and dark; resort fee is $25 per day; older property showing some wear. *Rooms from: $215* *2427 Kuhio Ave., Waikiki* *808/923–9805* *www.pacificmonarch.com* *216 rooms* *No Meals.*

**Prince Waikiki**

$$$$ | **HOTEL** | The sleek, modern Prince—which looks to Asia both in its high-style decor and such pampering touches as the traditional *oshiburi* (chilled hand towel) for refreshment upon check-in—has luxury oceanfront rooms and suites overlooking the Ala Wai Boat Harbor at Waikiki's *ewa* (western) edge. **Pros:** fantastic views from all rooms; excellent club lounge (available with certain rooms); two pools (including infinity pool). **Cons:** resort fee is $39 per day; beach is a 10-minute walk away; rooms don't have lanai. *Rooms from: $495 ✉ 100 Holomoana St., Waikiki ☎ 888/977–4623 toll-free for reservations, 808/956–1111 direct to hotel ⊕ www.princewaikiki.com 563 rooms No Meals.*

**Queen Kapiolani Hotel**

$$$ | **HOTEL** | With a contemporary look combined with a retro nod to the 1970s, the Queen Kapiolani Hotel is a short walk from the beach and is known for its stunning, unobstructed views of Diamond Head—a fabulous backdrop for its expansive pool deck. **Pros:** convenient Deck Bar by the pool; beach gear available at valet desk; large collection of museum-quality art. **Cons:** resort fee is $40 per day; bathrooms are small and a bit dated; noise from pool bar can be bothersome. *Rooms from: $320 ✉ 150 Kapahulu Ave., Waikiki ☎ 808/650–7841 ⊕ www.queenkapiolani.com 315 rooms No Meals.*

**The Ritz-Carlton Residences, Waikiki Beach**

$$$$ | **HOTEL** | The only Ritz-Carlton on Oahu welcomes well-heeled guests from across the globe with its signature elegance and impeccable service. **Pros:** very private setting; luxuriously appointed accommodations with kitchens; pampering service and pools with views. **Cons:** not close to the beach; pricey, particularly given distance from beach; families can sometimes overrun the facilities. *Rooms from: $699 ✉ 383 Kalaimoku St., Waikiki ☎ 808/922–8111 ⊕ www.ritzcarlton.com 552 units No Meals.*

**Royal Grove Waikiki**

$ | **HOTEL** | This pink, six-story hotel feels like a throwback to the days of boarding houses—when rooms were outfitted for function, not style, and offered with simple hospitality at a price that didn't break the bank. **Pros:** very economical Waikiki option; no resort fee; a bit of local flavor. **Cons:** no air-conditioning in some rooms; rooms and property are very dated; no on-site parking and minimum stays during busy seasons. *Rooms from: $150 ✉ 151 Uluniu Ave., Waikiki ☎ 808/923–7691 ⊕ www.royalgrovewaikiki.com 87 rooms No Meals.*

**★ The Royal Hawaiian, a Luxury Collection Resort, Waikiki**

$$$$ | **RESORT** | There's nothing like the iconic "Pink Palace of the Pacific," which is on 14 acres of prime Waikiki Beach and which has held fast to the luxury and grandeur that first defined it in the 1930s, when it became a favorite of the rich and famous. **Pros:** choice of rooms in historic wing or oceanfront tower; mai tais and sunsets are amazing; luxury and sense of history in a prime location. **Cons:** resort fee is $42 per day; high-traffic driveway entrance in center of Waikiki; very small swimming pool. *Rooms from: $525 ✉ 2259 Kalakaua Ave., Waikiki ☎ 808/923–7311, 866/716–8110 toll-free ⊕ www.royal-hawaiian.com 528 rooms No Meals.*

**Sheraton Princess Kaiulani**

$$ | **HOTEL** | **FAMILY** | The Princess Kaiulani sits across the street from the regal Moana Surfrider, without some of the more elaborate amenities (such as a spa or a kids' club), but with rates that are considerably kinder to the wallet. **Pros:** in the heart of everything in Waikiki, with the beach right across the street; beach service with chairs, towels, fruit, and water available; great value for the location. **Cons:** lobby area can feel like Grand Central Terminal; self parking is

$42 per night; resort fee is $37 per day. *Rooms from: $269 120 Kaiulani Ave., Waikiki 808/922–5811, 866/716–8109 toll-free marriott.com 1040 rooms No Meals.*

**★ Sheraton Waikiki Beach Resort**
**$$$$ | HOTEL | FAMILY** | Towering over its neighbors along the beachfront, this big, busy hotel offers stunning views from most of its modern rooms, which received a major renovation completed in 2023 that features neutral shades with splashes of color. **Pros:** fresh, modern guest rooms; variety of on-site activities and dining options; swimming pools often ranked among the Islands' best. **Cons:** busy atmosphere clashes with laid-back Hawaiian style; resort fee is $42 per day; room sizes and views vary. *Rooms from: $485 2255 Kalakaua Ave., Waikiki 808/922–4422, 866/716–8109 toll-free for reservations marriott.com 1636 rooms No Meals.*

**Shoreline Hotel Waikiki**
**$$$ | HOTEL** | Situated on bustling Seaside Avenue, this 14-story, 1970s-era property has been transformed into an urban-chic boutique hotel with both island and retro touches that playfully blend 20th-century style with modern necessities. **Pros:** great location in the middle of Waikiki; resort fee waived if you book direct; hipster decor a refreshing break from old-style Hawaiiana. **Cons:** if splashy colors aren't your thing, skip it; rooms are inconsistently sized and equipped; pool is accessed via two flights of stairs. *Rooms from: $379 342 Seaside Ave., Waikiki 808/931–2444, 855/931–2444 toll-free www.shorelinehotelwaikiki.com 135 rooms No Meals.*

**Surfjack Hotel & Swim Club**
**$$$ | HOTEL** | A surfing vibe and authentic, whimsical Hawaiian touches throughout (the lobby, for instance, evokes the living room of the interior designer's grandmother) set this hip boutique property apart from other modernized midcentury digs. **Pros:** hipster, urban-chic vibe that works; retro, locally designed decor; Ed Kenney restaurant on-site. **Cons:** resort fee is $25 per day; far from the beach; rooms can be inconsistent in terms of updates. *Rooms from: $325 412 Lewers St., Waikiki 808/923–8882 www.surfjack.com 112 rooms No Meals.*

## Condo Comforts

The local **Foodland** grocery-store chain has two locations near Waikiki, one in Market City in Kaimuki (*2939 Harding Ave. 808/734–6303*) and the other in the Ala Moana Center (*1450 Ala Moana Blvd. 808/949–5044*).

The popular ABC convenience stores have many locations. In addition to beach supplies, apparel, and just about everything else, some also sell packaged food, fruit, snacks, made-to-order meals, and alcoholic beverages.

**Twin Fin Hotel**
**$$$ | HOTEL | FAMILY** | A good choice for families, this recently refreshed (2022) high-rise hotel features a surf-inspired vibe and is directly across the street from a protected stretch of Kuhio Beach and near Kapiolani Park. **Pros:** fun for families, including on the pool deck; great beach access; Coconut Club lounge access for certain rooms/packages. **Cons:** active lobby area and crowded elevators; resort fee of $48 per day; rooms are dated. *Rooms from: $289 2570 Kalakaua Ave., Waikiki 808/922–2511 www.twinfinwaikiki.com 645 rooms No Meals.*

**Waikiki Beach Marriott Resort & Spa**
**$$$$ | RESORT | FAMILY** | Set on 5 acres across from Kuhio Beach and close to Kapiolani Park, the Honolulu Zoo, and the

Waikiki Aquarium, this flagship Marriott offers daily activities for children and adults and has an expansive pool deck with ocean views, several pools, plenty of cabanas and lounge chairs, and the large, outdoor Queensbreak restaurant. **Pros:** massive pool deck; lots of airy, tropical public spaces; central location in Waikiki. **Cons:** large impersonal hotel, requires lots of walking; self-parking is $45 per day; resort fee is $50 per day. *Rooms from: $399 ✉ 2552 Kalakaua Ave., Waikiki ☎ 808/922–6611, 800/367–5370 toll-free 🌐 marriott.com 1310 rooms No Meals.*

**Waikiki Malia**

**$$ | HOTEL** | Guests who return to this older property year after year appreciate its proximity to restaurants and shops and its easygoing "come as you are" vibe. **Pros:** convenient location; good value for the basics; on-site coin-operated laundry facilities. **Cons:** no views and small pool; property shows its age in places; resort fee of $30 per day. *Rooms from: $225 ✉ 2211 Kuhio Ave., Waikiki ☎ 808/923–7621 🌐 www.waikikimalia.com 332 rooms No Meals.*

**Waikiki Shore**

**$$ | HOTEL | FAMILY** | Nestled between Fort DeRussy Beach Park and the Outrigger Reef Resort, the only condo hotel directly on Waikiki Beach is beloved by some for its spaciousness and by others for its quieter, western-end location. **Pros:** desirable location on the beach; great views from spacious private lanai; units available in different sizes. **Cons:** some units are dated and amenities in them vary; extra cleaning fee can be hefty; two management companies rent here, so ask questions when booking. *Rooms from: $255 ✉ 2161 Kalia Rd., Waikiki ☎ 808/952–4500 Castle reservations, 808/922–3871 Outrigger reservations local, 800/688–7444 Outrigger reservations toll-free 🌐 www.castleresorts.com 168 suites No Meals.*

**Wayfinder Waikiki**

**$$$ | HOTEL** | This hotel refreshed in 2023 offers a fun vibe and lively design that mixes modern and traditional island elements, as well as close proximity to the beach, restaurants, and shops—all just three blocks away. **Pros:** fresh, colorful design; pool and hot tub; restaurant , bar, and coffee shop on-site. **Cons:** noise from the bar might annoy some; 10-minute walk to the beach; street noise from Ala Wai Boulevard can get loud. *Rooms from: $300 ✉ 2375 Ala Wai Blvd., Waikiki ☎ 808/922–4744, 800/247–1903 toll-free 🌐 www.wayfinderhotels.com/hotels/waikiki 214 rooms No Meals.*

## Nightlife

### BARS

**★ Duke's Waikiki Bar**

**BARS** | Making the most of its spot on Waikiki Beach, Duke's is a bustling destination featuring live music every day. This laid-back bar-and-grill's surf theme pays homage to Duke Kahanamoku, who popularized the sport in the early 1900s. Contemporary Hawaiian musicians like Henry Kapono and the Maunalua group have performed here, as have nationally known musicians like the late Jimmy Buffett. It's not unusual for surfers to leave their boards outside to step in for a casual drink after a long day on the waves. The cocktail menu is filled with Island-style drinks: try a sunset sour or coconut mojito while watching the Waikiki waves. *✉ Outrigger Waikiki, 2335 Kalakaua Ave., Suite 116, Waikiki ☎ 808/922–2268 🌐 www.dukeswaikiki.com.*

**Genius Lounge Sake Bar & Grill**

**BARS** | Removed from the tourist traps along Kalakaua Avenue, the Genius Lounge is tucked away on the third floor of a former apartment building on Lewers Street. The extensive drink menu offers beer and wine, cocktails, homemade sangria, and, of course, sake. Locally inspired dishes are also available. Though small, the space is open to the outdoors and furnished with dark woods and lit by candles, making an intimate setting for small gatherings and Friday-night dates. The crowd is mostly Asian visitors and transplants, but a daily happy hour (6–8 pm) lures office workers and pre-club prowlers. ✉ *346 Lewers St., 3rd fl., Waikiki* ☎ *808/626–5362* 🌐 *www.genius-loungehawaii.com.*

**Hideout**

**BARS** | Located at the Laylow Hotel, this indoor-outdoor mini-oasis has a firepit, tiki torches, comfy couches, and palm trees swaying overhead. Although there's a food menu, it's best to come here for expertly mixed cocktails or mocktails and some pupu (appetizers)—perhaps the poke tacos or the pork belly Brussels sprouts. A daily happy hour from 4:30 to 6:30 pm makes things easier on the wallet. Reservations are advised. ✉ *Laylow Hotel, 2299 Kuhio Ave., Waikiki* ☎ *808/628–3060* 🌐 *www.hideoutwaikiki.com.*

★ **Lewers Lounge**

**COCKTAIL BARS** | Set back from the main entrance of the Halekulani Hotel and decked out with dramatic drapes and cozy banquettes, Lewers Lounge is a great place for cocktails, both classic and contemporary. Standouts include Chocolate Dreams (made with Van Gogh Dutch Chocolate Vodka) and the Lost Passion (tequila, Cointreau, and fresh juices topped with champagne). Enjoy your libation with great nightly live jazz and tempting desserts, such as the hotel's famous coconut cake. ✉ *Halekulani Hotel, 2199 Kalia Rd., Waikiki* ☎ *808/923–2311* 🌐 *www.halekulani.com/dining/lewers-lounge.*

**Lulu's Waikiki**

**BARS** | Even if you're not a surfer, you'll love this place's retro vibe and unobstructed second-floor view of Waikiki Beach. The open-air setting, casual dining menu, and tropical drinks are all you need to help you settle into your vacation. The venue transforms from a nice spot for breakfast, lunch, dinner, or a drink (happy hour is 3 to 5 pm) into a bustling, high-energy club with live music lasting into the wee hours. ✉ *Park Shore Waikiki Hotel, 2586 Kalakaua Ave., Waikiki* ☎ *808/926–5222* 🌐 *www.luluswaikiki.com.*

★ **Mai Tai Bar at the Royal Hawaiian**

**BARS** | The bartenders here truly know how to mix up a fantastic mai tai. This is, after all, *the* establishment that first made the famous drink in the Islands. The pink umbrella–shaded tables at the outdoor bar are front-row seating for sunsets and also have an unobstructed view of Diamond Head. It's an ideal spot to soak in the island vibes just steps from the sand. Contemporary Hawaiian musicians hold jam sessions on stage nightly, and small bites are also available. ✉ *Royal Hawaiian Hotel, 2259 Kalakaua Ave., Waikiki* ☎ *808/923–7311* 🌐 *www.royal-hawaiian.com.*

★ **Maui Brewing Co.**

**BREWPUBS** | The craft beers produced by this Maui-based company are Island favorites, and a visit to this sprawling, indoor-outdoor brewpub adjacent to the Outrigger Waikiki Beachcomber Hotel's lobby means you don't have to island-hop to sample its offerings at the source. Ask about limited-release drafts to imbibe the brand's hidden gems, or order a flight of freshly brewed beers. Maui Brewing strives to source local ingredients for its beer and its food, and the menu here includes a poke bowl made with locally caught tuna, a kale salad that incorporates Waianae-based Naked Cow Dairy feta, and a Brewmaster pizza featuring Honolulu-based Kukui sausage. ✉ *Outrigger Waikiki Beachcomber Hotel, 2300 Kalakaua Ave., 2nd fl., Waikiki* ☎ *808/843–2739* 🌐 *www.mbcrestaurants.com/waikiki.*

**RumFire Waikiki Bar**

**BARS** | Locals and visitors head here for the convivial atmosphere, the trendy decor, and the million-dollar view of Waikiki Beach and Diamond Head. Come early to get a seat for happy hour (3–5 pm daily). If you're feeling peckish, there's a menu of tasty, Asian-influenced small plates. RumFire also features original cocktails, signature shots, and daily live music. On Friday and Saturday nights, the bar gets even livelier once local DJs start spinning. ✉ *Sheraton Waikiki, 2255 Kalakaua Ave., Waikiki* ☎ *808/922–4422* 🌐 *www.rumfirewaikiki.com.*

**Tiki's Bar**

**BARS** | Tiki torches light the way to this fun restaurant and bar overlooking Kuhio Beach in the Twin Fin Hotel. A mix of locals and visitors heads here for happy hour and, later, to enjoy its kitschy cool, casual vibe. There's great nightly entertainment by contemporary Hawaiian musicians playing lively and popular cover tunes. The drinks menu is extensive and (not surprisingly) tiki-focused. Don't leave without sipping on the Lava Flow (rum, coconut milk, pineapple juice, strawberry puree) or noshing on coconut shrimp, ahi poke, or macadamia-crusted fish of the day. And if you love the tiki vibe, you can purchase an array of whimsical merchandise, including the colorful tiki mugs. If you're here during the holidays, ask the host about the "Christmas bar." ✉ *Twin Fin Hotel, 2570 Kalakaua Ave., Waikiki* ☎ *808/923–8454* 🌐 *www.tikisgrill.com.*

**Waiolu Ocean Cuisine**

**BARS** | Hawaiian bars should have two things: stellar views of the sunset over the ocean and equally stellar mai tais. This lounge of this restaurant has both, as well as live music, ranging from contemporary to Hawaiian, Thursday through Sunday. Come for sunset or for the late-night happy hour, but seats are scarce once the music starts at 6:30 pm, and an attractive crowd starts showing up around 8. ✉ *Trump International Hotel, 223 Saratoga Rd., Waikiki* ☎ *808/683–7456* 🌐 *www.trumphotels.com/waikiki.*

## Mai Tais

Hard to believe, but the cocktail known all over the world as the mai tai has been around since 1944. Although the recipe has changed slightly over time, the original formula, created by bar owner Victor J. "Trader Vic" Bergeron, included 2 ounces of 17-year-old J. Wray & Nephew rum over shaved ice, ½ ounce of DeKuyper orange curaçao, ¼ ounce of Trader Vic's rock-candy syrup, ½ ounce of orgeat syrup, and the juice of one fresh lime. Done the right way, this tropical drink still lives up to the name "mai tai!," meaning "out of this world!"

**Wang Chung's Karaoke Bar**

**BARS** | Dubbed the "Friendliest Bar in Waikiki," this charming karaoke joint is a must-visit on any trip to the island. The positive vibe comes from owner Dan Chang, who personally welcomes his guests to this LGBTQ+-friendly establishment. The bar is in the lobby of the Stay Hotel and has a full kitchen cranking out Asian- and Latin-inspired dishes. It's known for a lively late-night crowd and innovative cocktails. The list of karaoke songs is extensive, and the place gets jammed, so arrive early if you really want to add your name to the list and sing a song. ✉ *Stay Hotel Waikiki, 2424 Koa Ave., Waikiki* ☎ *808/201–6369* 🌐 *www.wangchungs.com.*

### CLUBS

**Hula's Bar and Lei Stand**

**DANCE CLUB** | Hawaii's oldest and best-known gay-friendly nightspot offers panoramic views of Diamond Head by day and high-energy club music by night. Check out the all-day happy hour, which starts at 10 am. There's an abundance of drink specials on weekends and discounted pitchers of beer and cocktails on Sunday.

Food options include nachos, tacos, pork sliders, and more. Celebrity patrons have included Elton John, Adam Lambert, and Dolly Parton. ✉ *Waikiki Grand Hotel, 134 Kapahulu Ave., 2nd fl., Waikiki* ☎ *808/923–0669* 🌐 *www.hulas.com.*

**Sky Waikiki Raw & Bar**
**LIVE MUSIC** | This bar 19 stories above the city offers nearly 360-degree bird's-eye views of Diamond Head, the Waikiki beaches, and the classic coral Royal Hawaiian hotel. It's also one of the best spots to take in a Waikiki sunset. Be sure to order the popular SkyTai cocktail as you enjoy the views. There are also happy hour drink specials daily and a limited menu with fresh seafood. The indoor club, where resident DJs spin on Friday and Saturday nights, exudes contemporary-L.A. chic. ✉ *Waikiki Trade Center, 2270 Kalakaua Ave., Waikiki* ☎ *808/979–7590* 🌐 *www.skywaikiki.com.*

# Performing Arts

## LUAU

The luau is an experience that everyone, both local and tourist, should have. It's an exciting way to capture the "aloha spirit" and learn a bit about island culture. Today's luau offer traditional foods and entertainment, but they often incorporate fun, contemporary flair as well. At many, you can watch the roasted pig being carried out of its *imu,* a hole in the ground used for cooking food with heated stones.

Luau prices average around $150 per person, and several are held around the island, including a few in Waikiki. Reservations—and a camera—are a must.

**Royal Hawaiian Luau: Ahaaina**
**FOLK/TRADITIONAL DANCE** | **FAMILY** | With a beachfront location in the middle of Waikiki, the Royal Hawaiian's Ahaaina luau is an exceptional, upscale event with hula, fire dancing, live music, Hawaiian-inspired and luau-favorite dishes, and more. Options range from "standard dinner and show" to "premium dinner and show." The three-hour event is held two nights a week (Monday and Thursday); be sure to reserve in advance during the high season. ✉ *The Royal Hawaiian, a Luxury Collection Resort, 2259 Kalakaua Ave., Waikiki* ☎ *808/921–4600* 🌐 *www.royal-hawaiianluau.com* 🎟 *From $200.*

**Waikiki Starlight Luau**
**FOLK/TRADITIONAL DANCE** | **FAMILY** | This Waikiki luau is done spectacularly on the rooftop of Hilton Hawaiian Village. There isn't an *imu* ceremony, but the live entertainment is top-notch, and the views are unparalleled. Prices vary depending on your age and where you want to sit. The event also includes dinner with traditional specialties, games, and cultural activities, such as hula lessons and conch blowing. It's held Sunday, Monday, and Wednesday at 5 pm. ✉ *Hilton Hawaiian Village, 2005 Kalia Rd., Waikiki* ☎ *808/941–5828* 🌐 *www.hiltonhawaiianvillage.com* 🎟 *From $185.*

## MUSIC

★ **Blue Note Hawaii**
**MUSIC** | Music lovers adore this intimate venue, which draws local and national acts—jazz, rock, reggae, pop, and more—throughout the year. Comedy acts take the stage, too. Acoustics are fantastic, and seating is at tables, all with excellent views. The atmosphere is sophisticated, and the food here is excellent, too, with small and large plates offered (there's a $10 per person food or drink minimum). It's worthwhile to find out who's performing while you're in town so you can purchase tickets in advance, since the more popular acts sell out quickly. This 300-seat room is centrally located at the Outrigger Waikiki Beach Resort, so you can grab a drink at Duke's before or after the show. ✉ *Outrigger Waikiki Beach Resort, 2335 Kalakaua Ave., Waikiki* ☎ *808/777–4890* 🌐 *www.bluenotehawaii.com* 🎟 *From $35.*

**Honolulu Zoo Concerts**

**CONCERTS | FAMILY** | Since the early 1980s, the Honolulu Zoo Society has sponsored hour-long evening concerts, branded the "Wildest Show in Town," that are one of the best deals in town. They're held at 6 pm on Wednesday, June–August. Listen to local legends play everything from Hawaiian to jazz to Latin music. Take a brisk walk through the zoo, or join in the family activities. This is an alcohol-free event, and there's food for those who haven't brought their own picnic supplies. Gates open at 4:35. ✉ *Honolulu Zoo, 151 Kapahulu Ave., Waikiki* ☎ *808/971–7171* 🌐 *www.honoluluzoo.org* 🎟 *From $15.*

### THEATER

Hawaii can be an expensive gig for touring shows and music acts that depend on major theatrical sets. Not many manage to stop here, and those that do sell out fast. Oahu has developed several excellent local community theater companies that present first-rate, though not professional, entertainment all year long. (Anyone who attends is always surprised to learn that the Honolulu Theatre for Youth is the only professional troupe in the state.) Community support for these groups is strong.

**Diamond Head Theatre**

**THEATER** | Hawaii's oldest performing arts center offers a little of everything: musicals, dramas, and experimental productions. It opened in 1915 and is the third-oldest community theater in the United States. ✉ *520 Makapuu Ave., Diamond Head* ☎ *808/733–0274* 🌐 *www.diamondheadtheatre.com* 🎟 *From $15.*

## Shopping

Waikiki's hotels and malls or other shopping centers all have notable shops, and the abundance of name-brand and specialty items will be energizing or overwhelming, depending on your interest in shopping.

Clothing, jewelry, and handbags from Europe's top designers sit next to Hawaii's ABC Stores, a popular chain of convenience stores that sells groceries as well as souvenirs. Now more than ever, it's possible to find interesting, locally produced items and independent stores in Waikiki, but you must be willing to search beyond the expensive purses and the tacky wooden tikis to find innovation and quality.

Larger shopping centers (including the Royal Hawaiian Center) may offer some type of parking validation with purchase, so be sure to check or ask in advance.

### CLOTHING

**Blue Ginger**

**CLOTHING | FAMILY** | This little shop offers a great selection of Hawaii-made items for adults and children. Look for brightly colored, beach-casual clothing, bags, jewelry, and accessories in soft cotton and rayon aloha prints. ✉ *227 Lewers St., Waikiki* ☎ *808/924–7900* 🌐 *www.blueginger.com.*

**★ 88 Tees**

**CLOTHING** | Hip and fun, this shop stocks some of the island's coolest T-shirts, accessories, and apparel for women, men, and kids, featuring funky, retro Hawaii themes and designs. Bruno Mars famously wore a tank top from this eclectic shop on a *Rolling Stone* magazine cover in 2021. You may spend more time browsing—and buying—here than you might expect. A second location is nearby on Kuhio Avenue. Note that the store opens at 1 pm. ✉ *2168 Kalakaua Ave., Waikiki* ☎ *808/922–8832* 🌐 *www.88tees.com.*

**Newt at the Royal**

**HATS & GLOVES** | High-quality, handwoven Panama hats and tropical sportswear for men and women are the specialties here. ✉ *The Royal Hawaiian, 2259 Kalakaua Ave., Waikiki* ☎ *808/923–4332* 🌐 *www.newtattheroyal.com.*

**Oiwi Ocean Gear**

**CLOTHING** | Featuring stylish, high-quality activewear especially for ocean, paddling, and beach enthusiasts, this locally owned shop was founded in 1999 in the nearby beach town of Kailua. Its original designs for men, women, and children are created in-house and showcase the ocean, nature, and unique images of Hawaiian culture. These items include shirts, rash guards, board shorts, surf leggings, hats, accessories, and more. Most designs offer sun protection (UPF apparel). ✉ *Royal Hawaiian Shopping Center, 2201 Kalakaua Ave., Bldg. A, 1st fl., Waikiki* ☎ *808/263–7770* 🌐 *www.oiwioceangear.com.*

**Waikiki Beachboy Store**

**SWIMWEAR** | **FAMILY** | Tucked away in the Royal Hawaiian's lobby, this tiny shop is a great place to pick up a memento of your surf lesson. It's filled with a variety of high-quality Waikiki Beach Services gear, including the best-selling logo rash guards and T-shirts of the type worn by their beachboys and surf instructors. There's also a selection of locally designed bathing suits from Pualani Hawaii, swimwear from the Colombian brand Maaji, accessories, sunscreen, and original artwork. ✉ *The Royal Hawaiian, 2259 Kalakaua Ave., Shop 9, Waikiki* ☎ *808/922–2223* 🌐 *www.waikikibeachservices.com.*

## FOOD

**★ Honolulu Cookie Company**

**FOOD** | To really impress those back home, pick up a box of these locally baked, gourmet cookies. Choose from dozens of delicious flavors of premium shortbread delights packaged in a wide range of sizes, all designed for travel. In addition to the location in the Royal Hawaiian Center, the company has a number of stores in Waikiki, so you probably won't be able to avoid them—or their free samples—even if you try. ✉ *Royal Hawaiian Center, 2233 Kalakaua Ave., Waikiki* ☎ *808/921–3330* 🌐 *www.honolulucookie.com.*

## GALLERIES

**Ruby Mazur Gallery**

**ART GALLERY** | It's all about rock 'n' roll at this edgy, colorful gallery at the Waikiki Beach Walk. Ruby Mazur is known as the artist who created the original Rolling Stones logo (the famous lips and tongue), so it's no surprise that this space showcases an abundance of artwork featuring top musical performers such as Bruno Mars, Bruce Springsteen, and Taylor Swift, as well as many other classic and modern greats. ✉ *280 Beach Walk, Suite 104, Waikiki* ☎ *808/210–7024* 🌐 *rubymazurgallery.com/gallery.*

**Tabora Gallery Waikiki**

**ART GALLERY** | Pieces by local and international artists are featured here, including original paintings; limited-edition prints; works in wood, metal, glass, ceramic, and acrylic; and handcrafted jewelry. There's another branch on Oahu, in the town of Haleiwa, and one in Lihue on Kauai. ✉ *International Marketplace, 2330 Kalakaua Ave., 2nd fl., Waikiki* ☎ *8080/779–4339* 🌐 *taboragallery.com.*

**Wyland Galleries**

**ART GALLERY** | In addition to exhibiting the beautiful and inspiring work of the world-famous marine life artist Wyland, this expansive art gallery showcases works by a number of other artists, both lesser-known and highly acclaimed. There are also locations in the Oahu town of Haleiwa and on Kauai. ✉ *226 Lewers St., Waikiki* ☎ *808/924–1322* 🌐 *www.wyland.com/galleries.*

## GIFTS

**★ Aloha Collection**

**HANDBAGS** | Located in the Moana Surfrider hotel, the flagship store of this innovative company is filled with colorful, lightweight, "splash-proof" bags of all sizes, shapes, and styles—from tiny zippered travel pouches to eye-catching beach bags to oversize totes. The company continually offers new patterns and styles, so bag lovers will always find a unique beach- or travel-friendly option.

✉ *Moana Surfrider, 2369 Kalakaua Ave., Diamond Head Wing Shop #1, Waikiki* 🌐 *aloha-collection.com.*

### ★ House of Mana Up

**LOCAL GOODS** | The groundbreaking Mana Up organization promotes Hawaii-based entrepreneurs and shares many unique locally made products with consumers. Its retail store in the Royal Hawaiian Center not only showcases innovative, Hawaii-made items but also shares the stories of the makers behind them. It's fun to browse for gourmet chocolate, edible coffee bars, art, sustainable food wrappers, surf-inspired clothing, extra-comfy flip-flops (called slippers in Hawaii), children's books, and much more. All the profits are used to support these small businesses. ✉ *Royal Hawaiian Center, 2201 Kalakaua Ave., Space A111b (1st fl.), Waikiki* ☎ *808/425–4028* 🌐 *www.manauphawaii.com.*

### ★ Keep It Simple

**SPECIALTY STORE** | Founded by local entrepreneurs Jillian Corn and Hunter Long (who is also a professional skateboarder), Keep It Simple strives to promote a healthier planet by selling high-quality natural, organic, and/or vegan items with minimal (or zero) packaging. Look for sustainable beauty and bath products; beachwear, cover-ups, and accessories; and items for the kitchen and elsewhere in the home. ✉ *Waikiki Beach Walk, 240 Lewers St., Waikiki* ☎ *808/744–3115* 🌐 *www.keepitsimplezerowaste.com.*

## JEWELRY

### Na Hoku Gallery

**JEWELRY & WATCHES** | Like its larger sibling in the Ala Moana Center, this designer and island-lifestyle jewelry store sells Tahitian pearls and ocean- and marine-themed jewelry. Many beautiful Hawaii-inspired designs are featured here; the store also has branches around the Islands. ✉ *Outrigger Waikiki Beach Resort, 2335 Kalakaua Ave., Waikiki* ☎ *808/922–0556* 🌐 *www.nahoku.com.*

## SHOPPING CENTERS

### Luxury Row at 2100 Kalakaua

**MALL** | The ultimate destination for designer shopping in Hawaii is this elegant town house–style center, where high-end shops include Chanel, Coach, Tiffany & Co., Yves Saint Laurent, Bottega Veneta, Gucci, Hugo Boss, Miu Miu, and Moncler. ✉ *2100 Kalakaua Ave., Waikiki* ☎ *808/922–2246* 🌐 *www.luxuryrow.com.*

### ★ Royal Hawaiian Center

**MALL** | This three-block-long center has more than 110 establishments, including an Apple Store and ABC Store, as well as local gems, such as Oiwi Ocean Gear, Mana Up, Fighting Eel, Honolulu Cookie Company, Koi Honolulu, Hawaiian Island Arts, Island Soap & Candleworks, and Royal Hawaiian Quilts. In addition to a number of restaurants, you can dine at the Waikiki Food Hall. Complimentary cultural classes, a theater, and nightly outdoor entertainment round out the offerings. Note for drivers: the center offers free parking for three hours with validation at shops and restaurants. ✉ *2201 Kalakaua Ave., Waikiki* ☎ *808/922–0588* 🌐 *www.royalhawaiiancenter.com.*

### Waikiki Beach Walk

**MALL | FAMILY** | This open-air mall at the west end of Kalakaua Avenue and next to the Royal Hawaiian Center contains 70 locally owned stores and restaurants. Get reasonably priced, fashionable resort wear at Mahina or buy local delicacies from the Poke Bar. Of course, you can pick up T-shirts, bathing suits, and casual beach attire here, too. The mall also features free local entertainment on its outdoor fountain stage at least once a week. ✉ *226 Lewers St., Waikiki* ☎ *808/931–3591* 🌐 *www.waikikibeachwalk.com.*

## SKINCARE

### Love Renaissance

**SKINCARE** | This lovely and welcoming skincare boutique offers a wide array of serum-based beauty products from this highly acclaimed Japanese brand. The store offers excellent service, and the representative will demonstrate how to properly use their luxurious creams, lotions, and other items. The company's motto is to bring "beauty and happiness to everyone in the world," so shopping here can be a truly pampering experience. ✉ *Royal Hawaiian Center, 2301 Kalakaua Ave., Suite C117c, Waikiki* ☎ *808/923–0991* 🌐 *love-renaissance.shop.*

## SPAS

Excellent day and resort spas can be found throughout Oahu, primarily in the resorts of Waikiki. Individual treatments and day packages offer a wide choice of rejuvenating therapies, some of which are unique to the Islands. Try the popular lomilomi massage with kukui-nut oil (*lomi* meaning to rub, knead, and massage using palms, forearms, fingers, knuckles, elbows, knees, feet, even sticks). Add heated *pohaku* (stones) placed on the back to relieve sore muscles, or choose a facial using natural ingredients such as coconut, mango, papaya, ti leaf, Hawaiian honey, or ginger. Many full-service spas offer private treatment rooms for couples, fitness suites, yoga, and hydrotherapy pools.

### Abhasa Spa

**SPA** | Organic skin and body treatments are the highlights at this spa tucked away in the Royal Hawaiian's coconut grove. Vegetarian-lifestyle spa therapies, color-light therapy, and a facial fusing invigorating lomilomi (rubbing and kneading) technique with *pohaku* (heated stones) are all available. You can have your treatment in any of Abhasa's eight indoor rooms or in one of its three garden cabanas. ✉ *The Royal Hawaiian, a Luxury Resort, Waikiki, 2259 Kalakaua Ave., Waikiki* ☎ *808/922–8200* 🌐 *www.abhasa.com* 💳 *Massages from $185, facials from $200.*

### ★ Mandara Spa at Hilton Hawaiian Village Beach Resort & Spa

**SPA** | From its perch in the Kalia Tower, this outpost of a spa chain that originated in Bali overlooks the mountains, ocean, and downtown Honolulu. Hawaiian ingredients and traditional techniques are included in an array of services. Relieve achy muscles with a Thai poultice massage, perhaps with a reflexology or Balinese body polish add-on. This is one of the largest spas in Honolulu, with 25 treatment rooms, spa suites for couples, individual relaxation lounges with wet and dry saunas for men and women, Jacuzzis, traditional Japanese showers, a private infinity pool, fitness facilities, a salon, and a boutique. The delicately scented, candlelit foyer can fill up quickly with robe-clad conventioneers, so be sure to make a reservation. ✉ *Hilton Hawaiian Village Beach Resort & Spa, 2005 Kalia Rd., 3rd and 4th fl., Kalia Tower, Waikiki* ☎ *808/945–7721* 🌐 *www.mandaraspa.com* 💳 *Facials from $190, massages from $110.*

### Na Hoola Spa at the Hyatt Regency Waikiki Resort & Spa

**SPA** | The 16 rooms of Waikiki's premier resort spa are on two floors of the Hyatt on Kalakaua Avenue. Arrive early for your treatment to enjoy the serene, postcard-perfect beach views. You can choose from more than 15 different types of massages, including those for couples, and many of the treatments for body, face, and hair feature Hawaiian healing plants—noni, kukui, awa, and *kalo* (taro). This spa also has various day packages that last three to six hours. The small exercise room, however, is for use by hotel guests only. ✉ *Hyatt Regency Waikiki Resort & Spa, 2424 Kalakaua Ave., Waikiki* ☎ *808/923–1234, 808/237–6330 for reservations* 🌐 *www.hyatt.com/en-US/spas/Na-HoOla-Spa/home* 💳 *Massages from $180, treatments from $175.*

**Royal Kaila Spa**
**SPA** | The Marriott's spa, which faces Waikiki Beach, uses nature-based Aveda products to incorporate healing plant essences in its massage, facial, and body treatments. Linger with a cup of tea between treatments, and gaze through 75-foot-high windows at the activity outside. Lush Hawaiian foliage, sleek Balinese teak furnishings, and a mist of ylang-ylang and nutmeg in the air encourage relaxation. ✉ *Waikiki Beach Marriott Resort & Spa, 2552 Kalakaua Ave., Waikiki* ☎ *808/369–8088* 🌐 *www.spa-royalkaila.com/eng* 🎫 *Massages from $150.*

**SpaHalekulani**
**SPA** | Massages, body, and facial therapies at this intimate, tranquil spa are influenced by their "Art of Wellbeing" concept, which encompasses several pillars such as nourish, rest, explore, renew, and others. The exclusive line of bath and body products is scented by maile, lavender orchid, or coconut passion. Although the facilities are small, treatments are sublime and may include a Japanese *furo* bath or a steam shower. ✉ *Halekulani Hotel, 2199 Kalia Rd., Waikiki* ☎ *808/931–5322* 🌐 *www.halekulani.com* 🎫 *Bodywork from $225, facials from $253.*

# Pearl Harbor

*Approximately 9 miles west of downtown Honolulu, beyond Daniel K. Inouye International Airport.*

On December 7, 1941, the Japanese bombed Pearl Harbor, an act that was the catalyst for the United States' entrance into World War II. On that fateful day, more than 2,000 people died, and a dozen ships were sunk. Here, at what is still a key Pacific naval base, the attack is remembered every day by thousands of visitors. In recent years, the memorial has also been the site of reconciliation ceremonies involving Pearl Harbor veterans from both sides.

There are five distinct sights in Pearl Harbor, but only two are part of the Pearl Harbor National Memorial, with the others privately operated. Make reservations for the national park portion.

## Sights

**Battleship *Missouri* Memorial**
**MILITARY SIGHT | FAMILY** | Together with the *Arizona* Memorial, the USS *Missouri*'s presence in Pearl Harbor perfectly frames America's World War II experience, which began December 7, 1941, and ended on the "Mighty Mo's" starboard deck with the signing of the Terms of Surrender on September 2, 1945. To begin your visit on the fully restored vessel, pick up tickets online or at the Pearl Harbor Visitor Center. Then board a shuttle bus for the eight-minute ride to Ford Island and the teak decks and towering superstructure of the last American battleship ever built. Join a guided tour to learn more about the *Missouri*'s long and dramatic history. Two options for upgraded tours (an additional $30) provide an up-close look at areas not on the main tour, including the captain's cabin, the bridge, and engine and fire rooms.

The *Missouri* is 887 feet long and 209 feet tall, with nine 116-ton guns capable of firing up to 23 miles. Absorb these numbers during the tour, then stop to take advantage of the view from the decks. Near the entrance is a gift shop, as well as a lunch wagon and shave ice stand that serve casual fare. ✉ *Ford Island, 63 Cowpens St., Pearl Harbor* ✣ *You cannot drive directly to the USS Missouri; you must take a shuttle bus from Pearl Harbor Visitor Center* ☎ *808/455–1600* 🌐 *ussmissouri.org* 🎫 *From $35.*

**Pacific Fleet Submarine Museum**
**MILITARY SIGHT | FAMILY** | The expanded Pacific Fleet Submarine Museum,

opened in 2021, has as its centerpiece the USS *Bowfin,* which launched one year to the day after the Pearl Harbor attack and which claimed to have sunk 44 enemy ships during World War II. Like the *Arizona* Memorial, the so-called Pearl Harbor Avenger commemorates the lost, but the mood here is lighter. Perhaps it's the childlike scale of the boat, a metal tube just 16 feet in diameter and packed with ladders, hatches, and other obstacles, like the naval version of a jungle gym.

Compartments aboard the vessel are fitted out as though "Sparky" is away from the radio room just for a moment and "Cooky" might be back to his pots and pans any minute. Among the intriguing artifacts is an oversize, vintage dive suit known as JAKE that is now in the gift shop window. A guided audio tour is included with admission to this privately operated museum. A snack bar is also on-site.

For safety reasons, children under four are not allowed aboard the submarine, though they can visit the museum. You can also purchase shuttle tickets to access the USS *Oklahoma* Memorial at the *Bowfin*'s ticket counter, though you'll probably want to include that stop with a visit to the USS *Missouri* or the Pearl Harbor Aviation Museum, both of which are on Ford Island along with the sunken *Oklahoma* submarine. ✉ *11 Arizona Memorial Pl., Pearl Harbor* ☎ *808/423–1341* 🌐 *www.bowfin.org* 🎟 *$22* ☞ *Tickets available in advance or on arrival.*

**Pearl Harbor Aviation Museum**

**HISTORY MUSEUM | FAMILY** | This tribute to aviation in the Pacific battlefield of World War II is on Ford Island in Hangars 37 and 79, actual seaplane hangars that survived the Pearl Harbor attack. The museum consists of a theater where a short film on Pearl Harbor is shown, an education center, a restoration shop, a gift store, and a restaurant. Exhibits—many of which are interactive and feature sound effects—include an authentic Japanese Zero and various other vintage aircraft that help narrate such great battles as the Doolittle Raid on Japan, Midway, and Guadalcanal. The actual Stearman N2S-3 that President George H. W. Bush flew is housed in Hangar 79.

Ride in Fighter Ace 360 Flight Simulators, take a docent-led tour, and visit the Ford Island Control Tower for additional fees. Purchase tickets online, at the Pearl Harbor Visitor Center, or at the museum itself after you get off the shuttle bus that departs for the museum and the USS *Missouri* from the visitor center. ✉ *Ford Island, 319 Lexington Blvd., Pearl Harbor* ✣ *Access is only via the shuttle bus to Ford Island from the Pearl Harbor Visitor Center* ☎ *808/441–1000* 🌐 *pearlharboraviationmuseum.org* 🎟 *$26.*

★ **Pearl Harbor National Memorial**

**NATIONAL PARK | FAMILY** | Pearl Harbor is still a working military base as well as Oahu's most visited attraction, consisting of five distinct destinations. Managed by the National Park Service, the Pearl Harbor Visitor Center and USS *Arizona* Memorial make up the national memorial, where exhibits tell the story not only of the devastating Japanese attack on Pearl Harbor on December 7, 1941, but also of the wartime internment of Japanese Americans, World War II battles in the Aleutian Islands, and the occupation of Japan after the war. The history continues at three privately operated sights: the Pacific Fleet Submarine Museum (whose centerpiece is the USS *Bowfin*), the Battleship *Missouri* Memorial, and the Pearl Harbor Aviation Museum.

A valid government-issued photo ID is required to enter the base. You can walk to the visitor center or the submarine museum from the parking lot, but access to the USS *Arizona* requires a ferry ride (and ticket reservations via 🌐 *www.recreation.gov*), and access to other

*Continued on page 119*

USS *West Virginia* (BB48), 7 December 1941

# PEARL HARBOR

December 7, 1941. Every American then alive recalls exactly what they were doing when the news broke that the Japanese had bombed Pearl Harbor, the catalyst that brought the United States into World War II.

Although it was clear by late 1941 that war with Japan was inevitable, no one in authority seemed to have expected the attack to come in just this way, at just this time. So when the Japanese bombers swept through a gap in Oahu's Koolau Mountains in the hazy light of morning, they found the bulk of America's Pacific fleet right where they hoped it would be: docked like giant stepping stones across the calm waters of the bay named for the pearl oysters that once prospered there. More than 2,000 people died that day, including 49 civilians. A dozen ships were sunk. And on the nearby air bases, virtually every American military aircraft was destroyed or damaged. The attack was a stunning success, but it lit a fire under America, which went to war with "Remember Pearl Harbor" as its battle cry. Here, in what is still a key Pacific naval base, the attack is remembered every day by thousands of visitors, including many curious Japanese, who for years heard little World War II history in their own country. In recent years, the memorial has been the site of reconciliation ceremonies involving Pearl Harbor veterans from both sides.

## GETTING AROUND

**Pearl Harbor is both a working military base and the most-visited Oahu attraction. Five distinct destinations share a parking lot and are linked by footpath, shuttle, and ferry.**

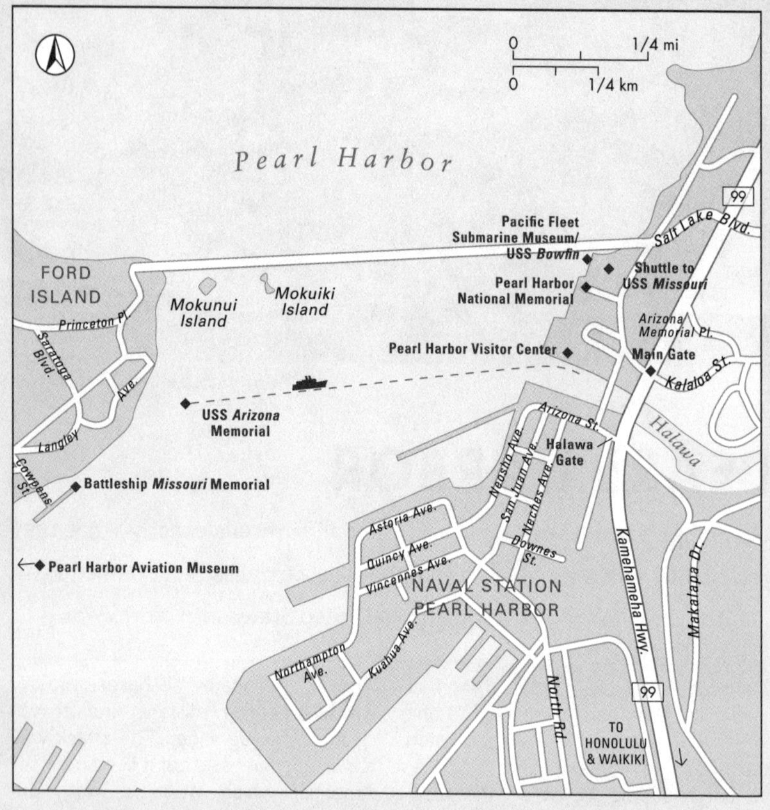


The visitor center is accessible from the parking lot. The USS *Arizona* Memorial itself is in the middle of the harbor; get tickets for the ferry ride online ahead of time. The Pacific Fleet Submarine Museum/USS *Bowfin* are also reachable from the parking lot. The USS *Missouri* is docked at Ford Island, a restricted area of the naval base. Vehicular access is prohibited. To get there, take a shuttle bus from the station near the *Bowfin*.

## USS *ARIZONA* MEMORIAL

**Snugged up tight in a row of seven battleships off Ford Island, the USS *Arizona* took a direct hit that December morning, exploded, and rests still on the shallow bottom where she settled.**

The swooping, stark-white memorial, which straddles the wreck of the USS *Arizona*, was designed to represent both the depths of the low-spirited, early days of the war, and the uplift of victory.

A visit here begins at the Pearl Harbor Visitor Center, which underwent a $58 million renovation in 2010. High-definition projectors and interactive exhibits were installed, and the building was modernized. From the visitor center, a ferry takes you to the memorial itself, and shuttles access the USS *Oklahoma*.

A somber, contemplative mood descends upon visitors during the ferry ride to the *Arizona*; this is a place where 1,177 crewmen lost their lives. Gaze at the names of the dead carved into the wall of white marble. Scatter flowers (but no lei—the string is bad for the fish). Salute the flag. Remember Pearl Harbor.

☎ *808/422–3399*
🌐 *www.nps.gov/perl*

Navy members, family, and friends visit the memorial's shrine with its wall of names.

# USS *MISSOURI* (BB63)

## BATTLESHIP *MISSOURI* MEMORIAL

Together with the *Arizona* Memorial, the *Missouri's* presence in Pearl Harbor perfectly bookends America's WWII experience, which began December 7, 1941, and ended on the "Mighty Mo's" starboard deck with the signing of the Terms of Surrender.

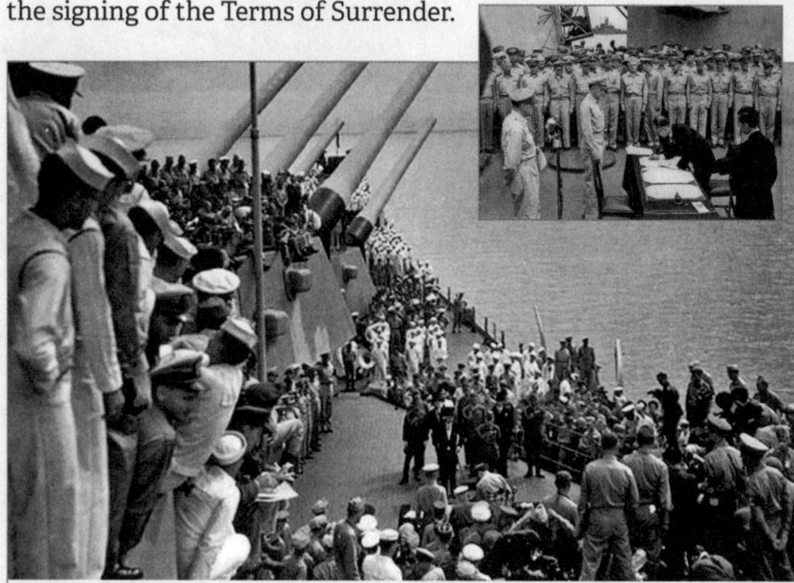

Surrender of Japan, USS *Missouri,* 2 September 1945

In the parking area behind the Pacific Fleet Submarine Museum, board a shuttle for an eight-minute ride to Ford Island and the teak decks and towering superstructure of the *Missouri*. The largest American battleship ever built, the *Missouri* famously hosted the final act of WWII, the signing of the Terms of Surrender. The commission that governs this floating museum has surrounded it with WWII-style buildings, among them a lunch wagon, a shave ice stand, and a souvenir shop.

**TIP→ Definitely hook up with a tour guide (no additional charge). Guides add a great deal to the experience.**

The *Missouri* is all about numbers: 209 feet tall, six 239,000-pound guns, capable of firing up to 23 miles away. Absorb these during the tour, then stop to take advantage of the view from the decks. The Mo is a work in progress, with only a handful of her hundreds of spaces open to view.

☎ *808/455-1600*

🌐 *www.ussmissouri.org*

# USS *BOWFIN* (SS287)

## PACIFIC FLEET SUBMARINE MUSEUM

Launched one year to the day after the Pearl Harbor attack, the USS *Bowfin* reportedly sank 44 enemy ships during WWII and now serves as the centerpiece of a museum honoring all submariners.

Although the *Bowfin* no less than the *Arizona* Memorial commemorates the lost, the mood here is lighter. Perhaps it's the childlike scale of the boat, a metal tube just 16 feet in diameter, packed with ladders, hatches, and other obstacles, like the naval version of a jungle gym. Or it might be the museum's touching displays—the penciled sailor's journal, the Vargas girlie posters. Aboard the boat nicknamed "Pearl Harbor Avenger," compartments are fitted out as though "Sparky" was away from the radio room just for a moment, and "Cooky" might be right back to his pots and pans. Reopened in 2021 after a major renovation, the adjacent submarine museum includes many artifacts to spark family conversations, among them a large vintage dive suit that is now in the gift shop window.

A caution: The *Bowfin* could be hazardous for very young children; no one under four allowed.

☎ *808/423–1341*
🌐 *www.bowfin.org*

## PEARL HARBOR AVIATION MUSEUM

This museum opened on December 7, 2006, as as a tribute to aviation in the Pacific. Located on Ford Island in Hangars 37 and 79, actual seaplane hangars that survived the Pearl Harbor attack, the museum is made up of a theater where a short film on Pearl Harbor kicks off the tour, an education center, a shop, and a restaurant. Exhibits—many of which are interactive and involve sound effects—include an authentic Japanese Zero in a diorama setting, vintage aircraft, and the chance to play the role of a World War II pilot using one of six flight simulators. Various aircraft are employed to narrate the great battles: the Doolittle Raid on Japan, the Battle of Midway, Guadalcanal, and so on. The Stearman N2S-3 in which President George H. W. Bush soloed is in Hangar 79.

The latest add-on tour takes you up the 15-story-tall Ford Island Control Tower for a panoramic view and a WWII history lesson.

☎ *808/441–1000*
🌐 *www.pearlharboraviationmuseum.org*

# PLAN YOUR PEARL HARBOR DAY LIKE A MILITARY CAMPAIGN

## DIRECTIONS

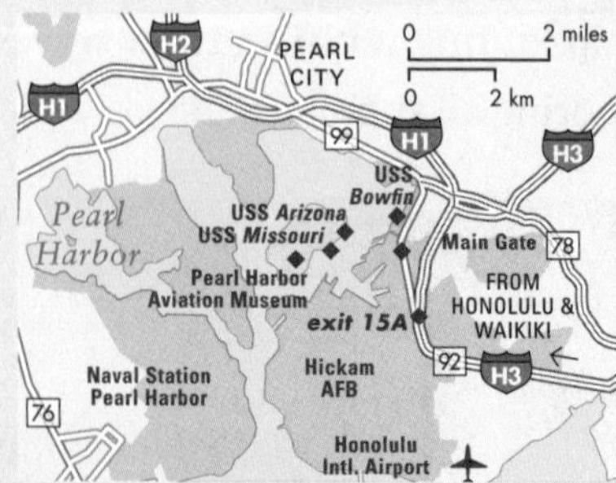


Take H–1 west from Waikiki to Exit 15A and follow signs. Or take TheBus route 20 or 47 from Waikiki. Beware high-priced private shuttles. It's a 30-minute drive from Waikiki. $7 parking fee.

### WHAT TO BRING

You must present a valid, government-issued, photo ID.

It's best to travel light. Only clear bags, wallets, and small clutches are allowed, so plan to carry cameras and stash cell phones and other items in pockets or to check bags at the visitor center ($7). Lines for this can be long, so allow plenty of time, particularly if you have timed-entry memorial tickets.

All you really need, though, are comfortable walking shoes, a light jacket, sunglasses, and sunscreen. One final note: Leave nothing in your car; theft is a problem despite security patrols.

### HOURS

Visitor center hours are 7 am to 5 pm daily. Most attractions don't open till 8 am, and some close at 3:30. Note, too, that last entry is often an hour before closing.

### TICKETS

***Arizona:*** Free. $10–$14 for museum audio tours; $1 per-person ticket reservation fee.

**Aviation:** $25.99 adults, $14.99 children; from $10.70 for flight simulator.

***Missouri:*** $34.99 adults, $17.49 children.

***Bowfin:*** $21.99 adults, $12.99 children. Children under 4 may go into the museum but not aboard the *Bowfin*.

**Passport to Pearl Harbor:** One-day access to all ships and exhibits; $89.99 adults (ages 13+), $44.99 children, $1 per-person reservation fee (buy at 🌐 *recreation.gov*).

### KIDS

This might be the day to enroll younger kids in the hotel children's program. Preschoolers chafe at long waits, and attractions involve some hazards for toddlers. Older kids enjoy the *Bowfin* and *Missouri*, especially.

### MAKING THE MOST OF YOUR TIME

You could see the highlights in half a day, but it would be rushed, so plan on a full day.

**Timed tickets for the USS *Arizona* Memorial can be reserved up to two months in advance.** Same-day, first-come, first-served tickets are no longer offered. The memorial is very popular, so do reserve as early as possible.

### SUGGESTED READING

*Pearl Harbor and the USS Arizona Memorial*, by Richard Wisniewski. 76-page magazine-size quick history.

*Bowfin*, by Edwin P. Hoyt. Dramatic story of undersea adventure.

*The Last Battleship*, by Scott C. S. Stone. Story of the Mighty Mo.

sites, including the USS *Missouri* and the aviation museum, requires a shuttle bus trip. ■ **TIP→ Advance reservations are required to access USS *Arizona* Memorial. There are no same-day tickets except rare standby spots.**

No bags of any kind except clear stadium ones—not even small purses—are allowed at any of the sights, though cameras, cell phones, and wallets can be hand-carried. A bag check is available. Children under four can visit the submarine museum, but for safety reasons, they are not allowed on the USS *Bowfin* itself. ✉ *Pearl Harbor Visitor Center, 1 Arizona Memorial Pl., Pearl Harbor* ☎ *808/422–3399 timed ticket reservations* 🌐 *www.nps.gov/perl* 🎫 *Visitor center and USS* Arizona *Memorial free (aside from $1 ticket reservation fee); fees for other sites; parking $7.*

**★ Pearl Harbor Visitor Center**

**VISITOR CENTER** | The gateway to the Pearl Harbor National Memorial and the starting point for visitors to this historic site has interpretive exhibits in two separate galleries (*Road to War* and *Attack*) that feature photographs and personal memorabilia from World War II veterans. There are also other exhibits, a bookstore, and a Remembrance Circle, where you can learn about the people who lost their lives on December 7, 1941. The visitor center is also where you start your tour of the USS *Arizona* Memorial if you have reserved in advance the requisite timed-entry ticket (🌐 *www.recreation.gov; $1 reservation fee*). ✉ *Pearl Harbor National Memorial, 1 Arizona Memorial Pl., Pearl Harbor* ☎ *808/422–3399* 🌐 *www.nps.gov/perl* 🎫 *Free (timed-entry ticket reservation fee $1).*

**★ USS *Arizona* Memorial**

**NATIONAL PARK | FAMILY** | Lined up tight in a row of seven battleships off Ford Island, the USS *Arizona* took a direct hit on December 7, 1941, exploded, and rests still on the shallow bottom where she settled. You must reserve tickets (🌐 *www.recreation.gov*) ahead of time to ensure access to the memorial; same-day tickets are no longer offered. As spaces are limited and tend to fill up, reserve as far ahead as possible; you can do so up to two months in advance. When your tour starts, you watch a short documentary film, then board the ferry to the memorial.

The swooping, stark-white structure, which straddles the wreck of the USS *Arizona,* was designed by Honolulu architect Alfred Preis to represent both the depths of the low-spirited, early days of the war and the uplift of victory. A somber, contemplative mood descends upon visitors during the ferry ride; this is a place where 1,177 people died. Gaze at the names of the dead carved into the wall of white marble. Look at oil on the water's surface, still slowly escaping from the sunken ship. Scatter flowers (but no lei—the string is bad for the fish). Salute the flag. Remember Pearl Harbor. ✉ *Pearl Harbor National Memorial, Pearl Harbor* ☎ *808/422–3399* 🌐 *nps.gov/perl* 🎫 *Free (advance reservation fee for timed-entry tickets $1); audio tours and other features cost extra.*

# Salt Lake

There's no longer a lake, salty or not, in this suburb of Honolulu. Instead you'll find a largely residential neighborhood with a commercial core at Salt Lake Shopping Center plus the oasis of Moanalua Gardens.

## Sights

**Moanalua Gardens**

**GARDEN** | This lovely and peaceful 24-acre park is a great place to spread out a blanket, have a picnic, take a snooze, fly a kite, or simply idle an afternoon away. Japanese visitors like taking pictures by

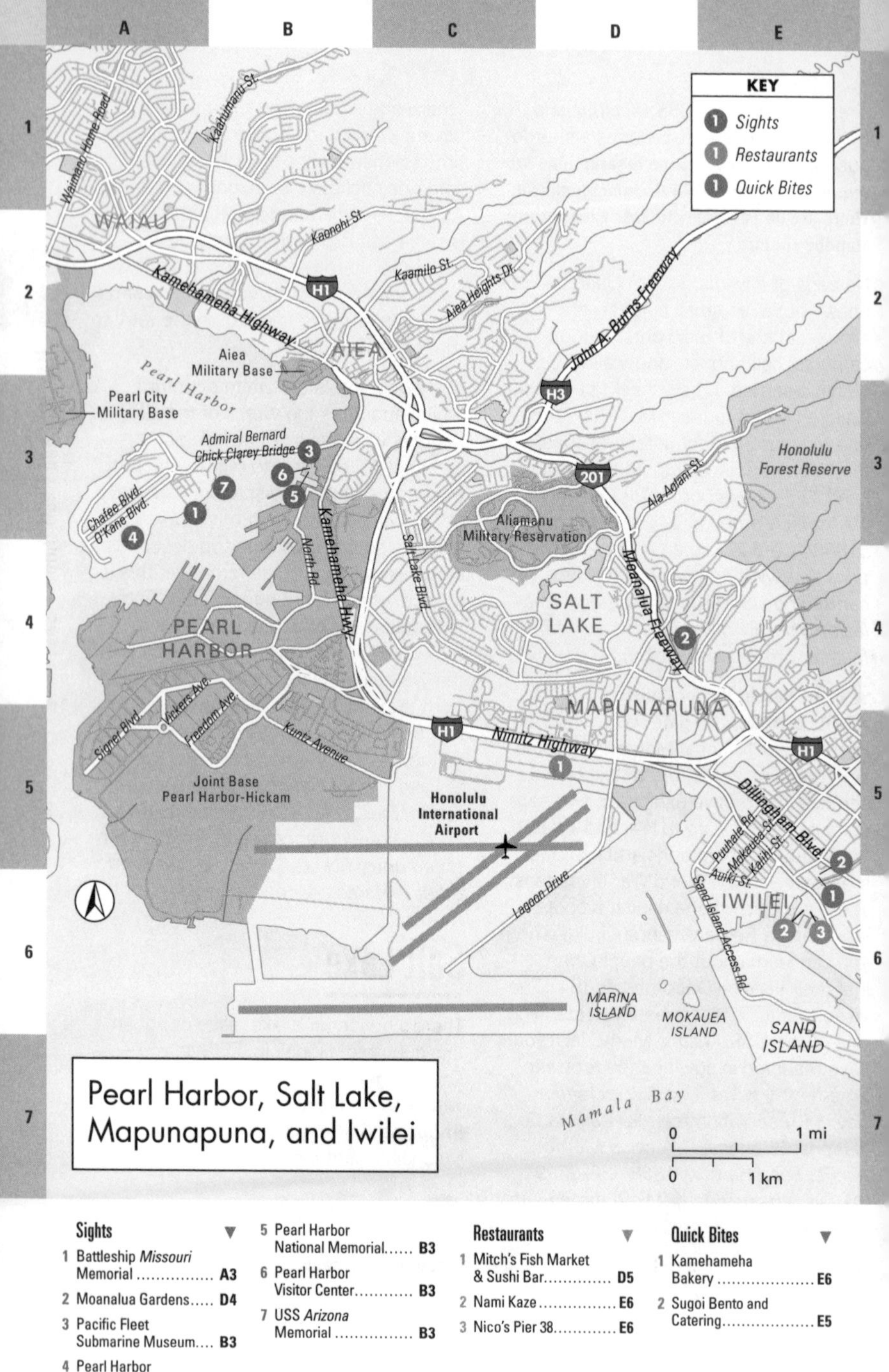


**Sights**

1 Battleship *Missouri* Memorial ........ **A3**
2 Moanalua Gardens ..... **D4**
3 Pacific Fleet Submarine Museum .... **B3**
4 Pearl Harbor Aviation Museum ....... **A3**
5 Pearl Harbor National Memorial ...... **B3**
6 Pearl Harbor Visitor Center ............ **B3**
7 USS *Arizona* Memorial ................ **B3**

**Restaurants**

1 Mitch's Fish Market & Sushi Bar .............. **D5**
2 Nami Kaze ................ **E6**
3 Nico's Pier 38 ............ **E6**

**Quick Bites**

1 Kamehameha Bakery .................... **E6**
2 Sugoi Bento and Catering .................... **E5**

a sprawling monkeypod tree nicknamed the Hitachi Tree; it's famous for advertising the Hitachi brand in Japan. There's a koi pond, a summer cottage once belonging to King Kamehameha V, a Chinese Hall, a taro patch, and a small gift shop. To reach Moanalua Gardens, take the Moanalua Freeway (78) westbound. Take the Tripler exit, then take a right on Jarrett White Road. Turn left at the first cross street onto Mahiole Street. The gardens are on the left, a serene pocket of green surrounded by busy roads. ✉ *2850 Moanalua Rd., Salt Lake* ☎ *808/834–8612* 🌐 *www.moanaluagardens.com* 🎫 *$10.*

# Mapunapuna

Mapunapuna is an area filled with factories and offices surrounding the airport. Tucked amid car dealerships, a Kaiser Permanente medical center, and warehouses are fast-food joints, a Chinese restaurant, local plate-lunch places, and Mitch's, a somewhat undiscovered gem of a sushi spot.

## Restaurants

**Mitch's Fish Market & Sushi Bar**
**$$$$** | **SUSHI** | Off the beaten path even for residents, this microscopic sushi bar is an adjunct of a wholesale seafood market and has a sort of cult following. The fish, air-freighted from around the world, is ultra-fresh, well-cut (into huge pieces—to the regret of those who follow the one-bite rule), and prepared for the serious sushi lover. **Known for:** hole-in-the-wall atmosphere; reservations are essential, and it's BYOB; otoro (fattiest part of tuna). $ *Average main: $60* ✉ *524 Ohohia St., Mapunapuna* ✣ *Near Daniel K. Inouye International Airport* ☎ *808/837–7774* 🌐 *mitchssushi.com.*

# Iwilei

Before the arrival of Captain Cook, Iwilei was a network of fishponds. After his arrival, it became home to a prison, railway depot, and houses of ill repute. (When the red-light district was shut down in 1916, one prostitute hopped a ship to Pago Pago. Also onboard was Somerset Maugham, who immortalized her as Sadie Thompson in his short story "Rain.")

Today, Iwilei is home to the busiest Costco in the world, some restaurants of note, and the Dole Cannery shopping complex, which was a pineapple cannery and now houses a multiplex.

## Restaurants

**★ Nami Kaze**
**$$** | **JAPANESE FUSION** | Chef Jason Peel's critically acclaimed Japanese fusion restaurant has an eclectic, creative, and often surprising mix of dishes from brunch through dinner, served in a bright, modern, high-ceilinged dining room or a smaller side dining space. Lots of local seafood, vegetables, and other island ingredients infuse the menu. Japanese breakfasts and omelets, plus twists on American brunch favorites, are served from morning to early afternoon. **Known for:** honey walnut shrimp; custard french toast; bustling restaurant. $ *Average main: $30* ✉ *1135 N. Nimitz Hwy., Iwilei* ☎ *808/888–6264* 🌐 *namikaze.com* ⏲ *Closed Mon. and Tues.*

**★ Nico's Pier 38**
**$$** | **SEAFOOD** | **FAMILY** | Lyonnais chef Nico Chaiz's harborside restaurant is steps from the Honolulu Fish Auction, which explains his "line-to-plate" concept—super-fresh fish dishes at a reasonable price. But he lets his French flag fly in dishes like steak *frites* and bouillabaisse, too. **Known for:** pan-seared ahi steak crusted in toasted seaweed and sesame

seeds; plate lunches and an excellent double cheeseburger; reservations aren't accepted. *Average main: $25* ✉ *1129 N. Nimitz Hwy., Pier 38, Iwilei* ☎ *808/540–1377* 🌐 *www.nicospier38.com.*

## Coffee and Quick Bites

**Kamehameha Bakery**

$ | **BAKERY** | **FAMILY** | This well-established bakery offers both old-school classics and newer treats, some of which have become cult favorites. You'll salivate as you stare at the cases filled with inexpensive pastries, doughnuts, cookies, and breads. **Known for:** variety of malasadas; Chantilly Roll (poi roll with sugar and frosting); opens early (before dawn) and sells out of many things by midmorning. *Average main: $1.50* ✉ *City Square Shopping Center, 1284 Kalani St., Unit D106, Iwilei* ☎ *808/845–5831* 🌐 *instagram.com/kamehamehabakeryhawaii.*

**Sugoi Bento and Catering**

$ | **MODERN HAWAIIAN** | Among the first of a new wave of plate-lunch places to take particular care with quality and nutrition, this breakfast-and-lunch spot in a strip mall offers brown rice and green salad as options instead of the usual white rice and mayo-loaded mac salad. Sweet-and-spicy garlic chicken and *mochiko* (rice-batter-dipped and fried) chicken, adapted from traditional Japanese dishes, are specialties that bring locals back again and again. **Known for:** cheerful service; grab-and-go for the beach; ample parking, no reservations. *Average main: $17* ✉ *City Square Shopping Center, 1286 Kalani St., Suite B-106, Iwilei* ☎ *808/841–7984* 🌐 *sugoihawaii.com* ⏲ *No dinner.*

## Performing Arts

**Ballet Hawaii**

**BALLET** | Established in 1976, Ballet Hawaii is a local company that's active throughout the year. Its annual, Hawaii-theme *The Nutcracker,* usually held at the Blaisdell Concert Hall (✉ *777 Ward Ave.*), is a local holiday tradition. Other shows take place at the Hawaii Theatre (✉ *1130 Bethel St.*) in Chinatown and elsewhere. ✉ *Dole Cannery Bldg., 735 Iwilei Rd., 2nd fl., Iwilei* ☎ *808/521–8600* 🌐 *ballethawaii.org.*

# Downtown

Throughout downtown, which is about 6 miles east of Daniel K. Inouye International Airport, the city's past and present are delightfully intertwined, as evidenced by the architecture. Postmodern glass-and-steel office buildings look down on the Aloha Tower, built in 1926 and, until the early 1960s, the tallest structure in Honolulu.

You'll also find history in the cut-stone, turn-of-the-20th-century storefronts on Merchant Street; the gracious, white-columned, American-Georgian manor that was the home of the Islands' last queen; the jewel-box palace occupied by the monarchy before it was overthrown; the Spanish-inspired stucco and tile-roofed Territorial Era government buildings; and the 21st-century glass pyramid of the First Hawaiian Bank Building.

### GETTING HERE AND AROUND

To reach downtown Honolulu from Waikiki by car, take Ala Moana Boulevard to Alakea Street, and turn right; three blocks up on the right, between South King and Hotel streets, there's a municipal parking lot in Alii Place. There are also public lots in buildings along Alakea, Smith, Beretania, and Bethel streets (Chinatown Gateway on Bethel Street is a good choice). The best parking downtown, however, is metered street parking along Punchbowl Street—when you can find it.

Another option is to take the highly popular and convenient TheBus to the Aloha Tower Marketplace. You can also take a trolley from Waikiki or use a ride-hailing service like Uber.

## Shangri La

The marriage of tobacco heiress Doris Duke (1912–93) to a much older man when she was 23 didn't last. But their around-the-world honeymoon did leave her with two lasting loves: Islamic art and architecture, which she first encountered on that journey; and Hawaii, where the honeymooners made an extended stay while Doris learned to surf and befriended Islanders unimpressed by her wealth.

Today, visitors to her beloved Oahu home—where she spent most winters—can share both loves by touring her estate. The sought-after tours are coordinated by and begin at the Honolulu Museum of Art in downtown Honolulu. A short van ride then takes small groups to the house itself, on the far side of Diamond Head.

⇨ *For more information, see the listing in the East (Windward) Oahu chapter.*

## Sights

**Hawaiian Mission Houses Historic Site and Archives**

**HISTORY MUSEUM** | Determined missionaries arrived in Hawaii in 1820, gaining royal favor and influencing much of Island life, and their descendants became leaders in government, business, and education. Here you can learn about their influence and walk through their original dwellings, including Hawaii's oldest Western-style wooden structure, a white-frame house that was prefabricated in New England and shipped around the Horn. A *hale pili* (traditional Hawaiian dwelling) sits nearby. **TIP→ Be sure to sign up in advance for one of the hourly guided tours: docents not only paint an excellent picture of what mission life was like, but they also take you to areas of the museum you wouldn't otherwise be able to see.** Special Hawaiian, architectural, and history tours are also offered on certain days, and you can take a self-guided tour of the cemetery across the street. Rotating displays showcase such arts as Hawaiian quilting, portraits, and even toys, and a rich archival library is also open to the public. ✉ *553 S. King St., Downtown* ☎ *808/447–3910* 🌐 *missionhouses.org* 🎫 *$10 general admission, $20 admission and guided tour* ⏲ *Closed Sun. and Mon.*

**Capitol Modern**

**ART MUSEUM** | Originally named the Hawaii State Art Museum, this fairly compact museum reopened after a renovation in late 2023 as Capitol Modern, a somewhat opaque name chosen to distinguish it as a contemporary art venue. The museum has four galleries that display art from the Hawaii-focused state art collection and the Hawaii State Foundation on Culture and the Arts. There's an outdoor sculpture garden and courtyard where events occur frequently, as well as The POD (Passion on Display), which presents artist-in-residence and temporary exhibitions. All galleries and programs at the museum are free; also check for free monthly events such as live entertainment.

Hawaii was the first state to legislate that a portion of the taxes paid on commercial building projects be set aside for the purchase of artwork. The state bought an ornate period-style building (at one time the Armed Services YMCA Building), and, in 2002, opened a 12,000-square-foot museum on the second floor dedicated to the art of Hawaii in all its ethnic diversity. ✉ *250 S. Hotel St., 2nd fl., Downtown* ☎ *808/586–0300* 🌐 *capitolmodern.org* 🎫 *Free* ⏲ *Closed Sun.*

**Hawaii State Capitol**

**GOVERNMENT BUILDING** | The capitol's architecture is richly symbolic: the columns resemble palm trees, the legislative chambers are shaped like volcanic cinder cones, and the central court is open to the sky, representing Hawaii's open society. Replicas of the Hawaii state seal, each weighing 7,500 pounds, hang above both its entrances. The building, which in 1969 replaced Iolani Palace as the seat of government, is surrounded by reflecting pools, just as the Islands are embraced by water. A pair of statues, often draped in lei, flank the building: one of the beloved Queen Liliuokalani and the other of the sainted Father Damien de Veuster, famous for helping Molokai's Hansen's disease (leprosy) patients. You can take a self-guided tour of the capitol using a brochure provided online or in person (room 415 at the capitol) by the governor's office. ✉ *415 S. Beretania St., Downtown* ☎ *808/586–0221* 🌐 *governor.hawaii.gov/contact-us/hawaii-state-capitol-tours* 🎟 *Free* ⏲ *Closed weekends.*

**Hawaii State Library**

**LIBRARY** | The Samuel Manaiakalani Kamakau Room, on the first floor in the library's *mauka* (Hawaiian for "mountain") courtyard, houses an extensive Hawaii and Pacific book collection and pays tribute to Kamakau, a missionary student whose 19th-century writings in English offer rare and vital insight into traditional Hawaiian culture.This beautifully renovated main library was built in 1913. ✉ *478 S. King St., Downtown* ☎ *808/586–3500* 🌐 *librarieshawaii.org* 🎟 *Free* ⏲ *Closed Sun.*

**Honolulu Hale**

**GOVERNMENT BUILDING** | This Mediterranean Renaissance–style building was constructed in 1929 and serves as the center of government for the City and County of Honolulu. Stroll through the shady, open-ceiling lobby with exhibits of works by local artists. During the winter holiday season, the Hale (Hawaiian for "house") becomes the focal point for the annual Honolulu City Lights, a display of lighting and playful holiday scenes spread around the campus, including the famous, gigantic Shaka Santa and Tute Mele. The mayor's office keeps a calendar of upcoming events. ✉ *530 S. King St., Downtown* ☎ *808/768–4385 for general city info* 🌐 *honolulu.gov/visitors* 🎟 *Free* ⏲ *Closed weekends.*

★ **Honolulu Museum of Art**

**ART MUSEUM** | The museum holds an impressive permanent collection that includes the third-largest assembly of Hiroshige's ukiyo-e Japanese prints in the country (donated by author James Michener); Italian Renaissance paintings; American and European art by Monet, Van Gogh, and Whistler, among many others; and a newer gallery of Hawaiian art. Originally built around the collection of a Honolulu matron who donated much of her estate to the museum, it is housed in a maze of courtyards, cloistered walkways, and quiet, low-ceiling spaces. The newer Luce Pavilion complex, nicely incorporated into the more traditional architecture of the museum, has a traveling-exhibit gallery, an excellent café, and a gift shop. The Doris Duke Theatre screens art films. This is also the jumping-off point for tours of Doris Duke's striking estate, which is now the Shangri La Museum of Islamic Art, Culture, and Design. ■ **TIP→ If you wish to visit Shangri La, you should reserve tickets well in advance.** ✉ *900 S. Beretania St., Downtown* ☎ *808/532–8700* 🌐 *honolulumuseum.org* 🎟 *$20* ⏲ *Closed Mon.–Wed.*

★ **Iolani Palace**

**CASTLE/PALACE** | America's only official royal residence, on the site of an earlier palace, was completed in 1882 and contains the thrones of King Kalakaua and his successor (and sister) Queen Liliuokalani. Bucking the stereotype of simple island life, the palace had electric lights even before the White House. Downstairs galleries showcase the royal

Take a guided tour of Iolani Palace, America's only royal residence, built in 1882.

jewelry, as well as a kitchen and offices that have been restored to the glory of the monarchy era. The palace gift shop and ticket office are in what was formerly the Iolani Barracks, built to house the Royal Guard. The palace has self-guided audio tours, docent-led tours, and specialty tours. ■ **TIP→ It's best to make reservations for guided tours a few days in advance.** ✉ *364 S. King St., Downtown* ☎ *808/522–0832* 🌐 *www.iolanipalace.org* 🎟 *$33 guided tour, $27 audio tour* ⏲ *Closed Sun. and Mon. (except for monthly Kamaaina Sun.).*

**Kamehameha I Statue**

**PUBLIC ART** | Honoring the Big Island chieftain who united all the warring Hawaiian Islands into one kingdom in the early 19th century, this statue, which stands with one arm outstretched in welcome, is one of two cast in Paris by American sculptor T. R. Gould. The original statue, lost at sea and replaced by this one, was eventually salvaged and is now in Kapaau, on the Big Island, near the king's birthplace. Each year on the king's birthday (June 11), the more famous copy is draped in fresh lei that reach lengths of 18 feet and longer. A parade proceeds past the statue, and Hawaiian civic clubs, women in hats and impressive long *holoku* dresses, and men in sashes and cummerbunds honor the leader, whose name means "The One Set Apart." ✉ *417 S. King St., outside Aliiolani Hale, Downtown* 🌐 *www.gohawaii.com/islands/oahu.*

**Kawaiahao Church**

**CHURCH** | Called Hawaii's Westminster Abbey, this historic house of worship was completed in 1842 and witnessed the coronations, weddings, and funerals of generations of Hawaiian royalty. Each of the building's 14,000 coral blocks was quarried from reefs offshore at depths of more than 20 feet and transported to this site. Interior woodwork was created from the forests of the Koolau Mountains, and the upper gallery displays paintings of the royal families. The graves of missionaries and of King Lunalilo are adjacent. Services in English, with songs and prayers in

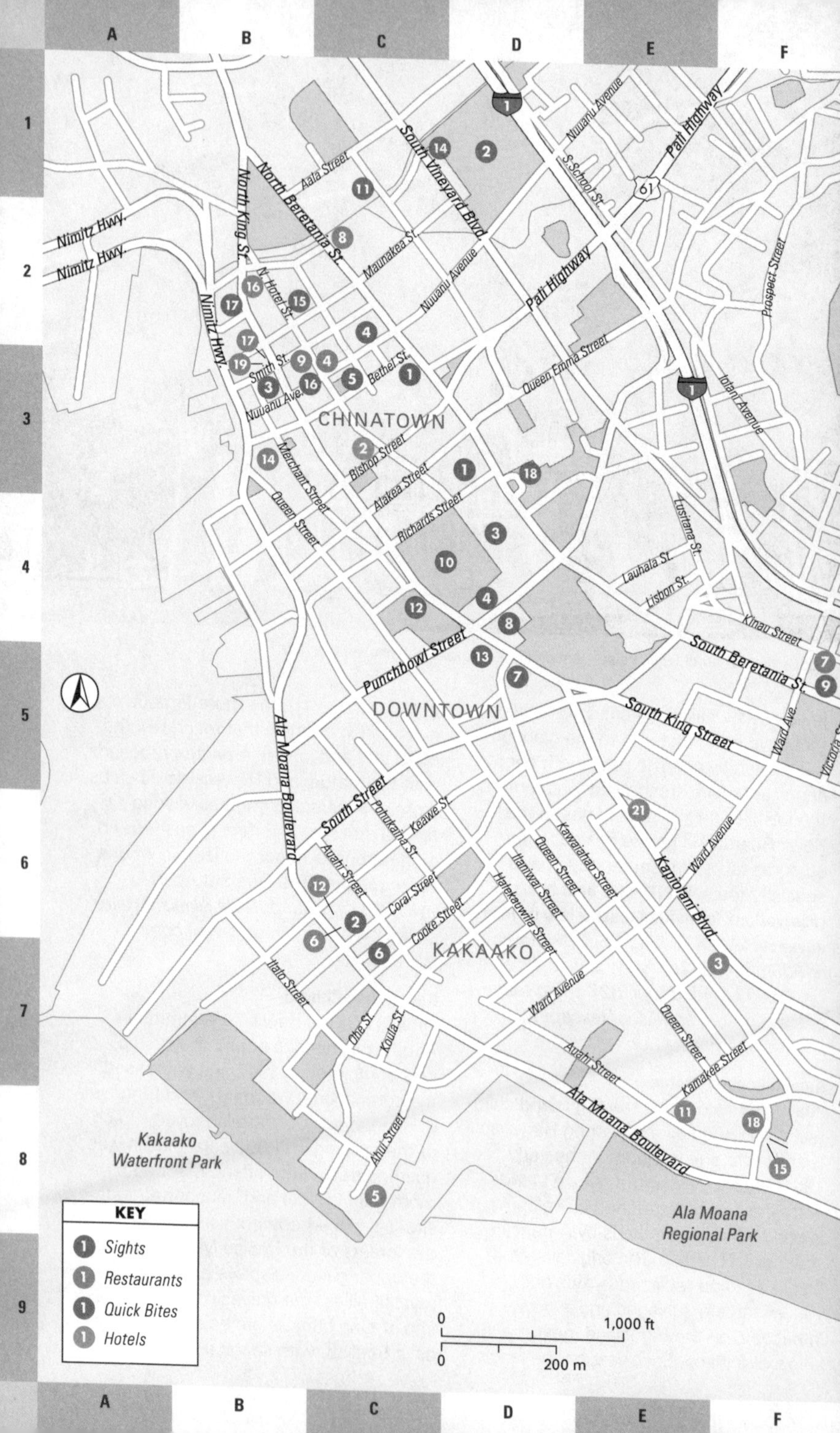

A
B
C
D
E
F
1
2
3
4
5
6
7
8
9
Nimitz Hwy.
Nimitz Hwy.
Nimitz Hwy.
North King St.
North Beretania St.
Aala Street
South Vineyard Blvd.
Maunakea St.
Nuuanu Avenue
Nuuanu Avenue
S. School St.
Pali Highway
Pali Highway
N. Hotel St.
Smith St.
Nuuanu Ave.
Bethel St.
Queen Emma Street
Prospect Street
Iolani Avenue
CHINATOWN
Bishop Street
Merchant Street
Queen Street
Atakea Street
Richards Street
Lusitana St.
Lauhala St.
Lisbon St.
Kinau Street
South Beretania St.
Punchbowl Street
DOWNTOWN
South King Street
Ward Ave.
Victoria St.
Ala Moana Boulevard
South Street
Pohukaina St.
Keawe St.
Auahi Street
Coral Street
Cooke Street
Halekauwila Street
Ilaniwai Street
Queen Street
Kawaiahao Street
Kapiolani Blvd.
Ward Avenue
KAKAAKO
Ilalo Street
Ohe St.
Koula St.
Ward Avenue
Auahi Street
Queen Street
Kamakee Street
Ala Moana Boulevard
Ahui Street
Kakaako Waterfront Park
Ala Moana Regional Park
KEY
Sights
Restaurants
Quick Bites
Hotels
0
1,000 ft
0
200 m

### Sights

1 Capitol Modern ......... **D3**
2 Foster Botanical Garden .................. **D1**
3 Hawaii State Capitol.... **D4**
4 Hawaii State Library.... **D4**
5 Hawaii Theatre........... **C3**
6 Hawaii Walls - World Wide Walls ....... **C7**
7 Hawaiian Mission Houses Historic Site and Archives ............ **D5**
8 Honolulu Hale ........... **D4**
9 Honolulu Museum of Art ...................... **F5**
10 Iolani Palace ............ **D4**
11 Izumo Taishakyo Mission of Hawaii ....... **C1**
12 Kamehameha I Statue ..................... **C4**
13 Kawaiahao Church..... **D5**
14 Kuan Yin Temple ......... **C1**
15 Maunakea Marketplace............. **B2**
16 Nuuanu Avenue......... **B3**
17 Oahu Market ............ **B2**
18 Washington Place...... **D3**

### Restaurants

1 Akasaka.................... **I8**
2 Bac Nam................. **G6**
3 Chef Chai ................. **F7**
4 Fête.......................... **C3**
5 53 By The Sea............ **C8**
6 Highway Inn Kakaako... **C6**
7 Honolulu Museum of Art Café ................ **F4**
8 Legend Seafood Restaurant................ **C2**
9 Livestock Tavern........ **B3**
10 Mariposa ................ **H8**
11 Merriman's Honolulu.... **E8**
12 Moku Kitchen ............ **C6**
13 MW Restaurant........... **I8**
14 PAI Honolulu ............ **B3**
15 Panya ...................... **F8**
16 Pho To Chau Restaurant............... **B2**
17 The Pig and the Lady... **B2**
18 Scratch Kitchen.......... **F8**
19 Senia ...................... **B3**
20 Sorabol Korean Restaurant................. **I7**
21 Yanagi Sushi.............. **E6**

### Quick Bites

1 Alii Coffee Co............. **C3**
2 Hank's Haute Dogs ...... **C6**
3 Local Joe ................ **B3**
4 Mei Sum Dim Sum .................. **C2**

### Hotels

1 Ala Moana Hotel by Mantra........... **I8**
2 Aston at the Executive Centre Hotel.............. **C3**

Hawaiian, are held each Sunday (Kawaiahao's affiliation is United Church of Christ). You can follow a free audio tour of the church and grounds or just look around by yourself. ✉ *957 Punchbowl St., at King St., Downtown* ☎ *808/469–3000* 🌐 *kawaiahaochurch.com* 🎫 *Free.*

**Washington Place**

**HISTORIC HOME** | This white-column mansion was built by sea captain John Dominis, whose son married Liliuokalani, the woman who became the Islands' last queen. Deposed by American-backed forces, the queen returned to the home—which is in sight of the royal palace—and lived there until her death. From 1922 to 2002, it was home to Hawaii's sitting governors. The nonprofit Washington Place Foundation now operates the gracious estate, which is open for only one public tour each Thursday. ✉ *320 S. Beretania St., Downtown* ☎ *808/586–0248* 🌐 *washingtonplace.hawaii.gov* 🎫 *Donations accepted* ⏲ *Closed Fri.–Wed.*

## Restaurants

**Honolulu Museum of Art Café**

**$$ | AMERICAN** | The Honolulu Museum of Art's cool courtyards and galleries filled with works by masters from Monet to Hokusai are well worth a visit, and, afterward, so is this popular lunch restaurant (reservations recommended). The open-air café is flanked by a burbling water feature and 8-foot-tall ceramic "dumplings" by artist Jun Kaneko—a tranquil setting in which to eat your salad or sandwich, shaded by a monkeypod tree. **Known for:** piadina pesto-caprese flatbread sandwich; limited but beautifully prepared menu of soups, salads, sandwiches, and mains; nice spot for Sunday brunch. 💲 *Average main: $20* ✉ *Honolulu Museum of Art, 900 S. Beretania St., Downtown* ☎ *808/532–8734* 🌐 *honolulumuseum.org/cafe* ⏲ *Closed Mon. and Tues. No dinner Sun., Wed., and Thurs.*

**PAI Honolulu**

**$$$$ | MODERN AMERICAN** | Michelin star–restaurant chef Kevin Lee and his general manager wife, Justine, are at the helm of the innovative, upscale Pai (short for *hoopai,* meaning "to encourage" in Hawaiian). The tantalizing and surprising fusion cuisine is served in a modern, arched dining room and patio tucked into the atrium of the Harbor Court condo building. **Known for:** attention to detail in everything served, including the homemade breads; superb cocktails and wine pairings; tasting menu and prix fixe menus. 💲 *Average main: $95* ✉ *Harbor Court, 55 Merchant St., Suite 110, Downtown* ☎ *808/744–2531* 🌐 *www.paihonolulu.com* ⏲ *Closed Sun.–Wed. No lunch.*

**Yanagi Sushi**

**$$ | JAPANESE** | Serving a complete menu until 1 am, this restaurant decorated with photos of food and people who have stopped by offers not only delicious sushi and sashimi around a small bar, but also *teishoku* (combination menus), tempura, stews, and cook-it-yourself shabu-shabu at tables. The fish can be depended on for freshness and variety. **Known for:** late-night happy hour; baked crabmeat volcano roll, spicy shrimp tempura roll, live abalone sashimi; local favorite. 💲 *Average main: $30* ✉ *762 Kapiolani Blvd., Downtown* ☎ *808/597–1525* 🌐 *www.yanagisushi-hawaii.com* ⏲ *Closed Sun.*

## Hotels

**Aston at the Executive Centre Hotel**

**$$ | HOTEL** | One of only two hotels in downtown Honolulu, this all-suites high-rise is in the center of the business district, within walking distance of the historic Capitol District, museums, and Honolulu's Chinatown, and a 10-minute drive from Daniel K. Inouye International Airport. **Pros:** friendly staff; close to many attractions; good spot for overnighting before or after a cruise. **Cons:** no beach within walking distance; suites are individually owned, so quality of room can vary; parking is very expensive. *Rooms from: $260* *1088 Bishop St., Downtown* *808/539–3000, 855/945–4090 toll-free reservations* *www.aquaaston.com/hotels/aston-at-the-executive-centre-hotel* *90 suites* *No Meals.*

## Nightlife

### BARS

**★ Bar Leather Apron**

**COCKTAIL BARS** | Winner of a James Beard Award for Outstanding Bar in 2023, this cocktail bar is oddly situated in the mezzanine of an office building and seats only six at the bar, along with a few other tables. You'll need some luck to snag reservations (or close watching of the Resy app) to enjoy bespoke cocktails that utilize only the finest liquors and ingredients. Owners Tom Park and Justin Park (no relation) have cultivated a reputation for their E Hoo Pau Mai Tai made with an eight-year-old, raisin-infused El Dorado rum and another 12-year-old El Dorado rum, as well as coconut water syrup, spiced orgeat, ohia blossom honey, lime, vanilla, and absinthe—all served with a kiawe wood–smoke presentation. *Topa Financial Center, 745 Fort St., Mezzanine Level, Suite 127A, Downtown* *808/524–0808* *www.barleather-apron.com.*

**Murphy's Bar & Grill**

**PUB** | On the edge of Chinatown and the financial district, this bar has served drinks to such locals and visitors as King Kalakaua and Robert Louis Stevenson since the late 1800s. The kind of Irish pub you would find in Boston, Murphy's offers a break from all the tropical, fruit-garnished drinks found in Waikiki, and it's definitely the place to be on St. Patrick's Day. Friendly bartenders and waitstaff serve Guinness on tap, pub food favorites, and Irish specialties like corned beef and cabbage and shepherd's pie. If you time it right, you can try their incredible house-made pies, which are served only on Friday and quickly sell out. *2 Merchant St., Downtown* *808/531–0422* *www.murphyshawaii.com* *Closed weekends.*

### DINNER CRUISES AND SHOWS

Most dinner cruises depart either from the piers adjacent to the Aloha Tower Marketplace in downtown Honolulu or from Kewalo Basin Harbor, near Ala Moana Beach Park, and head along the coast toward Diamond Head. There's usually a buffet-style dinner with local flavor, dancing, drinks, a sensational sunset, and even potential whale spotting between December and April. Some cruises offer discounts for online reservations. Most major credit cards are accepted. In all cases, reservations are essential.

**Atlantis Cruises**

**THEMED ENTERTAINMENT** | The sleekly high-tech *Majestic,* designed to sail smoothly in rough waters, powers farther along Waikiki's coastline than its competitors. Enjoy seasonal whale-watching trips between January and March during the day or year-round sunset cocktail and dinner cruises aboard the 400-passenger boat. (Atlantis is also known for its submarine tours off Waikiki.) The boat's dining room is elegantly laid out, and the standard Hawaiian buffet fare perfectly accompanies the tropical cocktails, sparkling wine, beer, or guava juice. Most passengers are honeymooners and those celebrating anniversaries and birthdays—or even the occasional proposal—and this, plus the Hawaiian music, makes the atmosphere festive. For the best view of Waikiki and the sunset, head to the top deck. *1 Aloha Tower Rd., Pier 6, Downtown* *808/973–9800, 800/381–0237 toll-free* *majestichawaii.com.*

**Star of Honolulu Cruises**

**THEMED ENTERTAINMENT** | The celebrated 1,500-passenger *Star of Honolulu* offers four sunset dinner-cruise packages, from a roast beef buffet and Polynesian show to a romantic, seven-course, fine-dining excursion with live music. The company also runs whale-watching and special holiday cruises. ✉ *Aloha Tower Marketplace, 1 Aloha Tower Dr., Pier 8, Downtown* ☎ *808/983–7730* 🌐 *starofhonolulu.com.*

### MUSIC

**Chamber Music Hawaii**

**MUSIC** | Consisting of four ensembles, this group has been around for decades and performs at the Honolulu Museum of Art's Doris Duke Theatre (✉ *901 S. Beretania St., Honolulu*), the Paliku Theatre at Windward Community College (✉ *45-720 Keaahala Rd., Kaneohe*), the University of Hawaii's West Oahu Library (✉ *1001 Farrington Hwy., Kapolei*), and other locations around Oahu. The season runs from fall through spring. ✉ *Downtown* ☎ *808/722–0172* 🌐 *chambermusichawaii.org* 🎟 *From $35.*

**Hawaii Opera Theatre**

**OPERA** | Locals refer to it as "HOT," probably because the Hawaii Opera Theatre has been turning the opera-challenged into opera lovers since 1961. All operas are sung in their original language, with a projected English translation. ✉ *Neal S. Blaisdell Center Concert Hall, 777 Ward Ave., Downtown* ☎ *808/596–7372 main office* 🌐 *hawaiiopera.org* 🎟 *From $20 or $30.*

### THEATER

**★ Honolulu Theatre for Youth**

**THEATER | FAMILY** | The only professional theater troupe in the state, this group stages delightful productions, with creative props and engaging stories, August through May. Local stories and themes are the focus, making for unique shows for visiting kids. Founded in 1955, it's one of the oldest children's theaters in the country, offering drama-education programs and school and family performances. ✉ *Tenney Theatre, 229 Queen Emma Sq., Downtown* ☎ *808/839–9885* 🌐 *www.htyweb.org* 🎟 *From $15.*

**Kumu Kahua Theatre**

**THEATER** | Focusing on plays written by local playwrights about Island life and Hawaiian experiences, this troupe stages five or six productions a year in an intimate, 100-seat auditorium. ✉ *46 Merchant St., Downtown* ☎ *808/536–4441* 🌐 *www.kumukahua.org* 🎟 *$25.*

## Shopping

The downtown shopping scene, like that in neighboring Chinatown, is ever changing. Focus on the small galleries—which have helped foster the area's arts and culture renaissance—and the burgeoning array of hip, home-decor stores tucked between restaurants serving food from around the world.

# Chinatown

Chinatown's original business district was made up of dry-goods and produce merchants, tailors and dressmakers, barbers and herbalists. The meat, fish, and produce stalls remain, but the mix is heavier now on gift and curio stores, lei stands, jewelry shops, and bakeries, with a smattering of noodle makers and travel agents and dozens of restaurants.

The name "Chinatown" here has always been a misnomer. Though three-quarters of Oahu's Chinese lived closely packed in these 25 acres in the late 1800s, even then the neighborhood was half Japanese. Today you hear Vietnamese and Tagalog as often as Mandarin and Cantonese, and there are voices of Japan, Singapore, Malaysia, Korea, Thailand, Samoa, and the Marshall Islands, as well.

Perhaps a more accurate name is the one used by early Chinese: *Wah Fau* (Chinese port), signifying a landing and jumping-off place. As soon as they finished their plantation contracts, Chinese laborers hurried into the city to start businesses here. It's a launching point for today's immigrants too: Southeast Asian shops almost outnumber Chinese establishments; stalls carry Filipino specialties like winged beans and goat meat; and you'll find Japanese, Cambodian, Laotian, Thai, and Korean cuisine and goods for sale.

In the half century after the first Chinese laborers arrived in Hawaii in 1852, Chinatown was a link to home for the all-male cadre of workers who planned to return to China rich and respected. Merchants did more than sell supplies: they held mail, loaned money, wrote letters, translated documents, sent remittances to families, served meals, offered rough bunkhouse accommodations, and were the center for news, gossip, and socializing.

Although much happened to Chinatown in the 20th century—beginning in January 1900, when almost the entire neighborhood was burned to the ground to halt the spread of bubonic plague—it remains a bustling, crowded, noisy, and sometimes odiferous place. The COVID-19 pandemic hit Chinatown and downtown Honolulu particularly hard. With locals working remotely, the area became a bit of a ghost town and still has not fully rebounded. More issues of homelessness and crime arose, and office vacancies remain above pre-pandemic levels. But Chinatown's status as a National Historic District and efforts at making improvements have been making a gradual impact, mostly for the good.

Those on a mission to keep Chinatown's revival moving along have big plans for the area: hotels in new and converted historic buildings and new eateries, retailers, and bars to replace those that didn't make it through the pandemic's economic downtown. Go with an open mind to discover the many hidden gems in the area.

## Buying Flowers and Fruit

You can bring home fresh pineapple, papaya, or coconut to share with friends and family. Orchids will also brighten your home and remind you of your trip to the Islands. By law, all fresh fruit and plant products must be inspected by the Department of Agriculture before export. Ask at the shop about agricultural rules so a surprise confiscation doesn't spoil your departure. Shipping to your home usually is best.



### GETTING HERE AND AROUND

Chinatown occupies 15 blocks immediately north of downtown Honolulu—it's flat, compact, and very walkable. Street parking can be hard to find depending on the time and day of the week. There are many paid municipal and private parking lots with varying rates.

**TIP→ Bring cash to use at the international markets, eateries, stores, and vendor stalls that don't accept credit cards or have a minimum spending amount to use one.**

## Sights

**Foster Botanical Garden**

**GARDEN** | Some of the trees in this 14-acre botanical garden, which opened in 1931, date from 1853, when Queen Kalama allowed a young German doctor to lease a portion of her land. More than 170 years later, you can see these trees and many others along with bromeliads, orchids, and other tropical plants, some of which are rare or endangered. Look out in particular for the cannonball tree and the redwood-size quipo tree. ✉ *180 N. Vineyard Blvd., Chinatown* ☎ *808/768–7135* 🌐 *www.honolulu.gov/parks/hbg/honolulu-botanical-gardens* 🎫 *$5.*

**Hawaii Theatre**

**PERFORMANCE VENUE** | Opened in 1922, this theater earned rave reviews for its neoclassical design, with Corinthian columns, marble statues, and plush carpeting and drapery. The so-called Pride of the Pacific was rescued from demolition in the early 1980s, underwent a massive renovation, and is now listed on both the State and National Registers of Historic Places. The 1,400-seat venue hosts concerts, theatrical productions, dance performances, and film screenings. Guided tours of the theater end with a miniconcert on the historical orchestral pipe organ and can be booked through the box office. If you're interested in the guided tours on Thursdays at 11 am, call a few days ahead to reserve. ⊠ *1130 Bethel St., Chinatown* ☎ *808/528–0506* ⊕ *www.hawaiitheatre.com* 🎟 *$25 for tour.*

**Izumo Taishakyo Mission of Hawaii**

**SHRINE** | From Chinatown Cultural Plaza, cross a stone bridge to the Izumo Taishakyo Mission of Hawaii to visit the shrine established in 1906. It honors Okuninushi-no-Mikoto, a *kami* (god) who is believed in Shinto tradition to bring good fortune if properly courted (and thanked afterward). ⊠ *215 N. Kukui St., Chinatown* ✣ *At the canal* ☎ *808/538–7778* ⊕ *izumotaishahawaii.com.*

**Kuan Yin Temple**

**TEMPLE** | A couple of blocks *mauka* (toward the mountains) from Chinatown is the oldest Buddhist temple in the Islands. Mistakenly called a goddess by some, Kuan Yin, also known as Kannon, is a bodhisattva—one who chose to remain on Earth doing good even after achieving enlightenment. Transformed from a male into a female figure centuries ago, she is credited with being particularly sympathetic to women. You will see representations of her all over the Islands: holding a lotus flower (beauty from the mud of human frailty), as at the temple; pouring out a pitcher of oil (like mercy flowing); or as a sort of Madonna with a child. Visitors are permitted but should be mindful that this is a practicing place of worship. ⊠ *170 N. Vineyard Blvd., Chinatown* ✣ *Park at Foster Botanical Garden* ☎ *808/533–6361.*

**Maunakea Marketplace**

**MARKET** | **FAMILY** | On the corner of Maunakea and Hotel streets is this busy plaza surrounded by shops and an air-conditioned indoor market and food court where you can buy fresh seafood and seasonal local produce or chow down on banana *lumpia* (spring rolls) and fruit smoothies or bubble tea (juices and flavored teas with tapioca balls inside). It gets packed during Chinese Lunar New Year. ⊠ *1120 Maunakea St., Chinatown* ⊕ *geyserholdings.com/maunakea.*

**Nuuanu Avenue**

**STREET** | **FAMILY** | Both Chinatown's main *mauka–makai* drag and Bethel Street, which runs parallel, are lined with art galleries, restaurants, tattoo parlors, bars and pubs, an antiques auctioneer, dress shops, one small theater/exhibition space (The ARTS at Marks Garage), and one historic stage (the Hawaii Theatre). You can also take in the unique early 1900s architecture of the buildings. ⊠ *Nuuanu Ave., Chinatown.*

**Oahu Market**

**MARKET** | **FAMILY** | In this tenant-owned market founded in 1904, you'll find a taste of old-style Chinatown, where you might spot a whole butchered pig, head intact, on display, and where glassy-eyed fish of every size and hue lie forlornly on ice. Magenta dragonfruit, ready-to-eat *char siu* (Cantonese barbecued pork) and pork belly, and bins brimming with produce add to the color. You'll find some of the cheapest Oahu prices on fruits and vegetables in this and other Chinatown markets. ⊠ *145 N. King St., Chinatown* ✣ *At Kekaulike St.*

## Restaurants

**Fête**

$$ | **AMERICAN** | At lunch, regulars pack into this tiny, brick-walled space for the burgers and specials; at dinner, they come for the pasta and locally sourced seafood dishes or the to-die-for twice-fried Kauai chicken with grits and collard greens. Here, you'll probably get cozy with the table next to you as waitstaffers glide between tables with full trays and great attitudes. **Known for:** Brooklyn-meets-Hawaii menu; great pau hana (happy hour) menu; craft cocktails and extensive drink menu. *Average main: $25 ✉ 2 N. Hotel St., Chinatown ☎ 808/369–1390 🌐 fetehawaii.com ⏲ Closed Sun.*

**Legend Seafood Restaurant**

$ | **CHINESE** | At this large Chinatown institution, the dim sum cart ladies stop at your table and show you their Hong Kong–style fare. If you come for breakfast dim sum, arrive before 9 am, especially on weekends, if you want to hear yourself think. **Known for:** still-warm custard tarts; dim sum, reasonably priced by the dish; easy parking in the cultural plaza parking lot. *Average main: $16 ✉ Chinese Cultural Plaza, 100 N. Beretania St., Suite 108, Chinatown ✥ In the Chinatown Cultural Plaza ☎ 808/532–1868 🌐 www.legendseafoodhonolulu.com.*

**Livestock Tavern**

$$$ | **MODERN AMERICAN** | Livestock Tavern scores big with its seasonal offerings of updated comfort foods and craft cocktails and its cowboy-minimalist decor. Although meat, including some of the best burgers in town, commands the menu, offerings like *burrata*, creative salads, sandwiches, and fish round out the possibilities. **Known for:** lively bar scene; good weekend brunch; fresh-cut fries. *Average main: $40 ✉ 49 N. Hotel St., Chinatown ☎ 808/537–2577 🌐 livestocktavern.com ⏲ No lunch weekdays.*

**Pho To Chau Restaurant**

$ | **VIETNAMESE** | This hole-in-the-wall storefront was the go-to spot for pho with all the trimmings long before hipsters and foodies found Chinatown. Many Vietnamese restaurants have since opened, and some have surpassed To Chau's quality—it's all in the broth—but eating habits die hard in this city. **Known for:** no-frills service and sometimes a wait for food once seated; old-school, 1970s decor, and no credit cards or reservations; large pho can be easily shared. *Average main: $10 ✉ 1007 River St., Chinatown ☎ 808/533–4549 ▭ No credit cards ⏲ No dinner.*

**★ The Pig and the Lady**

$$ | **ASIAN** | Chef Andrew Le's casual noodle house attracts downtown office workers by day and becomes a creative contemporary restaurant at night, pulling in serious chowhounds. Drawing on both his Vietnamese heritage and multicultural island flavors, the talented, playful Le is a wizard with spice and acid, turning out dishes of layered flavor. **Known for:** banh mi sandwiches at lunch and pho all day; house-made soft-serve custards and sorbets, including unexpected flavors; Hanoi-style egg coffee. *Average main: $30 ✉ 83 N. King St., Chinatown ☎ 808/585–8255 🌐 thepigandthelady.com ⏲ Closed Sun. and Mon.*

**★ Senia**

$$$ | **MODERN AMERICAN** | Every item on the modern American menu at this small, sophisticated, James Beard Award–nominated restaurant is carefully concocted and artfully plated. You can order à la carte or indulge in the pricey tasting menu at the Chef's Counter. **Known for:** ahi cigar rolls; sophisticated cocktails and an encyclopedic wine menu; creative presentation. *Average main: $34 ✉ 75 N. King St., Chinatown ✥ Between The Pig and the Lady and Smith & Kings ☎ 808/200–5412 🌐 restaurantsenia.com ⏲ Closed Sun. and Mon. No lunch.*

## Coffee and Quick Bites

**Alii Coffee Co.**

$ | **CAFÉ** | The specialties at this coffee spot are cold brew drinks and "Coff-tails," cold brew shaken with a mixture of milks, creams, and flavors. It's not just the drinks made with coffee roasted in-house that are yummy here: the café serves pastries and cold breakfast items like the Lomi Salmon Bagel, and toasted sandwiches, flatbreads, and salads. **Known for:** delicious Alii Veggie sandwich; ube (from a purple yam) latte; limited space, so good for grab and go. *Average main: $16 35 S. Beretania St., Chinatown 808/532–7928 aliicoffee.com No dinner.*

**Local Joe**

$ | **CAFÉ** | This is a great spot to stop for coffee and a light bite, including some breakfast items, salads, and sandwiches, before or after your explorations in Chinatown, downtown, and historic Honolulu. The coffee shop roasts its own beans and has a latte art "printer" that leaves detailed designs on your drink. **Known for:** delicious coffee; nice presentations; convenient location for sightseers. *Average main: $10 45 N. King St., Suite 110, Chinatown 808/536–7700 www.localjoehi.com Closed Sun. No dinner.*

**Mei Sum Dim Sum**

$ | **CHINESE** | In contrast to the sprawling, noisy halls where dim sum is generally served, Mei Sum is compact, shiny, and bright—it's also favored by locals who work in the area. Be ready to guess and point at the color photos of dim sum favorites or the items on the carts as they come by, or ask fellow diners for suggestions. **Known for:** deep-fried garlic eggplant; house special garlic rice; dim sum made fresh daily and served even in the morning. *Average main: $15 1170 Nuuanu Ave., Suite 102, Chinatown Next to post office 808/531–3268 Closed Wed.*

## Nightlife

### BARS

**EP Bar**

**COCKTAIL BARS** | Inspired by listening bars in Tokyo, this dimly lit, hip little spot serves some equally trendy cocktails. Sip a highball or house cocktail while a DJ spins vinyl nearby (no requests, please). Conversation is not banned, but a mellow mix of chatter and soaking up the sounds goes down best. Close to Hawaii Theatre, the bar is also a great place for a drink before or after a performance or show. Reservations are a good idea. *1150 Nuuanu Ave., Unit A, Chinatown 808/753–9720 epbar.co.*

**J. Dolan's**

**BARS** | The drinks and rotating beers on tap at this Irish, *Cheers*-like bar are reasonably priced by Honolulu standards, and its menu of New York–style pizzas, both classic and inventive, is a crowd-pleaser, too. *1147 Bethel St., Chinatown 808/537–4992 jdolans.com.*

**The Lei Stand**

**COCKTAIL BARS** | Come here to feel Hawaii hip. Named after the iconic lei sellers in Chinatown, this bar is part speakeasy, with a sign out front and an entryway that allude to those lei shops. You can buy lei here, and the bright white inner courtyard has two lei walls to enhance that vibe. The rest of the space, though, is a purple-hued, neon-tropical lounge that slays. On the menu are upscale cocktails and small plates, and there's plenty of great people-watching. *1115 Bethel St., Chinatown 808/773–7022 getleid.co.*

**The Manifest**

**COCKTAIL BARS** | With exposed red brick, big skylights, and rotating exhibitions of work by local photographers and painters, The Manifest has the vibe of an artist's loft. It's a café by day and a cocktail bar and night club by night, so it serves a good cup of joe as well as quality cocktails. ✉ *32 N. Hotel St., Chinatown* ☎ 🌐 *www.manifesthawaii.com* 🕑 *Closed Sun.*

**The Tchin Tchin! Bar**
**BARS** | This chill bar gets its name from the Chinese expression *"qing, qing"* (which means "please please"), often used as a toast; soldiers returning from the Chinese Opium Wars introduced it in France and throughout Europe. With an extensive wine menu—by the glass and the bottle—plus a selection of single malt bourbon, whiskey, and scotch, it's an ideal spot for a drink or tapas-style food. The bar's rooftop lanai, romantically lit with string lights and featuring a large living wall flourishing with ferns, is the best place to sit. ✉ *39 N. Hotel St., Chinatown* ☎ *808/528–1888* 🌐 *thetchintchinbar.com.*

## Shopping

Shopping in Chinatown, with its mix of the tacky and the unique, is a bustling cultural experience not to be missed. Tucked amid the produce stands are boutiques selling reasonably priced Asian silk clothing, curio shops with everything from porcelain statues to woks to Mao shoes, and apothecaries filled with glass jars of intriguing herbs.

Visit the Chinatown Cultural Plaza for fine-quality jade and the New Hong Kong Market for fresh fruit, crack seed (a popular dried-fruit snack), and boxed or tinned delicacies with names in various languages. Look for newer, hipper clothing, jewelry, books, art, and collectibles in stores along Nuuanu and Pauahi Streets.

Chinatown is also Honolulu's lei center, with shops strung along Beretania and Maunakea (locals all have their favorites where they're greeted by name). In spring, look for gardenia nosegays wrapped in ti leaves.

### BOOKS

**BAS Bookshop**
**BOOKS** | Specializing in books and media about design, architecture, art, and fashion, BAS (pronounced "base") is also part gallery and part shop, selling items that are uniquely local and sustainable. ✉ *1154 Nuuanu Ave., Chinatown* ☎ *808/545–8091* 🌐 *basbookshop.com.*

### CLOTHING

**Roberta Oaks**
**CLOTHING** | This boutique sells modern aloha wear for men, women, and children. Most of the prints and clothes are designed and made in Honolulu, and you'll also find accessories, bath and body items, and other local products. ✉ *1152 Nuuanu Ave., Chinatown* ☎ *808/526–1111* 🌐 *robertaoaks.com.*

### HOUSEWARES

**Place**
**HOUSEWARES** | Owner and interior designer Mary Philpotts McGrath creates a Hawaiian sense of place at this design studio/workshop known for its well-curated assemblage of sophisticated home items in all price ranges. You'll find a global collection of fine lighting, furniture, and textiles, as well as works by local artists and artisans. ✉ *54 S. School St., #100, Chinatown* ☎ *808/275–3075* 🌐 *www.placehawaii.com.*

# Kakaako

This 600-acre section of Honolulu between the Ala Moana Center and downtown is in the process of a redevelopment plan that began in 2012. It's definitely a neighborhood in transition, with everything from ramshackle mechanic shops to the University of Hawaii's medical school.

Luxury condos, trendy restaurants and breweries, local boutiques, and big-box retailers like T. J. Maxx are gradually replacing Kakaako's old warehouses and mom-and-pop storefronts. New events,

You won't soon forget the eye-popping murals the World Wide Walls collective has painted on the buildings in the redeveloping Kakaako neighborhood.

like those at the dining and shopping complex SALT at Our Kakaako, are also taking root.

## Sights

**Hawaii Walls – World Wide Walls**
**PUBLIC ART** | You can grab a bite and take in the unique street art here at any time of the year. Formerly known as the POW! WOW! Worldwide art collective, this project was founded in Hawaii in 2010 and has spread to cities globally. Its most visible Oahu endeavor is a multiblock area where colorful, eclectic, and innovative murals are painted on once-derelict-looking warehouses and other buildings. Every year, artists from all over come to refresh existing murals and add new ones. In 2023, the projects moved out of Kakaako for the first time (to Kalihi-Palama in the first year). ✉ *Kakaako* ✣ *Murals are centered on Cooke, Auahi, and Pohukaina Sts.* ☎ *808/223–7462* 🌐 *instagram.com/worldwidewalls.*

## Restaurants

**Chef Chai**
**$$$$** | **FUSION** | This contemporary dining room in a condo building across from the Blaisdell Center is the go-to spot before and after plays or concerts. The creative starters and seafood and meat entrées on the eclectic, global-fusion menu are healthier than the norm as they don't rely on butter or cream, with dishes like lobster bisque thickened instead with squash puree. **Known for:** early-bird and prix fixe menu options that will leave you stuffed; ahi tartare with avocado mousse in mini waffle cones; excellent desserts. $ *Average main: $45* ✉ *Pacifica Honolulu, 1009 Kapiolani Blvd., Ala Moana* ☎ *808/585–0011* 🌐 *chefchai.com* ⏲ *Closed Mon. and Tues. No lunch.*

**53 by the Sea**
**$$$$** | **CONTEMPORARY** | Housed in a McVilla aimed at attracting a Japanese wedding clientele, this restaurant serves contemporary Continental food that focuses primarily on beautifully plated,

well-prepared standards—albeit with a million-dollar view of Honolulu. Perched at the water's edge, with famed surf break Point Panic offshore, 53 by the Sea uses its setting to great advantage—the crescent-shape dining room faces the sea, so even if you're not at a table nestled against the floor-to-ceiling windows, you have a fine view. **Known for:** odd villa decor that somehow works; free valet parking, and reservations are essential; on-site wedding chapel in case the mood strikes. *$ Average main: $75 ✉ 53 Ahui St., Kakaako ☎ 808/536–5353 ⊕ 53bythesea.com ⏲ Closed Mon.*

### Highway Inn Kakaako

**$$ | HAWAIIAN | FAMILY** | This place focuses on what it does best: local favorites like *kalbi* ribs (Korean barbecue beef short ribs), *kalua* (roasted in an underground oven) pork sliders, beef stew, and old-fashioned hamburger steaks. It's also a great spot to try poi (the pudding-like dish made of pounded taro). **Known for:** signature combo plates; relatively close to the cruise terminal; no reservations except for groups of six or more, so there may be a wait. *$ Average main: $20 ✉ 680 Ala Moana Blvd., Kakaako ✣ In SALT complex ☎ 808/954–4955, ⊕ www.myhighwayinn.com.*

### Merriman's Honolulu

**$$$$ | BISTRO** | At this restaurant where fine dining comes without the fussiness, the cordial, well-trained servers present your "Bag O' Biscuits" or smoking oysters on the half shelf with equal aplomb and know all the details of each menu item. The large Hawaiian-French bistro has floor-to-ceiling windows and native wood accents throughout, and chef-owner Peter Merriman focuses on farm-to-table food, using Oahu-sourced ingredients as much as possible. **Known for:** lobster potpie; tableside poke; Waialua chocolate purse (a take on molten lava cake). *$ Average main: $45 ✉ 1108 Auahi St., Suite 170, Kakaako ☎ 808/215–0022 ⊕ merrimanshawaii.com.*

### Moku Kitchen

**$$ | HAWAIIAN | FAMILY** | In the hip SALT complex, Moku appeals to both foodies and families with authentic farm-to-table cuisine and a laid-back, urban setting. It's one of legendary chef Peter Merriman's restaurants (he's one of the founding chefs of Hawaii regional cuisine) and focuses on upcountry farm fare cooked in the on-site rotisserie; pizzas, salads, and sandwiches; and craft cocktails. **Known for:** lively happy hour; impressive list of craft cocktails, wine, and beer, including the signature monkeypod mai tai; live music every evening. *$ Average main: $25 ✉ SALT at Our Kakaako, 660 Ala Moana Blvd., Kakaako ☎ 808/591–6658 ⊕ www.mokukitchen.com.*

### Panya

**$$ | ECLECTIC** | Run by Hong Kong–born sisters Alice and Annie Yeung, this easy-breezy café is known for its pastries, desserts, and happy hours but also offers crowd-pleasing contemporary fare, both American (salads, sandwiches, pastas) and Asian (Thai-style steak salad, Japanese-style fried chicken, Singaporean seafood *laksa*). Dine inside for the air-conditioning and disco vibe, or choose a spot on the covered lanai. **Known for:** French-style pastries and cakes; eclectic and extensive menu; Japanese cheesecake. *$ Average main: $25 ✉ 1288 Ala Moana Blvd., Kakaako ☎ 808/946–6388 ⊕ www.panyabistro.com ⏲ Closed Mon.*

### Scratch Kitchen

**$$ | MODERN AMERICAN** | Tucked into the chic South Shore Market in Kakaako's Ward Village, Scratch Kitchen has wood-and-metal industrial-look decor, an open kitchen, and creative comfort food. It's popular for breakfast and brunch and has both small plates and generous entrées on its dinner menu. **Known for:** milk 'n' cereal pancakes; spicy (and good) chicken and waffles; large portions. *$ Average main: $25 ✉ South Shore Market at Ward Village, 1170 Auahi St., Kakaako ✣ Enter* *on side of building, along Queen St. ☎ 808/589–1669.*

## Coffee and Quick Bites

**Hank's Haute Dogs**

$ | **HOT DOG** | **FAMILY** | Owner Hank Adaniya's idea of a hot dog involves things like a duck and foie gras sausage with truffle mustard and stone fruit compote. Originally a true hole-in-the-wall, the gentrified Hank's in the SALT area is still a tiny spot where you can go classic with the Chicago Dog, made with the traditional fixings (including neon-green relish), or gourmet with the butter-seared lobster sausage topped with garlic-relish aioli. **Known for:** 12 varieties of dogs daily, plus a daily special; fries, truffle fries, and onion rings to die for; closes by 6 or 7 pm Fri.–Sun. *$ Average main: $12 ✉ 324 Coral St., Kakaako ☎ 808/532–4265 🌐 www.hankshautedogs.com ⏲ No dinner Mon.–Thurs. ☞ Remember to get parking validated.*

## Nightlife

### BREWPUBS

**Aloha Beer**

**BREWPUBS** | Grab a seat in either the industrial indoor taproom or the outdoor beer garden where dogs are welcome (and have their own menu). With more than a dozen beers on draft—including the Hop Lei IPA, Froot Loops, and Aloha Blonde—as well as wine, cocktails, and mocktails, you're likely to find something to your taste. For food, there's pizza and other standard pub fare plus a brunch menu. Get cocktails and more upscale offerings in the upstairs HI Brau Room, which has its own speakeasy-style entrance. A newer Aloha Beer location is in Waikiki. *✉ 700 Queen St., Kakaako ☎ 808/544–1605 🌐 alohabeer.com.*

**★ Hana Koa Brewing Co.**

**BREWPUBS** | One of the newer breweries to debut on Oahu, the modern, two-story brewhouse has its manufacturing area, a gift shop, a bar and more casual dining area downstairs, and an upscale mezzanine with exclusive cocktails. With 20 of its beers on tap (half of them IPAs), plus guest collaborations, cocktails, and mocktails, there's something for everyone. The food menu is just as extensive, including at Sunday brunch. *✉ 962 Kawaiahao St., Kakaako ☎ 808/591–2337 🌐 hanakoabrewing.com.*

**Honolulu Beerworks**

**BREWPUBS** | Oahu's brewing scene has erupted in Kakaako's industrial neighborhood, and one brewpub led the charge: Honolulu Beerworks. In a converted warehouse, owners Geoff and Charmayne Seideman and their crew brew 10 core beers—Kewalo's Cream Beer and South Shore Stout among them—in addition to limited releases with often spicy names. When you need some *ono grinds* (delicious food) with your local brew, they've got munchies, flatbreads, panini, and mac and cheese. Cocktails are also available. It's a regular spot for many locals, particularly on the weekends. You might just make new friends sitting at one of the bar's long picnic tables, made from reclaimed wood. *✉ 328 Cooke St., Kakaako ☎ 808/589–2337 🌐 www.honolulubeerworks.com.*

**Waikiki Brewing Company**

**BREWPUBS** | This company not only brews its own quality craft beer but also serves delicious food. This is its second location—the original is in Waikiki at 1945 Kalakaua Avenue—and it always offers nine beers on tap, including the Skinny Jeans IPA and the Hana Hou Hefe, to which orange peel and strawberry puree are added before fermentation. You can also buy six-packs at the bar to go. Barbecue sauces accompanying some of the smoked meat selections are made with Waikiki Brewing beer. Stop by for brunch on the weekends. *✉ 831 Queen St., Kakaako ☎ 808/591–0387 🌐 waikiki-brewing.com.*

## Performing Arts

### MUSIC

**Hawaii Symphony Orchestra**

**MUSIC** | The orchestra is the latest incarnation of the now-defunct Honolulu Symphony, with a mission to bring international talent to Hawaiian audiences of all ages. The orchestra performs at the Neal Blaisdell Concert Hall and the Waikiki Shell. ✉ *Honolulu* ☎ *808/380–7720* 🌐 *www.myhso.org* 🎫 *From $25.*

## Shopping

### CLOTHING

**Anne Namba Designs**

**CLOTHING** | This designer combines the beauty of classic kimonos with contemporary styles to make unique pieces for work and evening. In addition to women's apparel, Anne Namba designs a men's line. ✉ *324 Kamani St., Kakaako* ☎ *808/589–1135.*

### HOME DECOR

**fishcake**

**SPECIALTY STORE** | A place to find unusual art, this women-owned gallery hosts changing exhibitions and events showcasing works by designers and artists from near and far. It also offers interior design services and carries small and large home items you won't find anywhere else in Honolulu. There's a daily rotation of local eateries at its café. ✉ *307 Kamani St., Suite C, Kakaako* ☎ *808/800–6151* 🌐 *www.fishcake.us.*

**Indich Collection**

**HOME DECOR** | Bring home some aloha you can sink your bare feet into. Designs from this exclusive Hawaiian rug collection depict Hawaiian petroglyphs, banana leaves, heliconia, and other tropical plants or scenery. ✉ *550 Ward Ave., Kakaako* ☎ *808/596–7333* 🌐 *indichcollection.com.*

### SPORTING GOODS

**Boca Hawaii**

**SPORTING GOODS** | This triathlon shop near the Bike Factory offers training gear and bike rentals, classes, and nutritional products. ■ **TIP→ Inquire directly about the latest schedule of classes at the store, which is owned and operated by top athletes.** ✉ *330 Cooke St., Kakaako* ☎ *808/591–9839* 🌐 *bocahawaii.com.*

# Ala Moana

Ala Moana abuts Waikiki to the east (stopping at the Ala Wai Canal) and King Street to the north. Kakaako, Kewalo Basin Harbor, and the Blaisdell Center complex roughly mark its western edge. Probably its most notable attraction is the sprawling Ala Moana Center, jam-packed with almost any store you could wish for.

## Beaches

Honolulu proper has only one beach: Ala Moana. Popular with locals, it hosts everything from Dragon Boat competitions to the Lantern Floating Ceremony.

★ **Ala Moana Regional Park** (*Ala Moana Beach Park*)

**BEACH | FAMILY** | A protective reef makes Ala Moana essentially a ½-mile-wide saltwater swimming pool. Very smooth sand and no waves create a haven for families and stand-up paddleboarders. After Waikiki, this is the most popular beach among visitors, and the free parking area can fill up quickly on sunny weekends. On the Waikiki side is a peninsula called Magic Island, with shady trees and paved sidewalks ideal for jogging. Ala Moana Regional Park also has playing fields, tennis courts, and a couple of small ponds for sailing toy boats. The beach is for everyone, but only in the daytime; after dark, it's a high-crime area, with many unhoused people. **Amenities:** food and drink; lifeguards; parking (free); showers; toilets. **Best for:** swimming; walking.

✉ *1201 Ala Moana Blvd., Ala Moana* 🌐 *www.honolulu.gov/parks.*

## Restaurants

**Akasaka**

$$ | **JAPANESE** | Step inside this tiny sushi bar, tucked amid the strip clubs behind the Ala Moana Hotel, and you'll swear you're in an out-of-the-way Tokyo neighborhood. Don't be deterred by its dodgy neighbors or its reputation for inconsistent service—this is where locals come when they want the real deal, and you'll be greeted with a cheerful "*Irais-haimase!*" (Welcome!) before sitting at a diminutive table or perching at the small sushi bar. **Known for:** popular local spot for late-night food; spicy tuna roll; no pretense, nothing fancy. [$] *Average main: $25* ✉ *1646 Kona St., Suite B, Ala Moana* ☎ *808/942–4466* 🌐 *akasakahawaii.com* ⏲ *No lunch Sun.*

**Bac Nam**

$ | **VIETNAMESE** | Tam and Kimmy Huynh's menu ranges far beyond the usual pho and *bun* (cold noodle dishes) found at many Vietnamese restaurants. This welcoming, no-frills, hole-in-the-wall spot, which locals swear by, features crab curry, tapioca dumplings, head-on tamarind shrimp, and other dishes that hail from both northern and southern Vietnam. **Known for:** spring and summer rolls; limited free parking behind the restaurant; excellent crabmeat curry soup. [$] *Average main: $17* ✉ *1117 S. King St., Ala Moana* ☎ *808/597–8201* ⏲ *Closed Sun.*

**Mariposa**

$$$ | **HAWAIIAN** | Yes, the popovers and the wee cups of bouillon are available at lunch, but in every other regard, the menu at this Neiman Marcus restaurant departs from the classic model, incorporating a clear sense of Pacific place. The breezy, open-air veranda, with a view of Ala Moana Regional Park, the twirling ceiling fans, and the life-size hula-girl murals say "Hawaii." It's still a spot for ladies who lunch, but it also welcomes a more casual crowd. **Known for:** extensive cocktail menu, but note that it closes by 6 or 7 pm; corn chowder; reservations are essential. [$] *Average main: $35* ✉ *Neiman Marcus, Ala Moana Center, 1450 Ala Moana Blvd., Ala Moana* ☎ *808/951–3420* 🌐 *neimanmarcushawaii.com.*

★ **MW Restaurant**

$$$$ | **HAWAIIAN** | The "M" and "W" team of husband-and-wife chefs Michelle Karr-Ueko and Wade Ueko combine their collective experience (20 years alongside chef Alan Wong, a side step to the famed French Laundry, and some serious kitchen time at comfort food icon Zippy's) to create a uniquely local menu with a decidedly upscale twist. Michelle's flair for sweets has resulted in a dessert menu as long as the main one, including tropical fruit creamsicle brûlée, an MW candy bar, and the frozen *lilikoi* (Hawaiian passion fruit) soufflé. **Known for:** excellent fish dishes; nice craft cocktails; reservations are essential. [$] *Average main: $45* ✉ *888 Kapiolani Blvd., Suite 201, Ala Moana* ☎ *808/955–6505* 🌐 *www.mwrestaurant.com.*

**Sorabol Korean Restaurant**

$$ | **KOREAN** | Sorabol offers a vast menu encompassing the entirety of day-to-day Korean cuisine, plus sushi, in a light-filled dining room surrounded by windows. The restaurant, now in the Pagoda Hotel, is known for classic dishes including *bibimbap* (veggies, meats, and eggs on steamed rice), *kalbi* and *bulgogi* (barbecued meats), meat or fish *jun* (thin fillets battered with egg and then fried), and kimchi pancakes. **Known for:** late-night dining; simple but good Korean food; seafood pancake. [$] *Average main: $25* ✉ *Pagoda Hotel, 1525 Rycroft St., Ala Moana* ☎ *808/947–3113* 🌐 *instagram.com/sorabolhawaii.*

## Hotels

**Ala Moana Hotel by Mantra**

**$$ | HOTEL** | A decent value in a pricey hotel market, location is the hallmark of this property, which is connected to Oahu's largest mall, the Ala Moana Center, by a pedestrian ramp and is just a 10-minute walk from Waikiki, a two-minute stroll from Ala Moana Regional Park, and a block from the convention center. **Pros:** great value (and no resort fee); refreshed look; very convenient location. **Cons:** outside the heartbeat of Waikiki; Kona tower rooms are not fully refurbished and look tired; expensive parking. *Rooms from: $269 ✉ 410 Atkinson Dr., Ala Moana ☎ 808/955–4811, 800/367–6025 toll-free 🌐 www.alamoanahotelhonolulu.com 1100 rooms No Meals.*

## Nightlife

### BARS

**Eleven**

**COCKTAIL BARS** | Toward the back of Foodland Farms (located off Piikoi Street on the Ala Moana Center's first level), this small cocktail bar has an extensive menu of whiskey and other spirits. Both the drinks and the small plates use locally sourced ingredients. As a bonus, once you've enjoyed a drink and a snack, you can pick up some groceries in the main store on your way out. ✉ *Foodland Farms Ala Moana, 1450 Ala Moana Blvd., Ala Moana ☎ 808/949–2990 🌐 elevenhnl.com.*

**Mai Tai's**

**BARS** | After a long day of shopping at the Ala Moana Center, the casual, fourth-floor Mai Tai's is a great spot to relax. What you will find is live entertainment and happy hour specials for both food and drink. What you won't find is a cover charge or a dress code. To avoid waiting in line, arrive before 9 pm. ✉ *Ala Moana Center, 1450 Ala Moana Blvd., Ala Moana 🌐 instagram.com/maitaisalamoana.*

## Shopping

Getting to the hundreds of shops in the Ala Moana shopping area from Waikiki is quick and inexpensive thanks to TheBus and the Waikiki Trolley.

### BOOKS

**★ Na Mea Hawaii**

**BOOKS** | In addition to island-style clothing for adults and children, Hawaiian cultural items, and unusual artwork, such as Niihau-shell necklaces, this boutique's book selection covers Hawaiian history and language and includes children's books set in the Islands. Na Mea also has classes on Hawaiian language, culture, and history. A sister store, Native Books, is in Chinatown. ✉ *Ward Village, 1200 Ala Moana Blvd., Suite 270, Ala Moana ☎ 808/596–8885 🌐 www.nameahawaii.com.*

### CLOTHING

**Reyn Spooner**

**CLOTHING** | This is a good place to buy the aloha-print fashions residents wear. Look for the limited-edition Christmas shirt, a collector's item manufactured each holiday season. Reyn Spooner has seven locations statewide and offers styles for men and children and, sometimes, limited-edition women's wear. ✉ *Ala Moana Shopping Center, 1450 Ala Moana Blvd., Shop 2247, Ala Moana ☎ 808/949–5929 🌐 reynspooner.com.*

### FOOD

**★ Honolulu Cookie Company Ala Moana**

**FOOD** | Hugely popular with Islands residents and visitors, these pineapple-shaped shortbread cookies, half-dipped in milk or dark chocolate, come in an assortment of flavors from macadamia nut to mango and *lilikoi* (passion fruit). Made locally in Kalihi, these gourmet cookies are sold in boxes and tins of varying sizes at a number of locations in Ala Moana and Waikiki. ✉ *Ala Moana Shopping Center, 1450 Ala Moana Blvd., Ala Moana ☎ 808/945–0787 🌐 www.honolulucookie.com.*

## Inexpensive Local Souvenirs

Hawaii can be an expensive place. If you're shopping for souvenirs or gifts, consider the following relatively affordable items, which are sold all over the island.

Locally published, Hawaii-themed books for children and adults can be found at places like **Na Mea Hawaii/ Native Books** in Ward Village/Chinatown and **BookEnds** in Kailua.

Just when you thought peanut butter couldn't get any better, someone added coconut to it and made it even more delicious. The coconut peanut butter from **North Shore Goodies** makes a great gift.

If you are a fan of plate lunches, **Rainbow Drive-In** (several locations) has T-shirts with regular orders—"All rice" and "Gravy all over" are some of the sayings. They come packed in an emblematic plate-lunch box.

Relive your memories of tea on the veranda by purchasing Island Essence Tea at **Moana Surfrider** in Waikiki. Harvested from a salt farm on Molokai, **Hawaii Traditional Gourmet Sea Salts** come in a variety of flavors, including black lava, red alaea clay, and classic. They're colored to match their flavor, so they are beautiful as well as tasty.

**Foodland** makes insulated cooler bags that are decorated with uniquely local designs that go beyond tropical flowers and coconuts. Look for the pidgin or poke designs. The Hawaii-themed reusable totes at **Whole Foods** are also very popular.

Made with all-natural ingredients from the Islands, like kukui-nut oil and local flowers and herbs, and even seaweed, indigenous bar soap is available online or in stores like **Blue Hawaii Lifestyle** in Honolulu's Ala Moana Center.

**Longs Drugs**

**FOOD** | Try Longs at the Ala Moana Center (or one of its many other outposts) to stock up on chocolate-covered macadamia nuts, candies, cookies, Islands tea, and 100% Kona coffee—at reasonable prices—to carry home. ✉ *Ala Moana Shopping Center, 1450 Ala Moana Blvd., 2nd level, Ala Moana* ☎ *808/941–4010* 🌐 *longs.staradvertiser.com.*

### JEWELRY

**Na Hoku Ala Moana**

**JEWELRY & WATCHES** | If you look at the wrists of *kamaaina* (local) women, you might see Hawaiian heirloom bracelets fashioned in either gold or silver and engraved in a number of Islands-inspired designs. Na Hoku sells these and other traditional Hawaiian jewelry along with an array of modern Hawaii-influenced designs that capture the heart of the Hawaiian lifestyle in all its elegant diversity. There are a number of Na Hoku locations on Oahu, as well as on the other Islands and the Mainland. ✉ *Ala Moana Center, 1450 Ala Moana Blvd., Shop 2006, Ala Moana* ☎ *808/946–2100* 🌐 *www.nahoku.com.*

### LOCAL GOODS

**Blue Hawaii Lifestyle**

**LOCAL GOODS** | The Ala Moana store carries a large selection of locally made products, including soaps, honey, tea, salt, chocolates, art, and CDs. Every item is carefully selected from various Hawaiian companies, artisans, and farms—from the salt fields of Molokai to the lavender farms of Maui to the single-estate chocolate of Oahu's North Shore. An in-store café serves healthy smoothies, panini, tea, and espresso. ✉ *Ala Moana Shopping Center, 1450 Ala Moana Blvd., Shop 2312, Ala Moana* ☎ *808/949–0808* 🌐 *www.bluehawaiilifestyle.com.*

### SHOPPING CENTERS

**Ala Moana Shopping Center**

**MALL | FAMILY** | The world's largest open-air shopping mall is a five-minute bus ride from Waikiki. More than 350 stores and 160 dining options (including multiple food courts) make up this 50-acre complex, which is a unique mix of national and international chains as well as smaller, locally owned shops and eateries—and everything in between. The newer Lanai @ Ala Moana Center is worth stopping at for a range of casual dining options in one spot. More than 30 luxury boutiques are in residence, with stores such as Gucci, Louis Vuitton, and Christian Dior. All of Hawaii's major department stores are here, including the state's only Neiman Marcus and Nordstrom, plus Macy's, Target, and Bloomingdale's. ✉ *1450 Ala Moana Blvd., Ala Moana* ☎ *808/955–9517* 🌐 *www.alamoanacenter.com.*

**Ward Village**

**SHOPPING CENTER | FAMILY** | Heading west from Waikiki toward downtown Honolulu, you'll run into a section of town with distinct shopping-complex areas; there are more than 100 specialty shops and around 40 eateries here. The Ward Entertainment Center features 16 movie screens, including a state-of-the-art, 3D, big-screen auditorium, and all theaters have reclining chairs and access to an extended food menu and alcoholic beverages for those of age. The South Shore Market is a contemporary collection of local shops and restaurants, plus T. J. Maxx and Nordstrom Rack. For distinctive Hawaiian gifts, such as locally made muumuus, koa-wood products, and Niihau shell necklaces, visit Martin & MacArthur and Na Mea Hawaii. There's also free parking around the entire Ward Village, though sometimes you have to circle for a while to find a spot. Valet parking is also available. ✉ *1050–1200 Ala Moana Blvd., Ala Moana* ☎ *808/591–8411* 🌐 *www.wardvillage.com/shopping.*

## Koa Keepsakes

Items handcrafted from native Hawaiian wood make beautiful gifts. Koa and milo have a distinct color and grain. The scarcity of koa forests makes the wood extremely valuable, which is why there's a large price gap between koa-wood-veneer products and the real thing.

## Activities

### SPAS

**Hoala Salon and Spa**

**SPA** | This Aveda concept spa has everything from Vichy showers to hydrotherapy rooms to customized aromatherapy, as well as a hair salon. They'll even touch up your makeup for free before you leave. ✉ *Ala Moana Shopping Center, 3rd fl., 1450 Ala Moana Blvd., Ala Moana* ☎ *808/947–6141* 🌐 *www.hoalasalonspa.com* 🎫 *Facials from $55, massages from $75.*

# Makiki Heights

Makiki is home to the more unassuming neighborhood where former president Barack Obama grew up. Highlights include the exclusive Punahou School he attended and the notable Central Union Church, as well as the Tantalus area overlook.

## Sights

**The Liljestrand House**

**HISTORIC HOME** | Art, architecture, and history buffs will enjoy the 90-minute tours of the mid-century modern Liljestrand

House. Perched high on Tantalus Drive, with a spectacular view to match, this once-private home was built by famous Hawaii architect Vladimir Ossipoff. You'll learn about his "tropical modernism" building techniques, about the home's local art, and about Betty Liljestrand's dedication to creating the perfect, functional family home in collaboration with Ossipoff. Note that children under 10 are not permitted on the tours. ✉ *3300 Tantalus Dr., Makiki Heights* ☎ *808/537–3116* 🌐 *www.liljestrandhouse.org* 🎫 *$50.*

**Tantalus and Round Top Drive**

**SCENIC DRIVE** | **FAMILY** | A few minutes and a world away from Waikiki and Honolulu, this scenic drive shaded by vine-draped trees has frequent pullouts with views of Diamond Head and the *ewa* (western) side of Honolulu. It's a nice change of pace from urban life below. At Puu Ualakaa State Wayside (Tantalus), stop to see the sweeping view from Manoa Valley to Honolulu. To start the drive, go to the Punchbowl cemetery (National Memorial Cemetery of the Pacific), and follow Tantalus Drive uphill. You'll spot wild chickens, darting mongoose (the squirrels of Hawaii), and maybe the occasional wild boar along the road as you drive. ✉ *3200 Round Top Dr., Makiki Heights* 🌐 *dlnr.hawaii.gov/dsp/parks/oahu/puu-ualakaa-state-wayside.*

## Coffee and Quick Bites

**Honolulu Burger Company**

**$** | **BURGER** | **FAMILY** | Owner Ken Takahashi retired as a nightclub impresario on the Big Island to become a real-life burger king. This modest spot is the home of the locavore burger, made with range-fed beef, Manoa lettuce, tomatoes, and a wide range of toppings, all island-grown—and you can taste the difference. **Known for:** Miso Kutie Burger topped with red miso glaze and Japanese cucumber slices; Blue Hawaii Burger with blue cheese and bacon; a presence at local farmers' markets or elsewhere in its own food truck. 💲 *Average main: $15* ✉ *1295 S. Beretania St., Makiki Heights* ☎ *808/626–5202* 🌐 *honoluluburgerco.com* 🕑 *No dinner Sun. and Mon.*

# Kalihi-Liliha-Kapalama

North of downtown Honolulu, just off H1, is the tightly packed neighborhood of Kalihi. It's home to large industrial pockets but also the stellar Bishop Museum and great local eateries, like Mitsu-Ken. Local breweries have been spreading island-wide, and Kalihi Beer is one of the newest.

Liliha-Kapalama (that latter is sometimes referred to as just "Palama") is the sliver of land that runs from ocean to mountain (known as an *ahupuaa* in Hawaiian). It's presided over by famed Kamehameha Schools, which from its hillside perch looks down on a warren of modest homes and shops.

## Sights

★ **Bishop Museum**

**CULTURAL MUSEUM** | **FAMILY** | The state's designated history and culture museum, founded in 1889 by Charles R. Bishop as a memorial to his wife, Princess Bernice Pauahi Bishop, began as a repository for the royal possessions of this last direct descendant of King Kamehameha the Great. Today, its five excellent exhibit halls contain almost 25 million items that tell the history of the Hawaiian Islands and their Pacific neighbors.

Gain understanding of the entire region in the Pacific Hall, and learn about the culture of the Islands through state-of-the-art and often-interactive displays in the Hawaiian Hall. Spectacular artifacts—lustrous feather capes, bone fishhooks, the skeleton of a giant sperm whale, photography and crafts displays, and a well-preserved grass house—are displayed inside a three-story, 19th-century,

The Bishop Museum is Hawaii's state historical museum and the repository for the royal artifacts of the last surviving direct descendant of King Kamehameha the Great.

Victorian-style gallery. The building alone, with its huge turrets and immense stone walls, is worth seeing.

In the 16,500-square-foot science adventure wing, it's hard to miss the three-story simulated volcano where kids (young and young at heart) can make lava burble. A walk through the glowing black light tunnel is another fun feature. Also check out the planetarium, Hawaiian cultural and science demonstrations, special exhibits, and the Shop Pacifica. ✉ *1525 Bernice St., Kapalama* ☎ *808/847–3511* 🌐 *www.bishopmuseum.org* 🎫 *$29, planetarium shows $3; parking $5.*

## Restaurants

**Helena's Hawaiian Food**

**$** | **HAWAIIAN** | Started by Helen Chock and now run by her grandson, this casual, unassuming spot is an iconic stop for classic Hawaiian food. You can skip the hotel luau and come here for authentic *kalua* pig, *lomi lomi* salmon, poi, *pipikaula* (salted and dried) beef short ribs, *haupia* (a Jell-O-like coconut pudding), and more. **Known for:** long lines; juicy pipikaula (salted and dried) short ribs cured in the kitchen; knowledgeable staff can offer food recommendations. [$] *Average main: $10* ✉ *1240 N. School St., Kalihi* ☎ *808/845–8044* 🌐 *helenashawaiianfood.com* 🕒 *Closed Sat.–Mon.*

**Mitsu-Ken**

**$** | **HAWAIIAN** | The garlic chicken may haunt your dreams, so it's worth the trek to a downscale neighborhood to find this unprepossessing takeout joint. Line up, order the plate lunch with rice and salad, and sink your teeth into the profoundly garlicky masterpiece drizzled with a sweet glaze. **Known for:** delicious breakfast bentos; a local favorite with loyal fans; orders can be called in ahead of time. [$] *Average main: $12* ✉ *2300 N. King St., Kapalama* ☎ *808/848–5573* 🌐 *instagram.com/mitsukenokazu* 🕒 *Closed Sun.–Tues. No dinner.*

## Oahu's Best Shave Ice

Islands-style shave ice (never "shaved" ice—it's a pidgin thing) is said to have been born when neighborhood kids hung around the icehouse, waiting to pounce on the shavings from large blocks of ice, carved with ultrasharp Japanese planes that created an exceptionally fine-textured granita.

In the 1920s, according to the historian for syrup manufacturer Malolo Beverages & Supplies, Chinese vendors developed sweet fruit concentrates to pour over the ice.

The evolution continued with mom-and-pop shops adding their own touches, such as hiding a nugget of Japanese sweet bean paste in the center, placing a small scoop of ice cream at the bottom, and adding *li hing mui* powder (a Chinese seasoning used on preserved fruits). There's nothing better on a sticky, hot day.

Not all of Oahu's best shave ice is in or near Honolulu, but some are. **Waiola Shave Ice** (✉ *3113 Mokihana St., Kapahulu*), near Waikiki, is known for its finely shaved ice and varied flavors. The original location is in Moiliili. **Uncle Clay's House of Pure Aloha** (✉ *Aina Haina Shopping Center, 820 W. Hind Dr., Aina Haina*), near Hawaii Kai in a strip mall, specializes in all-natural syrups made with locally sourced fruits.

## Nightlife

### BREWPUBS

**Kalihi Beer**

**BREWPUBS** | Finding a brewery in Kalihi isn't what you'd expect from such a modest neighborhood, but this no-frills, hole-in-the-wall spot (formerly Broken Boundary Brewery) is home to a growing menu of "old school" beers (the Hi Fi is an ode to the original West Coast IPAs of the 2000s) that aficionados will appreciate. It's also a good place for a quick bite—sandwiches, burgers, tacos, and quesadillas are on the food menu—and a drink before or after a trip to the Bishop Museum or while picking up some food souvenirs at Diamond Bakery next door. ✉ *740 Moowaa St., Suite A, Kalihi* ☎ *808/888–2404* 🌐 *kalihibeer.com* Ⓜ *Kalihi.*

# Nuuanu

Immediately *mauka* of Kalihi, off the Pali Highway, are a renowned resting place and a carefully preserved home where royal families retreated during the doldrums of summer. In 1795, Nuuanu Pali was the sight of a famous battle that was key to King Kamehameha I's success in uniting all the Hawaiian Islands under his rule and becoming the Islands' first monarch. Nuuanu Valley is known for its lush, quiet beauty and has several notable cemeteries, churches, and embassies.

## Sights

**National Memorial Cemetery of the Pacific**

**CEMETERY** | Nestled in the bowl of Puowaina, or Punchbowl Crater, this 112-acre cemetery is the final resting place for more than 50,000 U.S. war veterans and family members and is a solemn reminder of their sacrifice. Among those buried here is Ernie Pyle, the famed

Puowaina, or the Punchbowl, is yet another extinct volcanic crater. It's home to the National Memorial Cemetery of the Pacific, the largest military cemetery in Hawaii.

World War II correspondent who was killed by a Japanese sniper on Ie Shima, an island off the northwest coast of Okinawa. Intricate stone maps provide a visual military-history lesson. Puowaina, formed 75,000–100,000 years ago during a period of secondary volcanic activity, translates as "Hill of Sacrifice." Historians believe this site once served as an altar where ancient Hawaiians offered sacrifices to their gods. **■ TIP→ The entrance to the cemetery has wide-open views of Waikiki and Honolulu—perhaps the finest on Oahu.** ✉ *2177 Puowaina Dr., Nuuanu* ☎ *808/532–3720* 🌐 *www.cem.va.gov/cems/nchp/nmcp.asp* 🎫 *Free.*

**Queen Emma Summer Palace**

**HISTORIC HOME** | Queen Emma, King Kamehameha IV's wife, used this small but stately New England–style home in Nuuanu Valley as a retreat from the rigors of court life in hot and dusty Honolulu during the mid- to late 1800s. Self-guided and docent-led tours highlight the residence's royal history and its eclectic mix of European, Victorian, and Hawaiian furnishings, most of which are original to the home. There are excellent examples of feather-covered *kahilis* (a standard), *umeke* (bowls), and koa-wood furniture. Visitors also learn how Queen Emma established what is today the largest private hospital in Hawaii, opened a school for girls, and ran as a widow for the throne, losing to King Kalakaua. **■ TIP→ Check online for special events like hula, quilting, and ukulele classes and a Hoonanea event including a tour, making a floral hairpiece, and picnic lunch.** A short drive away, you can visit the Royal Mausoleum State Monument, where Queen Emma, her husband, and their son, Albert, who died at age four, are buried beside many other Hawaiian royals. ✉ *2913 Pali Hwy., Nuuanu* ☎ *808/595–3167* 🌐 *www.daughtersofhawaii.org* 🎫 *$14, $20 docent-guided tour Sat. or by appointment and availability* 🕑 *Closed Sun., Mon., and Wed.*

A
B
C
D
E
F
1
2
3
4
5
6
7
8
9
LILIHA-
KAPALAMA
KALIHI
NUUANU
MAKIKI
HEIGHTS
CHINATOWN
DOWNTOWN
MOILILI
WAIKIKI
WEST
WAIKIKI
EAST
MOKAUEA
ISLAND
SAND
ISLAND
Likelike Highway
Pali Highway
Dillingham Blvd.
N. King St.
N. School St.
N. Kuakini St.
Liliha St.
Nuuanu Ave.
S. Vineyard Blvd.
Puuhale Rd.
Mokauea St.
Kalihi St.
Auiki St.
Waiakamilo Rd.
Sand Island Access Rd.
Smith St.
Punchbowl St.
South St.
Cooke St.
Queen St.
Ilalo St.
Ward Ave.
Pensacola St.
Piikoi St.
Wilder Avenue
S. Beretania St.
S. King St.
Kapiolani Blvd.
Ala Moana Blvd.
McCully St.
Isenberg St.
Manoa Road
Date Street
Ala Wai Boulevard
Kuhio Avenue
Kalakaua Ave.
Ala Moana
Beach Park
Magic Island
Lagoon Beach
Fort DeRussy
Beach
Waikiki Beach
Queen's Surf Beach
Kaimana Beach
Mamala Bay
201
H1
61
KEY
Sights
Restaurants
Quick Bites
Hotels
0
1 mi
1 km

### Sights

1 Bishop Museum .................. B3
2 Dolphin Quest at The Kahala Hotel & Resort ........ J8
3 The Liljestrand House .............. F4
4 Lyon Arboretum.................... H3
5 National Memorial Cemetery of the Pacific ....................... D5
6 Queen Emma Summer Palace .... E3
7 Tantalus and Round Top Drive................................ G3

### Restaurants

1 Chiang Mai Thai Cuisine........... F6
2 Helena's Hawaiian Food ...........C3
3 Hoku's...............................J8
4 Imanas Tei.......................... F6
5 Izakaya Nonbei .................... G7
6 Kapa Hale........................... I7
7 Koko Head Cafe.................... H7
8 Mitsu-Ken .......................... B3
9 Mud Hen Water.................... H7
10 Sasabune Hawaii...................E6
11 The Surfing Pig Hawaii............ H7
12 Threadfin Bistro.................... G7
13 Tokkuri Tei .......................... G7
14 Waioli Kitchen & Bake Shop ..... G4

### Quick Bites

1 Fukuya Delicatessen............... F6
2 Honolulu Burger Company ........ E6
3 Leonard's Bakery .................. G7
4 Morning Glass Coffee............. G5
5 Waiola Shave Ice................... F6

### Hotels

1 The Kahala Hotel & Resort ........ J8

# Moiliili

Packed into the neighborhood of Moiliili, about 3 miles from Waikiki, are flower and lei shops, restaurants, and little stores selling Hawaiian and Asian goodies. Most places of interest are along King Street, between Isenberg Street and Waialae Avenue.

##  Restaurants

**Chiang Mai Thai Cuisine**

$$ | **THAI** | Long beloved for its northern Thai classics, such as spicy curries and stir-fries and sticky rice in woven-grass baskets, made using family recipes, Chiang Mai is a short cab ride from Waikiki. Some dishes, like the signature barbecue Cornish game hen with lemongrass and spices, show how acculturation can create interesting pairings. **Known for:** spring rolls and Chiang Mai wings; limited parking in a small lot in back; local business-lunch favorite. *Average main: $25 ✉ 2239 S. King St., Moiliili ☎ 808/941–1151 ⊕ www.chiangmairestaurant.com ⊙ No lunch weekends.*

**Imanas Tei**

$$ | **JAPANESE** | *Nihonjin* (Japanese nationals) and locals flock to this tucked-away, bamboo-ceilinged restaurant for its tasteful, simple decor and equally tasteful—and perfect—sushi, sashimi, *nabe* (hot pots prepared at the table), and grilled dishes. You assemble your meal dish by dish, and the cost can add up if you aren't careful. **Known for:** simple food that some feel is better than in Japan; long waits (reservations are limited); traditional izakaya (casual, pub-like) dining experience. *Average main: $30 ✉ 2626 S. King St., Moiliili ☎ 808/941–2626 ⊕ imanastei.com ⊙ Closed Sun. No lunch.*

**Sasabune Hawaii**

$$$$ | **JAPANESE** | Try to get a coveted seat at the counter, and prepare for an unforgettable sushi experience—if you behave, as chef Seiji Kumagawa prefers that diners eat *omakase*-style, letting him send out his favorite courses (generally two pieces of sushi or six to eight slices of sashimi), each priced individually and each served with instructions ("please, no *shoyu* on this one" or "one piece, one bite"). People who've defied Kumagawa have been kicked out of the restaurant midmeal. **Known for:** one of Honolulu's top sushi spots, so reservations are essentials; fast service; lunch is takeout only. *Average main: $160 ✉ 1417 S. King St., Moiliili ☎ 808/947–3800 ⊕ sasabuneh.com ⊙ Closed Sun. and Mon.*

## Coffee and Quick Bites

**Fukuya Delicatessen**

$ | **JAPANESE** | Get a taste of local Japanese culture at this family operation on the main thoroughfare in Moiliili, a mile or so *mauka* (toward the mountains) out of Waikiki. Open since 1939, the delicatessen offers take-out breakfasts and lunches, Japanese snacks, noodle dishes, and confections—and it's a local favorite for catering, from parties to funeral gatherings. **Known for:** nori-wrapped chicken; mochi tray, offering samples of everything; kid-friendly menu. *Average main: $12 ✉ 2710 S. King St., Moiliili ☎ 808/946–2073 ⊕ fukuyadeli.com ⊙ Closed Mon. and Tues. No dinner.*

## Shopping

Although considered separate from the University of Hawaii's Manoa campus and in need of updating in places, Moiliili has a distinct college-town feel. A look past the tired exteriors reveals a haven of shops that have a loyal community following.

### JEWELRY

**Maui Divers Design Center**

**JEWELRY & WATCHES** | For a look into the harvesting and design of coral and black pearl jewelry, visit this shop and take a free tour at its adjacent factory near the Ala Moana Shopping Center. Note that it's closed on weekends. ■ **TIP→ Avoid the "Pick a Pearl" option at their other kiosk locations unless you're prepared to be upsold on a jewelry setting or two for the pearls "found" in your shells.** ✉ *1520 Liona St., Moiliili* ☎ *808/946–2929* 🌐 *www.mauidivers.com.*

# Kapahulu

Walk just a few minutes from the eastern end of Waikiki, and you'll find yourself in this very local main drag of restaurants, bars, and shops, where Bailey's Antiques & Aloha Shirts is the place for rare, wearable collectibles, and Leonard's Bakery is the place for *malasadas* (Portuguese deep-fried doughnuts rolled in sugar).

##  Restaurants

### Izakaya Nonbei

**$$ | JAPANESE** | Teruaki Mori designed this pub, one of the most traditional of Honolulu's izakayas, to make you feel that you're in a northern inn during winter in his native Japan. Dishes not to miss include *karei karaage* (delicate deep-fried flounder); fried *gobo* (burdock) chips; and the snow crab and avocado salad. **Known for:** frozen strawberry dream dessert; tiny spot with a huge menu; long waits (reservations strongly recommended). $ *Average main: $30* ✉ *3108 Olu St., Kapahulu* ☎ *808/734–5573* 🌐 *www.izakayanonbei.com* ⏲ *No lunch.*

### Threadfin Bistro

**$$$$ | MODERN HAWAIIAN** | This new prix fixe dining experience that incorporates local ingredients in a modern way is the creation of Jason Kiyota, who used to head up the fine-dining side of The Food Company in Kailua. The small restaurant, with its mid-century modern–inspired dining room, is tucked behind a discreet black door in the unassuming Kilohana Square strip mall. **Known for:** rotating menu of carefully sourced dishes; Kona abalone in a cognac butter sauce; ample parking. $ *Average main: $70* ✉ *Kilohana Square, 1014 Kapahulu Ave., Suite 140, Kapahulu* ☎ *808/692–2562* 🌐 *threadfinbistro.com* ⏲ *Closed Sun.–Wed. No lunch.*

### Tokkuri Tei

**$$$ | JAPANESE** | The playful atmosphere at this local favorite belies the food quality, originally created by its late founding chef Hideaki "Santa" Miyoshi. Best to just say "*omakase, kudasai*" ("chef's choice, please"), as Tokkuri Tea delivers creative options that can intimidate at first glance. Just be aware that some of the more rare seafood dishes can cost up to $45 (each). **Known for:** Japanese food that delivers time and again; salmon skin salad; ahi tartare poke, which is everything locals dream about. $ *Average main: $40* ✉ *449 Kapahulu Ave., #201, Kapahulu* ☎ *808/732–6480* 🌐 *www.tokkuritei-hawaii.com* ⏲ *Closed Mon. No lunch.*

## Coffee and Quick Bites

### Leonard's Bakery

**$ | BAKERY** | Whether you spell it *malasada* or *malassada,* when you're in Hawaii, you must try these deep-fried, holeless Portuguese doughnuts. Leonard's Bakery is the most famous of all the island establishments making them and was the first island bakery to commercialize their production. **Known for:** original and various filled malasadas; pão doce (Portuguese sweet bread); small parking lot and long lines. $ *Average main: $2* ✉ *933 Kaphalulu Ave., Kapahulu* ☎ *808/737–5591* 🌐 *leonardshawaii.com.*

### Waiola Shave Ice

**$ | HAWAIIAN | FAMILY** | Longtime local favorite Waiola Shave Ice, known for its super-soft and powdery shave ice (or snow cone) and wide variety of flavors, became nationally known through regular appearances on the reboot of the *Hawaii Five-0* TV show. It's a fast-moving line, so know your order when you get to the window. **Known for:** a large menu allowing for lots of customization; excellent example of a Hawaii classic; slightly brusque service. [$] *Average main: $4* ✉ *3113 Mokihana St., Kapahulu* ☎ *808/949–2269* 🌐 *facebook.com/WaiolaShaveIce.*

## Shopping

Kapahulu, like many older neighborhoods, should not be judged at first glance. It's full of variety; shops and restaurants are located primarily on Kapahulu Avenue. The area begins at the Diamond Head end of Waikiki and continues up to the H1 freeway.

### CLOTHING

**Bailey's Antiques & Aloha Shirts**

**ANTIQUES & COLLECTIBLES** | Vintage aloha shirts are the specialty at this kitschy store. Don't expect to find bargains, but rather unique designs you aren't likely to find elsewhere. Some shirts cost several hundred dollars. Thousands of them are used; others are creations by top designers. The tight space and musty smell are part of the thrift-shop atmosphere. **■ TIP→ Antiques hunters can also buy old-fashioned postcards, glassware, Hawaiian LPs, authentic military clothing, funky hats, and denim jeans from the 1950s.** ✉ *517 Kapahulu Ave., Kapahulu* ☎ *808/734–7628* 🌐 *www.alohashirts.com.*

### SPORTING GOODS

**Island Paddler**

**SPORTING GOODS** | Fashionable beach clothing and bags, bathing suits, hats, and rash guards supplement a huge selection of paddling accessories. **■ TIP→ Check out the wooden decorative paddles: they become works of art when mounted on the wall at home.** ✉ *716 Kapahulu Ave., Kapahulu* ☎ *808/737–4854* 🌐 *www.islandpaddlerhawaii.com.*

**Snorkel Bob's**

**SPORTING GOODS** | The chain, popular throughout the Islands, sells and rents gear—including fins, snorkels, wet suits, and beach chairs—and schedules ocean activities with other suppliers. It's also a good place to seek advice about the best snorkeling beaches and conditions, which vary considerably with the seasons. ✉ *700 Kapahulu Ave., Kapahulu* ☎ *808/735–7944* 🌐 *snorkelbob.com.*

### Take Home a Taste of Oahu

You don't necessarily have to buy a whole pineapple to enjoy Hawaii's fruit flavors back home. Tropical fruit jams are easy to pack and don't spoil. Coffee from Kona or Waialua (right here on Oahu) is another option. There are also dried-food products such as saimin, *haupia* (a type of coconut pudding) mixes, and teriyaki barbecue sauce. All kinds of cookies are available, as well as unusual teas, drink mixes, and pancake syrups. And don't forget the macadamia nuts and bottles of locally distilled liquor or handcrafted island beer.

# Kaimuki

Ten minutes beyond Kapahulu, this commercial thoroughfare runs through a neighborhood that, despite ongoing development, still has a good number of cool old Craftsman bungalows. Kaimuki has also become a food mecca, rivaled only by Chinatown, with perhaps Oahu's most diverse concentration of eateries. If you want to discover the island's culinary trends, this is the place to do it.

## Restaurants

**★ Koko Head Cafe**

**$$ | MODERN HAWAIIAN** | When Lee Anne Wong, best known as a competitor on the first season of Bravo's *Top Chef,* moved to the Islands, foodies waited with bated breath for this, her first restaurant. It's a lively yet laid-back café, where she took the concept of breakfast and flipped it, creating innovative dishes like Breakfast Bruschetta with vanilla cake rusks, local honey, and yogurt; also on offer are her signature dumplings, which change daily, and many other specials. **Known for:** cornflake french toast; creative cocktail menu; crazy busy weekends, but there is an online wait list. *Average main: $22 1120 12th Ave., Kaimuki 808/732–8920 kokoheadcafe.com No dinner.*

**Mud Hen Water**

**$$ | HAWAIIAN** | The name of this casual, homey restaurant is the English translation of *waialae* (meaning a gathering spot around a watering hole). Renowned chef Ed Kenney explores modern interpretations of the Hawaiian foods he remembers from his childhood with an ever-changing locavore menu. **Known for:** menu of creative small plates and snacks; beet poke; sorbetto and gelato. *Average main: $21 3452 Waialae Ave., Kaimuki 808/737–6000 www.mudhenwater.com Closed Mon. No lunch Mon.–Sat.*

**The Surfing Pig Hawaii**

**$$$ | BARBECUE** | The upscale sibling of the island's four Kono's barbecue spots focuses on Americana-tinged-with-Hawaiian food and drink served in a small, lofted space with a surfer-industrial vibe. Heaping portions of juicy smoked and grilled meats are the specialty, but the menu also has several great fish appetizers and entrées. **Known for:** smoked cocktails; pork, beef, and porchetta slider trio; a strong neighborhood brunch option. *Average main: $40 3605 Waialae Ave., Kaimuki 808/744–1992 thesurfingpighawaii.com.*

## Nightlife

### PUBS

**BREW'd Craft Pub**

**PUB** | Helping enliven the Kaimuki night scene is this pub, which stays open until midnight on Friday and Saturday. It's a small place—you have to squeeze between nearby patrons to get to and from your table—but the wait staff is friendly and knowledgeable about the menu of 150-plus beers. BREW'd also offers better versions of standard pub fare than you'll find at some places in town, including a good brisket poutine. *3441 Waialae Ave., Suite A, Kaimuki Corner of 9th and Waialae Aves. 808/732–2337 www.brewdcraftpub.com.*

## Shopping

### FLOWERS AND PLANTS

**Kawamoto Orchid Nursery**

**FLORIST** | Kawamoto grows all flowers on its 3½-acre orchid farm near downtown Honolulu. Their specialty is the cattleya, a favorite for Mother's Day, but they also grow hundreds of hybrids. The nursery now does the bulk of its business online, and they have decades of experience shipping temperamental orchids to the Mainland. *2630 Waiomao Rd., Kaimuki 808/732–5808 kawamotoorchids.com.*

### SPORTING GOODS

**Downing Hawaii**

**SPORTING GOODS** | Claiming to be the oldest surf shop in Hawaii, the store carries old-style Birdwell surf trunks here, along with popular labels, such as Quiksilver, Roxy, Dakine, and Billabong, which supplement Downing's own line of surf wear and surfboards. *3021 Waialae Ave., Kaimuki 808/737–9696 www.downingsurf.com.*

# Manoa

Manoa is probably best known as the home of the University of Hawaii's main campus. The surrounding area is chock-full of interesting coffee shops, restaurants, and stores supported by the collegiate and professorial crowd. History and beauty linger around verdant Manoa Valley at places like the Manoa Chinese Cemetery, Manoa Falls (⇨ *see Hiking in the Activities and Tours chapter*), and Lyon Arboretum. Manoa Valley Theatre puts on top-notch community productions year-round.

## Sights

**Lyon Arboretum**

**GARDEN** | Tucked all the way back in Manoa Valley, this is a gem of an arboretum operated by the University of Hawaii. Reservations are required to visit its almost 200 acres, where you can hike to a waterfall or sit and enjoy beautiful views of the valley while having a picnic. You'll also see an ethnobotanical garden, a Hawaiian *hale* (house) and garden, and one of the largest palm collections anywhere—all within a parklike setting. The arboretum's educational mission means there are often regular talks and walks, plus classes on lei-making, lauhala weaving, Hawaiian medicinal arts, and more, which you can take for an additional fee. ✉ *3860 Manoa Rd., Manoa* ☎ *808/988–0456* 🌐 *manoa.hawaii.edu/lyon* 🎟 *Suggested donation $10* ⏱ *Closed weekends.*

## Restaurants

**★ Waioli Kitchen & Bake Shop**

**$ | AMERICAN** | Dating from 1922, this historic café surrounded by the verdant Manoa Valley landscape is part of the Hawaii Salvation Army headquarters and has been independently operated by Ross and Stefanie Anderson since late 2018. A short menu of simple, delicious breakfast and lunch items are ordered at the counter and delivered to your chosen table, either inside the cozy, multiroom bungalow or on the covered lanai. **Known for:** braised short rib loco moco; assorted house-made pastries, scones, muffins, breads, jams, and jellies; peaceful garden setting. 💲 *Average main: $13* ✉ *Salvation Army Headquarters, 2950 Manoa Rd., Manoa* ☎ *808/744–1619* 🌐 *waiolikitchen.com* ⏱ *Closed Mon. and Tues. No dinner.*

## Coffee and Quick Bites

**Morning Glass Coffee**

**$ | CAFÉ** | Excellent, oversize breakfast items and pastries, accompanied by a versatile coffee and tea list, make this mostly open-air spot a good place to stop for breakfast (though they have lunch items like sandwiches) when you've got time for a leisurely meal. Get there early before food items start to sell out, and be ready to wait in a line that's often long and slow-moving. **Known for:** mac and cheese pancakes; wide range of customizable hot drinks; huge, delicious breakfast burrito. 💲 *Average main: $10* ✉ *2955 E. Manoa Rd., Manoa* ☎ *808/673–0065* 🌐 *morningglasscoffee.com* ⏱ *No dinner.*

## Performing Arts

### THEATER

**Kennedy Theatre**

**THEATER** | Eclectic programs—everything from Hawaiian language to musical theater to Bollywood—are offered at this space on the Manoa campus of the University of Hawaii. The theater, which opened in 1963, was designed by internationally renowned architect I. M. Pei. ✉ *1770 East-West Rd., Manoa* ☎ *808/956–7655 box office* 🌐 *manoa.hawaii.edu/liveonstage* 🎟 *From $25.*

**Manoa Valley Theatre**

**THEATER** | Wonderful performances grace this intimate community theater in lush

Manoa Valley. ✉ *2833 E. Manoa Rd., Manoa* ☎ *808/988–6131* 🌐 *www.manoavalleytheatre.com* 🎟 *From $25.*

# Kahala

Oahu's wealthiest neighborhood has streets lined with multimillion-dollar homes. Lanes at intervals along tree-lined Kahala Avenue provide public access to Kahala's quiet, narrow coastal beaches offering views of Koko Head. Kahala Mall includes restaurants, a movie theater, and a Whole Foods grocery store. Kahala is also the home of the private Waialae Country Club, where the golf course hosts the Sony Open PGA tournament in January.

## Sights

**Dolphin Quest at the Kahala Hotel & Resort**
**OTHER ATTRACTION** | **FAMILY** | This worldwide dolphin-encounter group has an Oahu location in the Kahala Hotel & Resort, where trained Atlantic bottlenose dolphins hold court in their outdoor lagoon adjacent to the pool area. Activities with the creatures go on throughout the day and can be watched from lanai, walkways, and even some rooms. Programs include kid-specific sessions where children can feed and interact with dolphins, fish, and other aquatic animals, as well as various interactive offerings for teens and adults. **■ TIP→ Advance reservations are highly recommended.** ✉ *The Kahala Hotel & Resort, 5000 Kahala Ave., Kahala* ☎ *808/739–8918* 🌐 *dolphinquest.com/oahu-hawaii* 🎟 *From $245.*

## Restaurants

**Hoku's**
**$$$$** | **ASIAN FUSION** | Everything about Hoku's speaks of quality and sophistication: the wall of windows with their beach views, the avant-garde cutlery and dinnerware, the solicitous staff, and the carefully constructed Euro-Pacific cuisine. Diners choose from several tasting menus, which change frequently and focus on seasonal cuisine made with fresh, local ingredients (including herbs from the hotel's on-site herb garden). **Known for:** relaxed elegance in the grande dame of Hawaii's social scene; reservations are essential, as is appropriate dress; setting and service that can outshine the food. $ *Average main: $124* ✉ *The Kahala Hotel & Resort, 5000 Kahala Ave., Kahala* ☎ *808/739–8760* 🌐 *www.hokuskahala.com* ⏲ *No lunch Mon.–Sat.*

★ **Kapa Hale**
**$$$** | **MODERN HAWAIIAN** | Putting a playful and inventive spin on Hawaii regional cuisine, Kapa Hale offers upscale food and cocktails by an outstanding Honolulu-born chef in a mid-century modern dining room. Menu items are changed seasonally and sourced locally, with fun, wordplay names for different dishes, and there's a focus on using local vegetables creatively in all dishes, as in an edible *lei poo* (a head lei). **Known for:** clever drink menu; chef's personal attention to detail; Naan Ya Business appetizer with grilled naan and tikka masala curry. $ *Average main: $40* ✉ *4614 Kilauea Ave., Suite 102, Kahala* ☎ *808/888–2060* 🌐 *www.kapahale.com* ⏲ *No lunch Mon. and Tues.*

## Hotels

★ **The Kahala Hotel & Resort**
**$$$$** | **RESORT** | **FAMILY** | Hidden away in the upscale residential neighborhood of Kahala (on the other side of Diamond Head from Waikiki), this elegant oceanfront hotel with top-notch service, opened in 1964 and one of Hawaii's first luxury resorts, has hosted celebrities, princesses, the Dalai Lama, and nearly every president since Lyndon Johnson. **Pros:** away from hectic Waikiki; top-notch Hoku's restaurant; heavenly spa on-site. **Cons:** far from Waikiki; in a residential

neighborhood, so not much to do within walking distance of hotel; small pool. *Rooms from: $563* ✉ *5000 Kahala Ave., Kahala* ☎ *808/369–9471, 800/367–2525 toll-free* 🌐 *www.kahalaresort.com* *338 rooms* *No Meals.*

# Shopping

Upscale Kahala, near the slopes of Diamond Head and a 10-minute drive from Waikiki, has a shopping mall and some gift stores.

## ART GALLERIES

### Nohea Gallery

**ART GALLERY** | This gallery represents hundreds of artisans who specialize in koa furniture, bowls, and boxes, as well as art glass and ceramics. Original paintings and prints—all with an Islands theme—add to the selection. The store also carries unique handmade Hawaiian jewelry, starting around $20, with ti leaf, maile, and coconut-weave designs. Home items like locally made kitchen towels and Tutu Nene hand-sewn native Hawaiian ducks make great souvenirs. ✉ *Kahala Mall, 4211 Waialae Ave., Kahala* ☎ *808/762–7407* 🌐 *noheagallery.com.*

## SHOPPING CENTERS

### Kahala Mall

**MALL** | **FAMILY** | This indoor mall has more than 100 stores and restaurants, with a mix of national retailers and not-to-be-missed, homegrown boutiques, clothing stores, and galleries. You can also browse local foods and products at Whole Foods. For post-shopping entertainment, see what movies are playing at the Consolidated Kahala Theatres, where you'll also find a full kitchen and bar. ✉ *4211 Waialae Ave., Kahala* ☎ *808/732–7736* 🌐 *www.kahalamallcenter.com.*

# Activities

## SPAS

### The Kahala Spa

**SPA** | Escape the hustle and bustle of metro Honolulu at the spa of the elegant yet homey Kahala Hotel & Resort, favored by celebrities and dignitaries. Nine spa suites have their own showers, soaking tubs, and changing areas. Custom treatments merge Hawaiian, Asian, and traditional therapies, and romance packages are also available. Relax in the private gardens, and use the fitness center's dry saunas, eucalyptus steam rooms, and outdoor whirlpools. ✉ *The Kahala Hotel & Resort, 5000 Kahala Ave., Kahala* ☎ *808/739–8938* 🌐 *www.kahalaresort.com* *Facials and massages from $195.*

Chapter 4

# WEST (LEEWARD) AND CENTRAL OAHU



Updated by
Cheryl Crabtree

| Sights | Restaurants | Hotels | Shopping | Nightlife |
|---|---|---|---|---|
| ★★★☆☆ | ★★★☆☆ | ★★★★★ | ★★★☆☆ | ★★★☆☆ |

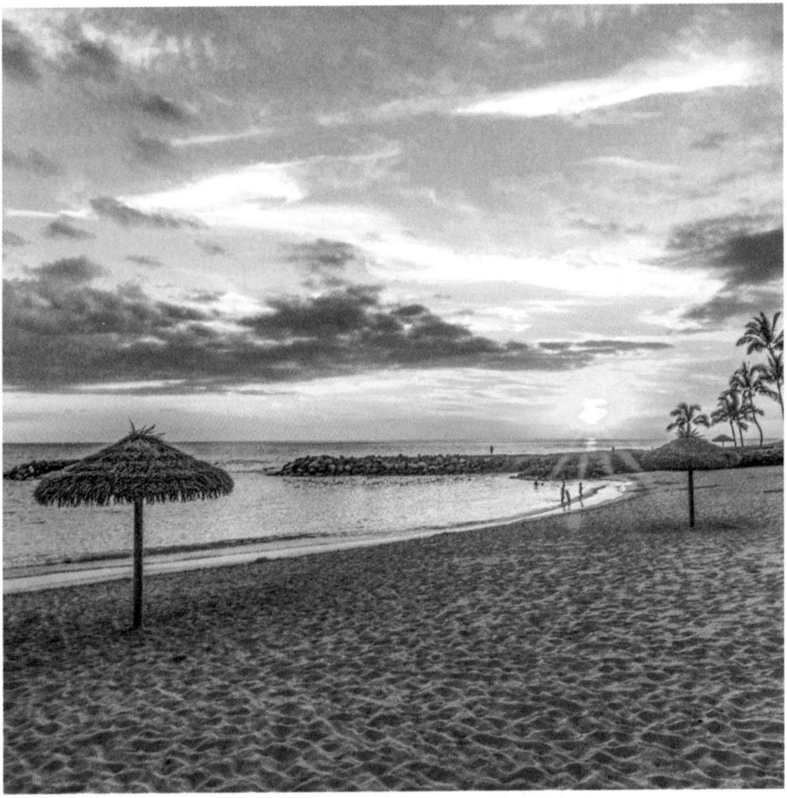

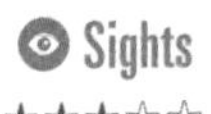

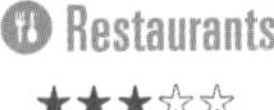

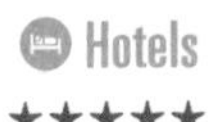

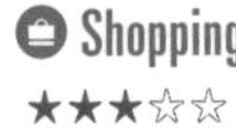

# WELCOME TO WEST (LEEWARD) AND CENTRAL OAHU

## TOP REASONS TO GO

★ **Gorgeous beaches:** From Pokai Bay and surf mecca Makaha to Keawaula Beach (Yokohama Bay), the leeward side of the island affords excellent opportunities to ditch tourist droves and connect with locals who live and play along a mostly undeveloped shoreline.

★ **Ko Olina:** A privately owned development on the southwest corner of Oahu, Ko Olina offers the region's best options for dining, nightlife, and golf.

★ **Shopping:** Head to Central Oahu for discounted traditional island souvenirs in premium outlets and big-box stores—where it's easier to find parking.

★ **Agricultural heritage:** Visit Hawaii's Plantation Village and Dole Plantation to learn about Oahu's commercial farming roots.

★ **Oahu's best sunsets:** The west-facing leeward side of the island is an ideal place to watch the sun dip into the Pacific at the end of the day.

Leeward and Central Oahu generally refer to the regions west and north of Pearl Harbor. Heading west from Honolulu, the H1 freeway leads to Oahu's "second city," Kapolei. From there, Farrington Highway continues west and north to the Ko Olina resorts and the Hawaiian communities of Nanakuli and Waianae, and then on to the beach and the end of the road at Keawaula, aka Yokohama Bay. Central Oahu occupies the fertile central valley, home to plantations, farms, military installations, and working-class towns like Wahiawa, as well as predominantly residential communities, such as Ewa Beach (home to the new Wai Kai Center), Mililani, and Waipio.

Oahu's commercial and residential future is expected to center here in the coming decades, and this area will expand and evolve more than any other region on the island. The central plateau in particular is meant to be a sustainable farming hub to ensure abundant fresh food supplies no matter what happens in the rest of the world. Phase one of the Skyline rail project runs for 10 miles between Halawa/Aloha Stadium, near Pearl Harbor, and East Kapolei, with trains making it somewhat easier to reach West Oahu attractions.

**1 Kapolei.** Hawaii's "second city" is a newish development meant to ease the burden of the congested Honolulu area and boost the future of the state.

**2 Ewa Beach.** Plantations and farms dominated this district, but today it holds residential communities and the busy Wai Kai Center, with its array of water activities.

**3 Ko Olina.** Protected lagoons and myriad lodging, dining, and activity options attract thousands of visitors to this privately owned community.

**4 Waianae.** Many native Hawaiians live in and around Waianae, a modest town that anchors the leeward side of the island.

**5 Wahiawa.** A small but busy town in the heart of Central Oahu, Wahiawa serves as an important center for military personnel and workers at nearby farms and the Dole Plantation.

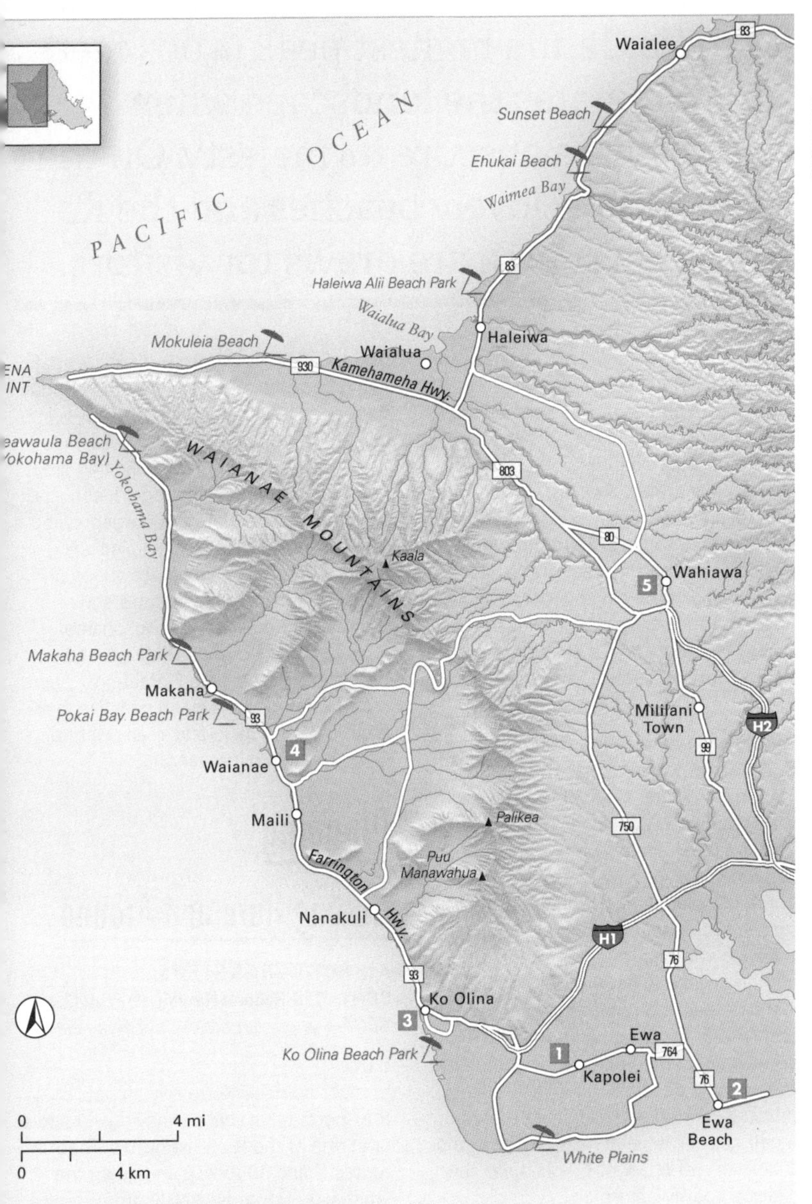
PACIFIC OCEAN
Waialee
Sunset Beach
Ehukai Beach
Waimea Bay
Haleiwa Alii Beach Park
Waialua Bay
Haleiwa
Mokuleia Beach
Waialua
Kamehameha Hwy.
Keawaula Beach (Yokohama Bay)
Yokohama Bay
WAIANAE MOUNTAINS
Kaala
Wahiawa
Makaha Beach Park
Makaha
Pokai Bay Beach Park
Mililani Town
Waianae
Maili
Palikea
Puu Manawahua
Farrington Hwy.
Nanakuli
Ko Olina
Ko Olina Beach Park
Ewa
Kapolei
Ewa Beach
White Plains
0 4 mi
0 4 km

The rugged Waianae Range bisects the island's leeward side from the central plateau. The queen of the range, Mount Kaala, is Oahu's highest peak (4,003 feet) and dominates the landscape when clouds fail to obscure its majesty. On the leeward side, lovely beaches and the Ko Olina resort area are draws for visitors.

The mountains shield the western slopes from trade winds and heavy rain that falls to the north and east. The western side thus appears drier, and its beaches are known for their pristine white sands and crystal clear waters that are excellent for snorkeling and diving. This geography (combined with flows from the western slopes of the parallel eastern Koolau Range) also results in abundant water flows to the fertile central valley plains—where much of Oahu's delectable agricultural bounty originates.

The region's eastern portion edges Pearl Harbor and includes the Aloha Stadium Swap Meet & Marketplace, Hawaii's Plantation Village, the Wet 'n' Wild Hawaii water park, and Waikele Premium Outlets near Waipio. Kapolei, Oahu's burgeoning "second city," lies due west of Pearl Harbor. It is a planned community, where, for years, the government has been trying to attract enough jobs to lighten inbound traffic to downtown Honolulu. A major mall and community center, Ka Makana Alii, opened here in 2017 to serve an expected influx of shoppers in the ensuing decades. Ko Olina—a lively, privately owned community centered on a golf course, several major resorts, and four man-made lagoons—occupies the island's southwestern tip.

Some locals avoid Leeward and Central Oahu because of traffic that tends to bottleneck at the intersection of the H1, H2, and H3 freeways. But those who time their travels to avoid the traffic find great rewards throughout the region, especially the chance to explore the gorgeous and remote west coast beaches, including the far-flung Hawaiian communities of Nanakuli and Waianae and the end of the road at Keawaula, aka Yokohama Bay. A visit to Ko Hana Distillers and a walk through the Dole Plantation's 3-acre maze (the world's largest) near Wahiawa are well worth including in any Central Oahu excursion itinerary.

## Planning

### Getting Here and Around

#### AIRPORT TRANSFERS

**CONTACTS Roberts Hawaii.** ☎ *808/439–8800* 🌐 *www.airportshuttlehawaii.com.*

#### BUS

It might be possible to rely on public transportation if you are staying in Kapolei or at one of the Ko Olina hotels. TheBus routes C and 40 run up and down the west side. Route 52 travels from the Ala

Moana Center in Honolulu to Wahiawa and Haleiwa on the North Shore; the trip takes about 1¼ hours to Wahiawa and about 1½ hours to Haleiwa.

### CAR

It's relatively easy to get to West Oahu, which begins at folksy Waipahu and continues past Makakilo and Kapolei on H1 and Highway 93, Farrington Highway. It takes about a half hour to reach Ko Olina from Waikiki, but rush hour traffic can create delays.

A couple of cautions as you head to the leeward side: Highway 93 is a narrow, winding, two-lane road, notorious for accidents. There's an abrupt transition from an expansive freeway to a two-lane highway at Kapolei. By the time you reach Nanakuli, it's a country road, so *slow down.* Also be aware of congestion between Ko Olina and Waianae during commuter hours.

### TAXI

If you don't rent a car, rideshares like Uber or Lyft are the most popular option in the region between Honolulu and Ko Olina. Roberts Hawaii also offers transportation to Waikele Premium Outlets and to Ko Olina.

## Beaches

The North Shore may be known as "country," but the west side is truly the rural area on Oahu. There are commuters from this side to Honolulu, but many people are born, live, and die over here with scarcely a trip to town. For the most part, there's little hostility toward outsiders, but occasional problems have flared up—generally on the order of car break-ins, not violence—mostly due to drug abuse, which has ravaged the fringes of the island. In short, lock your car when you stop to take in the breathtaking views, don't bring valuables, and enjoy the amazing beaches.

The beaches on the west side are expansive and empty. Most Oahu residents and tourists don't make it to this side simply because of the drive; in traffic it can take almost 90 minutes to make it to the end of the road at Yokohama Bay from downtown Honolulu. But you'll be hard-pressed to find a better sunset anywhere.

## Hotels

The full-service Ko Olina resorts and vacation rentals are your best options in this area, which doesn't have many short-term accommodations at all apart from basic motels. But be sure to factor in the hefty parking and resort fees at Ko Olina when comparing with lodgings elsewhere on the island.

### PRICES

⇨ *Hotel prices are the lowest cost of a standard double room in high season. Hotel reviews have been shortened. For full information, visit Fodors.com.*

**What It Costs in U.S. Dollars**

| | $ | $$ | $$$ | $$$$ |
|---|---|---|---|---|
| **HOTELS** | | | | |
| | under $200 | $200–$280 | $281–$380 | over $380 |

## Restaurants

Dining opportunities abound at the Four Seasons Resort Oahu, Aulani, and Marriott's Beach Vacation Club within the Ko Olina community. The new (opened 2023) Wai Kai complex in Ewa Beach also includes several dining options. The fear of traffic congestion on the freeways prevents some locals and visitors from driving to Ko Olina and Ewa Beach for dinner, but many come for lunch and happy hours, as well as to mark special occasions with a fancy meal and west-side sunset experience.

### PRICES

⇨ *Restaurant prices are the average cost of a main course at dinner or, if dinner is not served, at lunch. Restaurant reviews have been shortened. For full information, visit Fodors.com.*

| What It Costs in U.S. Dollars | | | |
|---|---|---|---|
| $ | $$ | $$$ | $$$$ |
| **RESTAURANTS** | | | |
| under $20 | $20–$30 | $31–$40 | over $40 |

## Safety

Car break-ins and beach thefts are common on the leeward side, so keep all your belongings in sight, and never leave anything in your car.

# Kapolei

*22 miles west of downtown Honolulu.*

The planned community of Kapolei, where, for years, the government has been trying to attract enough jobs to lighten inbound traffic to downtown Honolulu, is often called Oahu's "second city." It occupies much of 19th-century business mogul James Campbell's 41,000-acre Ewa plain estate, which once cultivated vast tracts of sugarcane and pineapple.

The first phases of Kapolei broke ground in the 1980s. Today, it is a thriving community with government centers, industrial parks, big-box malls, businesses small and large, and the West Oahu campus of the University of Hawaii. The Ko Olina complex to the west is officially part of the district and has a Kapolei zip code.

### GETTING HERE AND AROUND

From downtown Honolulu, you can get to Kapolei in 30 minutes by car. Note, though, that traffic can double or triple the driving time.

In 2023, Skyline trains began to run between Halawa/Aloha Stadium and East Kapolei, about a 42-minute trip, including stops. Three stations include park-and-ride lots.

**Hawaii's Plantation Village**

**HISTORY MUSEUM** | **FAMILY** | Starting in the 1800s, immigrants seeking work on the sugar plantations came to the Islands like so many waves against the shore, and this open-air museum examines the lives and cultures of the arrivals. Just 30 minutes from downtown Honolulu (without traffic), visit more than 25 authentically furnished buildings, original and replicated, that re-create and pay tribute to the plantation era. See a Chinese social hall; a Japanese shrine, sumo ring, and saimin stand; a dental office; and historic homes. You can explore on your own or take a guided tour (included in admission, but reserve ahead; several offered each day). ✉ *Waipahu Cultural Gardens Park, 94-695 Waipahu St., Waipahu* ☎ *808/677-0110* 🌐 *hawaiiplantationvillage.org* 🎫 *$17* 🕒 *Closed Sun.*

**★ White Plains Beach**

**BEACH** | **FAMILY** | Concealed from the public eye for many years as part of the former Barbers Point Naval Air Station, this beach is reminiscent of Waikiki but without the condos and the crowds. It is a long, sloping stretch with numerous surf breaks, but the beach is also mild enough at the shore for older children to play freely. It has views of Pearl Harbor and, over that, Diamond Head. Although the sand lives up to its name, the real impact of this beach comes from its history as part of a military property for the better part of a century. Expansive parking, great restroom facilities, and numerous tree-covered barbecue areas make it a great day-trip spot. As a bonus, a Hawaiian monk seal takes up residence here several months out of the year (seals are rare in the Islands). **Amenities:** lifeguards; parking (no fee); showers; toilets. **Best for:** surfing; swimming. ✉ *Essex Rd. and Tripoli Rd., Kapolei* ✣ *Take Makakilo Exit off H1 West, then turn left. Follow it into base gates, make left. Blue signs lead to beach.*

## Performing Arts

### LUAU

**Mauka Warriors Luau**

**FOLK/TRADITIONAL DANCE** | **FAMILY** | Unlike most island luau shows, Mauka Warriors at Hawaii Country Club goes beyond hula and fire-knife dances to tell the stories of King Kamehameha I, who aimed to unite the Hawaiian Islands, and also the warriors who populated islands throughout Polynesia. Tickets (three days a week) include a Polynesian buffet, various activities, and fascinating interactive performances. Transportation is available ($30 per person) from Honolulu and Waikiki. ✉ *94-1211 Kunia Rd., Waipahu* ☎ *808/646–3945* 🌐 *maukawarriorsluau.com* 🎟 *From $139.*

## Shopping

Kapolei is where people from the North Shore, Haleiwa, and Honolulu head to shop, as parking is ample and choices run the gamut. You can find some reasonably priced souvenir items, too. Choices include Ka Makana Alii, with more than 100 shops, and big-box options such as Target and T. J. Maxx.

### MARKETS

**Aloha Stadium Swap Meet & Marketplace**

**MARKET** | This thrice-weekly outdoor bazaar attracts hundreds of vendors and even more bargain hunters. Every Hawaiian souvenir imaginable can be found here, from coral shell necklaces to bikinis, as well as a variety of global wares, from Chinese brocaded dresses to Japanese pottery. There are also international foods, silk flowers, and luggage in aloha floral prints. That said, be prepared to wade through the usual sprinkling of used and counterfeit goods to find value. Wear comfortable shoes, use sunscreen, and bring bottled water. The flea market takes place in the parking lot of the (now-closed) Aloha Stadium Wednesday and Saturday 8–3 and Sunday 6:30–3. Admission is $2 per person ages 12 and up.

You can take either Uber or Lyft from your hotel. You might also ask your hotel concierge about shared shuttle services. For a cheaper but slower ride, take TheBus. The new Skyline trains connect Halawa/Aloha Stadium with East Kapolei. So you could shop at the swap meet and hop on the train, then walk or ride a bus 1½ miles to the Ka Makana Alii mall to treasure-hunt even longer—all without a car. ✉ *Aloha Stadium, 99-500 Salt Lake Blvd., Aiea* ☎ *808/486–6704* 🌐 *alohastadium.hawaii.gov.*

### SHOPPING CENTERS

**Ka Makana Alii — The Center for West Oahu**

**MALL** | This mall lures patrons with easy access from the H1 freeway, abundant free parking, and several island ware–focused stores, including Noeau, with an array of locally designed, handcrafted items. It also has plenty of familiar chain stores. Several buses run between the Skyline train stop in East Kapolei and Ka Makana Alii. ✉ *91-5431 Kapolei Pkwy., Kapolei* ☎ *808/628–4800* 🌐 *www.kamakanaalii.com.*

The LineUp at Wai Kai on Ewa Beach's waterfront includes a fun 100-foot wave pool and a large lagoon for paddling.

**Waikele Premium Outlets**
**MALL** | Armani Exchange, Calvin Klein, Coach, and Saks Fifth Avenue outlets anchor this discount destination of around 50 stores. ✉ *94-790 Lumiaina St., Waipahu* ☎ *808/676–5656* 🌐 *www.premiumoutlets.com/outlet/waikele.*

# Ewa Beach

*6 miles east of Kapolei.*

Ewa Beach—often just called Ewa—is a sprawling expanse of hot, dry plains on the southwest shore of Oahu, tucked between Pearl Harbor–Hickham Air Force Base on the east and the city of Kapolei to the west. Today it's a suburban hub with about 16,000 residents (a number that's rapidly growing), chockablock with residential developments and services, golf courses, and the new LineUp at Wai Kai wave pool and activities complex. In ancient times, it was a favorite vacation hangout for the alii, known for its balmy weather and excellent fishing. Later, the area was known for its sprawling sugar cane plantations and agricultural fields.

## Sights

**★ The LineUp at Wai Kai**
**OTHER ATTRACTION** | **FAMILY** | An all-in-one, surf-themed recreation complex at Hoakalei Resort (a master-planned community) on the Ewa Beach waterfront, the LineUp celebrates Hawaii's connection with water, surf, and cultural traditions. It centers around the Wai Kai Wave, a 100-foot wave pool that emulates river surfing, and there's also a 52-acre lagoon for paddling or floating. Wai Kai doesn't have a hotel yet, but it serves as a popular community hub, with three restaurants and numerous programs and activities, such as farmers markets, surfing classes, and performances. It's just a 10-minute drive from Kapolei and worth the drive to check out the complex. You can ride a shuttle to Wai Kai from West Oahu (Ko Olina, $35 round-trip) or Waikiki (from various resorts, $35 round-trip).

*✉ 91-1621 Keoneula Blvd., Ewa Beach ☎ 808/515–7873 ⊕ atthelineup.com 🎟 $50 for 4 hours at the Lagoon; from $60 for the Wave; $125 for Learn to Surf.*

## Restaurants

**★ The LookOut Food and Drink**

**$$ | HAWAIIAN** | Airy and modern, this hip, lively bar and restaurant overlooks the Wai Kai wave pool for fantastic views of Oahu's south shore, including Diamond Head, Honolulu, and Waikiki. The Hawaii-centric menu includes pizzas, salads, sandwiches, and a range of entrées, from a roasted veggie bowl and fish tacos to braised short rib *loco moco* (a comfort classic with white rice, meat such as a hamburger patty, fried eggs, and gravy); a dessert favorite is the strawberry guava parfait. **Known for:** kalua pork nachos and sliders, sashimi and ahi trio; good Sunday brunch; live or DJ music nightly. *$ Average main: $20 ✉ 91-1621 Keoneula Blvd., Ewa Beach ☎ 808/900–3579 ⊕ waikailookout.com.*

**Sessions Lifestyle & Apparel**

**SPECIALTY STORE** | Local, sustainably made specialty items fill the shelves of this small boutique in the Wai Kai complex, which features men's and women's clothing, children's gifts, and upscale souvenirs. *✉ The LineUp at Wai Kai, 91-1621 Keoneula Blvd., Ewa Beach ☎ 808/900–3579 ⊕ atthelineup.com.*

# Ko Olina

*5 miles west of Kapolei, 25 miles west of downtown Honolulu.*

For centuries, Hawaiian nobility rejuvenated at this pristine enclave on Oahu's southwestern edge, but today Ko Olina is a major visitor hub, part of a decades-long master plan to attract jobs to the leeward side. The privately owned, 642-acre complex is a community unto itself, with one guarded public entrance/exit off Farrington Highway. It includes a golf course, three natural lagoons, a series of four man-made lagoons, three major resorts (each with a range of restaurants, shops, and activities), 4½ miles of walking paths, and a shopping area with additional restaurants and cafés. Ko Olina is also home to the famed Paradise Cove Luau.

The Lanikuhonua Nature Preserve, with its pristine beach, edges the north end of the complex. The shoreline is public, but most of the 11-acre site belongs to the Lanikuhonua Cultural Institute, a nonprofit that preserves and promotes Hawaiian culture.

Ko Olina's lagoons are open to the public, but public parking is limited (first-come, first-served, sunrise to sunset). Arrive before 10 am to nab one of the prized spots. If you do manage to find a space, plan to walk at least a short bit to the lagoons along public access paths. Even resort guests pay hefty fees to park on-site.

### GETTING HERE AND AROUND

You can get to Ko Olina in 45 minutes from downtown Honolulu by car unless traffic is heavy, in which case it might take well over an hour.

**Wet 'n' Wild Hawaii**

**WATER PARK | FAMILY** | This 29-acre family attraction has waterslides, water cannons, and waterfalls. *✉ 400 Farrington Hwy., Ko Olina ✣ Off H1 at Exit 1 ☎ 808/674–9283 ⊕ wetnwildhawaii.com 🎟 $65, parking $20 per car.*

**Kahe Point Beach Park** (*Electric Beach*)

**BEACH** | Directly across from the electricity plant—hence its nickname, Electric Beach, this beach is a haven for

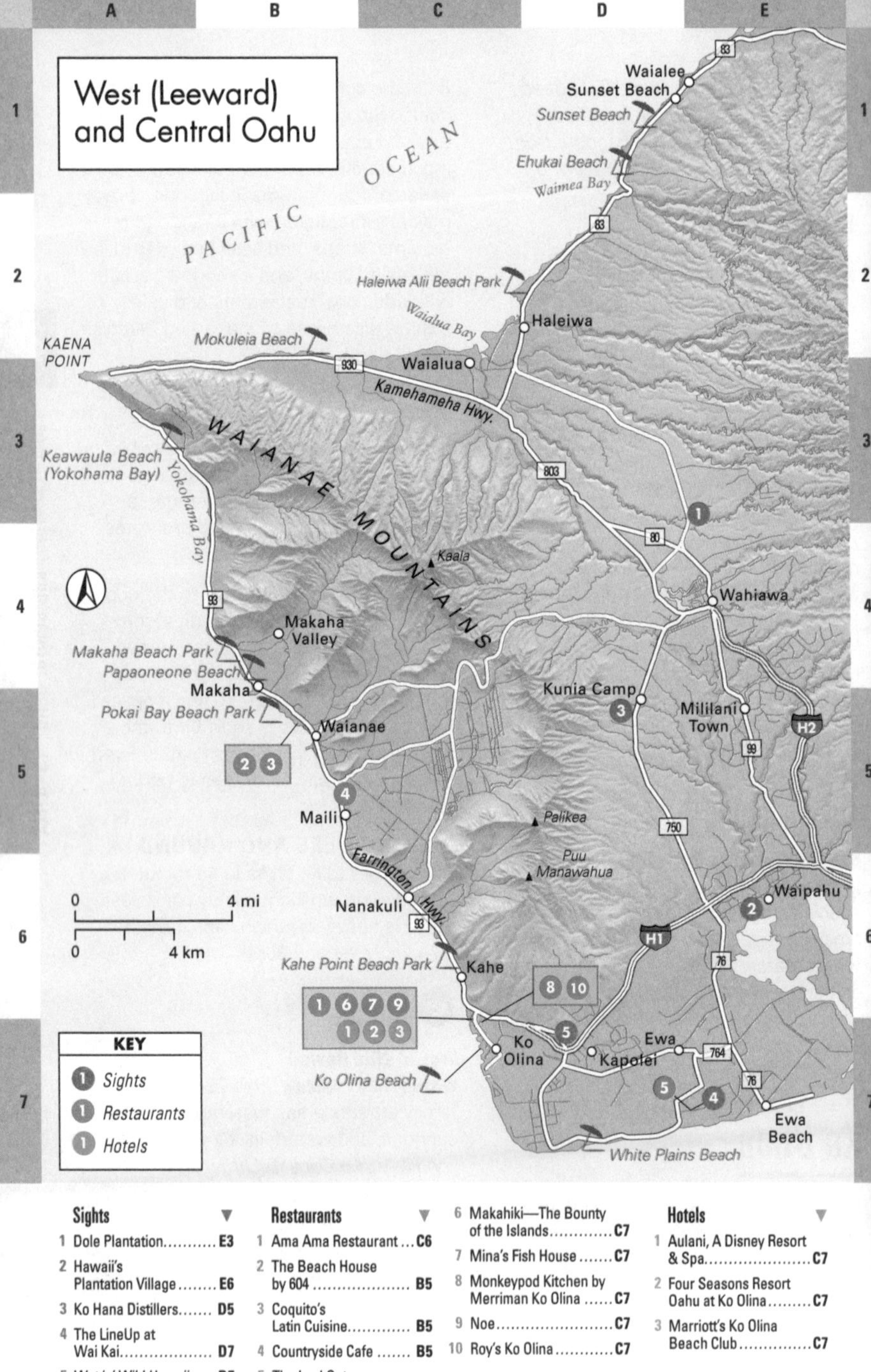


## Sights

1 Dole Plantation........... E3

2 Hawaii's Plantation Village........ E6

3 Ko Hana Distillers....... D5

4 The LineUp at Wai Kai.................. D7

5 Wet 'n' Wild Hawaii .... D7

## Restaurants

1 Ama Ama Restaurant ... C6

2 The Beach House by 604 .................... B5

3 Coquito's Latin Cuisine............. B5

4 Countryside Cafe ....... B5

5 The LookOut Food and Drink.......... D7

6 Makahiki—The Bounty of the Islands.............C7

7 Mina's Fish House .......C7

8 Monkeypod Kitchen by Merriman Ko Olina ......C7

9 Noe........................C7

10 Roy's Ko Olina ...........C7

## Hotels

1 Aulani, A Disney Resort & Spa.......................C7

2 Four Seasons Resort Oahu at Ko Olina.........C7

3 Marriott's Ko Olina Beach Club................C7

Ko Olina, a planned resort community on the island's southwestern shore, is the biggest tourist area on Leeward Oahu.

tropical fish, making it a great snorkeling spot. The expulsion of hot water from the plant raises the temperature of the ocean, attracting Hawaiian green sea turtles, spotted moray eels, and spinner dolphins. Although the visibility is not always the best, the crowds here are often small (though growing), and the fish are guaranteed. It's best to wear reef shoes here because of the sharp rocks. Unfortunately, there can be a strong current, so it's not very kid-friendly. This is also a great place to stop for a picnic and admire the views. **Amenities:** parking (no fee); showers; toilets. **Best for:** snorkeling; sunset. ✉ *Farrington Hwy., Ko Olina* ✣ *1 mile northwest of Ko Olina Resort.*

### ★ Ko Olina Beach

**BEACH** | **FAMILY** | This is the best spot on the island if you have small kids. The resort area commissioned a series of four man-made lagoons, but, as it has to provide public beach access, you are the winner. Huge rock walls protect the lagoons, making them perfect spots for the kids to get their first taste of the ocean without getting bowled over. The large expanses of seashore grass and hala trees that surround the semicircle beaches are made-to-order for nap time. A 1½-mile jogging track connects the lagoons. Due to its appeal for *keiki* (children), Ko Olina is popular, and the parking lot fills up quickly when school is out and on weekends. Try to get here before 10 am; the biggest parking lot is at the farthest lagoon from the entrance. There are actually four resorts here: Aulani (the Disney resort), Four Seasons Resort Oahu, Marriot's Ko Olina Beach Club (which has a time-share section as well), and Beach Villas at Ko Olina (condominiums with private vacation rentals). The area is 23 miles west of Honolulu. **Amenities:** food and drink; parking (no fee); showers; toilets. **Best for:** sunset; swimming; walking. ✉ *92 Aliinui Dr., Ko Olina* ✣ *Take Ko Olina exit off H1 West and proceed to guard shack.*

## Restaurants

### Ama Ama Restaurant

$$$$ | **MODERN HAWAIIAN** | There's nothing "Mickey Mouse" about the updated Hawaiian food at the prix fixe fine-dining restaurant of Aulani, the Disney resort, which has a reflecting pool and decor with beach house elements like a thatched roof. Add to that the views of the Ko Olina lagoons and Pacific Ocean—and nightly live music by top local performers in the adjacent bar—and you have an evening worth the pretty penny. **Known for:** four-course prix fixe menu, with plant-based option available for all courses; reservations are essential; hit-or-miss service. *Average main: $125 Aulani, a Disney Resort & Spa, 92-1185 Aliinui Dr., Ko Olina 808/674–6200 www.disneyaulani.com/dining Closed Tues. No lunch.*

### Makahiki — The Bounty of the Islands

$$$$ | **HAWAIIAN** | **FAMILY** | The main restaurant at Disney's Aulani resort offers three-course breakfast and dinner menus with a wide variety of locally produced items, as well as familiar dishes from stateside and the rest of the world. You'll find sustainable Hawaiian seafood, Asian selections, familiar grilled meats and vegetables. **TIP→ Arrive early for dinner and have a drink at the adjacent Olelo Room, where the staff are fluent in Hawaiian; you can get a language lesson along with your libation.** **Known for:** true reflection of Hawaii; many main-course choices, plus kids' menus for breakfast and dinner; reservations essential, including for popular Disney character breakfasts (which book up weeks in advance). *Average main: $75 Aulani, A Disney Resort & Spa, 92-1185 Aliinui Dr., Ko Olina 808/674–6200 www.disneyaulani.com/dining No lunch.*

### ★ Mina's Fish House

$$$$ | **SEAFOOD** | Chef Michael Mina, a James Beard Award winner, designed an exceptional line-to-table menu that celebrates the local catch in a space with panoramic views from indoor and lanai oceanfront tables. This might be the only restaurant in Hawaii (or the world) to have an on-site "fish sommelier," who guides you through the array of cooking techniques, flavorings, and portions—from fillet to whole fish—and helps you choose the best matches for your palate. **Known for:** charbroiled Hawaiian seafood tower; Kona lobster dishes and lobster pot pie; chili-miso glazed butterfish. *Average main: $60 Four Seasons Resort Oahu at Ko Olina, 92-1001 Olani St., Ko Olina 808/679–0079 www.michaelmina.net No lunch.*

### Monkeypod Kitchen by Merriman Ko Olina

$$ | **MODERN HAWAIIAN** | Local farm-to-table guru Peter Merriman is well-known throughout Hawaii for his inventive and popular restaurants, and this one captures his creativity and locally inspired food mantra perfectly. Hawaiian slack-key guitar music and the gentle buzz of diners kicking back make this a nice stop for a leisurely lunch—that could easily slide into happy hour. **Known for:** lobster deviled eggs and fresh fish tacos; indoor–outdoor setting; life-changing strawberry cream pie. *Average main: $30 Ko Olina Resort, 92-1048 Olani St., Ko Olina 808/380–4086 www.monkeypod-kitchen.com.*

### ★ Noe

$$$$ | **ITALIAN** | Classic dishes from southern Italy's Amalfi Coast dominate the menu at this sleek Four Seasons restaurant, with seating indoors, in various intimate and more social spaces, and outdoors overlooking a nature preserve. Locals come to celebrate special occasions, while guests from throughout the Ko Olina community come to feast on house-made pastas—especially the signature tagliatelle with truffle pesto and mushrooms—and multiple dishes that showcase Kona lobster. **Known for:** four-course tasting menu is an option; extensive Italian wine list; outdoor

nighttime dining experience. 💲 *Average main: $51* ✉ *Four Seasons Resort Oahu at Ko Olina, 92-1001 Olani St., Ko Olina* ☎ *808/679–3347* 🌐 *www.fourseasons.com/oahu* ⊗ *No lunch.*

**Roy's Ko Olina**

$$$$ | **MODERN HAWAIIAN** | The Ko Olina outpost of Roy's famed restaurant chain overlooks the 18th hole of the Ko Olina Golf Course and reflects a distinct local vibe, as most of the friendly staff come from this side of the island and exude an authentic aloha spirit. Dine on the Hawaii-Asia-Europe fusion signature dishes of Roy Yamaguchi and the chef's west side–influenced creations out on the patio or in the iconic wood-beam-and-concrete interior. **Known for:** braised short ribs and other Roy's signature dishes; great getaway from Ko Olina resort crowds; scenic golf course views. 💲 *Average main: $54* ✉ *Ko Olina Golf Club, 92-1220 Aliinui Dr., Kapolei* ☎ *808/676–7697* 🌐 *www.royyamaguchi.com.*

## Hotels

**★ Aulani, A Disney Resort & Spa**

$$$$ | **RESORT** | **FAMILY** | Disney's first property in Hawaii melds the Disney magic with breathtaking vistas, white sandy beaches, and sunsets that even Mickey stops to watch. **Pros:** tons to do on-site, including an upscale spa; family-friendly done right; Painted Sky: HI Style Studio makeovers for kids. **Cons:** a long way from Waikiki; Disney character breakfasts require advance reservations far in advance; areas and events can get really busy. 💲 *Rooms from: $764* ✉ *92-1185 Aliinui Dr., Kapolei* ☎ *866/443–4763 reservations, 808/674–6200 hotel operator* 🌐 *www.disneyaulani.com* *832 rooms* 🍽 *No Meals.*

**★ Four Seasons Resort Oahu at Ko Olina**

$$$$ | **RESORT** | At the first Four Seasons on the island, nearly every room or suite in the 17-story hotel offers floor-to-ceiling windows and a private lanai, all with an ocean view. **Pros:** luxurious and exclusive; secluded, even in the Ko Olina complex; amenities and options, such as a spa, abound. **Cons:** an hour from Waikiki; luxury doesn't come cheap; it doesn't always measure up to other Four Seasons. 💲 *Rooms from: $950* ✉ *92-1001 Olani St., in the Ko Olina complex, Ko Olina* ☎ *808/808–7053* 🌐 *www.fourseasons.com/oahu* *371 rooms* 🍽 *No Meals.*

**Marriott's Ko Olina Beach Club**

$$$$ | **RESORT** | **FAMILY** | Though primarily a time-share property, the Marriott here also offers nightly rentals, which range from hotel-style standard guest rooms to expansive and elegantly appointed one- or two-bedroom guest villa apartments, all within Ko Olina's 642-acre gated community. **Pros:** suites are beautifully decorated and have ample space for families; nice views; resort area offers entertainment, shopping, and dining options beyond the property. **Cons:** an hour to Honolulu and Waikiki; rooms and suites vary, so ask when booking; the coast beyond Ko Olina is rural without a lot for visitors to do. 💲 *Rooms from: $790* ✉ *92-161 Waipahe Pl., Ko Olina* ☎ *808/679–4700* 🌐 *www.marriott.com* *544 units* 🍽 *No Meals.*

## Performing Arts

### LUAU

**Paradise Cove Luau**

**FOLK/TRADITIONAL DANCE** | **FAMILY** | At one of the largest events on Oahu, you can stroll, drink in hand, through an authentic Hawaiian village, learn traditional arts and crafts, and play local games. The lively stage show includes a fire-knife dancer, singing emcee, and both traditional and contemporary hula and other Polynesian dances. A finale dance features participation from the audience. Admission includes the buffet, activities, and the show. You pay extra for table service, box seating, and shuttle transport to and from Waikiki—but the stunning sunsets are free. It starts daily at 5. ✉ *92-1089*

*Alii Nui Dr., Ko Olina* ☎ *808/842–5911* 🌐 *www.paradisecove.com* 🎫 *$150.*

## Activities

### SPAS

**Laniwai — A Disney Spa**

**SPA** | At this spa, every staff member—or "cast member," as they call themselves—is extensively trained in Hawaiian culture and history to ensure they are projecting the right *mana,* or energy, in their work. To begin each treatment, you select a special *pohaku* (lava rock) with words of intent, then cast it into a reflective pool. Choose from about 150 spa therapies, including some for younger family members, and indulge in Kula Wai, the only outdoor hydrotherapy garden on Oahu—with private vitality pools, a reflexology path, six different "rain" showers, whirlpool jet spas, and more. ✉ *Aulani, A Disney Resort & Spa, 92-1185 Aliinui Dr., Ko Olina* ☎ *808/674–6300* 🌐 *www.disneyaulani.com/spa-fitness* 🎫 *Facials from $185, masssages from $195, body treatments from $250.*

# Waianae

*9 miles north of Ko Olina.*

Waianae refers to both the town and the western (leeward) shores of Oahu, from Ko Olina up to Keawaula Beach (Yokohama Bay) and the end of the road near Kaena Point. It's mostly rural, without tourist traps and with few restaurants apart from fast-food outlets, tiny cafés, and hole-in-the-wall poke shacks. Still, the Waianae coast is well worth a day trip, mostly to experience an area where Hawaiians who are descendants of natives who populated the coast centuries before *haoles* (white people) arrived, live and play. The beaches boast crystal clear water. Turtles and dolphins swim near the shores, and when surf's up, Oahu's finest shredders show up to have fun and wow the watchers on the sand.

### GETTING HERE AND AROUND

Waianae is about 15 or 20 minutes north of Ko Olina by car along Highway 93.

## Beaches

**Keawaula Beach (Yokohama Bay)**

**BEACH** | **FAMILY** | You'll be one of the few outsiders at this Waianae coast beach at the very end of the road. If it weren't for the little strip of paved road, it would feel like a deserted isle: no stores, no houses, just a huge, sloping stretch of beach and some of the darkest-blue water off the island. Locals come here to fish and swim in waters calm enough for children in summer. Early morning brings with it spinner dolphins by the dozens just offshore. Although Makua Beach to the south (off Farrington Hwy.) is the best spot to see these animals, it's not nearly as beautiful or sandy as Keawaula. **Amenities:** lifeguards; parking (no fee); showers; toilets. **Best for:** solitude; sunset; swimming. ✉ *81-780 Farrington Hwy., Waianae* ✣ *About 7 miles north of Makaha.*

**Makaha Beach Park**

**BEACH** | **FAMILY** | This beach provides a slice of local life that most visitors don't see. Families string up tarps for the day, fire up hibachis, set up lawn chairs, get out the fishing gear, and strum ukulele while they "talk story" (chat). Legendary waterman Buffalo Keaulana can be found in the shade of the palms playing with his grandkids and spinning yarns of yesteryear. In these waters, Buffalo not only invented some of the most outrageous methods of surfing, but also raised his world-champion son, Rusty. He also made Makaha the home of the world's first international surf meet in 1954, and it still hosts his Big Board Surfing Classic. With its long, slow-building waves, the beach is a great spot to try out longboarding. The swimming is generally decent in summer, but avoid the big winter waves. The only parking is along the highway, but it's free. **Amenities:** lifeguards; showers; toilets. **Best for:** surfing;

In summer, when the surf is calm, Makaha is a great snorkeling destination; in winter, it's a popular surfing spot, especially for locals.

swimming. ⊠ *84-450 Farrington Hwy., Waianae* ✥ *Go 32 miles west of Honolulu on the H1, then exit onto Farrington Hwy. The beach will be on your left.*

**Papaoneone Beach**

**BEACH** | You may have to do a little exploring to find Papaoneone Beach, which is tucked behind three condos. Park on the street, and then duck through an easy-to-spot hole in the fence to reach this extremely wide, sloping beach that always seems to be empty. The waters are that eerie blue found only on the west side. Waves can get high here (it faces the same direction as the famed Makaha Beach), but, for the most part, the shore break makes for great, easy rides on your bodyboard or belly. The only downside is that all facilities, with the exception of a shower, are for the adjacent condos, so it's just you and the big blue. **Amenities:** showers. **Best for:** solitude; swimming. ⊠ *84-946 Farrington Hwy., Waianae* ✥ *In Makaha, across from Jade St.*

**Pokai Bay Beach Park**

**BEACH** | **FAMILY** | This gorgeous swimming and snorkeling beach is protected by a long breakwater left over from a now-defunct boat harbor. The entire length is sand, and a reef creates smallish waves perfect for novice surfers. **Amenities:** parking (no fee); showers; toilets. **Best for:** snorkeling; swimming. ⊠ *85-027 Waianae Valley Rd., Waianae* ✥ *Off Farrington Hwy.*

## Restaurants

**The Beach House by 604**

**$$** | **HAWAIIAN** | Housed in a former officer's dining hall right on the west-facing beach at Pokai Bay, the hip, casual, younger sibling of Pearl Harbor's Restaurant 604 is a great place to stop for a bite before or after a surf session at Makaha or a day trip up the west side to Yokohama Bay. The island-inspired menu focuses on comfort foods and includes everything from poke, burgers, fries, and pizza to traditional island plates with fish and rice. **Known for:** excellent sunset-viewing spot; buzzy happy hour; live music Tuesday through Saturday. *Average main: $22* *85-010 Army St., Waianae* *808/725–2589* *www.beachhouse604.com.*

**Coquito's Latin Cuisine**

$ | **LATIN AMERICAN** | A humble, family-run restaurant in a tiny roadside shack, Coquito's serves an eclectic array of traditional Puerto Rican and Latin American dishes, such as *arroz con gandules* (rice with peas), shrimp mofongo, *pastel borricúa* (ground green-banana masa stuffed with pork), Colombian empanadas, and Argentinian flank steak with chimichurri sauce. Order takeout for a picnic at a beach park, or dine in the small outdoor patio (no alcohol sold here, so you need to BYOB). **Known for:** Cuban sandwiches; various desserts, including tres leches cake and Puerto Rican flancocho, flan de coco, and tembleque (a coconut pudding); nearly everything prepared in-house. *Average main: $19* *85-773 Farrington Hwy., Waianae* *808/888–4082* *www.facebook.com/coquitoslatincuisinerest* *Closed Mon. No dinner Sun.*

**Countryside Cafe**

$ | **HAWAIIAN** | **FAMILY** | Escape the tourist traps and rub elbows with locals at this small, busy breakfast–brunch café, with outdoor porch seating and ocean views—but come early or order takeout, as it closes early afternoon. Island favorites dominate the menu, including corned beef hash *loco moco* (white rice, meat, fried eggs, and gravy) and *lilikoi* (passion fruit) pancakes for breakfast and garlic shrimp with mushrooms, fish tacos, and *kalbi* ribs for lunch. **Known for:** island-style eggs Benedict, pancakes, and French toast; fresh ingredients and large portions; friendly service. *Average main: $17* *87-70 Farrington Hwy., #104, Waianae* *808/888–5448* *www.countrysidecafe808.net* *No dinner.*

# Wahiawa

*Approximately 20 miles northeast of Ko Olina, 20 miles north of downtown Honolulu.*

Oahu's central plain is a patchwork of old towns and new residential developments, military bases, farms, ranches, and shopping malls, with a few noteworthy attractions and historic sites scattered about. Central Oahu encompasses the Moanalua Valley, residential Pearl City and Mililani, and the old plantation town of Wahiawa, on the uplands halfway to the North Shore.

James Dole first planted pineapples in the central plateau in the early 1900s, and the Dole Pineapple Plantation fields still border the northern limits of Wahiawa, a small town with a heavy military and working-class vibe. Lake Wilson (Wahiawa Reservoir) surrounds three sides of the town, and Highway 99 crosses two bridges (and several stoplights) to pass through.

Wahiawa is the commercial hub for several military bases, including Schofield Barracks, Wheeler Army Airfield, and the U.S. Naval Computer and Telecommunications Area Master Station Pacific. The main drag—a five-block stretch of Highway 99 where traffic often slows to a snail's pace—was once a fast-food mecca but in recent years has given birth to a handful of decent cafés and restaurants.

## GETTING HERE AND AROUND

For Central Oahu, all sights are most easily reached by either the H1 or the H2 freeway. Highway 99 goes through Schofield Barracks. Highway 80 goes through the town of Wahiawa.

*Continued on page 176*

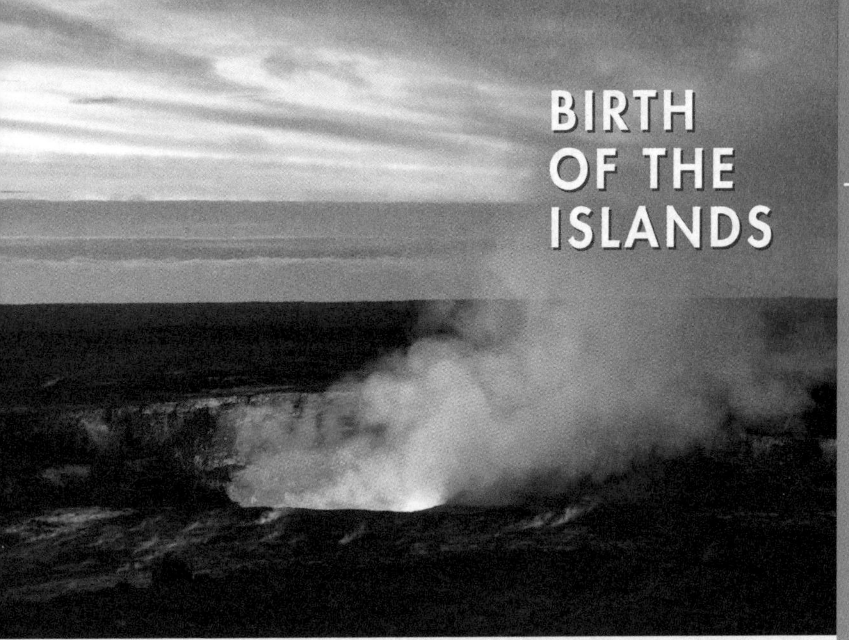

# BIRTH OF THE ISLANDS

How did the volcanoes of the Hawaiian Islands come to be here, in the middle of the Pacific Ocean? The ancient Hawaiians believed that the volcano goddess Pele's hot temper was the key to the mystery; modern scientists contend that it's all about plate tectonics and one very hot spot.

**Plate Tectonics and the Hawaiian Question:** The theory of plate tectonics says that the Earth's surface is comprised of plates that float around slowly over the planet's hot interior. The vast majority of earthquakes and volcanic eruptions occur near plate boundaries—the San Francisco earthquakes in 1906 and 1989, for example, were the result of activity along the nearby San Andreas Fault, where the Pacific and North American plates meet. Hawaii, more than 1,988 miles from the nearest plate boundary, is a giant exception. For years scientists struggled to explain the island chain's existence—if not a fault line, what caused the earthquakes and volcanic eruptions that formed these islands?

Kilauea erupting on the Big Island of Hawaii

**What's a Hot Spot?** In 1963, J. Tuzo Wilson, a Canadian geophysicist, argued that the Hawaiian volcanoes must have been created by small concentrated areas of extreme heat beneath the Pacific Plate. Wilson hypothesized that there is a hot spot beneath the present-day position of Hawaii Island (the "Big Island") and its heat produced a persistent source of magma. Magma is produced by rising-but-solid mantle rock that melts when it reaches about 100 km. At that depth, the lower pressure can no longer stop the rock from melting, and the magma rises to erupt onto the sea floor, forming an active seamount. Each flow caused the seamount to grow until it finally emerged above sea level as an island volcano. Plausible so far, but why then, is there not one giant Hawaiian island?

## THE JOURNEY OF PELE

Holo Mai Pele, often told through hula, is the Hawaiian story of how volcano goddess Pele sends her sister Hiiaka on an epic quest from the Big Island to fetch her lover Lohiau, living on Kauai. Overcoming many obstacles, Hiiaka reaches full goddess status and falls in love with Lohiau herself. When Pele finds out, she destroys everything dear to her sister, killing Lohiau and burning her sister's ohia groves. Each time lava flows from a volcano, ohia trees sprout shortly after, in a constant cycle of destruction and renewal.

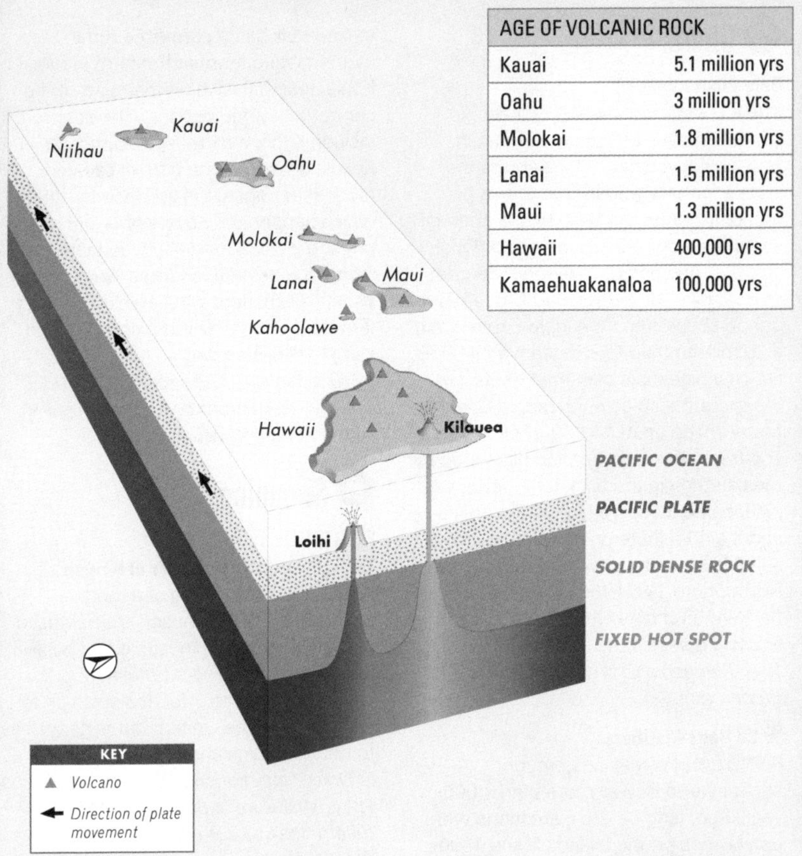


| AGE OF VOLCANIC ROCK | |
|---|---|
| Kauai | 5.1 million yrs |
| Oahu | 3 million yrs |
| Molokai | 1.8 million yrs |
| Lanai | 1.5 million yrs |
| Maui | 1.3 million yrs |
| Hawaii | 400,000 yrs |
| Kamaehuakanaloa | 100,000 yrs |

**Volcanoes on the Move:** Wilson further suggested that the movement of the Pacific Plate itself eventually carries the island volcano beyond the hot spot. Cut off from its magma source, the island volcano becomes dormant. As the plate slowly moved to the northwest, one island volcano would become extinct just as another would develop over the hot spot. After several million years, there is a long volcanic trail of islands and seamounts across the ocean floor. The oldest islands are those farthest from the hot spot. The exposed rocks of Kauai, for example, are about 5.1 million years old, but those on the Big Island are less than half a million years old, with new volcanic rock still being formed.

**An Island on the Way:** Off the coast of the Big Island of Hawaii, another volcano is still submerged but erupting. Geologists long believed it to be a retired seamount volcano, but in the 1970s they discovered both old and new lava on its flanks, and in 1996 it erupted with a vengeance. It is believed that thousands of generations from now, it will be the newest addition to the Hawaiian archipelago, so in July 2021 was given the name Kamaehuakanaloa, "the red child of Kanaloa."

## Sights

**Dole Plantation**

**OTHER ATTRACTION | FAMILY** | Pineapple plantation days are nearly defunct in Hawaii, but you can still celebrate the state's famous golden fruit at this promotional center with exhibits, a huge gift shop, a snack concession, educational displays, and one of the world's largest mazes. Take the self-guided Garden Tour, or hop aboard the Pineapple Express for a 20-minute train tour to learn a bit about life on a pineapple plantation. Kids love the more than 3-acre Pineapple Garden Maze, made up of 14,000 tropical plants and trees. If you do nothing else, stop by the cafeteria in the back for a delicious pineapple soft-serve Dole Whip. This is about a 40-minute drive from Waikiki, a suitable stop on the way to or from the North Shore. ✉ *64-1550 Kamehameha Hwy., Wahiawa* ☎ *808/621–8408* 🌐 *www.doleplantation.com* 🎟 *Plantation free, Pineapple Express $14, maze $10, garden tour $8.*

**★ Ko Hana Distillers**

**DISTILLERY** | Polynesians brought sugarcane to Hawaii more than 1,000 years ago, long before plantations were established on the Islands in the 1800s. Ko Hana grows 34 varieties of heirloom sugarcane and harvests it all by hand, then presses and distills the juice to make small-batch pure-cane rums. Stop by the tasting room at the farm in rural Kunia near Wahiawa, in the heart of the central valley, for tastings. Standout rums include Koho, a barrel-aged rum, and Kokoleka, made with pure cacao and raw honey. Sign up in advance for tours, which happen daily every hour until 4 pm and include a side-by-side tasting of white and barrel-aged rums. For a more in-depth experience, reserve a spot on a farm tour (Thursday morning at 10) and sample canes as well as rums. ✉ *92-1770 Kunia Rd., Kunia* ☎ *808/649–0830* 🌐 *www.kohanarum.com* 🎟 *Tasting $10, tour and tasting $25, farm tour $45.*

## Shopping

### FOOD

**Tropical Fruits Distributors of Hawaii**

**FOOD** | Avoid the hassle of airport inspections: this company specializes in packing inspected pineapple and papaya and will deliver to your hotel and to the airport check-in counter. It also ships to elsewhere in the United States as well as to Canada. Think about ordering online. ✉ *Dole Plantation, 64-1550 Kamehameha Hwy., Wahiawa* ☎ *800/697–9100* 🌐 *www.dolefruithawaii.com.*

Chapter 5

# NORTH SHORE

Updated by
Cheryl Crabtree

Sights
★★★★★

Restaurants
★★★☆☆

Hotels
★★★☆☆

Shopping
★★★☆☆

Nightlife
★☆☆☆☆

# WELCOME TO THE NORTH SHORE

## TOP REASONS TO GO

★ **Scenes of old Hawaii:** The wild, relatively undeveloped North Shore looks and feels more like the Oahu that existed centuries ago. Walk along bluff top and valley trails to discover ancient sites, and swim and fish in the crystal clear waters that sustained ancient communities.

★ **Farm-fresh bounty:** Oahu natives refer to the North Shore as the "country"—the source of much of the island's produce and seafood.

★ **World-famous beaches and waves:** Banzai Pipeline, Sunset (Paumalu) Beach, Waimea Bay—in winter they are the hallowed waters of surfing's greatest breaks. In summer, the glorious beaches provide the perfect setting for snorkeling and marine wildlife spotting.

★ **Laid-back vibe:** The North Shore is the antithesis of Waikiki. You won't find any high-rises or freeways here; outside of touristy Haleiwa, it's just miles of scenic coastline and country roads.

The main North Shore towns include Haleiwa (the hub), neighboring Waialua, Pupukea (just north of Waimea Bay), and the Kahuku district, which stretches from Kawela Bay and Kuilima/Turtle Bay to the small town of Kahuku.

**1 Waialua.** Life here once revolved around a sugar mill, but now it's a tranquil, mostly residential community that anchors the remote, uncrowded northwestern stretches of Oahu.

**2 Haleiwa.** The North Shore's touristy commercial hub reflects an early 1900s plantation-era vibe.

**3 Pupukea.** This is global surf culture's center of the universe, in the heart of a 7-mile stretch of the world's best breaks.

**4 Kahuku.** The easternmost North Shore district is home to legendary Turtle Bay Resort, famed shrimp shacks, and family-owned farms.

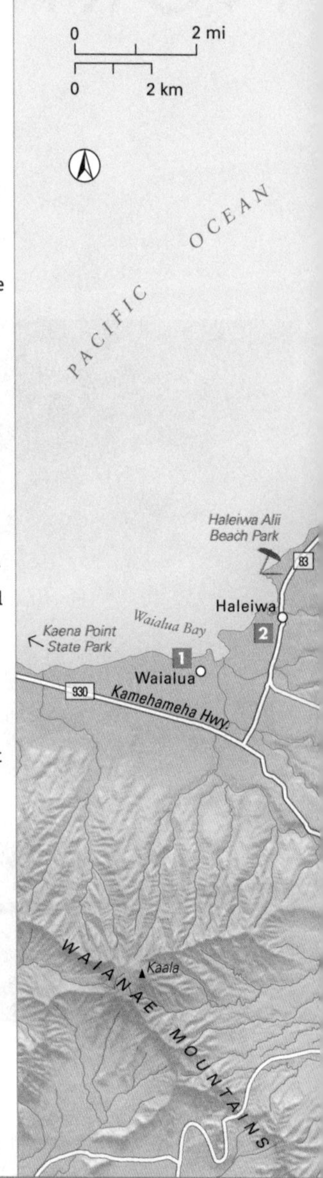

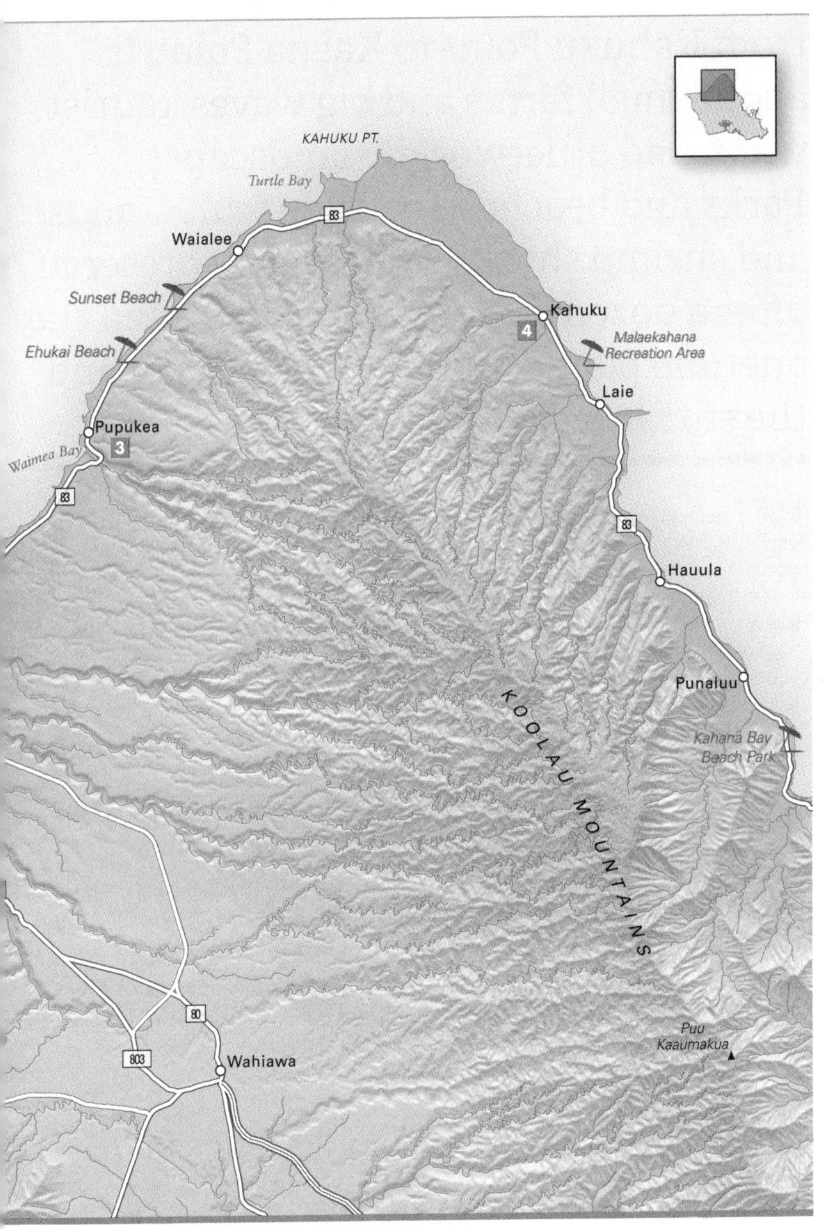
KAHUKU PT.
Turtle Bay
83
Waialee
Sunset Beach
Kahuku
4
Malaekahana Recreation Area
Ehukai Beach
Laie
Pupukea
3
Waimea Bay
83
83
Hauula
Punaluu
KOOLAU MOUNTAINS
Kahana Bay Beach Park
80
803
Wahiawa
Puu Kaaumakua

An hour from town (as locals refer to Honolulu) and a world away in atmosphere, Oahu's North Shore, roughly from Kahuku Point to Kaena Point, is about small farms and big waves, tourist traps, and otherworldly landscapes. Parks and beaches, roadside fruit stands and shrimp shacks, and a valley preserve offer a dozen reasons to stop between the onetime plantation town of Kahuku and the surf mecca of Haleiwa.

Haleiwa has had many lives, from resort getaway in the 1900s to plantation town through the 20th century to its life today as a surfer and tourist magnet. West of Haleiwa is the tiny village of Waialua; a string of beach parks; an airfield where gliders, hang gliders, and parachutists play; and, at the end of the road, Kaena Point State Park, which offers a brisk hike, striking views, and whale-watching in season.

Pack wisely for a day's North Shore excursion: swim and snorkel gear, light jacket and hat (the weather is mercurial, especially in winter), sunscreen and sunglasses, bottled water and snacks, towels and a picnic blanket, and both sandals and closed-toe shoes for hiking. A small cooler is nice; you may want to pick up some fruit or fresh corn. As always, leave valuables in the hotel safe, and lock the car whenever you park.

## Planning

### Getting Here and Around

#### AIR

North Shore Shuttle provides transportation, in private vehicles, to and from Honolulu International Airport and all North Shore destinations, and to and from Waikiki and the North Shore. Airport transfers to Haleiwa town are $95 per carload, east of Waimea Bay $110, and to Turtle Bay $120 per carload. Transportation between Waikiki and the North Shore costs $110 to $135 per carload.

**CONTACT North Shore Shuttle.** ☎ *808/465–7846* 🌐 *www.northshoreshuttle.net.*

### BUS

TheBus provides frequent daily service to the North Shore and is a practical way to get around, as parking is limited and fills quickly, especially in Haleiwa and at popular surf breaks. Nevertheless, bags must fit under your seat or on your lap, so TheBus is not an option if you have large checked bags and want to travel from the airport. (Surfboards aren't allowed either.)

Route 60 travels from Honolulu to Kaneohe and up the windward side to Turtle Bay, Pupukea, and Haleiwa and back. Route 52 transports riders from the Ala Moana Center to Haleiwa, traversing Central Oahu.

### CAR

From Waikiki, the quickest route to the North Shore is H1 west to H2 north, and then the Kamehameha Highway past Wahiawa. You'll hit Haleiwa in just under an hour. The windward route (H1 east, H3, Likelike or Pali Highway, through the mountains, then Kamehameha Highway north) takes at least 90 minutes to Haleiwa, but the drive is far prettier.

### TAXI

Taxis are very expensive and hard to find, but the rideshares Uber and Lyft have become popular options, especially for rides to and within the Haleiwa area. Most visitors who come up from Honolulu for day trips without a car sign up with a tour company.

## Beaches

"North Shore, where the waves are mean, just like a washing machine," sing the Kaau Crater Boys about this legendary side of the island. And in winter, they are absolutely right. At times, the waves overtake the road, stranding tourists and locals alike. When the surf is up, there are signs on the beach telling you how far to stay back so that you aren't swept out to sea. The most prestigious big-wave contest in the world, the "Eddie" (Eddie Aikau Big-Wave Invitational), is held at Waimea Bay on waves the size of a five- or six-story building. Major professional events take place across North Shore beaches in the winter months.

That all changes come summer, when this tiger turns into a kitten, with water smooth enough to water-ski on and ideal for snorkeling. The fierce Banzai Pipeline surf break becomes a great dive area, allowing you to explore the coral heads that, in winter, have claimed so many lives on the ultrashallow but big, hollow tubes created here. Even with the monster surf at a dull roar, this is still a time for caution: lifeguards are scarce, and currents don't subside just because the waves do.

That said, the North Shore is a place like no other on Earth and must be explored. From the turtles at Mokuleia to the tunnels at Shark's Cove, you could spend your whole trip on this side of Oahu and not be disappointed. A drive to the North Shore takes about an hour from Waikiki, but allot a full day to explore the beaches and Haleiwa, which, though burgeoning, retains a surf-town charm.

## Hotels

North Shore accommodation options are extremely limited compared to Honolulu and the southern shores of Oahu. Turtle Bay Resort is the only major hotel in the area, and the adjacent Kuilima condos provide legal short-term rentals. County of Honolulu law requires at least a 30-day minimum for most other vacation rental properties on the North Shore; currently, short-term rentals are legal only at condo complexes within 3,000 feet of a resort, and a license is required.

### PRICES

⇨ *Hotel prices are the lowest cost of a standard double room in high season. Hotel reviews have been shortened. For full information, visit Fodors.com.*

| What It Costs in U.S. Dollars | | | |
|---|---|---|---|
| $ | $$ | $$$ | $$$$ |
| **HOTELS** | | | |
| under $200 | $200–$280 | $281–$380 | over $380 |

## Restaurants

Most North Shore eateries cluster in the town of Haleiwa and at the Turtle Bay resort, which has options that range from casual poolside bars to the upscale Alaia restaurant. No North Shore trek is complete without a stop at a shrimp shack or truck and a slice of pie at Ted's Bakery. The classic shacks and food trucks are found mostly on the south side of Haleiwa and at the famed hub in Kahuku, at the North Shore's eastern limits, though some trucks travel to North Shore beaches and surf breaks during busy seasons.

### PRICES

⇨ *Restaurant prices are the average cost of a main course at dinner or, if dinner is not served, at lunch. Restaurant reviews have been shortened. For full information, visit Fodors.com.*

| What It Costs in U.S. Dollars | | | |
|---|---|---|---|
| $ | $$ | $$$ | $$$$ |
| **RESTAURANTS** | | | |
| under $20 | $20–$30 | $31–$40 | over $40 |

# Waialua

*30 miles northwest of Honolulu.*

A tranquil, multicultural burg with sleepy residential areas, uncrowded beach parks, and small mom-and-pop businesses, Wailua provides refuge from neighboring (and often tourist-choked) Haleiwa. In the 1900s, the Waialua Sugar Company attracted workers from around the world, and their descendants continue to live and work here. The former sugar operation buildings now hold a general store and eclectic, trendy shops, art studios, maker spaces for surfboard shapers and other craftspeople, and a coffee mill. Waialua is also the gateway to a wild and scenic coastline that includes Mokuleia Beach Park, Kaena Point State Park, and Kawaihapai Airfield (formerly known as Dillingham Airfield), where gliders and parachutists launch and land.

### GETTING HERE AND AROUND

Waialua, which is just west of Haleiwa, is about a 45-minute drive from Honolulu via the H2 and Highway 99 or Highway 803 through Central Oahu. TheBus Route 52 travels between Honolulu and Haleiwa, and Route 521 connects Haleiwa and Waialua.

## Sights

**Kaena Point State Park**

**STATE/PROVINCIAL PARK** | The name means "the heat," and, indeed, this windy, barren coast lacks both shade and fresh water (or any man-made amenities). Pack water, wear sturdy closed-toe shoes, don sunscreen and a hat, and lock the car. The hike is along a rutted dirt road, mostly flat and nearly 3 miles long (one-way), ending at a rocky, sandy headland. It is here that Hawaiians believed the souls of the dead met with their family gods and, if judged worthy to enter the afterlife, leapt off into eternal darkness at Leina Kauhane, just south of the point. Note that the point can also be accessed by trail (the hike is

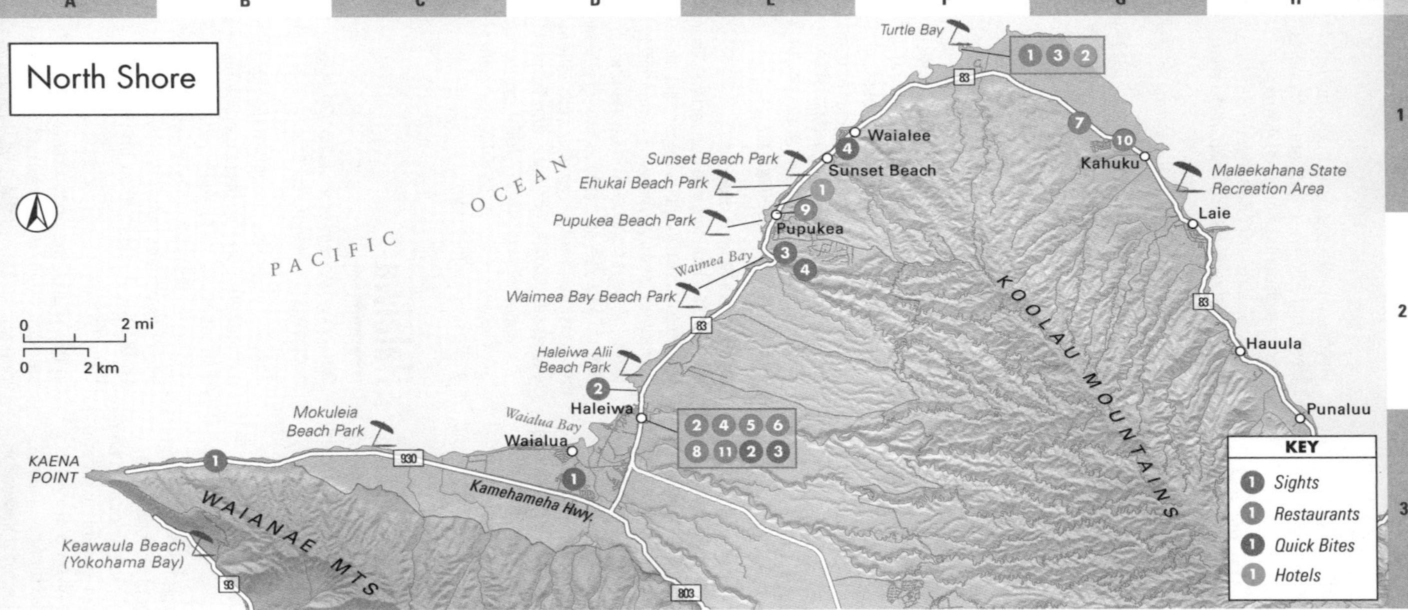


**Sights**

1 Kaena Point State Park .......... B3
2 Little Plumeria Farms .......... D2
3 Puu o Mahuka Heiau State Historic Site .......... E2
4 Waimea Valley .......... E2

**Restaurants**

1 Alaia .......... F1
2 Banzai Sushi Bar .......... D3
3 Beach House by Roy Yamaguchi .......... F1
4 Cholo's Homestyle Mexican Restaurant .......... D3
5 Haleiwa Beach House .......... D3
6 Haleiwa Joe's Seafood Grill .......... D3
7 Kahuku Farms Café .......... G1
8 Maya's Tapas & Wine .......... D3
9 Seven Brothers–Shark's Cove .......... E1
10 Thai Zapp .......... G1
11 Uncle Bo's Haleiwa .......... D3

**Quick Bites**

1 Island X Hawaii .......... D3
2 Kua Aina Sandwich Shop .......... D3
3 Matsumoto's Shave Ice .......... D3
4 Ted's Bakery .......... E1

**Hotels**

1 Ke Iki Beach Bungalows .......... E1
2 Turtle Bay Resort .......... F1

about the same length) from West Oahu at the Keawaula entrance, off another part of Farrington Highway.

In summer and at low tide, the small coves offer bountiful shelling; in winter, don't venture near the water. Rare native plants dot the landscape, and seabirds like the Laysan albatross nest here. If you're lucky, you might spot seals sunbathing on the rocks. From November through March, watch for humpback whales spouting and breaching. Binoculars and a camera are highly recommended. ✉ *69-385 Farrington Hwy., Waialua* 🌐 *dlnr.hawaii.gov/dsp/parks/oahu/kaena-point-state-park.*

## Beaches

**Mokuleia Beach Park**

**BEACH** | There is a reason why the producers of the TV show *Lost* chose this beach for their set: it's on the island's remote, northwest point and about 10 miles from the closest store or public restroom. Its beauty is in its lack of facilities and isolation—all the joy of being stranded on a deserted island without the trauma of the plane crash. The beach is wide and white, the waters bright blue (but a little choppy) and full of sea turtles and other marine life. Mokuleia is a great secret find; just remember to pack supplies and use caution, as there are no lifeguards. **Amenities:** parking (no fee). **Best for:** sunset, walking. ✉ *68-67 Farrington Hwy., Waialua* ✣ *West of Haleiwa town center, across from Kawaihapai (formerly Dillingham) Airfield.*

## Coffee and Quick Bites

**Island X Hawaii**

**$ | HAWAIIAN** | Recharge for more adventure with coffee, chocolate, shave ice, and boba drinks at this family-owned and operated spot in an old sugar mill garage. The owner crafts the all-natural syrups with organically grown mango, papaya, pineapple, and passion fruit. **Known for:** Hawaiian products used in the items; fresh ingredients; chocolate and coffee from neighboring fields. [$] *Average main: $5* ✉ *67-106 Kealohanui St., Unit C-1, Waialua* ☎ *808/637–2624* 🌐 *www.islandxhawaii.com.*

## Shopping

### GIFTS

**Island X Hawaii Shop**

**SOUVENIRS** | This eclectic store in a section of the Old Waialua Sugar Mill carries gifts, clothes, and local food items—especially coffee and chocolate that is produced in Waialua. The short unofficial tour of the coffee and cacao mill and roasting area just outside includes samples of coffee, cacao beans, and chocolate. ✉ *Waialua Sugar Mill, 67-106 Kealohanui St., Waialua* ☎ *808/637–2624* 🌐 *www.islandxhawaii.com.*

**North Shore Soap Factory**

**SOUVENIRS** | Housed in a converted silo in the historic Old Waialua Sugar Mill, this is a working factory where you can watch the soap as it's made. The soaps are all natural and use as many local ingredients as possible. The factory also sells lotions and essential oils, gift sets, and T-shirts. ✉ *Waialua Sugar Mill, 67-106 Kealohanui St., Waialua* ☎ *808/637–8400* 🌐 *northshoresoapfactory.com.*

# Haleiwa

*3 miles northeast of Waialua, 30 miles northwest of Honolulu.*

The North Shore's shopping, dining, and surf-culture hub has preserved its historic plantation-era roots and melded it with a laid-back 1960s vibe. The town sits amid a picture-perfect setting on Waialua Bay, where the Anahulu River empties into the harbor.

In the 1920s, the posh Haleiwa Hotel stood at the end of a railroad line (both long gone). During the '60s, hippies

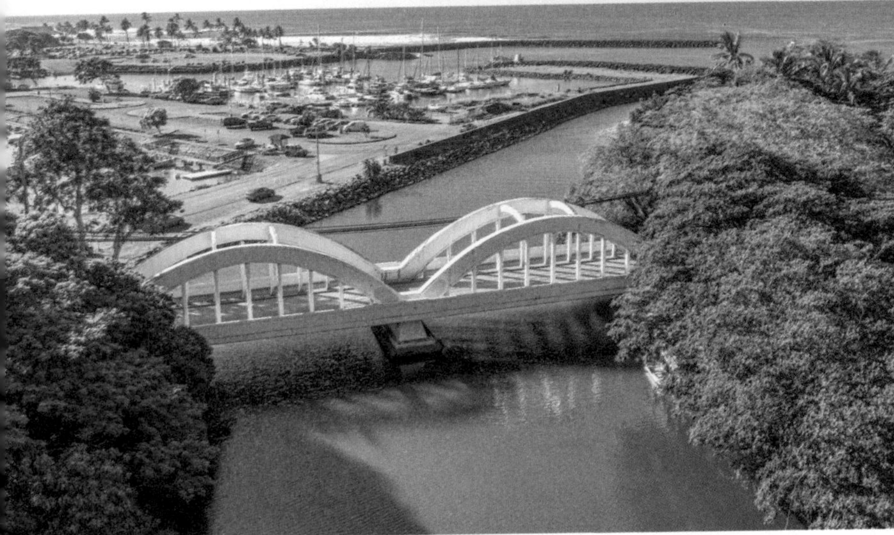

One landmark in the lively, water sports–focused town of Haleiwa is the double-arched, concrete Rainbow Bridge, built in 1921.

congregated here, followed by surfers from around the world. Today, the streets of historic Haleiwa Town reflect a fun mix of old and new, with charming general stores and contemporary boutiques, galleries, and eateries. Haleiwa Alii Beach Park and Haleiwa Beach Park border the bay and provide endless opportunities for water sports and other activities. Be sure to stop in at Liliuokalani Protestant Church, founded by missionaries in the 1830s. It's fronted by a large, stone archway built in 1910 and covered with night-blooming cereus (a type of cactus). Also check out the historic Rainbow Bridge, whose distinctive double arches appear in many local works of art.

### GETTING HERE AND AROUND

Haleiwa is about a 45-minute drive from Honolulu via the H2 and Highway 99 through Central Oahu. TheBus Route 52 transports passengers between Honolulu and Haleiwa via Central Oahu, and Route 60 travels around the windward side of the island, from Haleiwa to Kahuku and south to Kaneohe and Honolulu.

##  Sights

### Little Plumeria Farms

**FARM/RANCH** | Join an hour-long group tour of the Little family's farm, partly guided and the rest self-guided, through the nursery and gardens filled with rare hybrid plumeria trees. The tour (advance reservation required) includes the chance to pick your own blooms. The farm is on a hilltop overlooking the North Shore; pickup is at the North Shore Macadamia Nut Company in Haleiwa, across from Haleiwa Beach Park. ✉ *North Shore Macadamia Nut Company, 62-330 Kamehameha Hwy., for tour pickup, Haleiwa* ☎ *808/367–4119* 🌐 *littleplumeriafarms.com* 🎫 *Tours $45* ⏲ *No tours Nov.–Mar. and Wed. and Sun.*

## 

### ★ Haleiwa Alii Beach Park

**BEACH** | **FAMILY** | The winter waves are impressive here, but in summer, the ocean is like a lake, ideal for family swimming. The beach itself is big and tends to be full of locals. Its broad lawn off the highway is often the site of volleyball and Frisbee games, family barbecues, and art festivals and carnivals. Surf contests for amateurs and professionals regularly take place here. **Amenities:** lifeguards; parking (no fee); showers; toilets. **Best for:** surfing; swimming. ✉ *66-167 Haleiwa Rd., Haleiwa ⊕ North of Haleiwa town center and past harbor.*

## Restaurants

### ★ Banzai Sushi Bar

**$$ | JAPANESE FUSION** | An array of authentic Japanese dishes made with Hawaiian seafood and fresh, seasonal, mostly organic North Shore veggies and fruits attracts locals and visitors alike to this hip yet family-friendly sushi house. The extensive menu includes classic sashimi and tempura, standard and off-the-wall sushi rolls, Wagyu beef, broiled fish entrées, and various vegetarian and gluten-free options. **Known for:** full bar with good selection of Japanese whiskeys and sakes; rolls using macadamia nuts and island spices; some traditional Japanese seating. *Average main: $28* ✉ *North Shore Marketplace, 66-246 Kamehameha Hwy., Suite B, Haleiwa* ☎ *808/637–4404* 🌐 *banzaisushibarhawaii.com* ⏲ *Closed Mon. and Tues. No lunch.*

### Cholo's Homestyle Mexican Restaurant

**$ | MEXICAN | FAMILY** | There are only a couple of North Shore institutions that are considered gathering places—Foodland (the great grocery store) is one, and Cholo's is the other. Festively done up with Mexican tchotchkes, it serves decent rice-and-beans plates of Mexican standards (steak fajitas, burritos, enchiladas) at affordable prices. **Known for:** excellent ahi tacos; lively happy hour; fresh mango margaritas and more than 30 premium tequilas. *Average main: $19* ✉ *North Shore Marketplace, 66-250 Kamehameha Hwy., Haleiwa* ☎ *808/637–3059* 🌐 *www.cholos.mx.*

### Haleiwa Beach House

**$$ | AMERICAN | FAMILY** | This large, modern, two-story space on the North Shore takes full advantage of its epic water views; note that it doesn't take reservations. The menu is chock-full of surf-and-turf options, from juicy burgers to grilled steaks, blackened fish to red Thai curry with lobster and shrimp. **Known for:** view and setting (great for sunset) that can't be beat; loco moco, spicy tuna club sandwich; craft beers on draft and a nice wine list. *Average main: $26* ✉ *62-540 Kamehameha Hwy., Haleiwa* ☎ *808/637–3435* 🌐 *www.haleiwabeachhouse.com* ⏲ *No dinner Mon.–Thurs.*

### Haleiwa Joe's Seafood Grill

**$$$ | AMERICAN** | After the long drive to the North Shore, watching the boats and surfers come and go from the harbor while you enjoy a mai tai on the open-air lanai here may be just what you need. This casual little joint, just past the Rainbow Bridge, rarely changes (to some, that might feel dated, but regulars appreciate the familiarity); a more upscale Kaneohe location overlooks the lush Haiku Gardens. **Known for:** reliable food with a nice harbor setting; crunchy coconut shrimp and good daily fish specials; reservations not accepted. *Average main: $35* ✉ *66-011 Kamehameha Hwy., Haleiwa* ☎ *808/637–8005* 🌐 *www.haleiwajoes.com* ⏲ *No lunch Mon.–Sat.*

### ★ Maya's Tapas & Wine

**$$$ | TAPAS** | A cozy, romantic space with a slightly sophisticated (for the North Shore) vibe, Maya's serves up classic Spanish and Mediterranean dishes with island twists, including a variety of tapas as well as some larger plates. Here, seafood paella is made with local line-caught fish and shrimp, a burger showcases Kunoa beef, and hand-tossed flatbreads come with roasted local veggies and macadamia nut pesto. **Known for:** craft cocktails and sangria; savory paella and other specials; popular happy hour and weekend brunch. *Average main: $31*

⊠ *66-250 Kamehameha Hwy., Unit D-101, Haleiwa* ☎ *808/200–2964* 🌐 *www.mayastapasandwine.com* ⏲ *Closed Mon. No dinner Sun.*

**Uncle Bo's Haleiwa**

**$$ | HAWAIIAN | FAMILY** | One of the North Shore's liveliest eateries is set in a casual, contemporary space. It serves Hawaiian-style fare including pupus—from poke bowls and fresh wild-caught moonfish to nachos with ham and kalua pig on wonton chips—as well as pasta dishes, pizza, soups, and salads. **Known for:** something for everyone, plus extensive gluten-free menu; fun happy hour (weekdays 4 to 6 pm, weekends 2 to 6 pm); indoor–outdoor seating. $ *Average main: $28* ⊠ *66-111 Kamehameha Hwy., Unit 101, Haleiwa* ☎ *808/797–9649* 🌐 *www.unclebosrestaurant.com* ⏲ *No lunch weekdays.*

## Coffee and Quick Bites

**Kua Aina Sandwich Shop**

**$ | BURGER | FAMILY** | This North Shore spot has gone from funky burger shack (it first opened in 1975) to institution, with crowds of people standing in line to order the large, hand-formed burgers heaped with bacon, cheese, and pineapple. Frankly, there are better burgers to be had around the island, but this place commands a truly loyal following. **Known for:** a pilgrimage stop on the North Shore surf circuit; tourists by the busload, and locals too; decent burgers (in two sizes) and fries. $ *Average main: $13* ⊠ *66-160 Kamehameha Hwy., Haleiwa* ☎ *808/637–6067* 🌐 *kua-ainahawaii.com.*

**Matsumoto's Shave Ice**

**$ | CAFÉ | FAMILY** | For a real slice of Haleiwa life, stop at this family-run spot for cool treats that are available in every flavor imaginable. For something different, order a shave ice with house-made adzuki beans—the red beans are boiled until soft, mixed with sugar, and then placed in the cone with the ice on top. **Known for:** one of the most popular shave ice spots on Oahu; the Matsumoto with lemon, pineapple, and coconut syrup; in business since 1951. $ *Average main: $4* ⊠ *66-111 Kamehameha Hwy., Suite 605, Haleiwa* ☎ *808/637–4827* 🌐 *www.matsumotoshaveice.com.*

## Shopping

The North Shore has no major malls, but it does have a couple of open-air shopping complexes and numerous shops and makeshift stands—some on the side of the road, others a bit more hidden—with one-of-a-kind treasures. Eclectic shops are the best places to score skin-care products made on the North Shore, Hawaiian music CDs, sea glass and shell mobiles, coffee grown in the Islands, and clothing items unavailable elsewhere. Be sure to chat with the owners in each shop. North Shore residents are an animated, friendly bunch, with multiple talents. Stop in for coffee and a shopkeeper might reveal a little about his or her passion for creating distinguished pieces of artwork.

### CLOTHING

**The Growing Keiki**

**CHILDREN'S CLOTHING | FAMILY** | Frequent visitors return to this store year after year for a fresh supply of unique, locally made, Hawaiian-style clothing for youngsters. ⊠ *66-051 Kamehameha Hwy., Haleiwa* ☎ *808/637–4544* 🌐 *www.instagram.com/TheGrowingKeiki.*

★ **Silver Moon Emporium**

**CLOTHING** | The small boutique carries everything from Brighton jewelry and European designer wear to fashionable T-shirts, shoes, and handbags. Expect attentive and personalized yet casual service. The stock changes frequently, and there's always something wonderful on sale. No matter what your taste, you'll find something for everyday wear or special occasions. ⊠ *North Shore Marketplace,*

*66-250 Kamehameha Hwy., Haleiwa* ☎ *808/637–7710* 🌐 *www.instagram.com/silvermoon_emporium_haleiwa.*

### SHOPPING CENTERS

**Haleiwa Store Lots**

**SHOPPING CENTER** | **FAMILY** | The most notable tenant here is the legendary Matsumoto's Shave Ice. (You'll know it by the long line of people.) The shiny, open-air complex is also home to the locally operated Whaler's General Store and the casual beach-chic boutique Guava Shop, as well as surf photographer Clark Little's art gallery. ✉ *66-111 Kamehameha Hwy., Haleiwa* 🌐 *www.haleiwastorelots.com.*

**North Shore Marketplace**

**SHOPPING CENTER** | **FAMILY** | While playing on the North Shore, check out this open-air plaza that includes a number of art galleries, as well as clothing, gelato, and jewelry stores, among its tenants. And don't miss the Silver Moon Emporium for eclectic Islands fashions. People drive out of their way for the Coffee Gallery or for happy hour at Cholo's Homestyle Mexican Restaurant or Maya's Tapas and Wine. ✉ *66-250 Kamehameha Hwy., Haleiwa* ☎ *808/637–4416* 🌐 *northshoremarketplacehawaii.com.*

### SPORTING GOODS

**Surf N Sea**

**SPORTING GOODS** | **FAMILY** | This water-sports store has everything you need for an active vacation under one roof. Purchase rash guards, swimwear, T-shirts, footwear, hats, and shorts. Book scuba-diving tours and lessons and rent kayaks, snorkeling or scuba gear, spears for free diving, surfboards, stand-up paddleboards, and bodyboards. Experienced surfing instructors will take beginners to the small breaks on the North Shore beaches, with their notoriously huge (winter) or flat (summer) waves. Warning to fishing enthusiasts: a fishing pole is the one ocean apparatus this shop doesn't carry. ✉ *62-595 Kamehameha Hwy., Haleiwa* ☎ *800/899–7873* 🌐 *www.surfnsea.com.*

# Pupukea

*6 miles northeast of Haleiwa.*

Pupukea is a tiny village that anchors the Seven Mile Miracle, the legendary stretch of North Shore coast that faithfully serves up some of the world's best barrels and perfectly shaped waves every winter. It's also home to Foodland, the only grocery store between Kahuku/Laie and Haleiwa, which means you're likely to rub elbows in the checkout line with seasoned professional surfers and visiting celebrities, along with slipper-clad locals. Across the street are Shark's Cove and Three Tables, both excellent snorkeling and scuba sites when the winter swells abate. The Banzai Pipeline and Sunset (Paumalu) Beach are just a mile up the road. Drive up the hill behind Foodland to explore the sacred Puu o Mahuka Heiau, the largest shrine on the island.

### GETTING HERE AND AROUND

Pupukea is about a 70-minute drive from Honolulu via the H2 and Highway 99 through Central Oahu to Haleiwa, then east on Kamehameha Highway. TheBus route 60 is an option that travels the windward side. Traffic on Kamehameha Highway can slow to a snail's pace when waves are big and on weekends, when people head to the beaches.

## Sights

**Puu o Mahuka Heiau State Historic Site**

**RUINS** | Worth a stop for its spectacular views from a bluff high above the ocean overlooking Waimea Bay, this sacred spot spans 2 acres and is the largest *heiau* (place of worship) on Oahu. At one time it was used as a *heiau luakini*, or a temple for human sacrifices. Puu o Mahuka may have been built in the 17th century, and its use for religious purposes ended in 1819. The remnants of its stone walls are impressive, and the site is now on the National Register of Historic Places.

While Waimea Bay is known for its big winter waves and surf culture, the Waimea Valley is an area of great historical significance. It's also known for its botanical specimens, including big tropical trees.

Turn up the road at the Pupukea Foodland and follow it to the site. ✉ *Pupukea Rd., ½ mile north of Waimea Bay, Pupukea* ✣ *From Rte. 83, turn right on Pupukea Rd. and drive 1 mile uphill* 🌐 *dlnr.hawaii.gov/dsp/parks/oahu/puu-o-mahuka-heiau-state-historic-site* 🎟 *Free.*

### ★ Waimea Valley

**GARDEN | FAMILY** | Waimea gets lots of press for the giant winter waves in the bay, but the valley itself is a newsmaker and an ecological treasure, with a local nonprofit working to conserve and restore its natural habitat. Follow the Kamananui Stream up the valley through the 1,875 acres of gardens. The botanical collections here have more than 5,000 species of tropical flora, including a superb gathering of native Hawaiian and international plants. It's the best place on the island to see native species, such as the endangered Hawaiian moorhen. You can visit the restored Hale o Lono *heiau* (shrine) and other ancient archaeological sites as well; evidence suggests that the area was an important spiritual center. Daily activities include botanical walking tours and cultural tours. This is also the venue for the Haleiwa Farmers' Market every Thursday from 2 to 6. At the back of the valley (a ¾-mile walk one-way), Waihi Falls plunges 45 feet into a swimming pond. **■ TIP→ Bring your board shorts—a swim is the perfect way to end your hike, although the pond can get crowded. Bring mosquito repellent, too; it can get buggy.** ✉ *59-864 Kamehameha Hwy., Pupukea* ☎ *808/638–7766* 🌐 *www.waimeavalley.net* 🎟 *$25.*

## Beaches

### Ehukai Beach Park

**BEACH** | What sets Ehukai apart is the view of the famous Banzai Pipeline, where the winter waves curl into magnificent tubes, making it an experienced wave-rider's dream. It's also an inexperienced swimmer's nightmare. Spring and summer waves, on the other hand, are more accommodating to the average person, and there's good snorkeling. Except

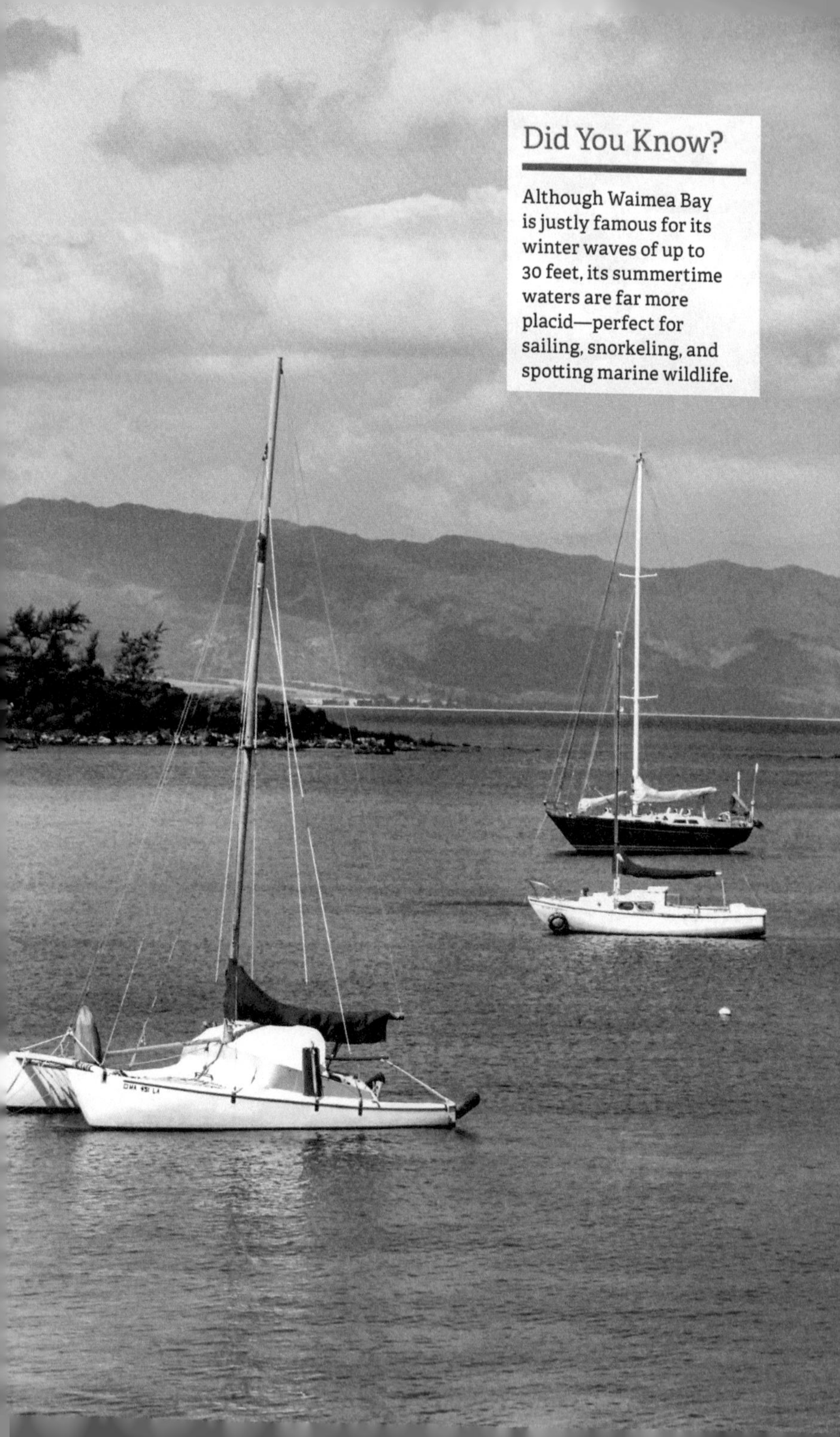

## Did You Know?

Although Waimea Bay is justly famous for its winter waves of up to 30 feet, its summertime waters are far more placid—perfect for sailing, snorkeling, and spotting marine wildlife.

when the surf contests are happening, there's no reason to stay on the central strip. Travel in either direction from the center, and the conditions remain the same but the population thins out, leaving you with a magnificent stretch of sand all to yourself. **Amenities:** lifeguards; parking (no fee); showers; toilets. **Best for:** snorkeling; surfing. ✉ *59-337 Ke Nui Rd., Pupukea* ✣ *1 mile north of Foodland at Pupukea.*

★ **Pupukea Beach Park** (*Shark's Cove*)
**BEACH** | Surrounded by shade trees, Pupukea Beach is pounded by surf in the winter months but offers great diving and snorkeling in summer (March through October). Its cavernous lava tubes and tunnels are great for both novice and experienced snorkelers and divers, though you must wear reef shoes at all times since there are a lot of sharp rocks. Sharp rocks also mean that this beach isn't the best for little ones. Some dive-tour companies offer round-trip transportation from Waikiki. Equipment rentals and dining options are nearby. **Amenities:** parking (no fee); showers; toilets. **Best for:** diving; snorkeling; swimming. ✉ *59-729 Kamehameha Hwy., Pupukea* ✣ *3½ miles north of Haleiwa, across street from Foodland.*

★ **Sunset Beach Park** (*Paumalu Beach Park*)
**BEACH** | The beach is broad, the sand is soft, the summer waves are gentle—making for good snorkeling—and the winter surf is crashing. Many love searching this shore for the puka shells that adorn the necklaces you see everywhere. **Amenities:** lifeguards; parking (no fee); showers; toilets. **Best for:** snorkeling; sunset; surfing. ✉ *59-144 Kamehameha Hwy., Pupukea* ✣ *1 mile north of Ehukai Beach Park.*

★ **Waimea Bay Beach Park**
**BEACH** | **FAMILY** | Made popular in that old Beach Boys song "Surfin' U.S.A.," this is a slice of big-wave (25 to 30 feet) heaven in winter. Summer is the time to swim and snorkel in the calm waters, and the beach is good for families then. The shore break is great for novice bodysurfers. Due to the beach's popularity, its postage-stamp parking lot is often full, but it's also possible to park along the side of the road and walk in. **Amenities:** lifeguards; parking (no fee); showers; toilets. **Best for:** snorkeling; surfing; swimming. ✉ *61-31 Kamehameha Hwy., Pupukea* ✣ *Across from Waimea Valley, 3 miles north of Haleiwa.*

## Restaurants

**Seven Brothers – Shark's Cove**
**$** | **HAWAIIAN** | **FAMILY** | The community-minded sons and the next generation of a Samoan-Californian couple run this casual eatery across from Shark's Cove, as well as other locations such as Kahuku and Haleiwa. Surfers and sightseers flock here for burgers, salads, fries, and, in some locations, seafood dishes; this location has outdoor seating. **Known for:** house-made sauces and dressings; Mom's banana bread topped with coconut and chocolate sauce; Polynesian salad, coconut macadamia-nut shrimp salad. $ *Average main: $17* ✉ *59-712 Kamehameha Hwy., Pupukea* 🌐 *sevenbrothersburgers.com* ⏲ *Closed Sun.*

## Coffee and Quick Bites

**Ted's Bakery**
**$** | **AMERICAN** | **FAMILY** | Sunburned tourists and salty surfers rub shoulders in their quest for Ted's famous chocolate *haupia* cream pie (layered coconut and dark chocolate puddings topped with whipped cream) and hearty plates such as garlic shrimp, gravy-drenched hamburger steak, and mahimahi. Parking spots and the umbrella-shaded tables are at a premium, so be prepared to grab and go; if you can't get enough of that haupia goodness, Foodland and other grocery chains typically stock a selection of the famous pies. **Known for:** Ted's pies, which

seem to show up at every Oahu potluck; reliable all-day dining; plate lunches. *Average main: $14 ✉ 59-024 Kamehameha Hwy., Pupukea ☎ 808/638–8207 🌐 www.tedsbakery.com.*

## Hotels

**Ke Iki Beach Bungalows**
**$$$$ | APARTMENT | FAMILY** | At this 1½-acre, sloped, beachfront lot with six duplex bungalows, you can choose from studios and one- or two-bedroom units—outfitted with breezy beach-house furnishings, individual grills, hammocks, and picnic tables—and enjoy access to a 200-foot strand of sugary white-sand beach running between the North Shore's famous Waimea Bay and Ehukai Beach (Banzai Pipeline). **Pros:** outdoor showers, meditation area, and beachfront seating for nightly stargazing; popular with families for reunions and weddings; steps to the beach and bike path to Sunset Beach and Waimea Bay. **Cons:** a bit far from restaurants and shopping in Haleiwa; high surf in winter months, no pool; some bungalows close to highway noise. *Rooms from: $395 ✉ 59-579 Ke Iki Rd. ☎ 808/638–8229 🌐 www.keikibeach.com 12 units No Meals.*

## Performing Arts

### LUAU

**Toa Luau at Waimea Valley**
**FOLK/TRADITIONAL DANCE | FAMILY** | Don a flower lei and feast on traditional Hawaiian luau fare while enjoying cultural activities and a Polynesian show, with a choice of start time at 12:30 or 5 on Monday and Wednesday through Friday. It's a three-hour experience, and tickets include a Waimea Valley pass so you can explore the gardens before the luau. *✉ 59-864 Kamehameha Hwy., Pupukea ☎ 877/778–0273 🌐 www.toaluau.com From $115.*

# Kahuku

*Kawela Bay is 5½ miles northeast of Pupukea, Kahuku is about 9 miles northeast of Pupukea.*

The Kahuku district, which stretches from Kahuku town to Kawela Bay, includes Kahuku Point, the northernmost point on Oahu. The area is best known for fresh fruits and veggies from local farms (watch for stands along the highway), shrimp shacks, and exceptional high school football stars who go on to play at top-tier colleges and in the NFL. Kahuku town has a collection of brand-name stores and tiny mom-and-pop shops amid modest residential neighborhoods filled with longtime island residents. Multimillion-dollar homes line the shores of the gated Kawela Bay community, but there's public beach access off Kamehameha Highway at Kawela Camp. Park on the side of the road, and walk about ¼ mile along a trail to get there.

### GETTING HERE AND AROUND

Kahuku is about a 70-minute drive from Honolulu via the Pali Highway, Likelike Highway, or the H3 east through the mountains, then north on Kamehameha Highway. TheBus route 60 serves the area, too.

## Beaches

**Turtle Bay** (*Kuilima Cove*)
**BEACH | FAMILY** | Now known more for its namesake resort than its magnificent beach at Kuilima Cove, Turtle Bay is mostly passed over on the way to the better-known beaches of Sunset and Waimea. But for those with average swimming capabilities, this is a good place to be. The crescent-shaped stretch is protected by a huge sea wall, so you can see and hear the fury of the northern swell while blissfully floating in cool,

*Continued on page 196*

# HAWAII'S PLANTS 101

Tropical hibiscus

Hawaii is a bounty of rainbow-colored flowers and plants. The evening air is scented with their fragrance. Just look at the front yard of almost any home, travel any road, or visit any local park and you'll see a spectacular array of colored blossoms and leaves. What most visitors don't know is that many of the plants they are seeing are not native to Hawaii; rather, they were introduced during the last two centuries as ornamental plants, or for timber, shade, or fruit.

Hawaii boasts nearly every climate on the planet, excluding the two most extreme: arctic tundra and arid desert. The Islands have wine-growing regions, cactus-speckled ranchlands, icy mountaintops, and the rainiest forests on earth.

The lush lowland valleys along the windward coasts are predominantly populated by non-native trees including yellow- and red-fruited **guava**, silver-leafed **kukui**, and orange-flowered **tulip trees.**

The colorful **plumeria flower**, very fragrant and commonly used in lei making, and the giant multicolored **hibiscus flower** are both used by many women as hair adornments, and are two of the most common plants found around homes and hotels. The umbrella-like **monkeypod tree** from Central America provides shade in many of Hawaii's parks including Kapiolani Park in Honolulu. Hawaii's largest tree, found in Lahaina, Maui, is a giant **banyan tree**, which survived the devastating fire there in 2023 despite major damage. Its canopy and massive support roots cover about two-thirds of an acre. The native **ohia tree**, with its brilliant red brush-like flowers, and the **hapuu**, a giant tree fern, are common in Hawaii's forests and are also used ornamentally in gardens.

Naupaka, Limahuli Garden

Bougainvillea
Guava 
Monkeypod 

Banyan
Ohia lehua* 
Tulip tree 

Plumeria
Pandanus 
Hibiscus 

Anthurium
Kukui 
Hapuu 

*Endemic to Hawaii

## DID YOU KNOW?

As many as 6,000 plant species are found in the Hawaiian Islands, but only about 1,400 are native. Of these, 366 are so rare, they are endangered. Hawaii's endemic plants evolved from ancestral seeds arriving in the Islands over thousands of years as baggage with birds, floating on ocean currents, or drifting on winds from continents thousands of miles away. Once here, these plants evolved in isolation, creating many new species known nowhere else in the world.

## Shrimp Shacks

No drive to the North Shore is complete without a shrimp stop. Stands dot Kamehameha Highway from Kahaluu north to Kahuku. For about $15, you can get a shrimp plate lunch or a snack of chilled shrimp with cocktail sauce, served from a rough hut or converted van (many permanently parked) with picnic-table seating.

The shrimp-shack phenomenon began with a lost lease and determined restaurateurs. In 1994, when Giovanni and Connie Aragona couldn't renew the lease on their Haleiwa deli, they began hawking their best-selling dish—an Italian-style scampi preparation involving lemon, butter, and lots of garlic—from a truck alongside the road. About the same time, aquaculture was gaining a foothold in nearby Kahuku, with farmers raising sweet, white shrimp and huge, orange-whiskered prawns in shallow freshwater ponds. The ready supply and the success of the first shrimp truck led to many imitators.

Although it has changed hands, that first business lives on as **Giovanni's Original Shrimp Truck**, parked in Kahuku town. Signature dishes include the garlic shrimp and a spicy shrimp sauté, both worth a stop. There's also a food truck in Haleiwa.

But there's plenty of competition: at least a dozen stands, trucks, or stalls are operating at any given time, with varying menus (and quality).

Not all that shrimp comes fresh from the ponds; much of it is imported. The only way you can be sure you're buying local, farm-raised shrimp is if the shrimp is still kicking. **Romy's Kahuku Prawns and Shrimp Hut** (Kamehameha Highway, near Kahuku) is an arm of one of the longest-running aquaculture farms in the area; it sells live shrimp and prawns and farm-raised fish along with excellent plate lunches.

calm waters. The convenience of this spot is also hard to pass up—a concession sells sandwiches and sunblock right on the beach. The resort has free parking for beach guests. **Amenities:** food and drink; parking (no fee); showers; toilets. **Best for:** sunset; swimming. ✉ *57-20 Kuilima Dr., 4 miles north of Kahuku, Kahuku* ✣ *Turn into Turtle Bay Resort and follow signs to public parking lot and beach access spots.*

## Restaurants

### Alaia

**$$$$ | HAWAIIAN** | The menus at Turtle Bay Resort's signature restaurant—a casual but chic open-air space overlooking Turtle Bay and the Seven Mile Miracle—showcase Hawaiian comfort food with a modern, upscale twist, for example, braised *kalbi* short ribs, roast chicken with macadamia nut mole, and Salanova lettuce. About 95% of the fresh produce, from lettuce, tomatoes, and breadfruit to apple bananas and kitchen herbs, comes from the 100-acre organic farm across the road and is grown in partnership with local farmers. **Known for:** special-occasion dinners; sweeping ocean views; Hawaiian bouillabaisse special. [$] *Average main: $45* ✉ *Turtle Bay Resort, 57-091 Kamehameha Hwy., Kahuku* ☎ *866/475–2569* 🌐 *www.turtlebayresort.com* ⏲ *No lunch.*

★ **Beach House by Roy Yamaguchi**
$$$$ | **MODERN HAWAIIAN** | Loyalists of Roy Yamaguchi's celebrated spots in Hawaii Kai and Waikiki are thrilled to find his North Shore outpost—a rustic, beam-and-concrete-floor pavilion literally on the sand at Turtle Bay. All the favorites are served at this more beach-casual spot, from miso deep-water black cod to beef short ribs, along with a more casual lunch menu. **Known for:** casual, romantic setting right on the beach; fresh North Shore ingredients; good for celebrations. *Average main: $56 ✉ Turtle Bay Resort, 57-091 Kamehameha Hwy., Kahuku ☎ 808/293–0801 🌐 www.royyamaguchi.com.*

★ **Kahuku Farms Café**
$ | **HAWAIIAN** | **FAMILY** | Fourth-generation descendants of Japanese sugarcane workers own and operate this casual café, set on the edge of a 140-acre farm north of the food truck village. Menu items include panini, pizzas, wraps, salads, iced drinks, and smoothies, all filled with homegrown ingredients, from *lilikoi* (passion fruit) and cacao to açai and sweet papaya; enjoy your meal or snack at outdoor shaded tables near a tree-studded lawn and gardens. **Known for:** hour-long wagon farm tour on select days, including fruit and chocolate tasting; seasonal açai bowls with apple bananas and berries; lots of veggie and vegan choices, can add chicken to many dishes. *Average main: $17 ✉ 56-800 Kamehameha Hwy., Kahuku ☎ 808/628–0639 🌐 kahukufarms.com ⊙ Closed Tues. and Wed. No dinner.*

**Thai Zapp**
$ | **THAI** | This casual eatery with tables inside and outdoors serves authentic Thai dishes in a tiny, unassuming spot in the Sugar Mill complex, next to Seven Brothers. It also operates a food truck nearby and is a good bet when the food trucks have closed for the day. **Known for:** adjustable spice levels; large portions, so count on bringing home leftovers; panang curry, pad Thai, drunken noodles. *Average main: $15 ✉ 56-565 Kamehameha Hwy., Kahuku ☎ 808/445–2719 ⊙ Closed Sun.*

## Hotels

★ **Turtle Bay Resort**
$$$$ | **RESORT** | **FAMILY** | Sprawling over nearly 1,300 acres of natural landscape on the edge of Kuilima Point in Kahuku, this resort has spacious guest rooms (averaging nearly 500 square feet) with lanai that showcase stunning peninsula views. **Pros:** fabulous open public spaces in a secluded area of Oahu; numerous amenities such as a beautiful spa and four outdoor pools; excellent location for exploring the North Shore. **Cons:** remote—even Haleiwa is a 20-minute drive; hefty resort fee; 24/7 resort living isn't for everyone. *Rooms from: $759 ✉ 57-091 Kamehameha Hwy., Kahuku ☎ 808/293–6000, 866/475–2567, 🌐 www.turtlebayresort.com 452 rooms No Meals.*

## Nightlife

★ **Off the Lip**
**COCKTAIL BARS** | West-oriented views (particularly stellar at sunset), creative cocktails incorporating fresh fruit and herbs from neighboring farms, house-made syrups and spirits, and live entertainment most nights draw locals and visitors to this classy, surf-themed lobby bar at Turtle Bay Resort. It's also the only nightlife choice on the North Shore east of Haleiwa, and night crawlers should know that the bar usually stops serving by 10 pm. *✉ Turtle Bay Resort, 57-091 Kamehameha Hwy., Kahuku ☎ 866/475–2569 🌐 www.turtlebayresort.com/dining/lip.*

### Kuilima Farm Stand

**MARKET | FAMILY** | Turtle Bay Resort purchased 468 acres of prime North Shore agricultural land near the entrance to the resort and created an organic farm to supply fresh ingredients to its restaurants, as well as to support 34 sustainably farmed community garden plots. A farm stand with multiple stalls shares the bounty with locals and visitors. Pull off the highway to pick up sustainably grown pineapple, papaya, corn, and other fruits and veggies, plus locally made souvenirs. The stand is open daily 9 to 5, and farm tours (from $25) are offered Wednesday, Thursday, and Friday mornings at 9 and 10:30. ✉ *57-146 Kamehameha Hwy., Kahuku* ✣ *Mauka (mountain) side of highway, across from Kawela Bay* ☎ *808/628–7400 farm, 808/753–7861 farm stand* 🌐 *kuilimafarm.com.*

## SPAS

### Nalu Spa at Turtle Bay

**SPA** | Luxuriate at the ocean's edge in this lovely spa at Turtle Bay Resort. Try one of the signature treatments, including a coconut *pohaku* (warm shell) massage or a Hawaiian sugar body polish. There are private spa suites, an outdoor treatment cabana that overlooks the surf, and a lounge area and juice bar. Spa guests may also join fitness classes for a fee. ✉ *Turtle Bay Resort, 57-091 Kamehameha Hwy., Kahuku* ☎ *808/447–6868* 🌐 *www.turtlebayresort.com* 🎟 *Massages and facials from $260.*

Chapter 6

# EAST (WINDWARD) OAHU



Updated by
Anna Weaver

| Sights | Restaurants | Hotels | Shopping | Nightlife |
|---|---|---|---|---|
| ★★★★☆ | ★★★☆☆ | ★☆☆☆☆ | ★★★☆☆ | ★☆☆☆☆ |

# WELCOME TO EAST (WINDWARD) OAHU

## TOP REASONS TO GO

★ **Beautiful beaches:** Although Oahu's windward side is known more for windsurfing than swimming, there are still some gorgeous beaches with magnificent views.

★ **Stunning emerald-green cliffs:** These are the kinds of dramatic backdrops that you see in movies.

★ **Fewer crowds:** Windward Oahu is primarily residential, so it just doesn't get the crowds of areas like Waikiki (or even Haleiwa on the North Shore).

★ **Local life:** If you want to see how Oahu locals really live, then make for the windward side, including some of the small villages that are still around.

★ **Polynesian Cultural Center:** The best Polynesian cultural experience on the island is here, in re-created villages on the 42-acre site.

Locals refer to the east side of Oahu as the windward side because of the east-to-west trade winds that carried sailing ships to the Islands in years gone by and that still keep Hawaii cooler and lower in humidity than other Polynesian islands in the South Pacific. Because this side of the island sees much more frequent—often daily—showers, it is cooler and greener than the leeward side, where most hotels are found. A day trip to the windward side feels like a visit to another island because of its slower pace, smaller crowds, and drop-dead gorgeous scenery.

1 **Hawaii Kai.** This strip mall–filled suburb on the southeast shore is a great place to stop for picnic supplies or lunch before heading to Hanauma Bay or beginning your cliff-hugging drive to the windward side.

2 **Waimanalo.** Nestled between the Koolau Mountains and a spectacular beach with turquoise-blue waters, this small village is where many Native Hawaiian families live.

3 **Kailua.** Two of Oahu's top beaches and plenty of upscale boutiques and great restaurants are here, making Kailua popular with locals and visitors alike.

4 **Kaneohe.** The sprawling suburb is the largest of Oahu's windward villages. It's next to the stunning Koolaus, which means restaurants and sights with a backdrop of incredible mountain scenery.

5 **Kaaawa.** It's so small a town that you may pass right through it before realizing you're there. Kaaawa's claim to fame is as the next-door neighbor to popular Kualoa Ranch.

6 **Laie.** Most folks trek to the windward side's northernmost village to spend a day and evening at the Polynesian Cultural Center.

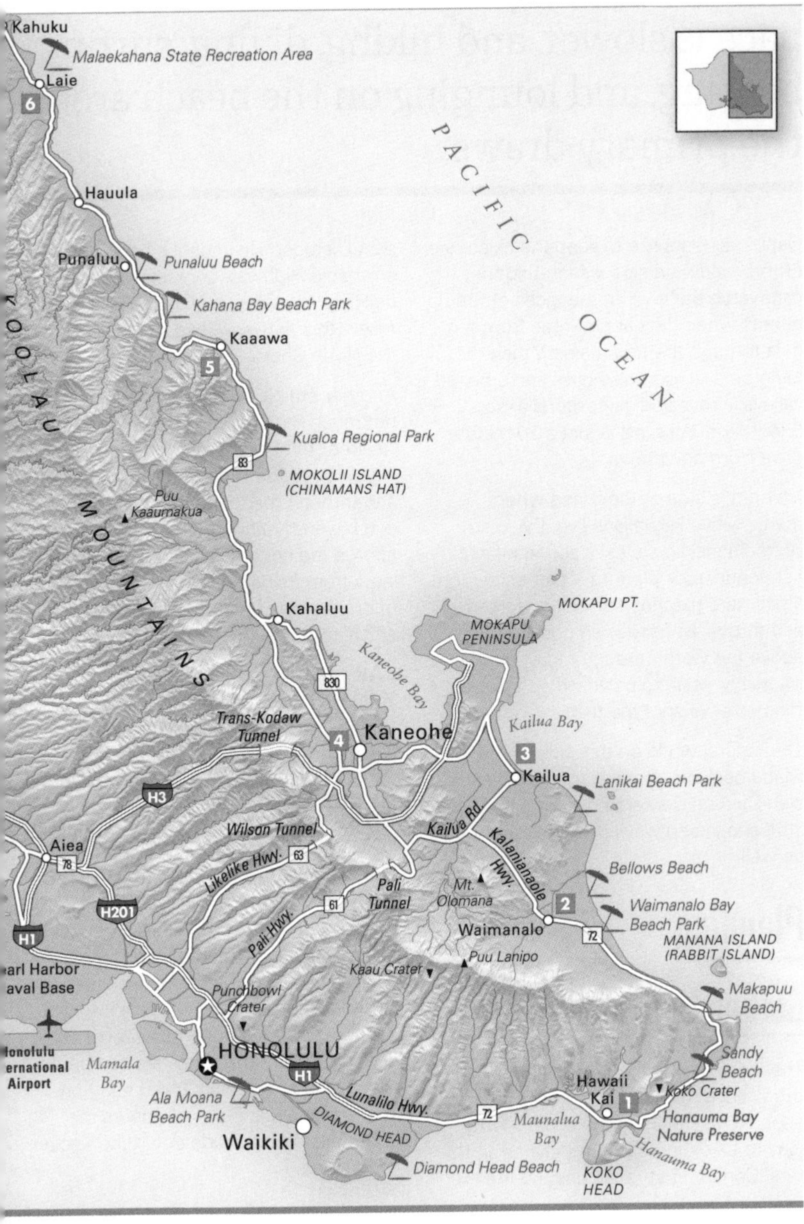
Kahuku
Malaekahana State Recreation Area
Laie
6
Hauula
Punaluu
Punaluu Beach
Kahana Bay Beach Park
Kaaawa
5
PACIFIC OCEAN
KOOLAU MOUNTAINS
Kualoa Regional Park
83
MOKOLII ISLAND
(CHINAMANS HAT)
Puu Kaaumakua
Kahaluu
MOKAPU PT.
MOKAPU PENINSULA
Kaneohe Bay
830
Trans-Kodaw Tunnel
4
Kaneohe
Kailua Bay
3
Kailua
Lanikai Beach Park
H3
Wilson Tunnel
Kailua Rd.
Kalanianaole Hwy.
Aiea
78
Likelike Hwy.
63
Bellows Beach
Mt. Olomana
Pali Tunnel
61
2
Waimanalo Bay Beach Park
H201
Pali Hwy.
Waimanalo
72
MANANA ISLAND
(RABBIT ISLAND)
H1
Puu Lanipo
Kaau Crater
Makapuu Beach
Punchbowl Crater
HONOLULU
Mamala Bay
H1
Sandy Beach
Hawaii Kai
1
Koko Crater
Ala Moana Beach Park
Lunalilo Hwy.
72
Maunalua Bay
Hanauma Bay Nature Preserve
DIAMOND HEAD
Waikiki
Hanauma Bay
Diamond Head Beach
KOKO HEAD

Looking at Honolulu's topsy-turvy urban sprawl, you would never suspect that the island's windward side exists. Here the pace is slower, and hiking, diving, surfing, boating, and lounging on the beach are the primary draws.

Oahu residents like to keep the existence of the windward side a secret so they can watch the awe on the faces of their guests when the car emerges from tunnels through the mountains. When the panorama of turquoise bays and emerald valleys is revealed, jaws literally drop. Every time. And this is just a 20-minute drive from downtown.

It's on this side of the island where many Native Hawaiians live. Evidence of traditional lifestyles is abundant in old fishponds, rock platforms that once were altars, taro patches still being worked, and throw-net fishermen posed stock-still above the water (though today, they're invariably wearing polarized sunglasses, the better to spot the fish).

The natural world on this side of the island beckons. But a visit to the Polynesian Cultural Center and poking through little shops and wayside stores are musts as well.

## Planning

### Getting Here and Around

There are a couple of ways to reach the windward side. One possibility is to spend a day hugging the coast all the way to Laie, home of the Polynesian Cultural Center. First, head east on the H1 past Diamond Head until it becomes Kalanianaole Highway. Look for Kamehameha Highway upon reaching Kaneohe, and follow this two-lane road all the way to the North Shore.

Another option that's just as spectacular but much more direct is taking the H1 to either the Pali Highway, the Likelike Highway, or the H3 across the mountains and through the tunnels to Kaneohe and beyond. Although the Pali Highway affords the opportunity to take in the view from its namesake lookout, the H3 offers the most breathtakingly beautiful arrival to this side of the island.

#### CAR

Though TheBus serves the entire island, you'll need a car to fully explore the windward side.

## Beaches

The windward side is ideal for sunbathing, swimming, and windsurfing or kiteboarding, or for the more intrepid, hang gliding. For the most part, the waves are mellow, and the beaches are all sand—perfect if you're traveling with younger kids. Although this side of Oahu gets more rain, the vistas are so beautiful that a little sprinkle shouldn't dampen your experience. Plus, it benefits the waterfalls that cascade down the Koolau Mountains.

## Hotels

Regulations severely limiting bed-and-breakfast and short-term vacation rentals on Oahu were adopted in 2019, largely driven by residents of the windward side. This translates into a scarcity of lodging options, but those you'll find are embedded within windward communities rather than tourist enclaves.

### PRICES

⇨ *Hotel prices are the lowest cost of a standard double room in high season. Hotel reviews have been shortened. For full information, visit Fodors.com.*

**What It Costs in U.S. Dollars**

| $ | $$ | $$$ | $$$$ |
|---|---|---|---|
| **HOTELS** | | | |
| under $200 | $200–$280 | $281–$380 | over $380 |

## Restaurants

Many folks on the windward side never travel to "town" (Honolulu) in search of great dining options. Join the locals for fine-dining in Hawaii Kai, locally brewed beer, fresh fish, and Hawaii regional cuisine in Kailua, and shave ice or Mediterranean-inspired pupu in a neighborhood spot.

### PRICES

⇨ *Restaurant prices are the average cost of a main course at dinner or, if dinner is not served, at lunch. Restaurant reviews have been shortened. For full information, visit Fodors.com.*

**What It Costs in U.S. Dollars**

| $ | $$ | $$$ | $$$$ |
|---|---|---|---|
| **RESTAURANTS** | | | |
| under $20 | $20–$30 | $31–$40 | over $40 |

# Hawaii Kai

*Approximately 10 miles southeast of Waikiki.*

Driving southeast from Waikiki on busy, four-lane Kalanianaole Highway, you'll pass a dozen bedroom communities tucked into the valleys at the foot of the Koolau Range, with fleeting glimpses of the ocean from a couple of pocket parks. Suddenly, civilization falls away, the road narrows to two lanes, and you enter the rugged coastline of Koko Head and Ka Iwi. This is a cruel coastline: dry and windswept, with rocky shores and untamed waves that are notoriously treacherous. While walking its beaches, do not turn your back on the ocean, don't venture close to wet areas where high waves occasionally reach, and heed warning signs.

At this point, you're passing through Koko Head Regional Park. On your right is the bulging remnant of a pair of volcanic craters that the Hawaiians called Kawaihoa, known today as Koko Head. To the left is Koko Crater and an area of the park that includes a hiking trail, a dryland botanical garden, a firing range, and a riding stable. Ahead is a sinuous shoreline with scenic pullouts and beaches to explore. Named the Ka Iwi Coast (*iwi*, "ee-vee," are bones—sacred to Hawaiians and full of symbolism) for the channel just offshore, this area was once home to a ranch and small fishing enclave that were destroyed by a tidal wave in the 1940s.

### GETTING HERE AND AROUND

Driving straight from Waikiki to Makapuu Point takes from a half to a full hour, depending on traffic. There isn't a huge number of sights per se in this corner of Oahu, so a couple of hours should be plenty of exploring time.

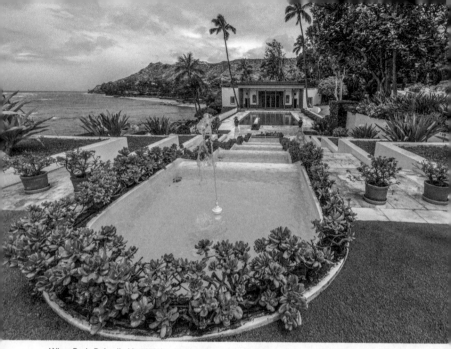

When Doris Duke died in 1993, her estate, Shangri La, became a museum of Islamic culture and art. Tours leave from the Honolulu Museum of Art in downtown Honolulu.

## Sights

### ★ Halona Blowhole

**VIEWPOINT** | Below a scenic turnout along the Koko Head shoreline, this oft-photographed lava tube sucks the ocean in and spits it out. Don't get too close, as conditions can get dangerous. **■ TIP→ Look to your right to see the tiny beach below that was used to film the wave-washed love scene in *From Here to Eternity*.** In winter, this is a good spot to watch whales at play. Offshore, the island of Molokai calls like a distant siren, and, every once in a while, Lanai is visible in blue silhouette. Take your valuables with you, and lock your car, because this popular scenic location is a hot spot for petty thieves. ✉ *Kalanianaole Hwy., Hawaii Kai* ✥ *1 mile east of Hanauma Bay.*

### Koko Crater Botanical Garden

**GARDEN** | If you've visited any of Oahu's other botanical gardens, Koko Crater will stand in stark contrast. Inside the tallest tuff (a type of volcanic rock) cone on Oahu, in one of the island's hottest and driest areas, the garden showcases dryland species of plants, including baobab trees, cacti, plumeria, and bougainvillea. **■ TIP→ Bring plenty of water, sunscreen, and a hat. Though it's close to Oahu's more lush windward side, this is a scorching spot.** ✉ *7491 Kokonani St., Hawaii Kai* ✥ *Entrance at end of Kokonani St.* ☎ *808/768–7135* 🌐 *honolulu.gov/parks/hbg* 🎟 *Free.*

### Lanai Lookout

**VIEWPOINT** | A little more than a ½ mile past Hanauma Bay as you head toward Makapuu Point, you'll see a turnout on the ocean side with some fine views of the coastline. In winter, you'll have an opportunity to see storm-generated waves crashing against lava cliffs. This is also a popular place for winter whale-watching, so bring your binoculars, some sunscreen, and a picnic lunch, and join the small crowd scanning for telltale white spouts of water only a few hundred yards away. On clear days, you should be able to see the islands of Molokai and Lanai off in the distance, hence the name. ✉ *Kalanianaole Hwy., Hawaii Kai* ✣ *Just past Hanauma Bay.*

### ★ Shangri La Museum of Islamic Art, Culture & Design

**HISTORIC HOME** | In 1936, heiress Doris Duke bought 5 acres at Black Point, down the coast from Waikiki, and began to build and furnish the first home that would be all her own. She called it Shangri La. For more than 50 years, the home was a work in progress as Duke traveled the world, buying art and furnishings, picking up ideas for her Mughal Garden, for the Playhouse in the style of a 17th-century Irani pavilion, and for the water terraces and tropical gardens. When she died in 1993, Duke left instructions that her home was to become a public center for the study of Islamic art.

Outside of minor conservation-oriented changes and 2017 renovations to the courtyard and pool, the house and gardens have remained much as Duke left them. To walk through them is to experience the personal style of someone who saw everything as raw material for her art. With her trusted houseman, Jin de Silva, she helped build the elaborate Turkish Room, trimming tiles and painting panels to retrofit the existing space (including raising the ceiling and lowering the floor) and building a fountain of her own design.

Among many aspects of the home inspired by the Muslim tradition is the entry: an anonymous gate, a blank white wall, and a wooden door that bids you, "Enter herein in peace and security" in Arabic script. Inside, tiles glow, fountains tinkle, and shafts of light illuminate artwork through arches and high windows. In 2014, after years of renovation, Duke's bedroom (the Mughal Suite) opened to the public. This was her private world, entered only by trusted friends. ■ **TIP → The house is open only via the guided tours that depart from downtown's Honolulu Museum of Art. Tours take about 2½ hours including transit time, and reservations are required.** Book your spot as early as possible, and note that children under eight are not permitted. ✉ *Honolulu Museum of Art, 900 S. Beretania St., Downtown* ✣ *Tours of Shangri La depart from museum* ☎ *808/532–3853 for Honolulu Museum of Art* 🌐 *shangrilahawaii.org* 🎫 *$25* ⏲ *Closed Sun.–Wed.* ☞ *$5 parking at Honolulu Museum of Art.*

##  Beaches

Much of Southeast Oahu is surrounded by reef, making most of the coast uninviting to swimmers, but the spots where the reef opens up are true gems. The drive along this side of the island is amazing, with its sheer lava-rock walls on one side and deep-blue ocean on the other. There are plenty of restaurants in the suburbs of Hawaii Kai and Kahala, so you can make a day of it, knowing that sustenance isn't far away.

### Halona Beach Cove

**BEACH** | Also known as Eternity Beach, this little beauty is never crowded due to the short, treacherous climb down to the sand. But what a treat it is for the intrepid—perfect for packing a lunch and holing up for the day. The beach is in a break in the ocean cliffs, with the surrounding crags providing protection from the wind. Open-ocean waves roll up onto the sand, but a gently sloping sand bottom takes much of the punch out of them before they hit the shore. Locals also call it "Cockroach Cove," but there's no consensus as to why. Turtles frequent the small cove, seeking respite from the otherwise blustery coast. ⚠ **The current is mellow inside the cove but dangerous once you get outside it. Amenities:** parking (no fee). **Best for:** sunrise. ✉ *8699 Kalanianaole Hwy., Hawaii Kai* ✣ *Below Halona Blow Hole Lookout parking lot.*

### ★ Hanauma Bay Nature Preserve

**BEACH** | **FAMILY** | Picture this as the world's biggest open-air aquarium: you

If you're a snorkeler, head straight for Hanauma Bay, the best and most popular place to snorkel on Oahu.

come to see fish, and fish you'll see. Due to their exposure to thousands of visitors every week, these fish are more like family pets than the skittish marine life you might expect. An old volcanic crater has created a haven from the waves where the coral has thrived. Note that there's a fee for nonresidents to enter the preserve; make reservations and prepay online ahead of time (locals have a morning time period where they can walk in without a reservation). You must also watch a nine-minute video about the nature preserve in its educational center before being allowed down to the bay. Snorkel equipment and lockers are available for rent, and you can walk the short distance from the parking lot or take a tram. ■ **TIP→ It's best to visit early in the morning (around 7), as it's difficult to park later in the day.** Need transportation? Take TheBus each way from anywhere on the island. **Amenities:** food and drink; lifeguards; parking (fee); showers; toilets. **Best for:** snorkeling; swimming. ✉ *7455 Kalanianaole Hwy., Hawaii Kai* ☎ *808/768–6861* 🌐 *hanaumabaystatepark.com* 🎫 *Nonresidents $25; parking $3 (cash only); snorkel rental $20* ⏲ *Closed Mon. and Tues.*

**★ Sandy Beach Park**

**BEACH** | Very popular with locals, this broad, sloping beach is covered with sunbathers who come to soak up the rays and watch "The Show"—a shore break that's like no other in the Islands. Monster ocean swells rolling into the beach combined with the sudden rise in the ocean floor cause waves to jack up and crash magnificently. Expert surfers and bodyboarders young and old brave the dangers to enjoy some of the biggest barrels around. ⚠ **Use extreme caution when swimming here. The stretch is nicknamed Break-Neck Beach for a reason: many neck and back injuries are sustained here each year.** **Amenities:** lifeguards; parking (no fee); showers; toilets. **Best for:** walking. ✉ *7850 Kalanianaole Hwy., Hawaii Kai* ✥ *Makai (toward ocean) of Kalanianaole Hwy., 2 miles east of Hanauma Bay.*

## Restaurants

**Roy's Hawaii Kai**

**$$$$ | MODERN HAWAIIAN** | Roy Yamaguchi is one of the 12 founding chefs of Hawaiian regional cuisine, a culinary movement that put the state on the foodie map back in 1991. Opened in 1988, his flagship restaurant across the highway from Maunalua Bay is still packed every night—reservations are essential—with food-savvy visitors and well-heeled residents, all of whom come for classics like smoked Szechuan baby back ribs or blackened ahi with soy mustard butter sauce. **Known for:** spectacular sunset views and a tiki torch–lit lanai and bar area; small and large portions available for many dishes; signature items like blackened ahi have a cultlike following. *Average main: $55* *Hawaii Kai Corporate Plaza, 6600 Kalanianaole Hwy., Hawaii Kai* *808/396–7697* *www.royyamaguchi.com* *No lunch.*

## Coffee and Quick Bites

**Kokonuts Shave Ice & Snacks**

**$ | ICE CREAM | FAMILY** | Why not stop for shave ice like President Barack Obama did while visiting the island after the 2008 election? This spot in Koko Marina Center serves fluffy shave ice, bubble drinks, ice cream, and more. **Known for:** shave ice with syrup flavors such as strawberry, coconut, and lilikoi (passion fruit); açai bowls; credit cards not accepted. *Average main: $5* *Koko Marina Center, 7192 Kalanianaole Hwy., Unit E121, Hawaii Kai* *808/396–8809* *No credit cards.*

**Uncle Clay's House of Pure Aloha**

**$ | HAWAIIAN | FAMILY** | Located in a strip mall in the residential neighborhood of Aina Haina, Uncle Clay's is a happy place. This shave-ice stand specializes in homemade, all-natural syrups made from cane sugar and locally sourced fruits, including "kalespin"—a combination of kale and spinach. **Known for:** shave ice that's gone trendy; fun, and kids love it; special Strawberry Dream with mochi and vanilla ice cream. *Average main: $5* *Aina Haina Shopping Center, 820 W. Hind Dr., Unit 116, Hawaii Kai* *Right off Kalanianaole Hwy.* *808/373–5111* *houseofpurealoha.com.*

## Nightlife

### BREWPUBS

**Kona Brewing Pub**

**BREWPUBS** | This massive Kona Brewing Co. restaurant and bar on the docks of Koko Marina has long been a hot spot. In addition to serving the company's signature brews with lunch and dinner, this authentic pub offers live music most nights. It's a lively spot, especially on weekends. *Koko Marina Center, 7192 Kalanianaole Hwy.* *808/396–5662* *konabrewinghawaii.com.*

# Waimanalo

*11 miles north of Hawaii Kai.*

Home to more Native Hawaiian families than Kailua to the north or Hawaii Kai to the south, this modest little seaside town flanked by chiseled cliffs draws visitors with its beautiful beaches, offering glorious views to the windward side. Bellows Field Beach Park is great for swimming, bodysurfing, and camping, and Waimanalo Bay Beach Park is also safe for swimming. Down the side roads, as you head *mauka* (toward the mountains), are little farms that grow a variety of fruits and flowers. Toward the back of the valley are small ranches with grazing horses. **TIP→ If you see any trucks selling corn, and you have a place to cook it, get some. It may be the sweetest you'll ever eat, and prices are the lowest on Oahu.**

### GETTING HERE AND AROUND

The drive from Waikiki in Honolulu takes approximately 30 minutes.

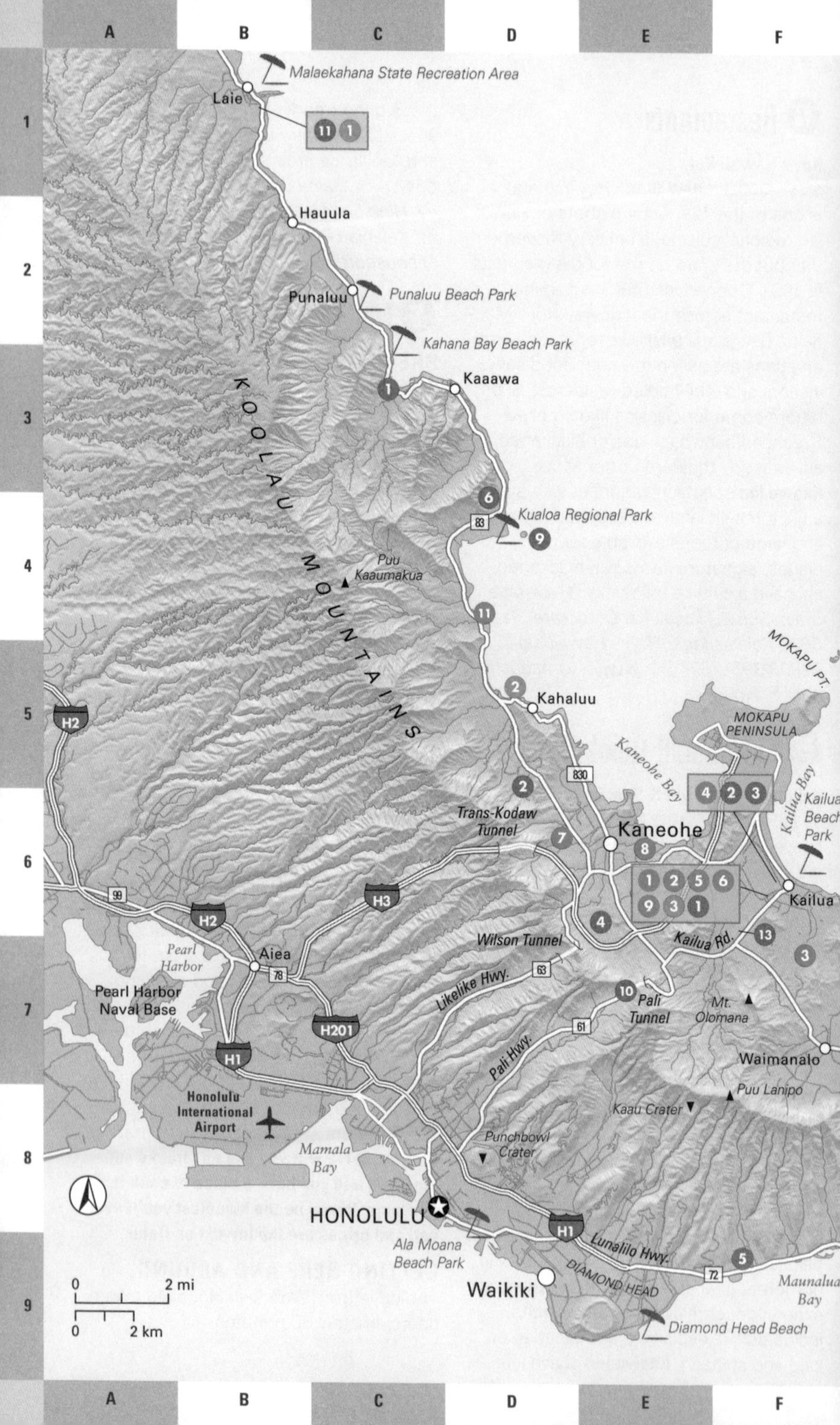
A
B
C
D
E
F
1
2
3
4
5
6
7
8
9
Malaekahana State Recreation Area
Laie
11 1
Hauula
Punaluu
Punaluu Beach Park
Kahana Bay Beach Park
Kaaawa
1
K O O L A U
M O U N T A I N S
6
83
Kualoa Regional Park
9
Puu Kaaumakua
11
2
Kahaluu
MOKAPU PT.
MOKAPU PENINSULA
Kaneohe Bay
830
2
4 2 3
Kailua Bay
Kailua Beach Park
Trans-Kodaw Tunnel
7
Kaneohe
8
1 2 5 6
9 3 1
Kailua
H2
99
H2
H3
4
Kailua Rd.
13
3
Pearl Harbor
Aiea
Wilson Tunnel
78
63
Likelike Hwy.
10
Pali Tunnel
Mt. Olomana
Pearl Harbor Naval Base
H201
61
Pali Hwy.
Waimanalo
H1
Honolulu International Airport
Puu Lanipo
Kaau Crater
Punchbowl Crater
Mamala Bay
HONOLULU
Ala Moana Beach Park
H1
Lunalilo Hwy.
5
72
Maunalua Bay
DIAMOND HEAD
Waikiki
Diamond Head Beach
0
2 mi
0
2 km

# East (Windward) Oahu

**KEY**
Sights
Restaurants
Quick Bites
Hotels

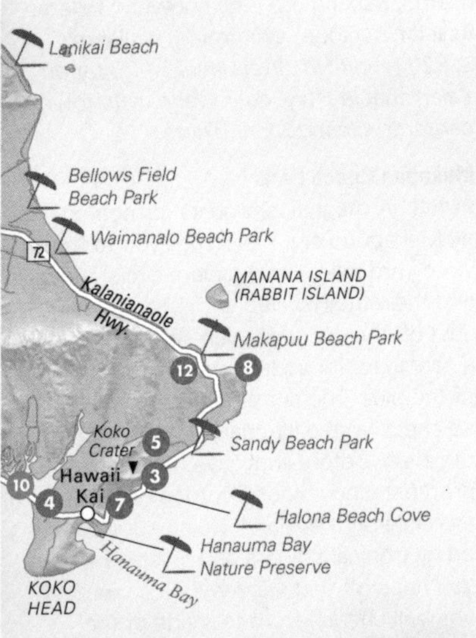


### Sights

1 Ahupuaa O Kahana State Park ........ C3
2 Byodo-In Temple........ D5
3 Halona Blowhole ....... G9
4 Hoomaluhia Botanical Garden........ E6
5 Koko Crater Botanical Garden....... G8
6 Kualoa Ranch.......... D3
7 Lanai Lookout.......... G9
8 Makapuu Point Lighthouse Trail........ H8
9 Mokolii.................. D4
10 Nuuanu Pali State Wayside .......... E7
11 Polynesian Cultural Center.......... B1
12 Sea Life Park Hawaii................... H8
13 Ulupo Heiau State Historic Site ....... F6

### Restaurants

1 Baci Bistro................ F6
2 Big City Diner............ F6
3 Boots & Kimo's Homestyle Kitchen ...... F7
4 Buzz's Original Steak House............. F6
5 Cinnamon's Restaurant................ F6
6 GOEN Dining + Bar ...... F6
7 Haleiwa Joe's Haiku Gardens .......... D6
8 Jolene's by the Bay Kaneohe ................. E6
9 Kalapawai Cafe & Deli .............. F6
10 Roy's Hawaii Kai ........ G9
11 Waiahole Poi Factory .............. D4

### Quick Bites

1 Agnes' Portuguese Bake Shop................ F6
2 Island Snow.............. F6
3 Kalapawai Market....... F6
4 Kokonuts Shave Ice & Snacks ................ G9
5 Uncle Clay's House of Pure Aloha............ F9

### Hotels

1 Courtyard by Marriott Oahu North Shore ...... B1
2 Paradise Bay Resort ... D5
3 Sheffield House Bed & Breakfast......... F6

## Sights

**★ Makapuu Point Lighthouse Trail**
**TRAIL | FAMILY** | This trail has breathtaking views of the ocean, mountains, and the windward Islands. The point of land jutting out in the distance is Mokapuu Peninsula, site of a U.S. Marine base. The spired mountain peak is Mt. Olomana. On the long pier is part of the Makai Undersea Test Range, a research facility that's closed to the public. Offshore is Manana Island (Rabbit Island), a picturesque cay said to resemble a swimming bunny with its ears pulled back. Ironically enough, Manana Island was once overrun with rabbits, thanks to a rancher who let a few hares run wild on the land. They were eradicated in 1994 by biologists who grew concerned that the rabbits were destroying the island's native plants.

Nestled in the cliff face is the Makapuu Lighthouse, which became operational in 1909 and has the largest lighthouse lens in the United States. The lighthouse is closed to the public, but near the Makapuu Point turnout is the start of a paved mile-long road (it's closed to vehicular traffic). Hike to the top of the 647-foot bluff to get a closer view of the lighthouse and, in winter, to do some whale-watching. **■ TIP→ Park in the free parking lot for the trail (it's busiest on the weekends), but don't attempt to continue driving to the gates for the military base since civilian vehicles are not allowed.** ✉ *Ka Iwi State Scenic Shoreline, Kalanianaole Hwy., Waimanalo* ✣ *At Makapuu Beach* 🌐 *dlnr.hawaii.gov/dsp/hiking/oahu* 🎫 *Free* ⏲ *Gates to the trail open daily 7 am–6:45 pm.*

**Sea Life Park Hawaii**
**AQUARIUM | FAMILY** | Dolphins leap and spin, and penguins frolic at this marine-life attraction 15 miles from Waikiki at scenic Makapuu Point. The park has a 300,000-gallon Hawaiian reef aquarium, a breeding sanctuary for Hawaii's endangered *honu* (sea turtles), penguin and Hawaiian monk seal habitats, an aviary, a seabird sanctuary, and many more marine attractions. Sign up for a dolphin, sea lion, or reef encounter to get up close and personal in the water with these sea creatures. The park also has its own luau show. ✉ *41-202 Kalanianaole Hwy., Waimanalo* ☎ *808/259–2500* 🌐 *sealifeparkhawaii.com* 🎫 *$45; parking $15.*

## Beaches

**Bellows Field Beach Park**
**BEACH** | Bellows is the same beach as Waimanalo, but it's under the auspices of the military, making it more friendly for visitors—though you need a Department of Defense ID to access one side of the beach. The park area is excellent for camping, and ironwood trees provide plenty of shade. There are no food concessions, but McDonald's and other take-out options are right outside the entrance gate; there's also a weekend farmers' market. **■ TIP→ The beach is best before 2 pm. After 2, trade winds bring clouds that get hung up on steep mountains nearby, causing overcast skies. Amenities:** lifeguards; parking (no fee); showers; toilets. **Best for:** solitude; swimming; walking. ✉ *520 Tinker Rd., Waimanalo* ✣ *Enter on Kalanianaole Hwy. near Waimanalo town center* ⏲ *Closed Mon.–Thurs.*

**Makapuu Beach Park**
**BEACH** | A magnificent beach protected by Makapuu Point welcomes you to the windward side. Hang gliders circle above, and the water is filled with bodyboarders. Just off the coast you can see Bird Island, a sanctuary for aquatic fowl, jutting out of the blue. The currents can be heavy, so check with a lifeguard if you're unsure of safety. Before you leave, take the prettiest (and coldest) outdoor shower available on the island. Being surrounded by tropical flowers and foliage while you rinse off that sand will be a memory you will cherish from this side of the

## Did You Know?

Windward Oahu's Makapuu Beach is protected by Makapuu Point, but currents are still strong, so be careful when in the water.

## Windward Oahu Villages

Tiny villages—generally consisting of a sign, a store, a beach park, possibly a post office, and not much more—are strung along Kamehameha Highway on the windward side. Each has something to offer. In **Waiahole,** look for fruit stands and the Waiahole Poi Factory, which is worth a stop for Hawaiian food and their famous poi. In **Kaaawa,** there's a convenience store/gas station. In **Punaluu,** get a plate lunch at Keneke's, or visit the venerable Chings' General Store. **Hauula** has the gallery of fanciful landscape artist Lance Fairly; the Shrimp Shack; Hauula Gift Shop, a clothing shop where sarongs wave like banners; and, at Hauula Kai Shopping Center, Tamura's Market, with excellent seafood and the last liquor before Mormon-dominated Laie.

rock. **Amenities:** lifeguards; parking (no fee); showers; toilets. **Best for:** sunrise; walking. ✉ *41-095 Kalanianaole Hwy., Waimanalo* ⊕ *Across from Sea Life Park Hawaii, 2 miles south of Waimanalo.*

**★ Waimanalo Bay Beach Park**

**BEACH | FAMILY** | One of the most beautiful beaches on Oahu, Waimanalo is a local pick, busy with picnicking families and active sports fields. Expect a wide stretch of sand; turquoise, emerald, and deep-blue water; and gentle shore-breaking waves that are fun for all ages. Theft is an occasional problem, so lock your car. **Amenities:** lifeguards; parking (no fee); showers; toilets. **Best for:** sunrise; swimming; walking. ✉ *41-849 Kalanianaole Hwy., Waimanalo* ⊕ *South of Waimanalo town center.*

# Kailua

*6 miles north of Waimanalo.*

Upscale Kailua, easily accessed from Honolulu via the Pali Highway, has two of Oahu's best beaches as well as great shopping and dining opportunities in its central core. You could easily spend a day visiting the stunning beaches, kayaking, exploring a hidden *heiau* (shrine), picnicking, or dining out with locals.

### GETTING HERE AND AROUND

The easiest way to reach Kailua from Waikiki, roughly 15 miles to the southwest, is to take the H1 interstate to Highway 61 (best known as the Pali Highway). On your way, stop for a breathtaking view at the Pali Lookout. Emerging from the tunnels, you'll immediately see what all the fuss is about—a turquoise bay lies to your left while you hug the emerald-green serrated mountains of the Koolau Range.

## Sights

**Ulupo Heiau State Historic Site**

**RUINS** | Find this spot—where signs near a *heiau* (shrine) also explain Kailua's early history—tucked next to the Windward YMCA. Although they may look like piles of rocks to the uninitiated, *heiau* are sacred stone platforms for the worship of the gods and date from ancient times; this one is 140 feet by 80 feet. *Ulupo* means "night inspiration," referring to the legendary Menehune, a mythical race of diminutive people who are said to have built the *heiau* under the cloak of darkness. ✉ *Kalanianaole Hwy. and Kailua Rd., Kailua* ⊕ *Behind Windward YMCA* 🌐 *dlnr.hawaii.gov/dsp/parks/oahu.*

## Did You Know?

If you're vacationing with kids, Kailua and Lanikai beaches are good choices, with calm waters and soft sand. Lanikai does not have bathrooms, but nearby Kailua does.

## Beaches

### ★Kailua Beach Park

**BEACH | FAMILY** | A cobalt-blue sea and a wide, continuous arc of powdery sand make this one of the island's best beaches, as illustrated by the crowds of local families who spend their weekend days here. The water is calm, a line of palms and ironwoods provides shade on the sand, and a huge park has picnic pavilions where you can escape the heat. This is also the "it" spot for windsurfing or kiteboarding, and you can rent kayaks nearby at Kailua Beach Adventures (✉ *130 Kailua Rd.*) for day trips to the Mokulua Islands. **Amenities:** lifeguards; parking (no fee); showers; toilets; water sports. **Best for:** swimming; walking; windsurfing. ✉ *437 Kawailoa Rd., Kailua* ✣ *Near Kailua town, turn right on Kailua Rd. After Kalapawai Market, cross bridge, then turn left into beach parking lot.*

### Lanikai Beach

**BEACH** | Think of the beaches you see in commercials: peaceful jade-green waters, powder-soft white sand, families and dogs frolicking, and offshore islands in the distance. It's an ideal spot for stretching out with a book. Though the beach hides behind multimillion-dollar houses, by state law there is public access every 400 yards. Street parking is available but very difficult to find (and prohibited on holiday weekends). Consider parking at Kailua Beach Park and walking along the paved pathway into Lanikai. Just don't block the boat ramp stalls. There are no shower or bathroom facilities here—but you'll find both at Kailua Beach Park. **■ TIP→ Look for walled or fenced pathways every 400 yards, leading to the beach. Do not park in the marked bike/jogging lane.** **Amenities:** none. **Best for:** sunrise; swimming; walking. ✉ *974 Mokulua Dr., Kailua* ✣ *Past Kailua Beach Park, heading south.*

## Restaurants

### Baci Bistro

**$$ | ITALIAN** | A long-time local favorite, the elegant, inviting bistro is a classic Italian restaurant offering an extensive range of pastas, antipasti, mains, and really excellent desserts. Consider the ravioli *del giorno* followed by *vitello* (veal) cooked with a variety of sauces. **Known for:** a wide variety of antipasti; housemade pasta; cozy, romantic setting. $ *Average main: $25* ✉ *30 Aulike St., Kailua* ☎ *808/262–7555* 🌐 *www.bacibistro.com.*

### Big City Diner

**$$ | DINER | FAMILY** | This outlet of the popular retro diner chain—with four locations, including one at Windward Mall in neighboring Kaneohe—is across the street from a small bird sanctuary and has outdoor lanai seating and a bar. It's a hot spot for breakfast and Sunday football; some popular dinner items on the lengthy menu are grilled steak with onions and mushrooms, baby back ribs, meatloaf, and salads. **Known for:** great loco moco; nice indoor and outdoor bar; big portions. $ *Average main: $20* ✉ *108 Hekili St., Kailua* ☎ *808/263–8880* 🌐 *bigcitydinerhawaii.com.*

### Boots & Kimo's Homestyle Kitchen

**$ | AMERICAN** | Sometimes you wait an hour for a table here while patrons clamor for the banana pancakes topped with a thick macadamia-nut sauce. At lunch, the signature dish is a plate of *pulehu* (grilled) ribs. **Known for:** worth going once for the mac-nut pancakes; more popular than food may warrant overall; no reservations, but quick table turnover. $ *Average main: $19* ✉ *1020 Keolu Dr., Suite D1, Kailua* ☎ *808/263–7929* 🌐 *bootsnkimos.com* ⏲ *Closed Tues. No dinner.*

### Buzz's Original Steak House

**$$$ | STEAK HOUSE** | Virtually unchanged since opening in 1967, this neighborhood institution opposite Kailua Beach Park is filled with the aroma of grilling steaks and plumeria blooms. It doesn't matter if you're a bit sandy and beach bedraggled (though bare feet are a no-no, as are tank tops after 4:30 pm)—just find a spot in the cozy maze of rooms; order a steak, a burger, teriyaki chicken, or the fresh fish special. **Known for:** reservations are essential; the views from the lanai at lunch; excellent fruity beach cocktails, including very strong mai tais. *Average main: $35 ✉ 413 Kawailoa Rd., Kailua ☎ 808/261–4661 🌐 buzzsoriginalsteakhouse.com.*

**Cinnamon's Restaurant**

$ | **AMERICAN** | **FAMILY** | Known for uncommon variations on common breakfast themes, this neighborhood favorite is tucked into a hard-to-find Kailua office park (call for directions). Local-style lunch plates are good, but the main attraction is breakfast, when you don't want to miss the guava chiffon and red velvet pancakes. (The Waikiki location in the Ilikai Hotel serves dinner, too.) Be prepared to wait. **Known for:** endless variations on pancakes, eggs Benedict, and waffles; original or macadamia-nut cinnamon rolls (of course); long waits. *Average main: $19 ✉ 315 Uluniu St., Kailua ☎ 808/261–8724 🌐 cinnamons808.com ⏲ No dinner.*

**GOEN Dining + Bar**

$$$ | **ASIAN FUSION** | **FAMILY** | This spinoff from famous chef Roy Yamaguchi serves elevated Hawaii regional cuisine and cocktails in the Lau Hala Shops complex, right where the old Macy's used to be. The kids' menu goes above and beyond the typical fare. **Known for:** open-air and patio seating; friendly, attentive service; yummy cocktails. *Average main: $35 ✉ 573 Kailua Rd., Kailua ☎ 808/263–4636 🌐 royyamaguchi.com ⏲ No lunch Mon.–Thurs.*

**Kalapawai Cafe & Deli**

$$ | **ECLECTIC** | **FAMILY** | The Dymond family, two generations of restaurateurs who have shaken up the windward food scene, created this one-stop, green-and-white, Mediterranean-leaning café, wine bar, bakery, and gourmet deli. Come in on your way to the beach for a cup of coffee and bagel, and stop back for a delicious pizza or bruschetta for lunch or a candlelight dinner at night. **Known for:** signature dishes, including fish and turf options, by night; good coffee and creative sandwiches by day; impressive wine list for such a small spot. *Average main: $25 ✉ 750 Kailua Rd., Kailua ☎ 808/262–3354 🌐 kalapawaimarket.com.*

## Coffee and Quick Bites

**★ Agnes' Portuguese Bake Shop**

$ | **BAKERY** | This food truck in the Manuhealii parking lot serves delicious, made-to-order *malasadas* (Portuguese doughnuts) that are crispy and dark brown on the outside and soft, chewy, and sweet on the inside. They're also denser than those found at some other bakeries on the island. **Known for:** authentic malasadas; no-fuss takeout; convenient location. *Average main: $2 ✉ 5 Hoolai St., Kailua ✥ In the parking lot of Manuhealii across from Kalapawai Cafe ☎ 808/284–4963 🌐 instagram.com/agnesbakeshop808 ⏲ Closed Sun. and Mon.*

**Island Snow**

$ | **ICE CREAM** | **FAMILY** | This hole-in-the-wall has been creating shave ice perfection in its tiny original spot since 1979, but when two young girls named Obama discovered the luscious flavors in 2008, it was really put on the map. A favorite spot for both locals and storied visitors (and these days lots of regular tourists), it makes a mean shave ice, whether you stick with standard flavors like cherry or go for *lilikoi* (passion fruit) guava with a snowcap on top. **Known for:** the best shave ice on the windward side; the Obama girls, who grew up on this stuff (look for their photos on the wall); long lines of locals and tourists. *Average main: $6 ✉ 130 Kailua Rd., Kailua ☎ 808/263–6339 🌐 islandsnow.com.*

**Kalapawai Market**

$ | **SANDWICHES** | **FAMILY** | Generations of children have purchased their beach snacks and sodas at Kalapawai Market near Kailua Beach. A Windward Oahu landmark since 1932, the green-and-white market has distinctive charm. **Known for:** takeout deli sandwiches for lunch or a light dinner; good coffee; great selection of wine. *Average main: $11* ✉ *306 S. Kalaheo Ave., Kailua* ☎ *808/262–4359* 🌐 *www.kalapawaimarket.com.*

## Hotels

**Sheffield House Bed & Breakfast**

$ | **B&B/INN** | Close to Kailua Beach, this cozy bed-and-breakfast has been around since the 1990s and has two suites that are attached to the main house but have their own private entrances. **Pros:** one of the few legal B&Bs in Kailua; near best beaches on the island; boutiques and dining abound in Kailua. **Cons:** B&Bs aren't for everybody; don't expect luxury; rental car a must. *Rooms from: $180* ✉ *131 Kuulei Rd., Kailua* ☎ *808/262–0721* 🌐 *www.hawaiisheffieldhouse.com* *2 rooms* *Free Breakfast* ☞ *Breakfast included on the first morning only.*

## Nightlife

### BARS

**The Boardroom**

**BARS** | Inside the tiny dining room and outside on the slightly bigger deck area, you can enjoy fancy cocktails, wine, and upscale food here. The parking lot outside has been converted to The Garden with picnic tables, a coffee cart, and more casual fare during the daytime only. The Boardroom is closed Monday and Tuesday, and reservations are recommended. ✉ *44 Kainehe St., Kailua* ☎ *808/807–5640* 🌐 *theboardroomkailua.com.*

**Sessions Bar + Lounge**

**BARS** | A replacement for a much seedier joint, this bar and live music venue has an entirely redone interior with a stage, pool table, and lounge seating in one room; the bar and high-tops are in the other room. One of the few venues for late-night live music in Kailua, Sessions is a welcome entry into this sleepier suburb's nightlife. Comedy shows and Sunday morning football watching (it's Hawaii time, after all) are also on the schedule. The excellent Whiskey Smoke BBQ provides food. It's closed Monday and Tuesday. ✉ *32 Maluniu Ave., Kailua* ☎ *808/261–6733* 🌐 *sessionshawaii.com.*

### BREWPUBS

**Tap & Barrel**

**BREWPUBS** | Lanikai Brewing Company's taproom features its island-centric beer, including seasonal varieties that incorporate unusual ingredients like Surinam cherry, mushrooms, and white tea. It also serves Valentina's wood-fired pizza and sometimes has a food truck out front. In addition to beer, there are spirits from the brewery's distillery line, house-made sangria, Paradise Ciders, and other sips from which to choose. Kids are welcome, and board games are available for playing. ✉ *167 Hamakua Dr., Kailua* 🌐 *www.lanikaibrewing.com.*

## Shopping

Shopping on the windward side is one of Oahu's best-kept secrets. The trip here takes a half hour by car or about an hour on TheBus. The real treats lie in the small boutiques and galleries in the heart of Kailua—the perfect place to find unique gifts. ■ **TIP→ Stop by Kalapawai Market, at Kailua Beach near the entrance to Lanikai, for sandwiches and cold drinks, as well as souvenirs, and finish the day relaxing on a less bustling white-sand beach.**

### BOOKS

★ **Bookends**

**BOOKS** | **FAMILY** | Shop for gifts or yourself at this cozy independent bookstore, which feels more like a small-town library, welcoming browsers to linger. It sells new and secondhand books, and the children's section is filled with both books and toys. ✉ *600 Kailua Rd., Unit 126, Kailua* ☎ *808/261–1996* 🌐 *instagram.com/bookendskailua.*

### CLOTHING

**Manuhealii**

**CLOTHING** | For modern and authentic aloha attire made in Hawaii, Manuhealii is your place. The Kailua storefront is one of two physical locations (the other is in Honolulu). The clothes for women, men, and children aren't inexpensive, but their quality is superb. ✉ *5 Hoolai St., Kailua* ☎ *808/261–9865* 🌐 *manuhealii.com.*

### HEALTH AND BEAUTY

**Lanikai Bath and Body**

**HEALTH & BEAUTY** | Take home the fragrances of the Islands with this shop's organic body lotions, hand creams, soaps, sprays, bath salts, and scrubs. Botanical extracts, such as papaya, mango, sea kelp, and calendula, are combined with essential oils, including from macadamia and kukui nuts, to produce the shop's refined line of products. ✉ *Kailua Shopping Center, 600 Kailua Rd., Suite 119, Kailua* ☎ *808/262–3260* 🌐 *lanikaibathandbody.com.*

# Kaneohe

*6 miles west of Kailua.*

The largest community on Oahu's windward side, Kaneohe (meaning "bamboo man" in Hawaiian) is a sprawling community with malls, car dealerships, and a few worthwhile restaurants. At the base of the Koolau Range, Kaneohe sees a lot more rain than neighboring Kailua and is the greener for it. Two noteworthy sights take advantage of their proximity to the mountains: the Byodo-In Temple and Hoomaluhia Botanical Garden.

### GETTING HERE AND AROUND

Kaneohe is a 30-minute drive or one-hour bus ride from Waikiki. If driving, you can take any of the three highways across the Koolau Mountains: the H3, the Pali, or the Likelike.

## Sights

**★ Byodo-In Temple**

**TEMPLE** | Tucked away in the back of the Valley of the Temples Memorial Park is a replica of the 11th-century temple at Uji in Japan, built in 1963. An impressive 2-ton, carved-wood statue of the Buddha presides inside the main building. Next to the temple are a meditation pavilion and gardens set dramatically against the sheer, green cliffs of the Koolau Mountains. You can ring the 5-foot, 3-ton brass bell for good luck; feed some of the hundreds of koi, ducks, and swans that inhabit the garden's 2-acre pond (buy fish food at the gift shop); and relax and enjoy the peaceful surroundings. ✉ *47-200 Kahekili Hwy., Kaneohe* ☎ *808/239–8811* 🌐 *byodo-in.com* 🎫 *$5.*

**★ Hoomaluhia Botanical Garden**

**GARDEN** | **FAMILY** | The name, which means "a peaceful refuge," describes the serenity and feeling of endless space you find in this verdant garden framed by the stunning Koolau Range. Its 400 acres contain specimens from such tropical areas as the Americas, Africa, Melanesia, the Philippines, and Hawaii. Not just for the botanist, Hoomaluhia has a 32-acre lake, easy walking trails, and open lawns ideal for picnicking and camping by permit. Families can also take advantage of the park's catch-and-release tilapia fishing program; free bamboo fishing poles are sometimes available for borrowing at the visitor center. If you see unusually dressed-up visitors, they are likely selfie seekers doing it for the 'gram. Hoomaluhia is very photogenic; just make sure you're not blocking the roadways in search of the perfect shot. ✉ *45-680 Luluku Rd., Kaneohe* ☎ *808/233–7323* 🌐 *www.honolulu.gov/parks/hbg* 🎫 *Free.*

### ★ Nuuanu Pali State Wayside

**VIEWPOINT** | This panoramic perch looks out to expansive views of Windward Oahu—from Kaneohe Bay to a small island off the coast called Mokolii ("little lizard," also known as Chinaman's Hat). It was in this region that King Kamehameha I drove defending forces over the edges of the 1,200-foot-high cliffs, thus winning the decisive battle for control of the island in 1795. Temperatures at the summit are several degrees cooler than in warm Waikiki, so bring a jacket along. Hang on tight to any loose possessions, and consider wearing pants; it gets extremely windy at the lookout, which is part of the fun. After arriving in the pay-to-park lot, remove valuables from your car and lock it. Break-ins have occurred here; this wayside is in the most trafficked state park in Hawaii. *Pali Hwy., Kaneohe* *At very top of Pali Hwy.* *dlnr.hawaii.gov/dsp/parks/oahu* *Parking $7 per car.*

## Restaurants

### ★ Haleiwa Joe's Haiku Gardens

**$$$** | **AMERICAN** | The Haleiwa location may be the namesake and claim the surf, but this windward-side branch offers knock-'em-dead views and a tiki torch–lit atmosphere after dark along with the friendly vibe and grilled seafood. In addition to surf-and-turf favorites, look for special preparations of each day's catch, which is delivered straight from the Honolulu Fish Auction. **Known for:** stunning views of Haiku Gardens; reliable for both seafood and meat; no reservations, so expect long lines for a table. *Average main: $35* *44-336 Haiku Rd., Kaneohe* *808/274–6671* *www.haleiwajoes.com/kaneohe-menu* *No lunch.*

### Jolene's by the Bay Kaneohe

**$** | **FUSION** | One of four Jolene's locations in Oahu, the Kaneohe restaurant with an open-air dining room and deck is next to the Bayview Golf Course and Bay View Mini-Putt and Zipline; the deck has a golf course view and a peek-a-boo glimpse of Kaneohe Bay. The eatery is best known for its lobster "buttah" rolls—toasted, buttery bread stuffed with pickled vegetables and lobster salad—and also has a range of coastal Atlantic hot and cold sandwiches, salads and burgers, many with some Asian spin, too. **Known for:** delicious corn chowder; lobster melt and other melt sandwiches; friendly service. *Average main: $17* *Bayview Golf Course, 45-285 Kaneohe Bay Dr., Kaneohe* *808/236–1010* *joleneshawaii.com/kaneohe.*

### ★ Waiahole Poi Factory

**$** | **HAWAIIAN** | The historic Waiahole Poi Factory, which made poi for 70 years before serving as an art galley and then a commercial kitchen, returned to its roots back in 2009 and now makes some of the island's freshest and best-tasting poi. Along with that Hawaiian food staple, you can get plate lunches with other classics like squid luau (a dish with taro leaves and coconut), *lomi lomi* salmon (pieces of salted salmon mixed with onion and tomatoes), chicken long rice, and *laulau* (meat or fish wrapped in leaves and cooked); outdoor seating is limited, so it's good for takeout. **Known for:** long line at some times, and it closes early at 5 or 6 pm; watching the poi pounders at work; authentic and fresh Hawaiian plate lunches. *Average main: $15* *48-140 Kamehameha Hwy., Kaneohe* *808/239–2222* *waiaholepoifactory.com* *Closes at 5 or 6 pm.*

## Hotels

### Paradise Bay Resort

**$$** | **RESORT** | Right on picturesque Kaneohe Bay amid the junglelike fauna of the windward side, this resort offers apartment-style units ranging from cozy studios to spacious two-bedroom suites with breathtaking views of the majestic Koolau Mountains; one stand-alone

Kualoa Point is in Kualoa Regional Park in Kaaawa, a beautiful but windy area overlooking Kaneohe Bay and the towering Koolau Mountains.

cottage is in a remote area not generally frequented by tourists. **Pros:** local, authentic experience; beautiful views over the bay; en suite kitchens or kitchenettes. **Cons:** remote location not near most other attractions; neighborhood is a bit run-down; rental car a necessity (but parking included in $38 nightly resort fee). *Rooms from: $220* *47-039 Lihikai Dr., Kaneohe* *808/239–5711* *www.paradisebayresort.com* *46 rooms* *No Meals.*

## Shopping

### HOME DECOR

**Jeff Chang Pottery & Fine Crafts**

**CRAFTS** | This family-owned and -operated gallery offers the artist's functional and decorative pottery as well as the works of approximately 200 other American artisans. Jeff has worked with clay for more than 40 years, and his wife, Karon, operates the gallery and selects other works, including jewelry, glass pieces, metal sculpture, wall art, wooden items, musical instruments, chimes, suncatchers, sand globes and pictures, holiday decor, and ornaments. *Windward Mall, 46-056 Kamehameha Hwy., 2nd fl., Theatre Wing, Kaneohe* *808/235–5150* *www.windwardmall.com/stores/jeff-chang-pottery.*

# Kaaawa

*14 miles north of Kaneohe.*

Less a village than a collection of homes, Kaaawa consists of little more than a post office, bus stop, and gas station—bookended by an elementary school and a fire station. Of course, there's a beach park, too.

### GETTING HERE AND AROUND

Kaaawa is located on Kamehameha Highway. You'll pass through it immediately before or after you pass sprawling Kualoa Ranch.

The 4,000-acre Kualoa Ranch may look familiar to you: it's been featured in several movies and TV shows. You can even take a tour of film locations around the ranch.

## Sights

**Ahupuaa O Kahana State Park**

**STATE/PROVINCIAL PARK | FAMILY** | This park offers the true Hawaiian experience: a beautiful windward bay sits a short walk away from the Huilua Fishpond, a National Historic Landmark where restoration efforts are ongoing. There are rain-forest hikes past many local fruit trees, a hunting area for pigs, and a coconut grove for picnicking. The water is suitable for swimming and bodysurfing, though it's a little cloudy for snorkeling. ✉ *52-222 Kamehameha Hwy., near Kahana Bay, Kaaawa* 🌐 *dlnr.hawaii.gov/dsp/parks/oahu* 🎫 *Free.*

**★ Kualoa Ranch**

**FARM/RANCH | FAMILY** | Encompassing 4,000 acres, this working ranch about 45 minutes by car from Waikiki offers a wide range of activities—from ATV and horseback tours to zip-lining or expeditions into the valley on an electric bike. The mountains that serve as the backdrop here may seem familiar: the ranch has served as the set for movies such as *Jurassic Park* and *Windtalkers*, as well as TV shows like *Magnum P.I.* and *Lost* (and you can take a film locations tour). From the grounds, you'll have a wonderful view of the ocean and Mokolii (Chinaman's Hat). ■ **TIP→ You can drop by the visitor center anytime, but it's best to book activities and tours two or three days in advance.** ✉ *49-560 Kamehameha Hwy., Kaaawa* ☎ *808/237-7321* 🌐 *www.kualoa.com* 🎫 *Tours and activities from $52.*

**Mokolii**

**ISLAND** | As you drive the windward and northern shores along Kamehameha Highway, a number of interesting geological features come into view. At Kualoa, look to the ocean at the uniquely shaped little island of Mokolii ("little lizard"), a 206-foot-high sea stack also known as Chinaman's Hat (for its hat-like shape). According to Hawaiian legend, the goddess Hiiaka, sister of Pele, slew the dragon Mokolii and flung its tail into the sea, forming the distinct islet. Other dragon body parts—in the form of rocks, of course—were scattered along the base of nearby Kualoa Ridge. Adventurous (and fit) folks can kayak out to Mokolii and scale its rocky sides, though it's not the easiest climb. ✉ *49-479 Kamehameha Hwy., Kaaawa.*

**Kahana Bay Beach Park**

**BEACH | FAMILY** | Local parents often bring their children here to wade safely in the very shallow, protected waters. This pretty beach cove, surrounded by mountains, has a long arc of sand that is great for walking and a cool, shady grove of tall ironwood and pandanus trees that is ideal for a picnic. An ancient Hawaiian fishpond, which was in use until the 1920s, is visible nearby. Note, though, that the water here is not generally a clear blue due to the runoff from heavy rains in the valley. **Amenities:** parking (no fee); showers; toilets. **Best for:** swimming; walking. ✉ *52-201 Kamehameha Hwy., Kaaawa* ✥ *North of Kualoa Park.*

★ **Kualoa Regional Park**

**BEACH** | Grassy expanses border a long, narrow stretch of sand with spectacular views of Kaneohe Bay and the Koolau Mountains, making Kualoa one of the island's most beautiful picnic, camping, and beach areas. Dominating the view is an islet called Mokolii, also known as Chinaman's Hat, which rises 206 feet above the water. You can swim in the shallow areas of this rarely crowded beach year-round. The one drawback is that it's usually windy here, but the wide-open spaces are ideal for kite flying. **Amenities:** lifeguards; showers; toilets. **Best for:** solitude; swimming. ✉ *49-479 Kamehameha Hwy., Kaaawa* ✥ *North of Waiahole.*

**Punaluu Beach Park**

**BEACH** | If you're making a circle of the island, this is a great place to stop, stretch your legs, and get your toes wet. It's nice (there is a sandy bottom and mostly calm conditions) and easy (the sand literally comes up to your parked car). Plus there are full facilities, shops for picnic supplies, and lots of shade trees. Often overlooked, and often overcast, Punaluu can afford you a moment of fresh air before you get back to your sightseeing. **Amenities:** food and drink; parking (no fee); showers; toilets. **Best for:** solitude; swimming. ✉ *53-400 Kamehameha Hwy., Hauula.*

# Laie

*10 miles north of Kaaawa, 33 miles north of Honolulu.*

Visiting Laie—over an hour by car and a world away from bustling Waikiki and Honolulu—is like taking a trip to another island. Home to a Mormon temple and the Mormon-founded Polynesian Cultural Center, Laie is a "dry town," meaning no alcohol is sold.

## GETTING HERE AND AROUND

From Waikiki, getting here will take a little more than an hour by car or up to two hours by bus. By car you can take the H2 past Haleiwa, until it joins the Kamehameha Highway. Along the route, you'll pass Haleiwa town and world-famous North Shore surf spots. Alternatively, take any of the highways going over the Koolau Range (Likelike, Pali, or H3) to Kaneohe and follow Highway 83 north. This road will then meet up with the two-lane Kamehameha Highway, which leads you to all points north.

**Polynesian Cultural Center**

**MUSEUM VILLAGE | FAMILY** | Re-created individual villages showcase the lifestyles and traditions of Hawaii, Tahiti, Samoa, Fiji, the Marquesas Islands, New Zealand, and Tonga. In addition, the 42-acre center, which is 35 miles from Waikiki and which was founded in 1963 by the Church of Jesus Christ of Latter-day

Saints, has restaurants, hosts luau, and demonstrates cultural traditions, such as hula, fire dancing, and ancient ceremonies. The Hukilau Marketplace carries Polynesian handicrafts.

There are multiple packages available, including luau and *Ha: Breath of Life* show options. Every May, the center hosts the World Fireknife Championships, an event that draws the top fireknife dance performers from around the world. Get tickets for that event in advance. **■ TIP→ If you're staying in Honolulu, see the center as part of a van tour so you won't have to drive home late at night after the two-hour evening show.** ✉ *55-370 Kamehameha Hwy., Laie* ☎ *800/367–7060* 🌐 *www.polynesia.com* 🎫 *From $120* ⏲ *Closed Sun. and Wed.*

## Beaches

**Malaekahana State Recreation Area**
**BEACH | FAMILY** | The big attraction here is tiny Goat Island, a bird sanctuary just offshore. At low tide the water is shallow enough—never more than waist-high—for you to wade out to it. Wear sneakers or aqua socks so you don't cut yourself on the coral. The beach itself is fairly narrow but long enough for a 20-minute stroll, one-way. The waves are never too big, and sometimes they're just right for novice bodysurfers. The entrance gates, which close at 7:45 pm in summer and 6:45 pm the rest of the year, are easy to miss, and you can't see the beach from the road. It's a great rural getaway: families love to camp in the groves of ironwood trees at Malaekahana State Park, and there are also cabins here, though they are undergoing renovation as of fall 2023, which may last a year. **■ TIP→ Unfortunately, theft is an increasingly serious issue here, so be aware of your surroundings and do not leave any personal property unattended.** **Amenities:** parking (no fee); showers; toilets. **Best for:** swimming; walking. ✉ *56-207 Kamehameha Hwy., Laie* ✣ *Enter at gates ½ mile north of Laie on Kamehameha Hwy.* 🌐 *dlnr.hawaii.gov/dsp/parks/oahu.*

## Hotels

**Courtyard by Marriott Oahu North Shore**
**$$$ | HOTEL | FAMILY** | This property offers reliable and affordable accommodations close to the Polynesian Cultural Center and a short drive to some of the North Shore's most iconic beaches and surfing spots. **Pros:** good bet for North Shore exploring; reliable, modern, and clean; near the beach. **Cons:** a long drive to the rest of Oahu's attractions; no alcohol served in the hotel or nearby establishments; a car is needed, and parking is not free. 💲 *Rooms from: $292* ✉ *55-400 Kamehameha Hwy., Laie* ☎ *808/293–4900* 🌐 *marriott.com* 🛏 *144 rooms* 🍽 *No Meals.*

Chapter 7

# ACTIVITIES AND TOURS



Updated by
Powell Berger

Although much is written about the water surrounding this little rock known as Oahu, there is as much to be said for the rock itself. It's a wonder of nature, thrust from the ocean floor thousands of millennia ago by a volcanic hot spot that is still spitting out islands today.

Hawaii is the most remote island chain on Earth, with creatures and plants that can be seen here and nowhere else. And there are dozens of ways for you to check them all out.

From the air, you can peer down into nooks and crannies in the mountains—where cars cannot reach and hikers don't dare to venture. Whether flitting here and there amid a helicopter's rush and roar or sailing by in the silence of a glider's reverie, you glimpse sights that few have experienced. Or, if you would rather, take a step back in time and take off from the waters of Keehi Lagoon in a World War II–era seaplane. Follow the flight path flown by the Japanese Zeros as they attempted to destroy Pearl Harbor and the American spirit.

If you prefer to stay grounded, Oahu is covered in hiking trails that traverse everything from tropical rain forest to arid desert. Even when in the bustling city of Honolulu, you are but minutes from hidden waterfalls and bamboo forests. Out west, you can wander a dusty path that has long since given up its ability to accommodate cars but is perfect for hikers. You can admire sea arches and gape at caves opened by the rock slides that closed the road. You can also camp out on many of these treks and beaches.

If somewhat less rugged and less vigorous exploration is more your style, how about letting horses do your dirty work? You can ride them on the beaches and in the valleys, checking out ancient holy sites, movie sets, and brilliant vistas.

Finally, there is the ancient sport of Scotland. Why merely hike into the rain forest when you can slice a 280-yard drive through it and then hunt for your Titleist in the bushy leaves instead? Almost 40 courses cover this tiny expanse, ranging from the target jungle golf of the Royal Hawaiian Golf Club to the pro-style links of Turtle Bay. There is no off-season in the tropics, and no one here knows your real handicap.

## Aerial Tours

Taking an aerial tour of the Islands opens up a world of perspective. Look down from the sky at the outline of the USS *Arizona*, where it lies in its final resting place below the waters of Pearl Harbor, or get a glimpse of the vast carved expanse of a volcanic crater—here are views only seen by an "eye in the sky." Don't forget your camera.

⚠ **All helicopter tour companies in Hawaii are under increasing legislative and regulatory scrutiny due to a number of fatal**

Take a helicopter tour for a unique perspective of the island.

**accidents since 2018, so it's possible that they will undergo further regulations and limitations in the future.**

## HONOLULU

### Blue Hawaiian Helicopters

**FLIGHTSEEING** | This company stakes its claim as Hawaii's largest helicopter operation, with tours on all the major Islands (including Maui) and more than two dozen choppers in its fleet. The 45-minute Oahu tour seats up to six passengers and includes narration from your friendly pilot along with sweeping views of Waikiki, the beautiful windward coast, and the North Shore. If you like to see the world from above or are just pinched for time and want to get a quick overview of the whole island without renting a car, this is the way to go. Discounts are available if you book online in advance. ✉ *99 Kaulele Pl., Airport Area* ☎ *808/745–2583* 🌐 *www.bluehawaiian.com* 🎫 *From $379.*

### ★ Magnum Helicopters

**FLIGHTSEEING** | For a once-in-a-lifetime adventure, this *Magnum P.I.*, doors-off helicopter tour offers sweeping views of Keehi Lagoon through urban Honolulu and the harbor, including the Aloha Tower and Waikiki Beach. Soar past and over Diamond Head Crater and up the scenic coast by Makapuu Lighthouse and Sandy Beach and over Windward Oahu's iconic Lanikai and Kailua beaches, complete with wind in your hair and jaw-dropping views. The breathtaking finale takes you inland to Sacred Falls, known for its stunning, 1,000-foot drop and its starring role in *Jurassic Park*, before returning to the airport via North Shore surf spots and a bird's-eye view of Pearl Harbor and the USS *Arizona* Memorial. If you're looking for more thrill (or a cool proposal site), opt for the exclusive mountaintop landing. And if water is your thing, your Navy SEAL guide will join you in plunging into the ocean for some scuba diving. **■ TIP→ If carrying a phone or camera on the tour, bring a strap to keep it closely secured.** ✉ *130 Iolana Pl., Airport Area* ☎ *808/833–4354* 🌐 *www.magnumhelicopters.com* 🎫 *From $350.*

### NORTH SHORE

Most aerial tour and skydiving operators on the North Shore work out of Kawaihapai Airfield (formerly known as Dillingham Airfield). Despite controversy and concern about possible closures, skydiving on Oahu is still alive and well, allowing people to plummet thousands of feet before soaring over breathtaking scenery. If you book a glider or skydiving adventure, definitely reconfirm with your outfitter closer to the time of any reservation to ensure it's still a go.

**Honolulu Soaring — The Original Glider Rides**

**FLIGHTSEEING** | "Mr. Bill" has been offering piloted glider (sailplane) rides over the northwest end of Oahu's North Shore since 1970. Scenic rides for one or two passengers are in sleek, bubble-top, motorless aircraft with aerial views of mountains, shoreline, coral pools, windsurfing sails, and, in winter, humpback whales. Seeking more thrills? You can also take a more acrobatic ride or take control yourself in a mini lesson. Flights run 15 minutes to an hour. The company's online booking platform shows days they are flying. Advance reservations are recommended. ✉ *Kawaihapai Airfield, 69-132 Farrington Hwy., Waialua* ☎ *808/637–0207* ✎ *mrbill@hawaii.rr.com* 🌐 *www.honolulusoaring.com* 🎫 *From $85.*

**Paradise Helicopters**

**FLIGHTSEEING** | Paradise offers tours on several islands, with Oahu tours departing from two helipads: Kalaeloa (near the Ko Olina resorts on the west side) and Turtle Bay Resort on the North Shore. Kalaeloa options range from a one-hour trip over Diamond Head to a two-hour island circle (daytime and sunset) to specialized trips that focus on World War II history. Turtle Bay choices include several 1½-hour North Shore adventures, with vistas of beaches as well as inland waterfalls. ✉ *Honolulu* ☎ *866/300–2294* 🌐 *paradisecopters.com* 🎫 *From $295.*

# Animal Encounters

Pods of dolphins surround the Islands and spotting them can be as easy as getting yourself out in—or on—the ocean. They are wild animals, of course, and do not follow a schedule, but a catamaran sail off Waikiki or the west side will usually net you a sighting. Dolphins also generally make appearances shortly after sunrise on the west shore and can be clearly observed from beaches like Makua and Makaha. And while they won't have the peppy music of SeaWorld in the background, their jumping and spinning is even more awe-inspiring when you realize they are doing it as a natural part of their lives rather than for a reward.

Some tour operators offer opportunities to swim with dolphins, but keep in mind that these are federally protected marine mammals, so you should always follow the instructions given by the tour operator on these trips. The National Oceanographic and Atmospheric Administration (NOAA) provides specific guidelines for tour operators encountering dolphins through their Dolphin Safe program.

The cost for dolphin encounters ranges from $150 for a chance to swim with wild dolphins on a snorkel cruise to $700 for getting in the pool with them as trainer-for-a-day. Both Dolphin Quest at The Kahala Hotel & Resort in Honolulu and Sea Life Park in Waimanalo offer opportunities to view and interact with captive dolphins. ⇨ *See Chapter 3, Honolulu and Pearl Harbor, and Chapter 6, East (Windward) Oahu, for more information.*

Similarly, you can also swim with sharks, though you do so in a protective cage.

### LEEWARD (WEST) OAHU

**Dolphin Excursions**

**WILDLIFE-WATCHING** | **FAMILY** | Oahu's leeward coast offers an abundance of spinner dolphins, as well as whales (in the winter months) and other marine wildlife.

This company's three-hour Dolphin Adventure departs from Waianae Boat Harbor and includes round-trip transportation from Waikiki and Ko Olina. Early morning tours are suggested for better dolphin sightings, and whale-watching tours in the winter, leading into sunset, are sure to take your breath away. Snorkeling adventures are also available. No more than 16 guests are booked on each boat, ensuring plenty of room for sightseeing. ✉ *Waianae Boat Harbor, 85-491 Farrington Hwy., Waianae ✣ Check in at Spinners Café ☎ 808/239–5579 🌐 dolphinexcursions.com 🎫 From $150.*

### NORTH SHORE

**North Shore Shark Adventures**

**WILDLIFE-WATCHING** | "You go in the cage, cage goes in the water, you go in the water. Shark's in the water." You remember these lines from *Jaws*, and now you get to play the role of Richard Dreyfuss, as North Shore Shark Adventures offers an interactive experience out of your worst nightmare. The tour allows you to swim and snorkel in a cage as dozens of sharks lurk just feet below and around you in the open ocean off the North Shore. No swimming is required. The company provides transportation from Waikiki for an additional charge, and discounts are available if you book online. ■ **TIP→ If you go, go early: the sea is calmer and clearer in the morning, and the sightings are more plentiful.** ✉ *Haleiwa Small Boat Harbor, 66-105 Haleiwa Rd., Haleiwa ✣ Check in at Shark Shack in harbor ☎ 808/228–5900 🌐 sharktourshawaii.com 🎫 From $80.*

# Bicycling

Oahu's coastal roads are flat, well-paved, and, unfortunately, awash in vehicular traffic. Frankly, biking is no fun in either Waikiki or Honolulu, but things are a bit better outside the city. Your best bet is to cycle early in the morning or get off the road to check out the island's bike trails. Biking on island roads is not recommended for families, but it is doable for those cyclists who are accustomed to busy roads that are not always welcoming to bike traffic.

**Honolulu City and County Bike Coordinator**

**BIKING** | This office can answer many of your biking questions concerning trails, permits, and state laws. ✉ *Honolulu* ☎ *808/768–8335 ✉ oryn.nakamura@honolulu.gov 🌐 www.honolulu.gov/bicycle.*

## BEST SPOTS

### HONOLULU

**Maunawili Demonstration Trail**

**BIKING** | Locals favor biking this 10-mile trail that has breathtaking views as you descend into Waimanalo. There are many flat portions, but the trail does have some uneven ground to negotiate unless you're willing to carry your bike for small stretches. The main trailhead is at the Pali Lookout on the blacktop of Old Pali Road. Be aware that the trail is also popular with hikers and dog walkers. Note, too, that there have been closures, so check ahead on the trail's status before heading out. ✉ *Nuuanu Pali Dr., at Pali Lookout, Honolulu.*

### NORTH SHORE

**Kaena Point Trail**

**BIKING** | If simply pedaling up a mountain road is not your idea of mountain biking, then perhaps Kaena Point Trail is better suited to your needs. This 10-mile trail takes you oceanside around the westernmost point on the island. You pass sea arches and a mini blowhole, then finish up with some motocross jumps right before you turn around. There's no drinking water available on this ride, so remember to bring your own, and then cool off at the Keawaula (also known as Yokohama) Beach showers. ✉ *69-385 Farrington Hwy., Waialua 🌐 dlnr.hawaii.gov/dsp/hiking/oahu/kaena-point-trail.*

**Kaunala Trail**

**BIKING** | Biking the North Shore may sound like a great idea, but the two-lane road is narrow and traffic-heavy. Consider trying the Kaunala Trail. It's a little tricky at times, but with the rain-forest surroundings and beautiful ocean vistas, you'll hardly notice your legs burning on the steep ascent at the end. It's about 5½ miles round-trip. Bring water because there's none on the trail unless it comes from the sky. Also remember that it gets really muddy and slippery after heavy rains. ✉ *59-777 Pupukea Rd., at the end of Pupukea Rd., Haleiwa* ✣ *Pupukea Rd. is next to Foodland, the only grocery store on the North Shore* 🌐 *hawaiitrails.hawaii.gov/trails/#/trail/kaunala-trail/171.*

**North Shore Bike Park**

**BIKING** | Wind around 12 miles of trails plus seven professionally designed, single-track loops at the North Shore's Turtle Bay Resort. Trails lead to protected wildlife areas and ancient Hawaiian sites, a World War II pillbox (a defensive structure), a giant banyan tree, and secluded beaches and bays. Purchase day passes at the Hele Huli Adventure Center, and rent bikes right on-site. ✉ *57-091 Kuilima Dr., Kahuku* ☎ *808/293–6024* 🌐 *www.turtlebayresort.com* 🎫 *Rates vary depending on season, trails, and bikes rented.*

## EQUIPMENT AND TOURS

### HONOLULU

**Bike Hawaii**

**BIKING** | Whether you want to tackle road tours on the North Shore or muddy off-road adventures in the Koolau Range, this company can help, and it offers combination packages that pair cycling with snorkeling, sailing, or hiking. Its Rainforest to Reef Tour (half- or full-day options) is often cited as one of the island's best outings, taking you 2,000 feet up into the Koolau Mountains so you can coast downhill through tropical woodlands before getting on a catamaran to swim and snorkel with turtles. Other options include a three-hour road excursion and a six-hour mountain-biking foray. Tours include equipment, transportation, and water; some also include lunch. The company will pick you up at central locations in Waikiki. The company's origins go back to 1948, when the founder played music in Waikiki and also offered suggestions to tourists. Several generations later, the family still calls the shots. ✉ *Honolulu* ☎ *808/734–4214* 🌐 *bikehawaii.com* 🎫 *Bike tours from $91.*

**Biki**

**BIKING** | In late 2017, nonprofit Bikeshare Hawaii launched a Honolulu bikesharing system equipped with 1,300 bikes docked at solar-powered kiosks throughout urban Honolulu. The comfortable, easy-to-maneuver bikes accommodate riders of all sizes and include a basket to carry your farmers' market goodies. Today, it's more popular than ever. The procedure is easy: pay at a kiosk, hop on a bike, and dock it at the kiosk closest to your destination. You can do a one-time rental for 30 or 60 minutes or pre-purchase a pool of minutes to use during the course of your trip. Helmets are not required by law, but you can purchase or rent one. ✉ *Honolulu* ☎ *888/340–2454* 🌐 *gobiki.org* 🎫 *From $4.*

**Hawaii Bicycling League**

**BIKING** | Don't want to go cycling by yourself? Visit this shop online, and you can get connected with rides and competitions, including the annual circle island ride. ✉ *3442 Waialae Ave., Suite 1, Honolulu* ☎ *808/735–5756* 🌐 *hbl.org.*

### NORTH SHORE

**North Shore Explorers**

**BIKING** | Rent cruisers, fat-tire bikes, mountain bikes, or mopeds at this outfitter's space at the Polynesian Cultural Center, where its Lunar Legends Tour offers a behind-the-scenes tour at the center and shares stories and history of the Islands. The company also rents bicycles and runs an often-changing array of guided adventure tours, introducing the North Shore to visitors. ✉ *Polynesian Cultural Center, 55-370 Kamehameha Hwy., Laie* ☎ *808/225–0522* ✍ *info@*

northshoreexplorers.com 🌐 northshore-explorers.com 💵 Bike rentals from $50.

# Birding

Independent birding can be accomplished by visiting 🌐 alltrails.com and finding the area that seems most interesting. Remember to bring all necessary equipment, water, and other supplies, incluing a portable charger for your phone, in case you get lost.

**Victor Emanuel Nature Tours**

**SPECIAL-INTEREST TOURS** | One of the most-respected companies in the world specializing in birding and nature tours has a limited number of Hawaii trips that take in Oahu, Kauai, and the Big Island. The cost includes double-occupancy accommodations, meals, interisland air, ground transportation, and guided excursions. Hawaii bird-watching tours often sell out, so book quickly. ☎ *800/328–8368* 🌐 *www.ventbird.com* 💵 *$7,995.*

# Boat Tours and Charters

Being on the water can be the best way to enjoy the Islands. Whether you want to see the fish in action or experience how they taste, there is a tour for you. For a sailing experience, you need go no farther than the beach in front of your Waikiki hotel. Strung along the sand are several catamarans that offer one-hour rides during the day (about $35) and 90-minute sunset sails ($49–$120). **TIP→ Feel free to haggle, especially with the smaller boats.**

Some operators provide drinks for free, some charge for them, and some let you pack your own, so keep that in mind when pricing the ride. Or choose to go the ultraluxe route and charter a boat for a day or week. These run from less than $100 per person per day to more than $1,000. ⇨ *See also: Deep-Sea Fishing.*

## HONOLULU

**Hawaii Nautical**

**BOATING** | With two locations—one in Waikiki and one on the Waianae coast—this outfitter offers a wide variety of cruise options, including guaranteed-sighting dolphin and whale-watching (in season), gourmet dinners, lunches, snorkeling, and sunset viewing. Three-hour cruises, including lunch and two drinks, depart from the Kewalo Basin Harbor just outside Waikiki. (The company's Port Waikiki Cruises sail from the Hilton Pier off the Hilton Hawaiian Village in Waikiki.) For those interested in leaving from the Waianae coast on the leeward side, snorkel tours are available from the Waianae Boat Harbor on Farrington Highway (✉ *85-471 Farrington Hwy.*). Prices include all gear, food, and two alcoholic beverages. The dock in the Waianae Boat Harbor is a little more out of the way, but this is a much more luxurious option than what is offered in Waikiki. Both morning and afternoon snorkel tours include stops for observing dolphins from the boat and a visit to a snorkel spot well populated with fish. All gear, snacks, sandwiches, and two alcoholic beverages make for a more complete experience. Pickup in Ko Olina is free. ✉ *Kewalo Basin Harbor, 1125 Ala Moana Blvd., Waikiki* ☎ *808/234–7245* 🌐 *www.hawaiinautical.com* 💵 *From $75.*

**Honolulu Sailing Company**

**BOATING** | With a select fleet of mono- and multihull sail and power boats, the Honolulu Sailing Company offers boat charters, sailing instruction opportunities, and other unique sailings as requested (including memorials and ash spreadings). Itineraries include private chartered day or sunset sails, snorkeling adventures, powerboating around Oahu, offshore fishing adventures, and special events like weddings. Remember that these are all private, full-ship charters, so you'll want at least a small group to make it affordable. ✉ *Kewalo Basin Yacht Harbor, 1025 Ala Moana Blvd., Ala Moana*

☎ *808/239–3900* 🌐 *honsail.com* 🎫 *From $599.*

**Maitai Catamaran**

**BOATING** | Taking off from the stretch of sand between the Sheraton Waikiki and the Halekulani, this 44-foot catamaran is the fastest and sleekest on the beach. There are a variety of tours, including a sunset sail, snorkel excursion, or even private sailings. If you have a need for speed and want a more upscale experience, this is the boat for you. ✉ *Sheraton Waikiki Beach Resort, 2255 Kalakaua Ave., Waikiki* ✣ *On beach behind hotel* ☎ *808/922–5665, 800/462–7975* 🌐 *www.maitaicatamaran.net* 🎫 *From $49.*

**Makani Catamaran**

**BOATING** | The 65-foot *Makani* is the top catamaran in Hawaii for luxury, from its Bose stereo system to its LCD TVs to its freshwater bathrooms. It sails out of Kewalo Basin four times daily, offering cruises that include lunch, afternoon "fun" sails, "Honolulu City Lights/Sunset" dinner cruises, and more. Some cruises may include the opportunity to snorkel; private charters, including snorkeling cruises, are another option. ✉ *Kewalo Basin Harbor, 1009 Ala Moana Blvd., Slip F31, Ala Moana* ☎ *808/591–9000* 🌐 *sailmakani.com* 🎫 *From $92.*

**Star of Honolulu Cruises**

**BOATING** | **FAMILY** | Founded in 1957, this company anchors Oahu's dinner-cruise market with its 232-foot *Star of Honolulu,* featuring four floors of walk-around decks and a 60-foot-high observation deck. Enjoy views, live entertainment, cocktails, and dinner. The company also offers several cruise experiences—from casual to luxury—to fit your needs and whims. On some cruises you can even learn how to string lei, play ukulele, or dance hula. Whale-watching cruises are another option. Transportation from all hotels on the island can be arranged. ✉ *1 Aloha Tower Dr., Pier 8, Downtown* ☎ *808/983–7730* 🌐 *starofhonolulu.com* 🎫 *From $117.*

**Tradewind Charters**

**BOATING** | This company's half-day private excursions can include sailing, snorkeling, reef fishing, sunset dinner cruises, sunrise mimosa ventures, whale-watching, and even spa treatments, all on luxury yachts that can accommodate 2 to 49 people. Traveling on these vessels not only gets you away from the crowds, but also gives you the opportunity to take the helm if you wish. The cruises may include snorkeling at an exclusive anchorage, as well as hands-on snorkeling and sailing instruction. All charters are for the full ship. ✉ *Kewalo Basin Harbor, 1125 Ala Moana Blvd., Ala Moana* ☎ *808/227–4956, 800/664–5493* 🌐 *www.tradewind-charters.com* 🎫 *From $495.*

# Bodyboarding and Bodysurfing

Bodyboarding (or sponging) has long been a popular alternative to surfing for a couple of reasons. First, the start-up cost is much less—a usable board can be purchased for $30–$40 or rented on the beach for $5 an hour to about $20 for up to three hours. Second, it's a whole lot easier to ride a bodyboard than a surfboard. All you have to do is paddle out to the waves, then turn toward the beach as the wave approaches and kick like crazy.

Most grocery and convenience stores sell bodyboards. Though these boards don't compare to what the pros use, beginners won't notice a difference in how they handle on smaller waves. Though they are not absolutely necessary for bodyboarding, fins do give you a tremendous advantage when you're paddling. If you plan to go out into bigger surf, get a leash, which reduces the chance you'll lose your board. The smaller, sturdier versions of dive fins used for bodyboarding sell for $25–$60 at surf and sporting-goods stores. Most beach

The windward side has many good spots for bodyboarding.

stands don't rent fins with the boards, so if you want them, you'll probably need to buy them.

Bodysurfing requires far less equipment—just a pair of swim fins with heel straps—but it can be a lot more challenging to master. Typically, surf breaks that are good for bodyboarding are good for bodysurfing.

If the direction of the current or dangers of the break are not readily apparent to you, don't hesitate to ask a lifeguard for advice.

### BEST SPOTS

Bodyboarding and bodysurfing can be done anywhere you find waves, but due to the paddling advantage surfers have over bodyboarders, it's usually more fun to go to surf breaks exclusively for bodyboarding. ⇨ *For more information on Oahu beaches, see the individual regional chapters.*

**Bellows Beach.** On Oahu's windward side, Bellows Field Beach Park has shallow waters and a consistent break that makes it an ideal spot for bodyboarders and bodysurfers. (Surfing isn't allowed between the two lifeguard towers.) But take note: the Portuguese man-of-war, a blue jellyfishlike invertebrate that delivers painful and powerful stings, is often seen here. ✉ *41-043 Kalanianaole Hwy., Waimanalo.*

**Kuhio Beach.** This beach park offers an easy spot for first-timers to check out the action. A break near the large pedestrian walkway called Kapahulu Groin is the quintessential bodyboarding spot. The soft, rolling waves make it perfect for beginners. Even during summer's south swells, it's relatively tame because of the outer reefs. ✉ *Waikiki Beach, between Moana Surfrider, a Westin Resort and Kapahulu Groin, Honolulu.*

**Makapuu Beach.** With its extended waves, this beach park on the windward side is a dream, though a somewhat challenging one. If you're a little more timid, go to the far end of the beach to Keiki's, where the waves are mellowed by Makapuu Point. Although the main break at Makapuu is much less dangerous than that at Sandy Beach, mind the ocean floor—the sands are always shifting, sometimes exposing coral heads and rocks. Always check (or ask lifeguards about) the currents, which can be strong. ✉ *41-095 Kalanianaole Hwy., across from Sea Life Park, Waimanalo.*

**Sandy Beach.** The best spot for advanced bodyboarding is Sandy Beach on Oahu's eastern shore. That said, even when the shore break here is small, it can be extremely dangerous. As lifeguards will attest, there are more neck injuries suffered here than at any other surf break in the United States. It's awesome for the advanced, but know its danger before paddling out. ✉ *8800 Kalanianaole Hwy., 2 miles east of Hanauma Bay, Honolulu.*

**Waimanalo Beach.** With the longest sand beach on Oahu's windward side, Waimanalo Bay Beach Park has a shallow sandbar at the water's edge that provides good waves for bodyboarding and bodysurfing. It's an ideal break for novices because of its soft waves. Like Walls in Waikiki, this area is protected by an outer reef. And like Bellows, it's favored by the dangerous Portuguese man-of-war. ✉ *Aloiloi St., Waimanalo.*

### EQUIPMENT

The more than 30 rental spots along Waikiki Beach all offer basically the same prices. But if you plan to bodyboard for more than just an hour or so, consider buying an inexpensive board for $30–$40 at an ABC Store—there are almost 40 in the Waikiki area—and giving it to a kid at the end of your vacation. It will be more cost-effective for you, and you'll be passing along some aloha spirit in the process.

## Deep-Sea Fishing

Fishing isn't just a sport in Hawaii—it's a way of life. A number of charter boats with experienced crews can take you on a sportfishing adventure throughout the year. Sure, the bigger yellowfin tuna (ahi) are generally caught in summer, and the coveted spearfish are more frequent in winter, but you can still hook them any day of the year. Plus, the dolphinfish (mahimahi), wahoo (ono), and skipjacks, not to mention the king—Pacific blue marlin—are ripe for the picking on any given day. The largest Pacific blue marlin ever caught, weighing in at 1,805 pounds, was reeled in along Oahu's coast.

When choosing a fishing boat in the Islands, look for veteran captains with decades of experience. Better yet, find those who care about Hawaii's fragile marine environment. Many captains now tag and release their catches to preserve the state's fishing grounds. Also remember that open ocean fishing can be challenging, so consider the ability and interest of everyone in your group before booking.

The general rule for the catch is an even split with the crew. Unfortunately, there are no "freeze-and-ship" providers in the state, so unless you plan to eat the fish while you're here, you'll probably want to leave it with the boat. Most boats do offer mounting services for trophy fish; ask your captain.

Prices vary greatly, but expect to pay from around $65 per person for a spot on a boat with more than 20 people to $2,000 for an overnight trip for up to six people. Besides the gift of fish, a gratuity of 10%–20% is standard, but use your own discretion based on the overall experience.

### BOATS AND CHARTERS

#### HONOLULU

**Maggie Joe Sport Fishing**

**FISHING** | The oldest sportfishing company on Oahu boasts landing one of the largest marlins ever caught out of Kewalo Basin. It offers a variety of offshore fishing packages, including exclusive or shared charters, and has a fleet of three boats. Half-day exclusives on the 41-foot *Sea Hawk* or the 38-foot *Ruckus* can accommodate up to six people and are the cheapest options for daytime fishing. The 53-foot *Maggie Joe* embarks on three-quarter- or full-day sails; can accommodate up to 15 anglers; and is equipped with air-conditioned cabins, hot showers, and cutting-edge gear. A marine taxidermist can mount the monster you reel in. ✉ *Kewalo Basin, 1025 Ala Moana Blvd., Ala Moana* ☎ *808/591–8888* 🌐 *www.maggiejoe.com* 🎫 *From $250.*

**Magic Sport Fishing**

**FISHING** | This 50-foot Pacifica fishing yacht, aptly named *Magic,* boasts a slew of sportfishing records, including some of the largest marlins caught in local tournaments and the most mahimahi hooked during a one-day charter. The yacht, which can accommodate up to six passengers for both shared or full charters, is very comfortable, with air-conditioning, a cozy seating area, two heads (bathrooms), private cabins, and a smooth ride thanks to twin diesel engines. ✉ *Kewalo Basin Harbor, 1125 Ala Moana Blvd., Slip G, Ala Moana* ☎ *808/596–2998* 🌐 *www.magicsportfishing.com* 🎫 *From $220 per person for a shared charter; from $1,190 for a private charter.*

# Golf

Unlike elsewhere in Hawaii, most of Oahu's golf courses aren't associated with hotels and resorts. In fact, of the island's more than three dozen courses, only five are tied to lodging, and none is in the tourist hub of Waikiki. The courses do offer some of the most spectacular views and vistas around the island, and several are quite challenging.

Although municipal courses are a good choice for budget-conscious golfers, they're more crowded than (and not always as well maintained as) private courses. Your best bet is to call the day you want to play and inquire about walk-on availability. Green fees are standard at city courses: walking rate $86 for visitors, riding carts $26 for 18 holes, pull carts $4.

Green fees listed here are the highest course rates per round on weekdays and weekends for U.S. residents. (Some courses charge non–U.S. residents higher prices.) Discounts are often available for resort guests and for those who book tee times online. Twilight fees are usually offered.

## HONOLULU

Ala Wai is the only spot to golf near Waikiki, and it is the busiest course in America. Although not a very imaginative layout, the price is right, and the advantage of walking from your hotel to the course is not to be overlooked. If you don't make a reservation, bring something to read because it will be a little while before you tee off. It's also frequented by local residents, so you might get some hot restaurant and local spot suggestions.

**Ala Wai Golf Course**

**GOLF** | Just across the Ala Wai Canal from Waikiki, this municipal golf course is said to host more rounds than any other U.S. course—up to 500 per day. Not that it's a great course, just really convenient. The best bet for a visitor is to show up and expect to wait at least an hour or call up to three days in advance for a tee time. (The jury is out on whether online reservations have made securing a time any easier.)

The course itself is flat, though Robin Nelson did some redesign work in the 1990s, adding mounding, trees, and a lake. The Ala Wai Canal comes into play on several holes on the back nine, including the treacherous 18th. There's also an on-site restaurant and bar, not fancy but they do the trick. ✉ *404 Kapahulu Ave., Waikiki* ☎ *808/207– 6856 for reservations*

## Tips for the Green

Before you head out to the first tee, there are a few things you should know about golf in Hawaii:

■ All resort courses and many daily-fee courses provide rental clubs. In many cases, they're the latest lines from Titleist, PING, Callaway, and the like. This is true for both men and women, as well as for left-handers, which means you don't have to schlep clubs across the Pacific.

■ Most courses offer deals varying from twilight deep-discount rates to frequent-visitor discounts, even for tourists. Ask questions when calling pro shops, and don't just accept the first quote—deals abound if you persist.

■ Pro shops at most courses are well stocked with balls, tees, and other accoutrements, so even if you bring your own bag, it needn't weigh a ton.

■ Come spikeless—very few Hawaii courses still permit metal spikes.

■ Sunscreen. Buy it, and apply it (minimum 30 SPF). The subtropical rays are intense, even in December. All sunscreen you use must be reef-safe, and any you buy in Hawaii is required to be.

■ Resort courses, in particular, offer more than the usual three sets of tees, sometimes four or five. So bite off as much or little challenge as you can chew. Tee it up from the tips, and you'll end up playing a few 600-yard par 5s and see a few 250-yard forced carries.

■ In theory, you can play golf in Hawaii 365 days a year. But there's a reason the Hawaiian Islands are so green. Rain is frequent and sometimes brings a deluge. Better to bring an umbrella and light jacket and not use them than not to bring them and get soaked.

■ Unless you play a muni or certain daily-fee courses, plan on taking a cart. Riding carts are mandatory at most courses and are included in green fees.

*www8.honolulu.gov/des/ala-wai-golf-course* *$66* *18 holes, 5861 yards, par 70.*

**Moanalua Golf Club**

**GOLF** | Said to be (not without dispute) the oldest golf club west of the Rockies, this 9-holer is semiprivate, allowing public play except on weekend and holiday mornings. Near Pearl Harbor and nestled in the hardwoods, this course will remind you more of golf in Pennsylvania than in the tropics, but it offers the lowest green fees in the area, and by the time you get here, you'll probably be over the whole palm-tree theme anyway. The course is a bit quirky, but the final two holes, a par 3 off a cliff to a smallish tree-rimmed green and a par 4 with an approach to a green set snugly between stream and jungle, are classic. Although carts are not required, they are recommended, as this course is a bit steep in places. *1250 Ala Aolani St., Salt Lake* *808/839–2411 for starter's office, 808/839–2311 for pro shop and clubhouse* *moanaluagolfclub.com* *$41* *9 holes, 2972 yards, par 36.*

### WEST (LEEWARD) OAHU

On the leeward side of the mountains, shielded from the rains that drench the Kaneohe side, West Oahu is arid and sunny and has a unique kind of beauty.

Indeed, golfers generally choose courses in Ewa and Kapolei because they provide a totally different landscape from that found in Waikiki or on the North Shore. Although west side resort courses are a longer drive from town, the beaches are magnificent, and you can find deals if you're combining a room with a round or two on the green. There's also a Disney hotel in the area, which is popular with families.

**Coral Creek Golf Course**

**GOLF** | On the Ewa Plain, 4 miles inland, this course is cut from ancient coral left from days long ago when this area was still underwater. Robin Nelson (1999) did some of his best work in making use of the coral—and of some dynamite—blasting out portions to create dramatic lakes and tee and green sites. They could just as easily call it Coral Cliffs because of the 30- to 40-foot cliffs Nelson created. They include the par-3 10th green's grotto and waterfall and the vertical drop-off on the right side of the par-4 18th green. An ancient creek meanders across the course, but there's not much water, just enough to be a babbling nuisance. Carts are required and are included in the green fee. ✉ *91-1111 Geiger Rd., Ewa Beach* ☎ *808/441–4653* 🌐 *www.coralcreekgolfhawaii.com* 💵 *$80 for 9 holes, $175 for 18 holes* 🏌 *18 holes, 6347 yards, par 72.*

**Ewa Beach Golf Club**

**GOLF** | A private course open to the public, Ewa is one of the delightful products of the too-brief collaboration of Robin Nelson and Rodney Wright (1992). Trees are very much part of the character here, but there are also elements of links golf, such as a double green shared by the 2nd and 16th holes. Carts are required and are included in the green fee. ✉ *91-050 Fort Weaver Rd., Ewa Beach* ☎ *808/689–6565* 🌐 *ewabeachgc.com* 💵 *From $190 ($140 after 12:30 pm)* 🏌 *18 holes, 5861 yards, par 72.*

**Hawaii Prince Golf Club**

**GOLF** | Affiliated with the Prince Waikiki hotel, the Hawaii Prince Golf Club (not to be confused with the Prince Course at Princeville, Kauai) has a links feel to it, and it is popular with local-charity fund-raiser golf tournaments. Arnold Palmer and Ed Seay (1991) took what had been flat, featureless sugarcane fields and sculpted 27 challenging, varied holes. Mounding breaks up the landscape, as do 10 lakes. Water comes into play on six holes of the A course, three of B, and seven of C. The most difficult combination is A and C (A and B from the forward tees). Carts are required and are included in the green fee. ✉ *91-1200 Fort Weaver Rd., Ewa Beach* ☎ *808/944–4567* 🌐 *www.hawaiiprincegolf.com* 💵 *From $210* 🏌 *A Course: 9 holes, 3138 yards, par 36. B Course: 9 holes, 3099 yards, par 36. C Course: 9 holes, 3076 yards, par 36.*

**Kapolei Golf Club**

**GOLF** | This is a Ted Robinson aquatic wonderland with waterfalls and four lakes—three so big they have names—coming into play on 10 holes. Set on rolling terrain, Kapolei is a serious golf course, especially when the wind blows. Carts are required and are included in the green fee. ✉ *91-701 Farrington Hwy., Kapolei* ☎ *808/674–2227* 🌐 *www.kapoleigolf.com* 💵 *$210* 🏌 *18 holes, 6586 yards, par 72.*

**Ko Olina Golf Club**

**GOLF** | Hawaii's golden age of golf-course architecture came to Oahu when Ko Olina Golf Club opened in 1989. Ted Robinson, king of the water features, went splash-happy here, creating nine lakes that come into play on eight holes, including the par-3 12th, where you reach the tee by driving behind a Disney-like waterfall. Tactically, though, the most dramatic hole is the par-4 18th, where the approach is a minimum 120 yards across a lake to a two-tiered green guarded on the left by a cascading waterfall. Today Ko

Olina has matured into one of Hawaii's top courses.

You can niggle about routing issues—the first three holes play into the trade winds (and the morning sun), as do two consecutive par 5s on the back nine play—but Robinson does enough solid design to make those of passing concern. The website offers a nice webcam and a lot of information so you can familiarize yourself with the course and its offerings. ■ **TIP→ The course provides free transportation from Waikiki hotels.** ✉ *92-1220 Aliinui Dr., Ko Olina* ☎ *808/676–5300* 🌐 *koolinagolf.com* 💵 *$255* ⛳ *18 holes, 6432 yards, par 72.*

**Makaha Valley Country Club**

**GOLF** | This course (William F. Bell, 1968), known locally as Makaha East, is indeed a valley course, taking great advantage of the steep valley walls and natural terrain. The double-dogleg, downhill-uphill, par-5 18th is a doozy of a closer. Carts are required and are included in the green fee. ✉ *84-627 Makaha Valley Rd., Waianae* ☎ *808/695–7111* 🌐 *www.makahavalleycc.com* 💵 *$67 for 9 holes, $89 for 18 holes* ⛳ *18 holes, 6260 yards, par 71.*

**West Loch Golf Course**

**GOLF** | Possibly the best of Honolulu's municipal courses, this Robin Nelson (1991) design plays along Pearl Harbor's West Loch. In the process of building the course, wetlands were actually expanded, increasing bird habitat. At the time of this writing, there is no pro shop or restaurant, and twilight play is not available. ✉ *91-1126 Okupe St., Ewa Beach* ☎ *808/675–6076* 🌐 *www8.honolulu.gov/des/west-loch-golf-course* 💵 *$86* ⛳ *18 holes, 6335 yards, par 72.*

## CENTRAL OAHU

In Central Oahu, plantations morphed into tract housing, and golf courses were added to anchor communities. The vegetation is much sparser, but some of the best greens around can be found here. Play early to avoid the hot afternoons. If, however, you can handle the harsh afternoon sun, many courses offer substantial discounts for twilight hours.

**Hawaii Country Club**

**GOLF** | Also known as Kunia—but not to be confused with Royal Kunia a few miles away—this course is in the middle of former sugarcane fields and dates from plantation times. Several par 4s are drivable, including the 9th and 18th holes. Views in the distance of the Koolau Mountains, Pearl Harbor, and Diamond Head offer an occasional distraction. This is a fun course, but it's a bit rough around the edges. The course is often noted as a good spot for beginners. You can walk it on weekdays only. Reservations can be made online two weeks in advance. ✉ *94-1211 Kunia Rd., Wahiawa* ☎ *808/621–5654* 🌐 *www.hawaiicountryclubgolf.com* 💵 *$65* ⛳ *18 holes, 5910 yards, par 71.*

**Mililani Golf Club**

**GOLF** | Located on Oahu's central plain, Mililani is usually a few degrees cooler than downtown, 25 minutes away. Designers Bob and Robert L. Baldock (1966) make good use of an old irrigation ditch reminiscent of a Scottish burn. The eucalyptus trees through which the course plays add to the cool factor, and stands of Norfolk pines give Mililani a "Mainland course" feel. The views of the Waianae Mountains and the Koolau Mountains in the distance, however, remind you that you're a long way from home. Carts are required and are included in the green fee. ✉ *95-176 Kuahelani Ave., Mililani* ☎ *808/623–2222* 🌐 *mililanigolf.com* 💵 *$160* ⛳ *18 holes, 6274 yards, par 72.*

**Pearl at Kalauao**

**GOLF** | Carved in the hillside high above Pearl Harbor, the 18 holes here are really two courses. The front nine rambles out along gently sloping terrain, while the back nine zigzags up and down a steeper portion of the slope as it rises into the

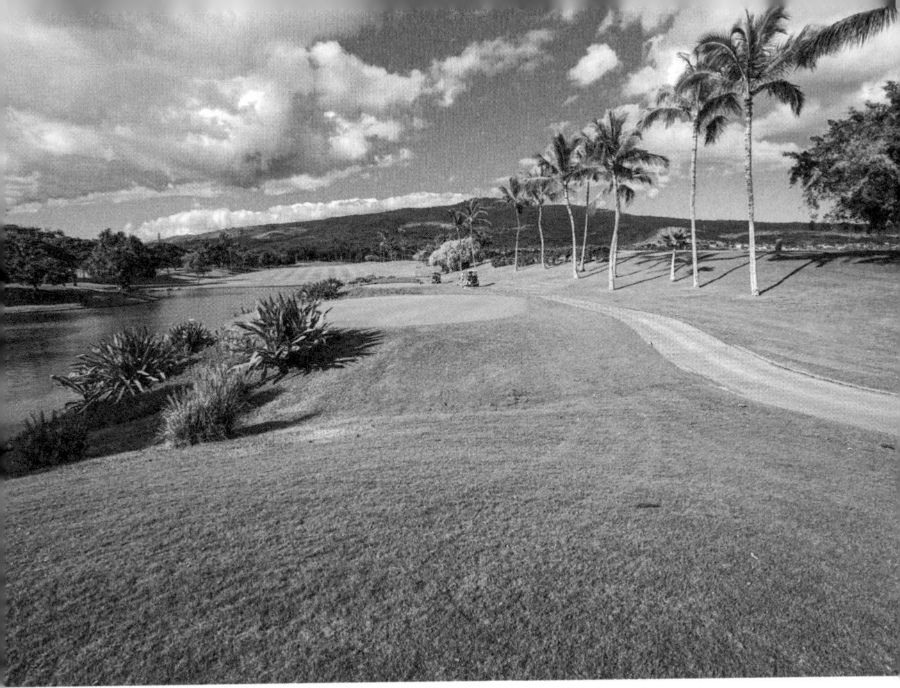

**The North Shore's Turtle Bay Resort attracts golfers who come for the prized Palmer Course.**

Koolau Mountains. The views of Pearl Harbor are breathtaking. Hawaii residents routinely rank it their #1 choice in the *Honolulu Star-Advertiser* annual rankings of state courses. Carts are required and are included in the green fee. At the time of this writing, the site (formerly Pearl Country Club) is undergoing a major renovation during 2024. Call ahead to confirm its status before you visit. Prices may change after renovation, too. ✉ *98-535 Kaonohi St., Aiea* ☎ *808/487–2460* 🌐 *pearlatkalauao.com* 🎟 *$120* 🏌 *18 holes, 6232 yards, par 72.*

**Royal Kunia Country Club**

**GOLF** | At one point, the PGA Tour considered buying the Royal Kunia Country Club and hosting the Sony Open here. It's that good. Robin Nelson's eye for natural sight lines and his dexterity with water features add to the visual pleasure. ■ **TIP→ Every hole offers fabulous views including Diamond Head, Pearl Harbor, and the nearby Waianae Mountains.** Carts are required and are included in the green fee. ✉ *94-1509 Anonui St., Waipahu* ☎ *808/688–9222* 🌐 *www.royalkuniacc.com* 🎟 *$150* 🏌 *18 holes, 6507 yards, par 72.*

**Ted Makalena Golf Course**

**GOLF** | The flat layout of this bare-bones municipal course with Bermuda grass fairways appeals to all levels of players, but especially those just starting to learn the sport. At the time of this writing, twilight play has been suspended until further notice. ✉ *93-059 Waipio Point Access Rd., Waipahu* ☎ *808/207–6735 for reservations, 808/675–6052* 🌐 *www8.honolulu.gov/des/ted-makalena-golf-course* 🎟 *$86* 🏌 *18 holes, 5976 yards, par 71.*

**Waikele Country Club**

**GOLF** | Outlet stores are not the only draw in Waikele. The adjacent, daily-fee golf course offers a private club–like atmosphere and a terrific Ted Robinson (1992) layout. Robinson's water features are less distinctive here but define the short par-4 4th hole—with a lake running down the left side of the fairway and guarding the green—and the par-3 17th, which plays across a lake. The par-4 18th is a terrific closing hole, with a lake lurking on the right side of the green. Carts are required and are included in the green fee. ✉ *94-200 Paioa Pl., Waipahu* ☎ *808/676–9000* 🌐 *www.golfwaikele.com* 💳 *$185* ⛳ *18 holes, 6261 yards, par 72.*

## NORTH SHORE

The North Shore has both the cheapest and the most expensive courses on the island. You can play nine holes in your bare feet, and you can chunk up the course played by both the LPGA and Champions Tour here, too. Don't try to go the barefoot route on the LPGA course, or the only course in the Islands you may be allowed on will be the Kahuku muni.

### Kahuku Golf Course

**GOLF** | The only true links course in Hawaii, this 9-hole municipal course is not for everyone. Maintenance is an ongoing issue, and, in summer, it can look a bit like the Serengeti. It's walking-only (a few pull carts are available for rent); there's no pro shop, just a starter who sells lost-and-found balls; and the 19th hole is a soda machine and a covered picnic bench. And yet the course stretches out along the blue Pacific where surf crashes on the shore, the turf underfoot is spongy, sea mist drifts across the links, and wildflowers bloom in the rough. ✉ *56-501 Kamehameha Hwy., Kahuku* ☎ *808/293–5842* 🌐 *www.honolulu.gov/des/golf-courses* 💳 *$43 for two 9-hole rounds; $30 for 9 holes* ⛳ *9 holes, 2699 yards, par 35.*

### Turtle Bay Resort

**GOLF** | When the Lazarus of golf courses, the Fazio Course (George Fazio, 1971), rose from the dead in 2002, Turtle Bay on Oahu's rugged North Shore became a premier golf destination. Two holes had been plowed under when the Palmer Course (Arnold Palmer and Ed Seay, 1992) was built, while the other seven lay fallow, and the front nine remained open. Then new owners re-created holes 13 and 14 using Fazio's original plans, and the Fazio became whole again. At the time of this writing, the Fazio Course is temporarily closed, and the gem at Turtle Bay is the Palmer. The front nine is mostly open as it skirts Punahoolapa Marsh, a nature sanctuary, while the back nine plunges into the wetlands and winds along the coast. The short par-4 17th runs along the rocky shore, with a diabolical string of bunkers cutting diagonally across the fairway from tee to green. Carts are required and are included in the green fee. ✉ *57-091 Kamehameha Hwy., Kahuku* ☎ *808/293–8574* 🌐 *www.turtlebayresort.com* 💳 *$220* ⛳ *Palmer Course: 18 holes, 7200 yards, par 72.*

## HAWAII KAI

Prepare to keep your ball down on this windy corner of Oahu. You'll get beautiful ocean vistas, but you may need them to soothe you once your perfect drive gets blown 40 yards off course by a gusting trade wind.

### Hawaii Kai Golf Course

**GOLF** | The Championship Golf Course (William F. Bell, 1973) winds through a Honolulu suburb at the foot of Koko Crater. Homes (and the liability of a broken window) come into play on many holes, but they are offset by views of the Pacific and a crafty routing of holes. With several lakes, lots of trees, and bunkers in all the wrong places, Hawaii Kai really is a "championship" golf course, especially when the trade winds howl. Green fees for this course include a mandatory cart. The Executive Course (1962), a par-54 track, is the first of only three courses in Hawaii built by Robert Trent Jones Sr. Although a few changes have been made to his original design, the usual Jones attributes are here, including raised greens and lots of risk-reward options. ✉ *8902 Kalanianaole Hwy.* ☎ *808/395–2358* 🌐 *hawaiikaigolf.com* 💳 *Championship Course: $165 (twilight $125); Executive Course: $65* ⛳ *Championship Course: 18 holes, 6207 yards,* *par 72. Executive Course: 18 holes, 2196 yards, par 54.*

### EAST (WINDWARD) OAHU

Windward Oahu is what you expect when you think of golfing in the Islands. Lush, tropical foliage will surround you, with towering mountains framing one shot and the crystal-blue Pacific framing the next. Although it's a bit more expensive and a good deal wetter on this side, the memories and pictures you take on these courses will last a lifetime.

**Olomana Golf Links**

**GOLF** | Bob and Robert L. Baldock are the architects of record for this layout, but so much has changed since it opened in 1969 that they would recognize little of it. A turf specialist was brought in to improve fairways and greens, tees were rebuilt, new bunkers were added, and mangroves were cut back to make better use of natural wetlands. But what really puts Olomana on the map is that this is where wunderkind Michelle Wie West learned the game. A cart is required at this course and is included in the green fee. ✉ *41-1801 Kalanianaole Hwy., Waimanalo* ☎ *808/259–7926* 🌐 *www.olomanalinks.com* *$90* *18 holes, 6306 yards, par 72.*

**Pali Golf Course**

**GOLF** | Panoramic views of the Koolau Mountains and Kaneohe Bay enhance the many challenges at this popular municipal course between Kaneohe and Kailua. ✉ *45-050 Kamehameha Hwy., Kaneohe* ☎ *808/207–7099 reservations, 808/262–2911 pro shop* 🌐 *www8.honolulu.gov/des/pali-golf-course* *$86* *18 holes, 6524 yards, par 72.*

**★ Royal Hawaiian Golf Club**

**GOLF** | In the cool, lush Maunawili Valley, Pete and Perry Dye (1993) created what can only be called target jungle golf. In other words, the rough is usually dense jungle, and you may not hit a driver on three of the four par 5s, or several par 4s, including the perilous 18th that plays off a cliff to a narrow green protected by a creek. It's a jungle out there, so don't be shocked by mud or rain. Mount Olomana's twin peaks tower over the course. At the time of this writing, the driving range and restaurant are closed until further notice. **TIP→ The back nine wanders deep into the valley and includes an island green (par-3 11th) and perhaps the loveliest inland hole in Hawaii (par-4 12th).** ✉ *770 Auloa Rd., at Luana Hills Rd., Kailua* ☎ *808/262–2139* 🌐 *royalhawaiiangc.com* *$165* *18 holes, 5541 yards, par 72.*

## Hiking

The trails of Oahu cover a full spectrum of environments: desert walks through cactus, slippery paths through bamboo-filled rain forest, and scrambling rock climbs up ancient volcanic calderas. Hikes are generally on the shorter side, with many trails that won't take you more than half a day. In addition, many of the prime hikes are within 10 minutes of downtown Waikiki, meaning that you won't have to spend your whole day getting back to nature.

When choosing hiking trails, be realistic about your ability and that of your companions. Some of the best vistas come at the end of a steep, often treacherous climb, while others pose heat exhaustion and other issues. Always hike with plenty of water, a charged phone, and lots of time and patience.

**Hawaii Department of Land and Natural Resources**

**HIKING & WALKING** | Go to the website for information on all major hiking trails on Oahu. You can also obtain camping permits for state parks here. **TIP→ Always follow DLNR recommendations regarding personal safety and environmental impact in these fragile areas.** ✉ *1151 Punchbowl St., Room 310, Downtown* ☎ *808/587–0300* 🌐 *dlnr.hawaii.gov/dsp/hiking/oahu.*

## Tips for the Trail

- When hiking the waterfall and rainforest trails, use insect repellent. The dampness draws swarms of bloodsuckers that can ruin a walk.
- Volcanic rock is porous and therefore likely to be loose. Rock climbing is discouraged, as you never know which ledge is going to go.
- Avoid hiking after heavy rains and check for flash-flood warnings. Keep in mind that those large boulders in the idyllic pools beneath the waterfalls were carried by torrential flows high up in the mountains.
- Always let someone know where you're going, and never hike alone. The foliage gets dense, and, small as the island is, hikers have been known to get lost for a week or longer.
- Bring a well-charged phone.

**Na Ala Hele Trail & Access Program**
**HIKING & WALKING** | Contact the Na Ala Hele (Trails to Go On) folks for a free hiking-safety guide and trail information. The interactive website has maps and information about the current status of trails on all the Islands. You can also stop in at their office for free printed maps and information. ✉ *1151 Punchbowl St., Room 325, Downtown* ☎ *808/587–0166* 🌐 *hawaiitrails.ehawaii.gov/trails/#.*

### BEST SPOTS

### HONOLULU

**Aiea Loop Trail**
**HIKING & WALKING** | This 4.8-mile loop begins and ends in the Keaiwa Heiau State Recreation Area, running along the ridge on the west side of Halawa Valley. It's a fairly easy hike that lasts about 2½ to 3 hours and brings many rewards, including views of the southern coastline of Oahu from Pearl Harbor and the Waianae Range to Honolulu and Diamond Head. Foresters replanted this area with various trees in the 1920s, so scents of lemon eucalyptus, pine, koa, and other trees enhance the trek. There's ample parking near the trailhead, close to restrooms and a picnic pavilion. ✉ *Aiea District Park, 99-350 Aiea Heights Dr., Aiea* ✥ *At upper east corner of park, at top of Aiea Heights Rd.* ☎ *808/587–0300* 🌐 *dlnr.hawaii.gov/dsp/hiking/oahu/aiea-loop-trail.*

★ **Diamond Head State Monument**
**HIKING & WALKING** | Climbing Diamond Head is high on the list of things to do on Oahu. It's a moderately easy hike if you're in good physical condition, but be prepared to climb many stairs along the way, particularly at the top, when you may be most tired. Also be sure to bring a water bottle, because it's hot and dry. Only a mile up, a clearly marked trail with handrails scales the inside of this extinct volcano. At the top, the fabled final 99 steps take you up to the pillbox overlooking the Pacific Ocean and Honolulu. It's a breathtaking view and a lot cheaper than taking a helicopter ride for the same photo op. Last entry for hikers is 4:30 pm. **■ TIP→ Visitors must now make a reservation (up to 30 days in advance; reserve early as this is very popular) and pay online to do the hike.** ✉ *Diamond Head Rd. at 18th Ave., Diamond Head* ✥ *Enter on east side of crater; there's limited parking inside, so most park on street and walk in* ☎ *808/587–0300* 🌐 *dlnr.hawaii.gov/dsp/parks/oahu/diamond-head-state-monument* 🎫 *$5 per person, $10 to park.*

★ **Manoa Falls Trail**
**HIKING & WALKING** | Travel up into the valley beyond Honolulu to make the Manoa

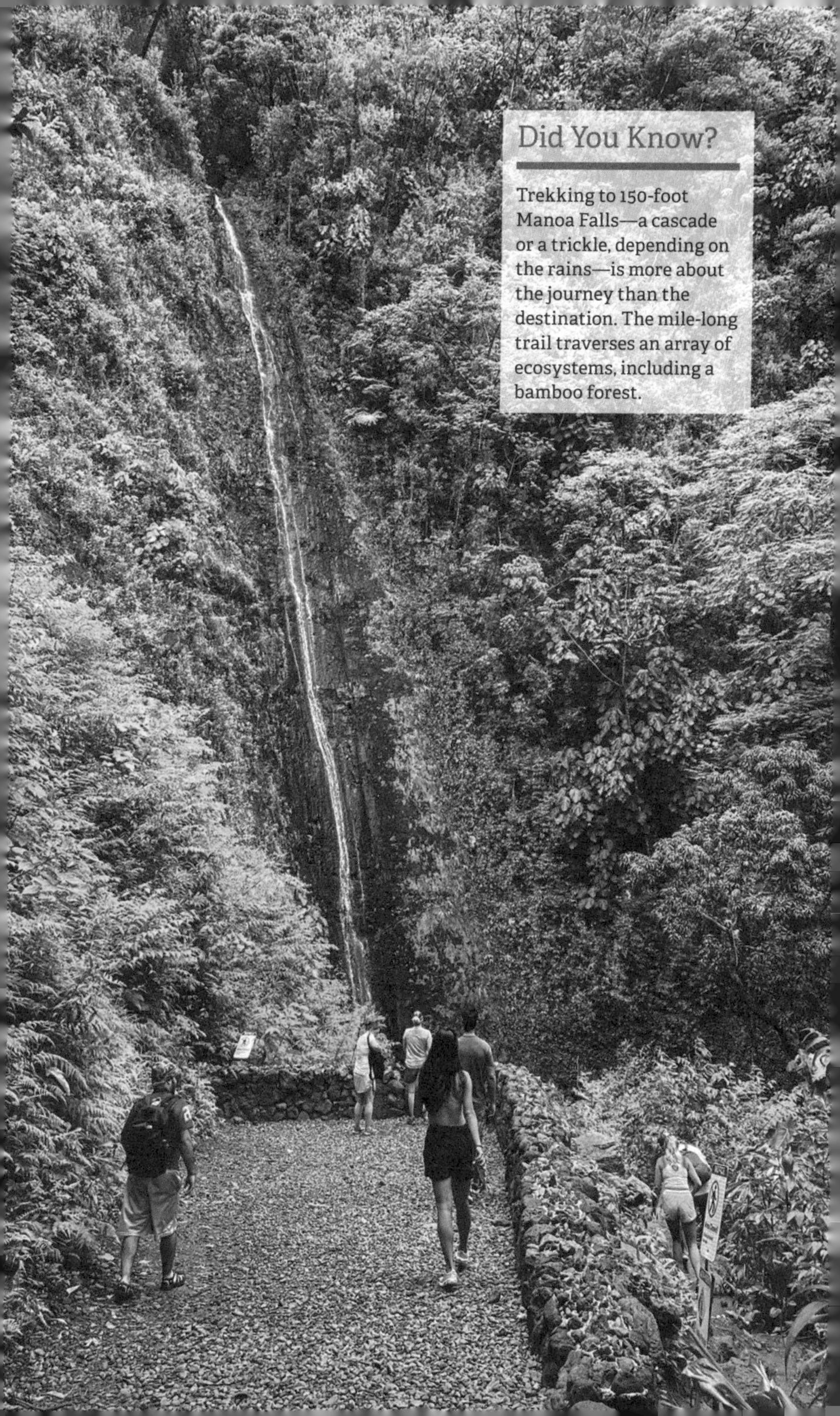

## Did You Know?

Trekking to 150-foot Manoa Falls—a cascade or a trickle, depending on the rains—is more about the journey than the destination. The mile-long trail traverses an array of ecosystems, including a bamboo forest.

Falls hike. Though only a mile long, this well-trafficked path, with an estimated 100,000 visitors a year, passes through so many different ecosystems that you feel as if you're in an arboretum—and you're not far off. The beautiful Lyon Arboretum is right near the trailhead, if you want to make another stop. Walk among the elephant ear (*ape*) plants, ruddy fir trees, and a bamboo forest straight out of China. At the top is a 150-foot waterfall, which can be an impressive cascade or, if rains have been light, little more than a trickle, but this hike is more about the journey than the destination. Bring mosquito repellent because they grow 'em big up here. The trail can get muddy and slippery after it rains, so plan accordingly. ✉ *3998 Manoa Rd., Manoa* ✣ *West Manoa Rd. is behind Manoa Valley in Paradise Park. Take West Manoa Rd. to end, park on side of road or in parking lot for a small fee, follow trail signs* 🌐 *hawaiitrails.ehawaii.gov/trails/#.*

## LEEWARD (WEST) OAHU

### ★ Kaena Point Trail

**HIKING & WALKING** | Kaena Point is one of the island's last easily accessible pockets of nature left largely untouched. The state protects nearly 60 acres of land at the point, previously as a nature preserve and now as an ecosystem restoration project for endangered and protected coastal plants and seabirds. The uneven 5-mile trail around the point can be accessed from two locations—Keawaula Beach (aka Yokohama Bay) at the end of Farrington Highway on Oahu's western coastline, or Mokuleia at the same highway's northern coast endpoint. Both entry points are on the same road, but the trail divides the two sides, so there's no way to drive all the way around. It's a rugged coastline hike without much shade, so bring water and sunscreen. (Or, better yet, start early!) ■ **TIP→ Keep a lookout for the Laysan albatrosses. These enormous birds may come in for a closer look at you, too.** ✉ *81-780 Farrington Hwy., Waianae* ✣ *Take Farrington Hwy. to its end at Yokohama. Hike in on old 4x4 trail* 🌐 *dlnr.hawaii.gov/dsp/hiking/oahu/kaena-point-trail.*

## NORTH SHORE

### Maunawili Falls

**HIKING & WALKING** | Want to find a waterfall that you can actually swim in? Then Maunawili Falls is your trip. In fact, plan on getting wet even if that's not your goal: you have to cross Maunawili Stream several times to get to the falls, and the route is pretty muddy. Along the 1½-mile trek, enjoy the ginger, vines, and heliconia before greeting fern-shrouded falls that are made for swimming. The water is not the clearest, but it's cool and refreshing after battling the bugs (wear repellent) to get here. Walking sticks are helpful; if you don't have one, use the loaner sticks often left by hikers at the trailhead. ■ **TIP→ On weekends, the trail can be crowded. Prepare to park far from the trailhead as regulations are strictly enforced, and do not block driveways or streets.** ✉ *1221 Kelewina St., Kailua* ✣ *Take Pali Hwy. (Rte. 61) from Honolulu through tunnels, then take 3rd right onto Auloa Rd., then take left fork immediately. At dead end, climb over vehicle gate to find trailhead.*

### Trails at Turtle Bay Resort

**HIKING & WALKING** | When on the North Shore, check out Turtle Bay Resort, which has more than 12 miles of trails and oceanside pathways. Maps of the property are available, and staff offer great tips and suggestions. ✉ *57-091 Kamehameha Hwy., Kahuku* ☎ *808/293–8811* 🌐 *www.turtlebayresort.com.*

## HAWAII KAI

### Makapuu Lighthouse Trail

**HIKING & WALKING** | For the less adventurous hiker and anyone looking for a great view, this paved trail that runs up the side of Makapuu Point in southeastern Oahu fits the bill. Early on, the trail is surrounded by lava rock, but as you ascend, foliage—the tiny white koa haole flower, the cream-tinged spikes of the kiawe, and, if

## Camping in Oahu

If you are looking for a more rugged escape from the resorts of Waikiki, consider pitching a tent on the beach or in the mountains, where you have easy access to hiking trails and the island's natural features.

■ TIP→ **Camping here is not as highly organized as it is on the Mainland: expect few marked sites, scarce electrical outlets, and nary a ranger station.**

What you find instead are unblemished spots in the woods and on the sand. Both the Division of Forestry and Wildlife and the Division of State Parks offer recreation areas at which you can camp. All such campsites can now be reserved up to 90 days in advance online (⊕ *www.hawaiistateparks.org*). The fees run from $20 to $50 per night, based on the number of people and space requested.

As for the county spots, there are 17 campgrounds currently available, and all require a permit. The good news is that the permits are only $32 for three days and $52 for five days, always beginning on a Friday, with no camping allowed on Wednesday or Thursday. They are also easy to obtain, as long as you're not trying to go on a holiday weekend. Visit ⊕ *camping.honolulu.gov* for more information.



you go early enough, the night-blooming cereus—begins taking over the rock. At the easternmost tip of Oahu, where the island divides the sea, this trail gives you a spectacular view of the cobalt ocean meeting the land.

To the south is the lighthouse; to the east are the Manana (Rabbit) and Kaohikaipu islets, two bird sanctuaries just off the coast. The 2-mile round-trip hike is a great break on a circle-island trip. From late December to early May, this is a marvelous perch to see migrating humpback whales. You can no longer access the tidal pools here because the steep descent to them is treacherous), and rogue waves swept people out to sea. ■ TIP→ **Heed trail closure signs. Also, don't leave valuables in your car; break-ins, even in the parking lot, are common.** ✉ *Makapuu Lighthouse Rd., Hawaii Kai* ✣ *Take Kalanianaole Hwy. to base of Makapuu Point, then look for parking lot* ⊕ *dlnr.hawaii.gov/dsp/hiking/oahu/makapuu-point-lighthouse-trail.*

### GOING WITH A GUIDE

#### NORTH SHORE

**North Shore Eco Tours**

**HIKING & WALKING** | Native Hawaiians own and operate this business, the only one allowed to lead guided small-group adventures in private conservation lands. This group gets you out in nature and up close with the land and its history. Options range from 2- and 3½-mile round-trip hikes to pools and waterfalls (lunch included) to an off-road expedition in all-terrain vehicles. Community service opportunities are also an option. Excursions have minimum age requirements for children. The pickup point for hikes is the North Shore Marketplace in Haleiwa town; off-road tours begin in Waimea Valley. ✉ *North Shore Marketplace, 56-250 Kamehameha Hwy., Haleiwa* ☎ *877/521–4453* ⊕ *www.northshoreecotours.com* 🎫 *From $95.*

# Horseback Riding

A great way to see the island is atop a horse, leaving the direction to the pack while you drink in the views of mountains or the ocean.

## NORTH SHORE

### Turtle Bay Stables

**HORSEBACK RIDING | FAMILY** | Trail rides follow the 12-mile-long coastline and even step out onto sandy beaches fronting this luxe resort on Oahu's fabled North Shore. The stables here are part of the resort but can be utilized by nonguests, and the sunset ride is a must. Private rides, group rides, and educational (horsemanship) classes are among the many options. Children ages 7 and up are allowed. A basic trail ride lasts 45 minutes and visits filming sites for ABC's *Lost* and the film *Pirates of the Caribbean.* ✉ *Turtle Bay Resort, 57-091 Kamehameha Hwy., Kahuku* ☎ *808/293–6024* 🌐 *turtlebayresort.com* 🎫 *From $100.*

## EAST (WINDWARD) OAHU

### Gunstock Ranch

**HORSEBACK RIDING | FAMILY** | This working cattle ranch encompasses nearly 800 acres on the northeastern shore, in the foothills of the Koolau Mountains. It reflects the country life of Hawaii in its offerings, including eco-tours, tree plantings, and off-road adventures as well as trail rides. Choose among 5 to 10 small-group guided trail rides a day (1–2½ hours, or longer) for riders of all skill levels. Rides are designed to replicate the experience of the *paniolo,* or Hawaiian cowboy. Some climb high enough to view (on clear days) 30 miles of coastline—sometimes as far as Maui and Molokai. The ranch also offers private 30-minute horse experiences for ages two to seven, private and group advanced trail rides, and private romantic tours for couple that include picnics. Reservations are required. ✉ *56-250 Kamehameha Hwy., Kahuku* ✣ *2 miles north of the Polynesian Cultural Center, between Laie and Kahuku* ☎ *808/341–3995* 🌐 *gunstockranch.com* 🎫 *Trail rides from $99.*

### Kualoa Ranch

**HORSEBACK RIDING | FAMILY** | This 4,000-acre working ranch across from Kualoa Beach Park offers two-hour trail rides in the breathtaking Kaaawa Valley, which was the site of such movie back lots as *Jurassic Park, Godzilla,* and *50 First Dates,* as well as numerous television shows, including *Lost.* Kualoa has other activities—bus, boat, and Jeep tours; electric mountain bike tours; kayak adventure tours; ATV trail rides; canopy zip line tours; and children's activities—that may be combined for full-day package rates. The minimum age for horseback rides is 10. ✉ *49-479 Kamehameha Hwy., Kaneohe* ☎ *800/231–7321, 808/237–7321* 🌐 *www.kualoa.com* 🎫 *Trail rides $145.*

# Jet Skiing and Waterskiing

## HONOLULU

### Aloha Jet Skis

**JET SKIING** | Skip across the surface of the immense Keehi Lagoon as planes from Daniel K. Inouye International Airport soar above you. After an instructional safety session, you can try your hand at navigating the buoyed course. The Yamaha deluxe wave runners can be operated either tandem or solo. Reservations are required. ✉ *Keehi Lagoon, 1640 Sand Island Access Rd., Honolulu* ☎ *808/721–1754* 🌐 *www.alohajetski.com* 🎫 *From $126.*

### Hawaii Water Sports Center

**JET SKIING | FAMILY** | This company transforms Maunalua Bay into a water park with activities for all ages. You can bounce around in a bumper tube, zoom around on Jet Skis, wakeboard, waterski, scuba dive, or ride the six-person banana boats. Another option is to choose a multi-ride pass and do it all. ✉ *Koko Marina Center, 7192 Kalanianaole Hwy., Honolulu* ☎ *808/395–3773* 🌐 *hawaiiwatersportscenter.com* 🎫 *$79 for Jet Skiing.*

### HAWAII KAI

**H2O Sports Hawaii**

**WATER SPORTS | FAMILY** | Jet Skiing, snorkeling, and scuba diving, plus banana boats, bumper boats, and packages: this company offers a wide variety of activities on the water, suitable for different ages. All of them launch in Maunalua Bay near Hawaii Kai. ■ **TIP→ Make your reservations early.** ✉ *Hawaii Kai Shopping Center, 377 Keahole St., near Longs Drugs, Hawaii Kai* ☎ *808/396–0100* 🌐 *www.h2osportshawaii.com* 🎫 *Jet Skiing from $75.*

# Kayaking

Kayaking is an easy way, even for novices, to explore the ocean—and Oahu's natural beauty—without much effort or skill. It offers a vantage point not afforded by swimming or surfing and a workout you won't get lounging on a catamaran. The ability to travel long distances can also get you into trouble. ■ **TIP→ Experts agree that rookies should stay on the windward side.** Their reasoning is simple: if you get tired, break or lose an oar, or just plain pass out, the onshore winds will eventually blow you back to the beach. The same cannot be said for breezes off the North Shore and West Oahu.

Kayaks are specialized: some are suited for riding waves while others are designed for traveling long distances. Your outfitter can address your needs depending on your skill level, leading to a more enjoyable—and safer—experience. Expect to pay from $35 for a half-day single rental; guided kayak tours are also available. Tandem kayaks are an option for sharing your adventure with a friend. Some kayaking outfitters also rent stand-up paddleboards. ⇨ *See also: Stand-Up Paddleboarding.*

### BEST SPOTS

**Bellows Field Beach Park,** near Waimanalo Town Center on the windward side, and **Mokuleia Beach Park,** across from Kawaihapai Airfield (formerly Dillingham Airfield) on the North Shore, are two great spots to try surf kayaking. Hard-to-reach breaks, the ones that surfers exhaust themselves trying to reach, are easily accessed by kayak. The buoyancy of the kayak also lets you catch the wave earlier and get out in front of the white wash. If you're green, stick to Bellows with those onshore winds. Also, you don't want to be catching waves where the surfers are (in Waikiki, however, pretty much anything goes).

Because of its calm waters and onshore winds, **Lanikai Beach,** tucked away in a windward side residential area, is popular with amateur kayakers. More adventurous paddlers can head to the Mokulua Islands, two islets less than a mile from the beach. You can land on Moku Nui, which has surf breaks and small beaches great for picnicking. Take a dip in Queen's Bath, a small saltwater swimming hole. Take care to not venture onto the back side of the islets, where waves can create dangers.

For something a little different, try Windward Oahu's Kahana Stream, which empties into the ocean at **Kahana Bay Beach Park.** The riverlike stream may not have the blue water of the ocean, but the majestic Koolau Mountains, with waterfalls during rainy months, make for a picturesque backdrop. It's a short jaunt, about 2 miles round-trip from the beach. Bring mosquito repellent.

### EQUIPMENT, LESSONS, AND TOURS

#### HONOLULU

**Go Bananas Kayaks**

**KAYAKING** | At the island's largest outfitter, staffers make sure that you rent the appropriate kayak for your abilities, and the company can also outfit your rental car with soft racks (included in the rental fee) to transport your boat to the beach. You can rent either a single or a double kayak. The store also carries clothing and kayaking accessories and rents stand-up paddleboards. ✉ *799 Kapahulu Ave., Kapahulu* ☎ *808/737–9514* 🌐 *gobananaskayaks.com* 🎫 *From $35.*

**NORTH SHORE**

**Surf N Sea**

**KAYAKING** | This outfitter is located in a rustic wooden building on the beach, so in minutes you can start paddling on a single or double kayak. ■**TIP→ These plastic boats are great from spring to fall, but winter weather can be hazardous for even veteran kayakers. This outfitter's proximity to a protected stream makes kayaking in any sea conditions possible.** In addition to kayaking, this company also offers just about any surf-related activity you can imagine on the North Shore. ✉ *62-595 Kamehameha Hwy., Haleiwa* ☎ *808/637–9897* 🌐 *www.surfnsea.com* 🎫 *From $60 for a half-day kayak rental.*

**EAST (WINDWARD) OAHU**

**Hawaiian Watersports**

**KAYAKING** | **FAMILY** | This multifaceted outfitter emphasizes ocean safety with fully guided 90-minute tours to either the Mokes or Flat Island that include both instruction and equipment rental. Experienced paddlers can also rent a single or double kayak and venture out on their own. In addition, the company rents windsurfing equipment, surfboards and bodyboards, snorkel equipment, and stand-up paddleboards. Discounts are available if you reserve online. ✉ *171 Hamakua Dr., Kailua* ☎ *808/262–5483* 🌐 *pwhawaii.org* 🎫 *Rentals from $64, single-person lesson from $176.*

**Kailua Beach Adventures**

**KAYAKING** | **FAMILY** | One of the best places for beginners to kayak is Kailua Beach, and this outfitter has an ideal location just across the street from it. The company offers two- and five-hour guided kayak tours (the longer tour includes lunch, time for kayaking, and time for the beach). More adventurous visitors can rent a kayak (double, single, or triple for a half or full day), take it out onto the beach, and venture to the Mokulua Islands off Lanikai. Other rental options include snorkeling equipment, stand-up paddleboards, and bikes. Discounts are given if booked online. ✉ *Kailua Beach Shopping Center, 130 Kailua Rd., Kailua* ☎ *808/262–2555* 🌐 *www.kailuasailboards.com* 🎫 *Rentals from $69.*

### Kayaking to The Mokes

The Mokulua Islands (aka The Mokes) are two islets off Lanikai Beach on the windward side. The larger Moku Nui is a perfect kayaking destination and a popular place for picnics. (The islands are state-protected bird sanctuaries.) Some outfitters offer guided tours. But as it's impossible to miss the islets and the water between them is typically calm, spend your money on sunscreen and snacks instead, and enjoy the paddle. Avoid the back side of the islets: rogue waves can sometimes be dangerous.

## Running

In Honolulu, the most popular places to jog are the two parks at either end of Waikiki, Kapiolani and Ala Moana. In both cases, the loop around the park is just less than 2 miles. You can also run a 4-mile ring around Diamond Head Crater, past scenic views, luxurious homes, and herds of other joggers.

### BEST SPOTS

#### HONOLULU

**Honolulu Marathon**

**RUNNING** | The Honolulu Marathon is thrilling for spectators as well as participants. Join the throngs who cheer at the finish line at Kapiolani Park as local and internationally famous runners tackle the 26.2-mile challenge. It's held on the second Sunday in December and is sponsored by the Honolulu Marathon Association. ✉ *Honolulu* ☎ *808/734–7200* 🌐 *www.honolulumarathon.org.*

**Running Room**

**RUNNING** | Once you leave Honolulu, it gets trickier to find places to jog that are both scenic and safe. It's best to stick to the well-traveled routes, or ask the experienced folks at this outpost of the international apparel and shoe chain for advice. Note that it's closed on Monday. ✉ *819 Kapahulu Ave., Kapahulu* ☎ *808/737–2422* 🌐 *www.runningroomhawaii.com.*

## Scuba Diving

Not all of Hawaii's beauty is above water. What lurks below can be just as magnificent. Although snorkeling provides adequate access to this underwater world, nothing gives you the freedom—or depth, quite literally—as scuba. The diving on Oahu is comparable with any you might do in the tropics, but its uniqueness comes from the isolated environment of the Islands. There are literally hundreds of species of fish and other marine life that you can find only in this chain. In fact, about 25% of Hawaii's marine life can be seen here only—nowhere else in the world. Adding to the singularity of diving off Oahu is the human history of the region. Military activities and tragedies of the 20th century filled the waters surrounding Oahu with wreckage that the ocean creatures have since turned into their homes.

Although instructors certified to license you in scuba are plentiful in the Islands, it's best to get your PADI certification before coming, as a week of classes may be a bit of a commitment on a short vacation. Expect to pay around $150 for a two-tank boat dive (provided that you are certified; remember to bring your paperwork). ■ **TIP→ You can go on short, shallow introductory dives without the certification, but the best dives require it and cost a bit more.**

### BEST SPOTS

**Hanauma Bay Nature Preserve.** On Oahu's southeast shore, about a 30-minute drive east of Waikiki, this preserve is home to more than 250 different species of fish, a quarter of which can be found nowhere else. While it's beloved for snorkeling, this volcanic crater bay is also one of the state's most popular dive sites. It's a long walk from the parking lot to the beach—even longer lugging equipment—so consider hooking up with a licensed operator. If you go on your own, make the required reservation (they sell out quickly) and pay in advance; see 🌐 *honolulu.gov/parks-hbay/home.* Preservation efforts have aided the bay's delicate ecosystem, so expect to see various butterfly fish, surgeonfish, tangs, parrotfish, and endangered Hawaiian sea turtles. ✉ *7455 Kalanianaole Hwy., Hawaii Kai* ☎ *808/768–6861* 🎫 *$25 per person and $3 parking.*

***Mahi* Wreck.** Hawaii's waters are littered with shipwrecks, but one of the most intact and accessible is this 165-foot minesweeper that was sunk in 1982 off the leeward coast. It lies upright in about 90 feet of calm, clear water, encrusted in coral and patrolled by white-spotted eagle rays and millet-seed butterfly fish. The wreck also serves as an artificial reef for such Hawaii aquatic residents as blue-striped snappers, puffer fish, lionfish, moray eels, and octopuses. Visibility averages about 100 feet, making this one of the most popular dives on the island. ✉ *Waianae.*

**Maunalua Bay.** Stretching about 7 miles, from Portlock Point to Black Point, and teeming with marine life, this bay has several accessible dive sites of varying difficulty. The shallow-water Turtle Canyon is home to endangered Hawaiian green sea turtles. Fantasy Reef is another shallow dive, with three plateaus of volcanic rock lined with coral that is home to fish, eels, and sea turtles. In about 85 feet of water, *Baby Barge* is an easy-to-access sunken vessel encrusted in coral. An advanced dive, the wreck of a Vought F4U Corsair attracts garden eels and stingrays. ✉ *Southeast Oahu.*

**100 Foot Hole.** Once an ancient Hawaiian fishing ground reserved for royalty, this cluster of volcanic boulders, which is accessible from shore, features ledges, caves, and a large, open-ended cavern perfect for diving. The spot attracts octopuses, manta rays, and the occasional white-tip shark. ✉ *Off Diamond Head, Honolulu.*

**Shark's Cove.** Oahu's best shore dive is accessible only during the summer months. Shark's Cove, on the North Shore, churns with monster surf during the winter, making this popular snorkeling and diving spot extremely dangerous. In summer, the cavernous lava tubes and tunnels are great for both novices and experienced divers. Some dive-tour companies offer round-trip transportation from Waikiki. ✉ *Haleiwa.*

**Three Tables.** A short walk from Shark's Cove is Three Tables, named for a trio of flat rocks running perpendicular to shore. There are lava tubes to the right of these rocks that break the surface and extend out about 50 feet. Although this area isn't as active as Shark's Cove, you can still spot octopuses, moray eels, parrotfish, green sea turtles, and the occasional shark. ✉ *Haleiwa.*

### EQUIPMENT, LESSONS, AND TOURS

#### NORTH SHORE

**Surf N Sea**

**SCUBA DIVING** | This is the North Shore headquarters for all things water-related, including diving. One interesting perk: upon request, the dive guides can shoot a video of your adventure. It's hard to see facial expressions under the water, but it still might be fun for those who want to prove that they took the plunge. The outfitter caters to divers of all abilities, from first-timers to advanced divers. ✉ *62-595 Kamehameha Hwy., Haleiwa* ☎ *808/637–3483* 🌐 *www.surfnsea.com* 🎫 *Two-tank shore dives from $120.*

#### EAST (WINDWARD) OAHU

**Aaron's Dive Shop**

**SCUBA DIVING** | This friendly and well-equipped dive shop caters to everyone. Take an "introductory" dive if you're not certified, get certified, or sign up for an offshore day or night dive excursion if you're experienced. In addition to organized group dives, the company's "dive concierge" can arrange private charters for those who want a completely customized experience. Snorkelers can go along on many dives as well. ✉ *307 Hahani St., Kailua* ☎ *808/262–2333* 🌐 *www.aaronsdiveshop.com* 🎫 *Two-tank dive from $155.*

## Snorkeling

If you can swim, you can snorkel. You don't need any formal training, and you can do it anywhere there's enough water to stick your face in. A mask, snorkel, and fins will run you about $35 at any corner ABC Store. At the other end of the price spectrum, luxurious snorkel cruises cost up to $175, including lunch and drinks.

Conditions at each snorkeling spot vary, depending on the weather and time of

*Continued on page 254*

# SNORKELING IN HAWAII

Molokini Crater

The waters surrounding the Hawaiian Islands are filled with life—from giant manta rays cruising off the Big Island's Kona Coast to humpback whales giving birth in the waters around Maui. Dip your head beneath the surface to experience a spectacularly colorful world: pairs of milletseed butterflyfish dart back and forth, redlipped parrotfish snack on coral algae, and spotted eagle rays flap past like silent spaceships. Sea turtles bask at the surface while tiny wrasses give them the equivalent of a shave and a haircut. The water quality is typically outstanding; many sites afford 30-foot-plus visibility. On snorkel cruises, you can often stare from the boat rail right down to the bottom.

Certainly few destinations are as accommodating to every level of snorkeler as Hawaii. Beginners can tromp in from sandy beaches while more advanced divers descend to shipwrecks, reefs, craters, and sea arches just offshore. Because of Hawaii's extreme isolation, the island chain has fewer fish species than Fiji or the Caribbean—but many of the fish that live here exist nowhere else. The Hawaiian waters are home to the highest percentage of endemic fish in the world.

The key to enjoying the underwater world is slowing down. Look carefully. Listen. You might hear the strange crackling sound of shrimp tunneling through coral, or you may hear whales singing to one another during winter. A shy octopus may drift along the ocean's floor beneath you. If you're hooked, pick up a waterproof fish-key from Long's Drugs. You can brag later that you've looked the Hawaiian turkeyfish in the eye.

*Endemic to Hawaii

## POLYNESIA'S FIRST CELESTIAL NAVIGATORS: HONU

*Honu* is the Hawaiian name for two native sea turtles, the hawksbill and the green sea turtle. Little is known about these dinosaur-age marine reptiles, though snorkelers regularly see them foraging for *limu* (seaweed) and the occasional jellyfish in Hawaiian waters. Most female honu nest in the uninhabited Northwestern Hawaiian Islands, but a few sociable ladies nest on Maui and Big Island beaches. Scientists suspect that they navigate the seas via magnetism—sensing the earth's poles. Amazingly, they will journey up to 800 miles to nest—it's believed that they return to their own birth sites. After about 60 days of incubation, nestlings emerge from the sand at night and find their way back to the sea by the light of the stars.

## SNORKELING

Many of Hawaii's reefs are accessible from the shore.

**The basics:** Sure, you can take a deep breath, hold your nose, squint your eyes, and stick your face in the water in an attempt to view submerged habitats . . . but why not protect your eyes, retain your ability to breathe, and keep your hands free to paddle about when exploring underwater? That's what snorkeling is all about.

**Equipment needed:** A mask, snorkel (the tube attached to the mask), and fins. In deeper waters (any depth over your head), life jackets are advised.

**Steps to success:** If you've never snorkeled before, it's natural to feel a bit awkward at first, so don't sweat it. Breathing through a mask and tube, and wearing a pair of fins take getting used to. Like any activity, you build confidence and comfort through practice.

If you're new to snorkeling, begin by submerging your face in shallow water or a swimming pool and breathing calmly through the snorkel while gazing through the mask.

Next you need to learn how to clear water out of your mask and snorkel, an essential skill since splashes can send water into tube openings and masks can leak. Some snorkels have built-in drainage valves, but if a tube clogs, you can force water up and out by exhaling through your mouth. Clearing a mask is similar: lift your head from water while pulling forward on mask to drain. Some masks have built-in purge valves, but those without can be cleared underwater by pressing the top to the forehead and blowing out your nose (charming, isn't it?), allowing air to bubble into the mask, pushing water out the bottom. If it sounds hard, it really isn't. Just try it a few times and you'll soon feel like a pro.

Never touch or stand on coral.

Now your goal is to get friendly with fins—you want them to be snug but not too tight—and learn how to propel yourself with them. Fins won't help you float, but they will give you a leg up, so to speak, on smoothly moving through the water or treading water (even when upright) with less effort.

Flutter kicking is the most efficient underwater kick, and the farther your foot bends forward the more leg power you'll be able to transfer to the water and the farther you'll travel with each stroke. Flutter kicking movements involve alternately separating the legs and then drawing them back together. When your legs separate, the leg surface encounters drag from the water, slowing you down. When your legs are drawn back together, they produce a force pushing you forward. If your kick creates more forward force than it causes drag, you'll move ahead.

Submerge your fins to avoid fatigue rather than having them flailing above the water when you kick, and keep your arms at your side to reduce drag. You are in the water—stretched out, face down, and snorkeling happily away—but that doesn't mean you can't hold your breath and go deeper in the water for a closer look at some fish or whatever catches your attention. Just remember that when you do this, your snorkel will be submerged, too, so you won't be breathing (you'll be holding your breath). You can dive head-first, but going feet-first is easier and less scary for most folks, taking less momentum. Before full immersion, take several long, deep breaths to clear carbon dioxide from your lungs.

If your legs tire, flip onto your back and tread water with inverted fin motions while resting. If your mask fogs, wash condensation from the lens and clear water from your mask.

## TIPS FOR SAFE SNORKELING

- Snorkel with a buddy and stay together.
- Plan your entry and exit points prior to getting in the water.
- Swim into the current on entering and then ride the current back to your exit point.
- Carry your flippers into the water and then put them on, as it's difficult to walk in them, and rocks may be slippery.
- Make sure your mask fits properly and is not too loose.
- Pop your head above the water periodically to ensure you aren't drifting too far out, or too close to rocks.
- Think of the water as someone else's home—don't take anything that doesn't belong to you, or leave any trash behind.
- Don't touch any sea creatures; they may reveal hidden stingers.
- Wear a rash guard; it will help you from being fried by the sun..
- When in doubt, don't go without a snorkeling professional; try a guided tour.
- Don't go in if the ocean seems rough.

Green sea turtle (honu)

Hanauma Bay in Southeast Oahu has more than 250 different species of marine life; you'd be hard-pressed to find a better place to snorkel.

year, so consult with the purveyor of your gear for tips on where the best viewing is that day. The North Shore should be attempted only when the waves are calm, namely in the summertime. Also, put plenty of sunscreen on your back (or better yet, wear a T-shirt or rash guard): once you start gazing below, your head may not come back up for hours, but your back will be exposed to the sun.

## BEST SPOTS

**Electric Beach.** This haven for tropical fish is on the island's west side, directly across from an electricity plant, hence the name (aka Kahe Beach Park). The expulsion of hot water from the plant raises the temperature of the ocean, attracting Hawaiian green sea turtles, spotted moray eels, and spinner dolphins. Although visibility is not always the best, the crowds are small, and the fish are guaranteed. ✉ *Farrington Hwy., 1 mile west of Ko Olina Resort, Kapolei.*

**Hanauma Bay Nature Preserve.** What Waimea Bay is to surfing, Hanauma Bay in Southeast Oahu is to snorkeling. It's home to more than 250 different species of marine life. Due to the protection of the narrow mouth of the cove and the prodigious reef, you would be hard-pressed to find a place you would feel safer while snorkeling. Reservations and payment online are required to enter if you're on your own, versus being on a tour; see 🌐 *honolulu.gov/parks-hbay/home.* ✉ *7455 Kalanianaole Hwy.*, Honolulu ☎ *808/768–6861* 🎫 *$25 per person and $3 parking.*

**Queen's Surf Beach.** On the edge of Waikiki, between the Kapahulu Groin and the Waikiki Aquarium, this marine reserve isn't as chock-full of fish as Hanauma Bay, but it has its share of colorful reef fish and the occasional Hawaiian green sea turtle. Just yards from shore, it's a great spot for an escape if you're stuck in Waikiki and have grown weary of watching the surfers. ✉ *Kalakaua Ave., Honolulu.*

**Shark's Cove.** Great shallows protected by a huge reef make Shark's Cove on the North Shore a prime spot for snorkelers, even young ones, in the summer. You'll find a plethora of critters, from crabs to octopuses, in water that's no more than waist deep. When the winter swells come, this area can turn treacherous. ✉ *Kamehameha Hwy., across from Foodland, Haleiwa.*

### EQUIPMENT AND TOURS

#### HONOLULU

**Snorkel Bob's**

**SNORKELING | FAMILY** | This place has all the stuff you'll need—and more—to make your water adventures more enjoyable. Bob makes his own gear and is active in protecting reef fish species. Remember to ask the staff about good snorkeling spots, as the best ones can vary with weather and the seasons. You can either rent or buy gear (and reserve it in advance online). ✉ *700 Kapahulu Ave., Kapahulu* ☎ *808/735–7944* 🌐 *snorkelbob.com* 🎫 *Snorkel gear rental packages from $8 per day, $24 per wk.*

#### WEST (LEEWARD) OAHU

**Hawaii Nautical**

**SNORKELING** | With operations throughout the Islands, this eco-focused operator follows strict guidelines to protect marine mammals and wildlife. Besides cruises, its offerings include snorkeling and whale-watching tours, with two- and three-hour snorkeling tours departing from Waianae Harbor in West Oahu and Kewalo Harbor in Waikiki. Some tours include lunch. ✉ *Waianae Boat Harbor, 85-491 Farrington Hwy., Waianae* ☎ *808/234–7245* 🌐 *www.hawaiinautical.com* 🎫 *Snorkeling tours from $99.*

#### HAWAII KAI

**★ Hanauma Bay Rental Stand**

**SNORKELING | FAMILY** | You can rent masks, fins, and snorkels here; just be sure to make an online reservation and pay ahead to enter Hanauma Bay (🌐 *honolulu.gov/parks-hbay/home*). The stand also has lockers that are just large enough to stash your valuables. Bring ID or car keys as a deposit for rental. ✉ *Hanauma Bay Nature Preserve, 7455 Kalanianaole Hwy., Hawaii Kai* ☎ *808/396–3483* 🌐 *hanaumabaystatepark.com* 🎫 *Rentals from $20, lockers from $10* 🕒 *Closed Mon. and Tues.*

## Stand-Up Paddleboarding

From the lakes of Wisconsin to the coast of Lima, Peru, stand-up paddleboarding (or SUP, for short) is taking the sport of surfing to unexpected places. Still, the sport remains firmly rooted in the Hawaiian Islands. Back in the 1960s, Waikiki beachboys would paddle out on their longboards using a modified canoe paddle. It was longer than a traditional paddle, enabling them to stand up and stroke. It was easier this way to survey the ocean and snap photos of tourists learning to surf. Eventually it became a sport unto itself, with professional contests at world-class surf breaks and long-distance races across treacherous waters.

Stand-up paddleboarding is easy to learn—though riding waves takes some practice—and most outfitters on Oahu offer lessons for all skill levels starting at about $55. It's also a great workout; you can burn off yesterday's dinner buffet, strengthen your core, and experience the natural beauty of the island's coastlines all at once. Once you're ready to head out on your own, half-day rentals start around $50.

If you're looking to learn, go where there's already a SUP presence. Avoid popular surf breaks, unless you're experienced, and be wary of ocean and wind conditions. You'll want to find a spot with calm waters, easy access in and out of the ocean, and a friendly crowd that doesn't mind the occasional stand-up paddleboarder.

## Did You Know?

Shark's Cove is a wonderful place on the North Shore for young snorkelers to spend time exploring the ocean's bottom in shallow waters, as the area is protected by a huge reef just offshore.

### BEST SPOTS

**Ala Moana Beach Park.** About a mile west of Waikiki, Ala Moana is the most SUP-friendly spot on the island. In fact, the state installed a series of buoys in the flat-water lagoon to separate stand-up paddlers and swimmers. There are no waves here, making it a great spot to learn, but beware of strong trade winds, which can push you into the reef.

**Anahulu Stream.** Outfitters on the North Shore like to take SUP beginners to Anahulu Stream, which empties into Waialua Bay near the Haleiwa Boat Harbor. This area is calm and protected from winds, plus there's parking at the harbor, and surf shops nearby rent boards.

**Waikiki.** Several south shore outfitters take beginners into the waters off Waikiki. Canoes, the surf break fronting the Duke Kahanamoku statue, and the channels between breaks are often suitable for people learning how to maneuver their boards in not-so-flat conditions. But south swells here can be menacing, and ocean conditions can change quickly. Check with lifeguards before paddling out, and be mindful of surfers in the water.

**White Plains Beach.** If you've got a car with racks, you might want to venture to White Plains, a fairly uncrowded beach about 27 miles west of Waikiki near Barbers Point. It's a long, sandy beach with many breaks and plenty of room for everyone. There are lifeguards, restrooms, and lots of parking, making this a great spot for beginners and those just getting comfortable in small waves. ✉ *Essex Rd. and Tripoli Rd, Kapolei.*

### EQUIPMENT AND LESSONS

#### HONOLULU

**Hans Hedemann Surf School**

**STAND UP PADDLEBOARDING | FAMILY** | Get professional instruction in stand-up paddleboarding right in Waikiki, where the sport originated. This school offers group lessons, semiprivate lessons, and private training. Instruction is also offered at Turtle Bay Resort in Kahuku on the North Shore. ✉ *Queen Kapiolani Hotel, 150 Kapahulu Ave., Waikiki* ☎ *808/924–7778* 🌐 *www.hhsurf.com* 🎟 *Two-hour rental from $25, two-hour group lesson from $95.*

#### NORTH SHORE

**Rainbow Watersports Adventures**

**STAND UP PADDLEBOARDING | FAMILY** | When you spot this company's colorful van at the bay near Haleiwa Beach Park, you'll know you're in the right place. You can get a two-hour private or group lesson on Oahu's North Shore. All lessons are held in a spot popular with the resident green sea turtles. The company also offers a 3½-hour coastal eco-adventure trip, including snorkeling and lunch. Its Twilight Glow Paddle lets you glide through calm waters illuminated by lights mounted to your board. ✉ *Haleiwa Beach Park, Kamehameha Hwy., Haleiwa* ☎ *800/470–4964, 808/470-4332* 🌐 *rainbowwatersports.com* 🎟 *Group lessons from $99; private lessons from $119.*

**Surf N Sea**

**STAND UP PADDLEBOARDING | FAMILY** | With stand-up paddleboarding lessons for every skill level, Surf N Sea is a great place to start. Beginners can take the introductory lesson to learn proper paddling technique. A one-hour session focuses on honing your skills. More advanced paddlers can book surf trips out to several North Shore breaks. ✉ *62-595 Kamehameha Hwy., Haleiwa* ☎ *808/637–3008, 800/899–7873* 🌐 *www.surfnsea.com* 🎟 *Rentals $20 per hour, $60 per day (includes paddle); lessons from $55.*

#### EAST (WINDWARD) OAHU

**Hawaiian Watersports**

**STAND UP PADDLEBOARDING | FAMILY** | Paddle off the shore of picturesque Kailua Beach. This safety-conscious outfitter offers both equipment rentals and 90-minute and 3-hour group or individual lessons. The one-stop shop for water sports also offers kiteboarding, surfing, and windsurfing lessons as well as kayak tours and equipment rentals. Discounts are available online if you book ahead. ✉ *171 Hamakua Dr., Kailua* ☎ *808/262–5483* 🌐 *pwhawaii.org* 🎫 *Rentals from $64; lessons from $90.*

# Submarine Tours

## HONOLULU

### Atlantis Submarines

**BOATING | FAMILY** | Here is an underwater adventure for the unadventurous. Not fond of swimming, but want to see what you've been missing? Board this high-tech 64-passenger vessel for a ride past shipwrecks, turtle breeding grounds, and coral reefs. Little kids really seem to love it, though there's a 36-inch height minimum. The tours, which depart from the pier at the Hilton Hawaiian Village, are available in several languages, and discounts are available if booked online. ✉ *Hilton Hawaiian Village Waikiki Beach Resort, 2005 Kalia Rd., Waikiki* ☎ *808/973–9800, 800/381–0237 for reservations* 🌐 *atlantisadventures.com* 🎫 *From $148.*

# Surfing

Perhaps no word is more associated with Hawaii than surfing. Every year, the best of the best gather on Oahu's North Shore to compete in major surfing events. The pros dominate the waves for a month, but the rest of the year belongs to folks just trying to have fun. Oahu is unique because it has so many famous spots: Banzai Pipeline, Waimea Bay, Kaiser Bowls, Sunset Beach, and others. These spots, however, require experience and are often populated with well-known surfers who can be both territorial and intimidating. Waikiki is a great place for beginners to learn or for novice surfers to catch predictable waves. Group lessons on Waikiki Beach start at $50, but if you really want to fine-tune your skills, you can pay up to $500 for a daylong private outing with a former pro.

The island also has miles of coastline with surf spots that are perfect for everyday surfers. But remember this surfer's credo: when in doubt, don't go out. If you're unsure about conditions, stay on the beach, and talk to locals to get more info about surf breaks before trying yourself.

⚠ **To avoid a confrontation with local surfers, who can be very territorial about their favorite breaks, try some of the alternate spots listed below. They may not have the name recognition, but their waves can be just as great.**

## BEST SPOTS

**Makaha Beach Park.** If you like to ride waves, try this west side beach. It has legendary, interminable rights that allow riders to perform all manner of stunts: from six-man canoes with everyone doing headstands to Bullyboards (oversize bodyboards) with whole families along for the ride. Mainly known as a longboarding spot, it's predominantly local but respectful to outsiders. Use caution in winter, as the surf can get huge. It's not called Makaha—which means "fierce"—for nothing. ✉ *84-369 Farrington Hwy., Waianae.*

**Sunset Beach Park.** If you've got some skills, impress your surfing buddies back home by catching a wave at the famous Sunset Beach on Oahu's North Shore. Two of the more manageable breaks are Kammie Land (or Kammie's) and Sunset Point. Thick waves and long rides await, but you'll need a thick board and a thicker skull. Surf etiquette here is a must, as it's mostly local. ✉ *59-104 Kamehameha Hwy., 1 mile north of Ehukai Beach Park, Haleiwa.*

**Ulukou Beach.** In Waikiki you can paddle out to Populars—or Pops—a break at

This surfer is doing a stellar job of riding the world-famous Banzai Pipeline on Oahu's North Shore.

Ulukou Beach. Nice and easy, it never breaks too hard and is friendly to both newbies and veterans. It's one of the best places to surf during pumping south swells, as thick waves break in open ocean, making it more rideable. The only downside is the long paddle out from Kuhio Beach, but that keeps the crowds manageable. ✉ *Waikiki Beach, in front of Sheraton Waikiki Beach Resort, Honolulu.*

**White Plains Beach.** Known among locals as "mini Waikiki," the surf at White Plains breaks in numerous spots, preventing the logjams that are inevitable at many of Oahu's more popular spots. It's a great break for novice to intermediate surfers, though you do have to watch for wayward boards. ✉ *From the H1, take the Makakilo exit. Off H1, Kapolei.*

## EQUIPMENT AND LESSONS

### HONOLULU

#### Aloha Beach Services

**SURFING** | **FAMILY** | It may sound like a cliché, but there's no better way to learn to surf than from the iconic beachboys in Waikiki, a Waikiki fixture since 1959. In fact, it's often where locals take their visitors who want to surf because it's really got it all. And there's no one better than Harry "Didi" Robello, a second-generation beachboy and owner of Aloha Beach Services. Learn to surf in an hour-long group or semiprivate lesson or with just you and an instructor. You can also rent a board here. ✉ *2365 Kalakaua Ave., on beach near Moana Surfrider, Waikiki* ☎ *808/922–3111 ask for Aloha Beach Services* 🌐 *www.alohabeachservices.com* 🎫 *Lessons from $100, board rentals from $20.*

#### Faith Surf School

**SURFING** | **FAMILY** | Professional surfer Tony Moniz started his own surf school in 2000, and since then, he and his wife, Tammy, have helped thousands of people catch their first waves in Waikiki. The Moniz family is iconic in Hawaii's surf culture, and their stories are as good as their lessons. The 90-minute group lessons include all equipment and are the cheapest option. You can pay more (sometimes a lot more) for semiprivate lessons with up to three people or for private lessons. You can also book an all-day surf tour with Moniz, riding waves with him at his favorite breaks. ✉ *Outrigger Waikiki Beach Resort, 2335 Kalakaua Ave., Waikiki* ☎ *808/931–6262* 🌐 *faithsurfschool.com* 🎫 *Lessons from $95, board rental from $20.*

### NORTH SHORE

**Hans Hedemann Surf School**

**SURFING | FAMILY** | Hans Hedemann spent 17 years on the professional surfing circuit. He and his staff offer surfing, bodysurfing, and stand-up paddleboarding instruction; multiday intensive surf camps; and fine-tuning courses with Hedemann himself. Two-hour group lessons are the cheapest option, but private lessons are also available. There are also locations on the North Shore. ✉ *Queen Kapiolani Hotel, 150 Kapahulu Ave., Waikiki* ☎ *808/924–7778* 🌐 *hhsurf.com* 🎫 *Lessons from $95.*

**Surf N Sea**

**SURFING** | This is a one-stop shop for surfers (and other water-sports enthusiasts) on the North Shore. Rent a short or long board by the hour or for a full day. Two-hour group lessons are offered, as are four- to five-hour surf safaris for experienced surfers. ✉ *62-595 Kamehameha Hwy., Haleiwa* ☎ *800/899–7873* 🌐 *www.surfnsea.com* 🎫 *Lessons from $85, rentals from $35 per day.*

## Tennis

Although tennis has given way to golf as the biggest resort attraction, and many hotel courts have closed, there are still locations in Waikiki to get your tennis match on. Both sides of Waikiki are framed by tennis complexes, with 10 courts at Ala Moana Beach Park and four at Kapiolani Regional Park. Play is free at public courts, which are readily available during the day—but they tend to fill up after the sun goes down and the asphalt cools off. If pickleball is your thing, courts can usually be found (see 🌐 *honolulu.gov* and 🌐 *oahupickleballassociation.org*).

### HONOLULU

**Ala Moana Beach Park Tennis Courts**

**TENNIS** | The 10 public courts in Ala Moana Beach Park are the closest to the *ewa* (west) end of Waikiki. ✉ *1201 Ala Moana Blvd., Ala Moana* ☎ *808/768–3029.*

**Diamond Head Tennis Center**

**TENNIS** | Across the street from Kapiolani Park, this center has 10 courts open to the public. ✉ *3908 Paki Ave., Waikiki* ☎ *808/971–2525.*

**Kapiolani Tennis Courts**

**TENNIS** | There are four lighted courts for play here, just beyond Waikiki Beach. ✉ *2740 Kalakaua Ave., Waikiki* ☎ *808/765–4626.*

## Volleyball

With no shortage of sand, beach volleyball remains an extremely popular sport in the Islands.

### BEST SPOTS

There are sand-volleyball courts in Waikiki near **Fort DeRussy.** These are open to the public, so talent levels vary; however, the winner-plays-on policy here guarantees a higher level of play as the day progresses. For more advanced play, go to **Queen's Beach,** where you must bring your own net (which can lead to court possessiveness). This is the area where college kids and pros come when they're in town.

## Whale-Watching

December is marked by the arrival of snow in much of North America, but in Hawaii it marks the return of humpback whales. These migrating behemoths move south during winter for courtship and calving, and they put on quite a show. Watching males and females throwing themselves out of the ocean and into the sunset awes even the saltiest of sailors. Newborn calves riding next to their 2-ton mothers will stir you to your core. These gentle giants can be seen from the shore, but there's nothing like having a boat rock beneath you in the wake of a whale's breach. Whales are gone by May, but while they are in Hawaii, they captivate everyone.

The whales show up when and where they want, so although seasonal whale-watching tours are a good option, it's entirely possible you'll see some on any occasion that you're out on the water. Ask staff about whale sightings when you're booking any water activity.

### HONOLULU

**Atlantis Majestic Cruises**

**WILDLIFE-WATCHING** | **FAMILY** | The 150-foot cruise vessel *Majestic* bills itself as the smoothest whale-watching tour on Oahu and guarantees a whale sighting. The boat is big, with three decks where you can choose indoor or outdoor viewing while listening to Hawaiian music. An onboard naturalist provides information, adding history and local color during the 2½-hour lunchtime cruise. Departures are from the Aloha Tower Marketplace at Pier 6. Transportation from Waikiki can be arranged. **■ TIP→ Check-in begins 30 minutes before departure. Arrive early to get a table near a window for the best views while you eat.** ✉ *Aloha Tower Marketplace, 1 Aloha Tower Dr., Pier 6, Downtown* ☎ *800/381–0237* 🌐 *www.atlantisadventures.com* 💲 *From $79.*

### WEST (LEEWARD) OAHU

**Wild Side Specialty Tours**

**WILDLIFE-WATCHING** | **FAMILY** | Boasting a marine-biologist/naturalist crew, this company takes you to undisturbed snorkeling areas, and you may well spot dolphins and turtles along the way. The company promises a sighting of migrating whales year-round on some itineraries. The boat is well appointed and ideal for smaller groups. Tours may depart as early as 8 am from Waianae, so plan ahead. The three-hour deluxe wildlife tour is the most popular option. ✉ *Waianae Boat Harbor, 85-471 Farrington Hwy., Waianae* ☎ *808/306–7273* 🌐 *sailhawaii.com* 💲 *From $205.*

## Windsurfing and Kiteboarding

Those who call windsurfing and kiteboarding cheating because they require no paddling have never tried hanging on to a sail or kite. It will turn your arms to spaghetti quicker than paddling ever could, and the speeds you generate earn these sports the label of "extreme."

Windsurfing was born in the Islands. For amateurs, the windward side is best because the onshore breezes will bring you back to land even if you're not a pro. Kiteboarding is tougher but more exhilarating, as the kite will sometimes take you in the air for hundreds of feet before bringing you back to the ocean. **■ TIP→ Changes to local laws restrict lessons on the beach, so outfitters offering lessons are few and far between.**

### EAST (WINDWARD) OAHU

**Hawaiian Watersports**

**WINDSURFING** | Learn to kiteboard, windsurf, kayak, surf, or ride a stand-up paddleboard with this multifaceted outfitter. This is the only shop to offer kiteboarding and windsurfing lessons on Oahu, and the location of your lessons—off Kailua Beach—is one of the best and most beautiful on the island. (It's also where kitesurfing was invented.) For experienced kitesurfers, rentals are available, and the company offers equipment rentals for other water sports. Discounts are available for booking lessons or rentals online in advance. ✉ *171 Hamakua Dr., Kailua* ☎ *808/262–5483* 🌐 *pwhawaii.org* 💲 *Lessons $299.*

# Index

## F



## G



## H



## I



## J



## K

# Photo Credits

**Front cover:** Robertharding/Alamy Stock Photo [Descr.: Duke Paoa Kahanamoku, Waikiki Beach, Honolulu, Oahu, Hawaii, United States of America, Pacific]. **Back cover, from left to right:** Elias Bitar/iStockphoto. Leigh Anne Meeks/ Shutterstock. Rradams/Dreamstime. Spine: Bennyartist/Shutterstock. **Interior, from left to right:** Santonius Silaban/ Alamy Stock Photo (1). Eddy Galeotti/Shutterstock (2-3). Cathy Locklear/Dreamstime (5). **Chapter 1: Experience Oahu:** Tomas del amo/Shutterstock (6-7). Nataliya Hora/Dreamstime (8-9). O'ahu Visitor's Bureau (9). Dave/Flickr (9). Dana Edmunds/Hawaii Tourism Authority (10). Segawa7/Shutterstock (10). Jennifer Boyer/Flickr (10). RobertaLouise/Shutterstock (10). Lynn Watson/Dreamstime (11). Patrick Evans/Dreamstime (11). Joshua Rainey Photography/Shutterstock (12). Ashmephotography/Dreamstime (12). Shane Myers Photography/Shutterstock (12). Paparico/Dreamstime (12). 7maru/ Shutterstock (13). Westin Hotels & Resorts (14). Westin Hotels & Resorts (14). Adeliepenguin/Dreamstime (14). Dana Edmunds/Hawaii Tourism Authority (14). Joshua Mcdonough/Dreamstime (15). Esusek/Dreamstime (15). Follow2find/ Shutterstock (16). Bhofack2/Dreamstime (16). Phillip B. Espinasse/Shutterstock (16). Phillip B. Espinasse/Shutterstock (16). Nalukai/Dreamstime (17). Christian Mueller/Shutterstock (22). Leigh Anne Meeks/Shutterstock (23). Shane Myers Photography/Shutterstock (24). Dshumny/Shutterstock (24). Segawa7/iStockphoto (24). Norbert Turi/Shutterstock (25). Cupertino10/Dreamstime (25). Marilyn Gould/Dreamstime (26). Douglas Peebles Photography/Alamy Stock Photo (26). Ancha Chiangmai/Shutterstock (26). Pr2is/Dreamstime (26). Vfbjohn/Dreamstime (26). Eddygaleotti/Dreamstime (27). Koondon/Shutterstock (27). Caner CIFTCI/Dreamstime (27). Elmar Langle/iStockphoto (27). Kirk Lee Aeder/Big Island Visitors Bureau (27). Brent Hofacker/Shutterstock (28). Hawaii Tourism (28). Dana Edmunds (28). Magdanatka/Shutterstock (29). Kirk Lee Aeder/Big Island Visitors Bureau (29) Lost Mountain Studio/Shutterstock (30). Brooke Dombroski/Hawaii Tourism Authority (30). Alla Machutt/iStockphoto (30). Temanu/Shutterstock (30). Mongkolchon Akesin/Shutterstock (30). Heather Goodman/Hawaii Tourism Authority (31). Olgakr/iStockphoto (31). Dana Edmunds/Hawaii Tourism Authority (31). Hawaii Tourism Authority (31). Heather Goodman/Hawaii Tourism Authority (31). Cathy Locklear/Dreamstime (35). Hawaii Visitors and Convention Bureau (36). Thinkstock LLC (37). Linda Ching/Hawaii Visitors and Convention Bureau (39). Sri Maiava Rusden/Hawaii Visitors and Convention Bureau (39). Leis of Hawaii/leisofhawaii.com (40). Kelly Alexander Photography (40). Leis of Hawaii /leisofhawaii.com (40). Leis of Hawaii/leisofhawaii.com (40). Leis of Hawaii/ leisofhawaii. com (40). Kelly Alexander Photography (40). Tim Wilson/ Flickr (41). Douglas Peebles Photography/Alamy Stock Photo (42). Douglas Peebles Photography/Alamy Stock Photo (42). Dana Edmunds/ Polynesian Cultural Center's Alii Luau (42). Douglas Peebles Photography/Alamy Stock Photo (42). Purcell Team/Alamy Stock Photo (42). Hawaii Visitors and Convention Bureau (43). Hawaii Visitors and Convention Bureau (43). Hawaii Visitors and Convention Bureau (43). Oahu Visitors Bureau (43). **Chapter 3: Honolulu and Pearl Harbor:** Izabela23/Shutterstock (69). HelioSanMiguel_DiamondHead (77). 7maru/iStockphoto (92). Library of Congress (113). Madrabothair/Dreamstime (115). Operation 2022/Alamy Stock Photo (115). Army Signal Corps Collection in the U.S. National Archives (116). USS *Missouri* Memorial Association (116). Bennymarty/Dreamstime (117). 7maru/Shutterstock (125). Rico Leffanta/Dreamstime (136). 7maru/Shutterstock.com (145). MH Anderson Photography/Shutterstock (147). **Chapter 4: West (Leeward) and Central Oahu:** Hpbfotos/ Dreamstime (157). Courtesy of The LineUp at Wai Kai (164). Harry Beugelink/Shutterstock (167). Dudarev Mikhail/ Shutterstock (171). Alexander Demyanenko/Shutterstock (173). Maria Luisa Lopez Estivill/Dreamstime (174). **Chapter 5: North Shore:** Phillip B. Espinasse/Shutterstock (177). Steve Heap/Shutterstock (185). MNStudio/Shutterstock (189). Malachi Jacobs/Shutterstock (190). Cphoto/Dreamstime (193). Kauai Visitors Bureau (194). Jack Jeffrey (195). **Chapter 6: East (Windward) Oahu:** Cloudia Spinner/Shutterstock (199). Phillip B. Espinasse/Shutterstock (204). Eddygaleotti/Dreamstime (206). Damien Verrier/Shutterstock (211). Hipho/iStockphoto (213). Ppictures/Shutterstock (219). Malgorzata litkowska/Alamy Stock Photo (220). **Chapter 7: Activities and Tours:** Anna Bryukhanova/ iStockphoto (223). Blue Hawaiian Helicopters (225). Mlenny/iStockphoto (231). Wellych/Dreamstime (237). Life/ iStockphoto (241). Ron Dahlquist/HVCB (249). Shane Myers Photography/Shutterstock (250). Orxy/Shutterstock (252). Gert Vrey/Dreamstime (252). Shane Myers Photography/Shutterstock (253). Mitgirl/Dreamstime (254). Photo Resource Hawaii/Alamy Stock Photo (256). Karen Wilson (259). **About Our Writers:** All photos are courtesy of the writers except for the following: Marla Cimini, courtesy of Andréa Cimini Photography, 2014.

*Every effort has been made to trace the copyright holders, and we apologize in advance for any accidental errors. We would be happy to apply the corrections in the following edition of this publication.

# Notes

# Notes

# Notes

# Fodor's OAHU

**Publisher:** Stephen Horowitz, *General Manager*

**Editorial:** Douglas Stallings, *Editorial Director;* Jill Fergus, Amanda Sadlowski, *Senior Editors;* Brian Eschrich, Alexis Kelly, *Editors;* Angelique Kennedy-Chavannes, Yoojin Shin, *Associate Editors*

**Design:** Tina Malaney, *Director of Design and Production;* Jessica Gonzalez, *Senior Designer;* Jaimee Shaye, *Graphic Design Associate*

**Production:** Jennifer DePrima, *Editorial Production Manager;* Elyse Rozelle, *Senior Production Editor;* Monica White, *Production Editor*

**Maps:** Rebecca Baer, *Map Director;* Mark Stroud (Moon Street Cartography) and David Lindroth, *Cartographers*

**Photography:** Viviane Teles, *Director of Photography;* Namrata Aggarwal, Neha Gupta, Payal Gupta, Ashok Kumar, *Photo Editors;* Jade Rodgers, Shanelle Jacobs, *Photo Production Intern*

**Business and Operations:** Chuck Hoover, *Chief Marketing Officer;* Robert Ames, *Group General Manager*

**Public Relations and Marketing:** Joe Ewaskiw, *Senior Director of Communications and Public Relations*

**Fodors.com:** Jeremy Tarr, *Editorial Director;* Rachael Levitt, *Managing Editor*

**Technology:** Jon Atkinson, *Executive Director of Technology;* Rudresh Teotia, *Associate Director of Technology;* Alison Lieu, *Project Manager*

---

**Writers:** Powell Berger, Marla Cimini, Cheryl Crabtree, Anna Weaver

**Editors:** Linda Cabasin, Douglas Stallings

**Production Editor:** Monica White

---



10th Edition

ISBN 978-1-64097-690-0

ISSN 1559-0771

All details in this book are based on information supplied to us at press time. Always confirm information when it matters, especially if you're making a detour to visit a specific place. Fodor's expressly disclaims any liability, loss, or risk, personal or otherwise, that is incurred as a consequence of the use of any of the contents of this book.

**SPECIAL SALES**

This book is available at special discounts for bulk purchases for sales promotions or premiums. For more information, e-mail SpecialMarkets@fodors.com.

PRINTED IN CANADA

10 9 8 7 6 5 4 3 2 1

# About Our Writers

**Powell Berger** lives in the heart of Honolulu's Kakaako neighborhood, where she's ever in search of the best poke bowl. When not in Honolulu, she's in Durham, North Carolina, where she enjoys family, beaches that are lovely but don't measure up to Hawaii's, and no decent poke bowls. Her wanderlust has taken her to more than 50 countries around the world, and her writing appears in numerous state and regional publications, AAA magazines, *The Atlantic,* and various websites, in addition to Fodor's. Powell updated the Activities and Tours chapter for this edition.

**Marla Cimini** (🌐 *www.marlacimini.com*) is an award-winning writer with a passion for travel, beaches, music, and culinary adventures. As an avid globetrotter and frequent Oahu visitor, she has covered topics such as Hawaii's luxury hotels, fascinating and fun surf culture, and the innovative restaurant scene on the Islands. She appreciates Oahu's unique dichotomy, and enjoys the bustling Waikiki neighborhood as much as exploring the island's quieter beaches. And she's always up for surfing or an outrigger canoe ride in Waikiki! Marla's articles have appeared in numerous publications worldwide, including *USA Today*. Marla updated the Experience Oahu chapter, Travel Smart, and the Waikiki portion of the Honolulu and Pearl Harbor chapter.

**Cheryl Crabtree** first visited Hawaii as a kindergartner, a trip that sparked a lifelong passion for the Islands and led to frequent visits. She spends months at a time in residence on the North Shore and updated the North Shore and the West (Leeward) and Central Oahu chapters for this edition. Cheryl has also contributed to *Fodor's California* for more than two decades and is a regular updater for *Fodor's National Parks of the West* and *Complete National Parks*. She also contributes to numerous regional, national, and international publications.

Writer and multimedia journalist **Anna Weaver** was born and raised in Kailua, Oahu, and is proud of her Portuguese immigrant roots in the Islands. She can never get enough of Spam *musubi, malasadas,* or the gorgeous Koolau Mountains in her home state. Anna has written for Slate, Simplemost, and Hawaii publications such as the *Honolulu Star-Advertiser, Honolulu Magazine,* and *Pacific Business News*. In this guide, she updated the East (Windward) Oahu chapter and all sections but Waikiki in the Honolulu and Pearl Harbor chapter.